STEAL not this book for fear of shame, for here you see the owner's n a m e

Sally McKee

*A State of Deference*

University of Pennsylvania Press
MIDDLE AGES SERIES
*Edited by*
*Edward Peters*
Henry Charles Lea Professor
of Medieval History
University of Pennsylvania

A listing of the available books
in the series appears at the
back of this volume

# A State of Deference: Ragusa/Dubrovnik in the Medieval Centuries

Susan Mosher Stuard

*upp*

University of Pennsylvania Press

Philadelphia

Copyright © 1992 by Susan Mosher Stuard
All rights reserved
Printed in the United States of America

Library of Congress Cataloging-in-Publication Data
Stuard, Susan Mosher.
    A state of deference: Ragusa/Dubrovnik in the medieval centuries
/ Susan Mosher Stuard.
        p.   cm. — (Middle Ages series)
    Includes bibliographical references and index.
    ISBN 0-8122-3178-3
    1. Dubrovnik (Republic)—Civilization.   I. Title.   II. Series.
DR1645.D8S78   1992
949.7′2—dc20                                              92-12164
                                                            CIP

# Contents

Preface   vii

1. Introduction: An Ancient Town   1

2. The Old Republic   15

3. The Noble Circle   59

4. Women in Ragusa   100

5. Ragusan Households   115

6. Community   140

7. Fortunes   171

8. Fame   203

Appendix 1: Timeline   229
Appendix 2: The Later Centuries of the Republic of Ragusa   233
Appendix 3: Text of 1377 Law Establishing a *Trentino*   239

Bibliography   241
Index   259

# Preface

*Illyrici ora mille amplius insulis frequentator.*
Pliny the Younger, *Nat. Hist.* III, c.xxvi

I have many people to thank. Dr. Zdravko Šundrica, Archivist at the Dubrovnik State Archives for many years, taught me to read charters, as he taught so many others. The staff of the archives and Dr. Foretić have been unfailingly gracious and helpful. Three fellow researchers at the archives deserve special thanks: Dušanka Dinić-Knežević of the University of Novi Sad, David Rheubottom of the University of Manchester, and Josip Lučić of the University of Zagreb. They have all enriched my understanding of the old republic of Ragusa. Professor Lučić, in particular, has generously shared knowledge, books hard to obtain outside Yugoslavia, even his excellent historical maps with me. Allen Stahl of the American Numismatic Society allowed me to examine Serbian *grossi* firsthand. I am grateful as well to Troian Stoianovich of Rutgers University for his help. A year as Fellow at the Institute of Advanced Study at Princeton, New Jersey, allowed me to give structure to this study. Danila Spielman read the entire manuscript to my great benefit, and Donald Queller of the University of Illinois gave cogent criticisms and suggestions. Thomas Wagner produced photographs, and Kay Warren helped type the manuscript. Haverford College has been consistently supportive of my scholarship, and I am grateful for the Provost's Office subsidy that aided this book's publication. Since I now publish a third book with the University of Pennsylvania Press in the Middle Ages Series, those good people certainly deserve my gratitude for their support and judgment. Any errors in the text are, of course, my own.

 I first ventured to Dubrovnik, the modern name of the old republic of Ragusa, to search the archives for information about the medieval economy. I returned as it became clear to me that Ragusa had followed a remarkable course of social development that promoted economic growth over the medieval centuries. That is the story I attempt to tell in this monograph. Ragusa once comforted Western thinkers in the fond belief that people offered up deference to their betters voluntarily, in cheerful acceptance that others were better equipped to direct and lead than they were themselves. But my mind is firmly set in a postmodern age so I seriously doubt that deference is ever paid without instruction or coercion. This study is the result of my quest into how the endogamous elite of old Ragusa brought to pass a semblance of deference so convincing that Renaissance thinkers held them up as an ideal, an Illyrian utopia of fact, not fiction.

Because old Ragusans were rather closemouthed, I have tried to burrow beneath the placid surface of chroniclers' accounts and minutes of Council to pursue the strategies of noble citizen families. As a result, my study is somewhat episodic rather than a smooth march of events such as the reader might expect in a monograph on a medieval city-state. I find that the patricians of Ragusa were quite conscious of the factors that kept their polity free from most social turmoil and exhausting foreign wars. If they were prudent to such a marked degree, they also enjoyed social solidarity based on endogamous marriage which was the exception, not the rule, in late medieval Europe. The history of old Ragusa sank from notice in Western circles as belief in deference as a "natural" trait died, making it all the more intriguing to assess this poorly remembered history in the light of modern skepticism about whether aristocratic republics have ever practiced deference.

So it is time to reconsider how this city-state could survive as an independent polity more than a thousand years, practice endogamy for the documented portion of that span, and become one of the most prosperous commercial carriers of our early modern capitalist centuries. Unfortunately, this book appears as Yugoslavia fragments. Perhaps this is also a moment to reconsider Ragusa as a community that did not base its political identity on ethnicity but on the more sound foundation of avowing their constitution and the self-conscious principles of republicanism.

The New World "Mille Isles," or Thousand Islands, the name Pliny first applied to the lovely islands of the Dalmatian coast and that Champlain later transferred to the islands of the St. Lawrence River where I sit now, remind me that a resolute people might well follow an independent course sustained in such an environment.

Squaw Island
Gananoque, Ontario

# 1. Introduction: An Ancient Town

A classic city-state—surely Ragusa, present-day Dubrovnik, won that epithet fairly, boasting more than a thousand-year allegiance to republicanism in its pristine form.[1] But some view this as social stasis and a contraindication of growth in comparison to medieval city-states in the Mediterranean basin that changed dramatically in political form and social composition through the medieval centuries. Ragusa remained essentially "medieval," Maurice Aymard stated, and never saw an elaborate increase in bureaucratic functions or felt the great weight of government intervention as Venetians did.[2] According to Fernand Braudel, sixteenth-century Ragusa was a "perfectly preserved" city-state, in fact the "living image of thirteenth century Venice."[3] He found a "stable kind of humanity rather than a stable society" here, begging the question perhaps because he could not imagine the dynamic economic growth he ascribed to the city unaccompanied by significant social turmoil.[4]

The very qualities that allowed Renaissance commentators to understand the town in utopian terms—a completed society, hierarchical in character, stable and prosperous—became stumbling blocks for more recent evaluators who see the dynamic of a community in its capacity to change. In point of fact, the development of the economy is the component of Ragusan life best documented in the historical literature. This is understandable, since the urban economy did evolve in the late medieval centuries, conforming more closely than other aspects of communal life to modern assumptions about dynamic change. What still remains is the conundrum of an accompanying stasis in human relations and political institutions; this has eluded explanations. It is my intention to examine this problem of stasis, real or perceived, in this monograph.

In its environs, Dalmatia, the Adriatic littoral, and the West Balkans, Ragusa's importance was undisputed, and substantial documentation exists to record the early story of the city. Ragusa inhabited a spot midway along the *intra-culfum* sea route from Venice to the wider Mediterranean, and lay on an east-west axis between Italy and Constantinople, providing the community a nearly endless string of strategic opportunities to participate in Adriatic affairs in this, the most unified of the Mediterranean Seas.[5] While the Mediterranean remained the heart of a developing European civilization, Ragusans were participants in a long string of events of historical importance.[6]

Tradition placed Ragusa's founding in the seventh century and identified refugees as the first inhabitants. They had fled from nearby Epidaurus (today Cavtat) trying to escape marauders. The Anonymous Chronicler of Ravenna corroborates this tradition with these terse words: "Epidaurus now is Ragusium."[7] Twelve hundred years later in May 1806, the republic of Ragusa capitulated to Napoleon's troops who were on their journey south to Catar (Kotor), then held by the Russians. During the intervening centuries, the Ragusan citizenry often accepted the suzerainty of great powers like the Byzantines and even more often paid tribute to appease a menacing neighbor or buy protection. The town lived through two periods of occupation, first by the Normans in the late eleventh and twelfth centuries, and later by the Venetians, from 1204 until 1358. After that time, and despite the nominal overlordship of Hungary and tribute to the Turks, Ragusans pursued their own affairs as an autonomous republic.

The commune's white flag bore the proud word *Libertas,* not to flaunt absolute independence but rather to assert a claim to setting communal agendas largely free from meddling by foreigners. Three aristocratic councils, aided by a weak executive authority vested first in a count, later a rector, and aided by the Small Council, governed at home and directed foreign policy. The town jealously guarded its archiepiscopal seat, gained through protracted politicking in the late tenth and eleventh centuries. In time that see became the easternmost independent outpost of the Catholic Church in the Balkans.

For Ragusan chroniclers, who began to write in the later medieval centuries, the enduring features of urban life had taken on a sacrosanct character. By the fifteenth century, classically educated citizens had begun to stretch their claims for worthy antecedents beyond their seventh-century founding. They claimed direct descent, through the link of Illyrian Epidaurus, to fifth-century Athens. Thus the myth of Ragusa was born. Medieval chroniclers and citizens alike made a proud bid for the longest continuous history of all cities in western Christendom, even outstripping the claims of the eternal city of Rome. In their "golden century," which began in the late fifteenth century, Ragusans themselves lauded stability and hierarchy, placing those values at the heart of community life.

Specifically, Ragusans claimed that their pacific history, that is, the virtual lack of recorded rebellion, sedition, or factional strife, sprang out of a special inheritance from the distant past. They saw themselves as the inheritors of an ancient Greek republicanism so well preserved that while other medieval communes readily capitulated to autocracy, Ragusans were ensured against such a fate. This line of argument served to convince others as well as themselves. Ragusa was lauded as Europe's prime surviving example of an unadulterated republic until its last days as an independent city-state: a *republica perfetta* with the backward-looking arguments of the Ragusan chroniclers cited to explain the phenomenon. Renaissance Ragusa arose as a *città felice* maintaining that "carefully measured equality in the distribution of powers and dignities among aristocrats" that utopian writers sought and applauded.[8]

Abetting the persuasiveness of notions of stasis, the community failed to increase in population and urban scale in the medieval centuries, as had the Italian city-states across the Adriatic Sea. Many environmental reasons help explain why this was so (and they will be noted in Chapter 2), but there is little dispute that constraint applies to urban numbers as well as the geographical perimeters of the town. Ragusa became a late medieval city-state of restricted territory, enclosed by walls that had been built in the thirteenth century (see Figure 1), and although it was further fortified it never expanded. It contained a peak population of possibly 7,000 inhabitants in the town with 25,000 more in the Astarea (coastal land outside the walls) and the islands under the commune's jurisdiction.[9] An explanation for economic growth that moves beyond typical numerical and spatial arguments is needed to explain how Ragusa became a major carrier of trade, competing in carrying capacity with the likes of the great cities of Genoa and Venice. Late fifteenth-century Ragusa rivaled in wealth cities ten or more times its population, which administered vast territories and resources. Ragusa's commerce in its "golden century," the last years of the fifteenth and the beginning years of the sixteenth centuries, succeeded so far beyond the expectations one normally brings to the achievements of small city-states that it clamors for explanation.

Ragusans participated in European cultural life with enthusiasm. Some of the earliest extant records of the Great Council noted efforts to bring teachers of Latin to town to instruct youth. The brightest of these young men were sent off to Italian, and later Spanish, universities at town expense to complete their educations. A high level of literacy characterized civic life, with instruction in Latin predominating through most of the

Figure 1. City wall, Tower of St. Jacob, thirteenth century. From Lukša Beritić, *Utvrđenja grada Dubrovnika* (Zagreb: JAZU, 1955).

medieval period, although an active Slavic notariat lodged in the town chancellery promoted Slavic literacy as well. Slavic Renaissance literature was born here. Marin Držić (1508–67) produced comedies of lasting popularity for the stage. Ragusa's most famous poet and tragedian, Ivan Gundulić (1589–1638), lived in a generation in which Ragusa's small circle of patrician and bourgeois families produced numerous scholars and writers. Ancient learning from the Greek as well as the Latin classics was cultivated, and Ragusans made contributions to the fields of mathematical science and geography. Through contacts with humanist circles in Italy, and praises in

Figure 2. Aerial view of the city.

Figure 3. Arsenal and ancient port of the town. From Lukša Beritić, *Utvrđenja grada Dubrovnika* (Zagreb: JAZU, 1955).

verse composed in the town's honor by the well-regarded humanist and Ragusan archbishop, Luigi Beccadelli, (1555–63), Ragusans maintained their ties to the cultural life of the northern Italian city-states as well as a bilingual literary tradition. In the fifteenth century they had won renown through the popular *Della mercatura et del mercante perfetto* of a native son, Benedetto Cotrugli, and in the sixteenth century their chronicles attracted the attention of that perceptive and critical political theorist, Jean Bodin. However, most local authors wrote primarily in Slavic after the sixteenth century; for that reason Ragusan humanists contributed substantially to the vernacular tradition in early Slavic literature, but at the expense of remaining accessible to a western European audience.

Ragusa receded from notice as the late seventeenth and eighteenth centuries progressed. However, after the fall of the republic, South Slav nationalists rediscovered the town's early history and recorded it in Serbo-Croatian, augmented by a few studies and translations in Viennese German. As a result Ragusan historiography developed largely independent of the comparative *topos* that was imposed on the various histories of city-states of Italy proper. Irredentist claims to an Italian Ragusa did not prevail over a Slavic Dubrovnik. The city's history came to figure in the greater project of Yugoslav social science, that is, the self-discovery, and in a sense the legitimation, of native South Slav elites.[10] The legal scholar Valtlazar Bogišić edited Ragusa's statute law with the Czech-born historian Constantine Jireček as part of his greater project of understanding the relationship of traditional legal systems to modern South Slav law codes. In other regards, the city-state's proud heritage transcended the confines of national history because the town had harbored the first school of Slavic literature. Ragusa's Renaissance writers became the acknowledged founders of a Pan-Slav literary tradition.

Meanwhile, historians with training in scientific evaluation of sources expressed a growing skepticism that a "pure" aristocracy, such as Ragusa was claimed to have been, had ever existed within the early modern European state system. Over time Venetian historiography has influenced Western opinion against that possibility, with revelations that Venice had never been the successfully functioning early modern aristocratic republic that her mythmakers had projected.[11] Could the opinions of Ragusa's own rigorously trained critical school of historians be heard over the new terms of Western historical discourse when they asserted that their town had been a successful aristocratic republic for over a thousand years? Could they be heard when they wrote, for the most part, in a language inaccessible to a

Western public? The largely local interpreters of medieval Ragusa continued to back their assertion that the city-state succeeded at aristocratic republicanism even in the face of commercial prosperity and despite the pressures of its role as a Mediterranean power. The project of establishing Ragusa's republicanism has occupied generations of Yugoslav scholars. In order to further that goal, they edit and publish, even republish, political sources when that project has been all but abandoned elsewhere in European scholarship.[12]

If clear benefit accrued to the South Slav national cause because of the incorporation of Ragusa's proud history into a shared Yugoslav past, this has also meant that Ragusa has remained ripe for rediscovery by the West for well over a century. In the 1870s a young and exuberant Arthur Evans hiked over the Balkan highlands of Bosnia and the Herzegovina, developing an increasing sympathy for the nationalist South Slav cause that was directed against foreign occupation. Insights about the troubled history of the Balkans occurred to the scholarly, well-read Evans as he gazed down from a mountain pass upon the walled seaport of Dubrovnik, as the republic of Ragusa was then known. His excitement about the centrality of the city-state's role in regional development grew when he settled in the town and read everything he could lay hands on, both history and tantalizing myths. In the first flush of his enthusiasm he resolved to write the entire history of Ragusa from prehistoric times to the present.

If Evans had completed his project rather than faced arrest, jail, and then banishment by Austrian officials for complicity in nationalist agitation, Crete might have lost its pioneer archaeologist and publicist, and Ragusa might have gained one instead. Sir Arthur Evans's vision of Ragusa transcended a "scientific" history, because he saw the community in metahistorical terms as the inheritor of classical values, which the town preserved and transmitted to eastern Europe when those values were jeopardized by Turkish occupation, war, and turmoil.[13]

Such romance eluded the city-state. Only a faint notion of that glamorous possibility has clung to the city's history after Evans took his remarkable skills as publicist further south in the Mediterranean. Ragusa did not capture the attention of a wider European audience again until the World War II era. Then Ragusa fairly catapulted to scholarly attention because Fernand Braudel incorporated the history of its golden century into his great vision of the Mediterranean, paying out some highly flattering compliments to Ragusa in his narrative. Since then the story of the community's economy and accomplishments have received some recognition in general histories.[14]

If we have come to consider this city in the wider context of European development only recently, then perhaps there lies a reason for some lingering misconceptions. "A life with no risks and no history," Alberto Tenenti dourly observed in 1967 when comparing Ragusa to "the old city state of Venice and its refusal to give way to the predominance of any power."[15] His allegation of "no risk" may be easily disproved; "no history" is a considerably more serious charge, since it allows the possession of a history only to those who show clear evidence of change and strife in the readily observable institutions of public life. By Tenenti's criteria Ragusans' proudest boast is turned against them. In a community where the most extraordinary accomplishments were a smooth tenor for political and social life, and a foreign policy based on diplomacy that avoided wars and armed aggression, Tenenti perhaps missed the locus of the city's dynamism and often confused successful social programs with stasis. One might better look within and behind the public record of accomplishments at Ragusa to seek answers about how that record was achieved.

For this reason, it is worth investigating whether Ragusa's meaningful history occurred at a less readily observable level of community life. Ragusa was a medieval city-state that may be better served by the new techniques and methods of late-twentieth-century historical investigation than it has been by the more traditionally organized histories that devote their attention to change wrought in the public sphere. That is to say, this may be a story more accurately told by methods of investigation that look to the internal history of family, family networks, and their impact on community life. This social history produces collective portraits, or what is now commonly called a prosopography of a community. It is possible that in Ragusa, consequential policies were often planned and effected within the private confines of the household or through ostensibly casual meetings in streets, on corners, or at the harbor. If so, this is the proper arena for historical investigation, and it is a contention of this study that through analyzing informal, occasional, and familial systems a new internal chronology, one sometimes congruent with events in the public sphere, sometimes distinct from them, may be constructed. This amended chronology may reveal a picture of intense urban dynamism.

Methods devised for dealing with notarial charters that can extract from these "documents of practice" evidence on the conduct of social life and business are relevant. Charters survive in plentiful and organized series in the town's archives. Since private notarized instruments recorded lives at critical junctures, they may be collated, quantified, and studied over a sufficiently long span so that dominant patterns of behavior and informal remedies for community problems may be in part, at least, known. It is appropriate, for example, to study how the touted equality in the distribution of powers among aristocrats was achieved. It is also useful to give weight to aristocratic women's influence because their private world of household and neighborhood in many ways remained the locus of power and afforded them a role in momentous decision making. Such an emphasis enriches the general history of any community, but it may provide a unique entry point into the dominant aristocratic culture at Ragusa. The private institutions of marriage, family, and family networks appear to have provided the very tools that allowed Ragusans to create in the private sphere what other cities accomplished through the elaboration of complex public institutions.

This results in an episodic history, as various aspects of communal life yield to investigation in the documented decades following the codification of statute law in 1272. Such an approach sacrifices the anticipated organization of a city-state history, however; burrowing into the components of urban life interrupts the stately course of Ragusan achievement presented to the outside world in the minutes of councils and the histories of chroniclers. These records may confound as well as illuminate, because Ragusans saw little reason in sharing their ways and means with the outside world.

Constructing an internal history of the community cannot, however, be undertaken in the common sense in which it is understood today, that is, as a history of the private values and familial world of the city's inhabitants. This avenue of approach into Ragusan history, useful as it has proved elsewhere, is closed by a lack of personal, revelatory sources that allow glimpses of private life. For fourteenth-century Florentines, or fifteenth-century Venetians, highly personal histories may be composed for individuals and their families through consulting private letters, sermons, manuals of advice to relatives and friends. In the case of Florence even *ricordanze* and *ricordi* exist. Perhaps some Ragusans kept such records—there are a few references to fourteenth-century *quaderni* that may have contained more than business accounts—but these have not survived for any period earlier than the sixteenth century, and even then there appear to have been few. There are references in sixteenth-century histories to one private archive of the aristocratic Bobali family, but these documents no longer exist and they cannot be reconstructed in any usable form from the histories that were based on them.[16] This is a loss because historians have made valuable discoveries by heeding the words of Lucien Febvre when he stated in 1942 that the study of family history is one of the surest devices for understanding an age.[17] Attempts to investigate personal values in order to understand the inner life and vitality of the family organism have enriched our understanding of urban life and development in important ways, but they are not very practicable for this study if they rely on intimate revelations. One rather negative benefit balances against this scarcity of private, revelatory papers. Because of a lack of "garrulous" accounts of private life, homilies, or sermons on conduct, there is little temptation to read idealized accounts of family life, or admonitions, as norms within medieval Ragusa. Notarial records, all that survive to record private lives in this community, compensate for the fragmented evidence they provide on people's lives with their rather bland neutrality: they record acts or intended acts unadorned by putative motives. For that reason they are less likely to prejudice us.

One procedure that has been followed in the past in an attempt to investigate Ragusan history has been to construct genealogies, that is, to collect and connect together the names of cognate groups, particularly those known to be members of the powerful Ragusan patriciate. This effort has been inspired by the concerns of political history. It represents an attempt to augment the public record and illuminate the official histories of the community by revealing more about lineages and associations of powerful political figures. Although this approach yields some information on family, it is of limited use since it is based on the unexamined assumption that a traceable cognate group was family in a meaningful sense. Therefore, this study looks instead at how Ragusans understood family relations and what they perceived as correct in regard to family rights and obligations.

In concrete terms, I shall ask questions about the informal life of the community, which may be investigated by reference to the surviving notarial charters, then correlate findings with what is known about change in the public sphere. What behavior allowed the community to achieve its success without the highly visible conflicts, turnings points, confrontations, wars, and creation of complex bureaucratic institutions that mark the histories of other noteworthy city-states? The question could also be phrased in this way: Was there an alternative, workable way to conduct community life and business that, over the long term, achieved successes comparable to those achieved by Ragusa's nearby Italian neighbors? In particular, the critical role marriage negotiations played in the economic and political strategies of the community requires attention. I also consider the customary methods for problem solving that were available to Ragusan families. Through the legitimating act of drawing up personal transactions before the notary—

wills, dowry contracts, *fraterna*, and various forms of partnerships—how could individuals work toward the goal of social solidarity? Ragusans envisioned broad applications for these ordinary contractual agreements in common use throughout southern Europe. Notarial evidence sometimes hints at a consensus that underlay economic and political initiatives.

An internal reconstruction of Ragusa's documented medieval centuries would not then be a study of genealogies of political personages, or the personal accounts of its families' lives, but rather a study of that coherent group of citizen families who by the thirteenth century, if not before, had formed themselves into a marrying group (Slavic *prijateljstvo*) and whose contours as an elite group with a monopoly of political power were not disturbed until the disastrous earthquake of 1667. It is possible to argue that even after that devastating event this endogamous group of families (or "friendship circle," as it is sometimes translated from the Serbo-Croatian) remained the core of the community until the fall of the republic. By identifying the aristocratic *prijateljstvo* as a critical unit of study in the investigation of the community, the society of the entire city may be constructed from this core outward: the public and more intimate lives of group members, then the lives of related households, inter-related neighborhoods, roles of servants, clients, and friends; and through this approach lay open to analysis the community at large. This provides a vantage point from which to examine the long-planned effort to launch a Ragusan bid for preeminence among the commercial powers in Mediterranean trade. From such a vantage point Ragusa's twelve-hundred-year history as a republic may be better understood. An internal reconstruction that builds from this social core outward may have the effect of fleshing out Ragusa's story in such a way that its longevity as a republic, its late medieval economic success, and its consequence in the greater Mediterranean world are clarified.

No doubt groups of friends, who over generations chose their marriage partners largely or exclusively from within their own numbers, existed elsewhere in the Balkans and in medieval Europe. But over the centuries these groups were likely to fade away when more formal political institutions grew powerful enough to provide an alternative point of identity. Occasionally a friendship circle survived as a locus of power where factional politics promoted group intermarriage or a distrusted political regime was imposed by an occupying power on a homogeneous population. Ragusa underwent prolonged periods of occupation in the centuries before 1358. In defense against external intervention the aristocratic *prijateljstvo,* and the republican institutions its members preferred, were cultivated side by side, effectively avoiding the most corrosive effects of internal faction through constant attention to resolution of divisive issues. In sum, patricians deferred to each other in deepening commitment to a shared destiny. After Ragusa became an independent city-state, noble Ragusans continued their simultaneous reliance on their informal circle, with its ties cemented by marriage, and republicanism as their preferred form of government. This was a remarkable departure from what occurred in Italy among urban people who developed new understandings of political identity as city-states and broke free from allegiance to monarchs, popes, and emperors.

Ragusa's distinct political evolution meant that noble citizens respected their own notion of the proper distinction between the public and the private spheres and what should be accomplished within each. The appropriate devolution of public and private matters were pressing concerns in city-states and landed realms throughout Europe in the late medieval centuries; however, the distinction emerging at Ragusa was in some sense unique and underlay a social experiment that finds few parallels among Western polities. The friendship or marrying circle continued to bear the principal responsibility for obtaining political, social, and economic consensus while councils of state and organs of government implemented Ragusans' civil and foreign policies, often significantly, as Aymard observed, employing medieval statecraft rather than an inflated modern state apparatus.

Studying this friendship or marrying circle and constructing community relations from this core outward allow a glimpse of the imaginative way in which Ragusans apportioned responsibilities for private or public concerns in the course of their everyday lives. This approach in no way denies the significance of the public record, which has until now provided the major corpus of the community's recorded history. In order to introduce the reader to the internal life of the community, it is perhaps best to first provide some acquaintance with the history of public institutions of the city-state and what historians have had to say about them. This history may in turn serve as a point of departure for inquiring into the internal dynamics of community life.

*   *   *

Was a state of deference—a desired but unrealizable vision to most Renaissance men who sought it—realized in the old Republic of Ragusa? And if so, how?

*Notes*

1. Bariša Krekić, *Dubrovnik in the Fourteenth and Fifteenth Centuries* (Norman: University of Oklahoma, 1972).

2. Maurice Aymard, *Venise, Raguse et le commerce du blé pendant la seconde moitié du XVIe siècle* (Paris: SEVPEN, 1966), p. 73.

3. Fernand Braudel, *The Mediterranean and the Mediterranean World in the Age of Philip II*, trans. Siân Reynolds (New York: Harper, 1973), vol. 1, p. 340.

4. Fernand Braudel, *The Mediterranean*, vol. 1, p. 58.

5. The Venetians coined the term *inter-culfum* to refer to the area of the Adriatic gulf north of Corfu on the east and the heel of Italy's boot on the west, which they saw as within their sphere of influence. Dominance over the gulf figured importantly in Venetian politics from the eleventh century onward.

6. Surveys on Ragusa/Dubrovnik in western European languages are scarce. Constantine Jireček, "Die Bedeutung von Ragusa in der Handelgeschichte des Mittelalters," in *Almanach der Kaiserlichen Akademie der Wissenschaften in Wien*, 49, Jg. S. (Vienna, 1899), pp. 362–452 has not been replaced. Milan Prelog and Jorjo Tadić provide surveys in *Historija naroda Jugoslavije* I (1953), pp. 654–60 and pp. 629–54 (in Serbo-Croatian); and "Dubrovnik," *Enciklopedija Jugoslavije*, 3 (Zagreb: JAZU, 1958), pp. 121–27 is useful. Recently Vinko Foretić has produced *Povijest Dubrovnika*, 2 vol. (Zagreb: JAZU, 1980). In English, F. W. Carter, *Dubrovnik: The Classic City-State* (London: Seminar Press, 1972) is not entirely reliable and is largely based on the nineteenth-century work by Luigi Villari, *The Republic of Ragusa* (London: J. M. Dent, 1904). Bariša Krekić, *Dubrovnik in the Fourteenth and Fifteenth Centuries* (Norman: University of Oklahoma Press, 1972) and *Dubrovnik, Italy, and the Balkans in the Late Middle Ages* (London: Variorum, 1980) are valuable.

7. *Ravenatis Anonymi Cosmographia*, ed. M. Pinder and G. Parthey (Berlin: F. Nicolai, 1860), p. 208.

8. Frank E. Manuel and Fritzie P. Manuel, *Utopian Thought in the Western World* (Cambridge, Mass.: Belknap Press, 1979), p. 153.

9. J. Tadić, "Le Port de Raguse au moyen âge. Le navire et l'économie maritime du moyen âge au XVIIIᵉ siècle" (Paris: SEVPEN, 1958), p. 18.

10. E. A. Hammel and Joel M. Halpern, "Observations on the Intellectual History of Ethnology and Other Social Sciences in Yugoslavia," *Comparative Studies in Society and History* 7 (1969): 17–26.

11. Compare Edward Muir, *Civic Ritual in Renaissance Venice* (Princeton, N.J.: Princeton University Press, 1981) for a review of the myth of Venice.

12. Recently see Ilija Mitić, *Dubrovačka država u medunarodnoj zajednici (od. 1358 do 1815)* (Zagreb: JAZU, 1988). See also the scholarly edition of Ragusa's *Liber Viridis* by Branislav Nedeljković (Belgrade: SAN, 1984), and more recently Josip Lučić's re-editing of the first extant chancellery notebooks, *Spisi dubrovačke kancelarije*, Monumenta Historica Ragusina III (Zagreb: JAZU, 1988).

13. Sir Arthur Evans, *Illyrian Letters, Correspondence Addressed to the Manchester Guardian during 1877* (London: Longmans, Green, 1878) and *Through Bosnia and the Herzegovina on Foot* (London: Longmans, Green, 1876). See D. B. Harden, *Sir*

*Arthur Evans, A Memoir, 1851–1941* (London, 1876; reprint Oxford: Ashmolean Museum, 1983), and Sylvia Horwitz, *The Find of a Lifetime* (London: Weidenfed and Nicolson, 1983), pp. 5off.

14. Dražen Budiša, "Humanism in Croatia" appears in *Humanism Beyond Italy*, vol. 2 of *Renaissance Humanism*, ed. Albert Rabil (Philadelphia: University of Pennsylvania Press, 1988), pp. 265–92, but until recently Slavic literature was not routinely included in anthologies and general studies of humanist literature.

15. Alberto Tenenti, *Piracy and the Decline of Venice,* trans. J. Pullan and B. Pullan (Berkeley: University of California Press, 1967), pp. xvii–xviii.

16. John Fine, *The Bosnian Church, A New Interpretation* (New York and London: East European Quarterly, distrib. Columbia University Press, 1975), pp. 41–112.

17. Lucien Febvre, "Ce que peuvent nous apprendre les monographies familiales," *Mélanges d'histoire sociale* 1 (1942): 31–34.

# 2. The Old Republic

## Origin Myths and Early History

The first centuries at Ragusa yield few records. For the tenth century that situation alters dramatically. In his *De Administrando Imperio,* Constantine Porphyrogenitus described Ragusa among the Adriatic tributaries of the Byzantine empire. This imperial source and certain other early versions of the town's origins share a curious anomaly: they account for the town's founding in various unresolvable ways. Both a Latin origin story and a Greek origin story survived in Porphyrogenitus's account; locally composed medieval chronicles presented a Slavic origin story and Renaissance accounts provided the community with mythic Greek origins from the dawn of recorded time. None, however, make the usual claims that theirs was the "true" story, or that the various accounts may be merged into one authoritative text.

In the tenth century Constantine Porphyrogenitus stated first that Ragusa's earliest inhabitants came from Greek-speaking Epidaurus across the bay, then added that they came from Latin-speaking Salona to the north. No note or comment attempted to resolve these contradictory assertions. Although, in a certain sense, not enough was known about the community's early history, too much has been offered by way of explanation without resolution of glaring inconsistencies.

Constantine Porphyrogenitus's royally edited and abridged series of ambassadorial and officials' reports, known as *De Administrando Imperio,* devoted one full paragraph to the origin and history of his distant appendage, Ragusa. Because it is by far the earliest as well as most complete reference to the community it is worth quoting in full:

> The city of Ragusa is not called Ragusa in the tongue of the Romans but because it stands on cliffs, it is called in Roman speech "the cliff, lau"; whence they are called "Lausioi" i.e. "those who have their seat on the cliff." But vulgar usage, which frequently corrupts names by altering their letters, has changed the denomination and called them Rausaioi. These same Rausaioi used of old

to possess the city that is called Pitaura; and since when the other cities were captured by the Slavs that were in the province, this city too was captured, and some were slaughtered and others taken prisoner, those who were able to escape and reach safety settled in the almost precipitous spot where the city now is; they built it small to begin with, and afterwards enlarged it, and later still extended its wall until the city reached its present size, owing to their gradual spreading out and increase in population. Among those who migrated to Ragusa are: Gregory, Arsaphius, Victorinus, Vitalius, Valentine, the arch-deacon, Valentine the father of Stephen the Protospatharius. From their migration from Salona to Ragusa, it is 500 years till this day, which is the 7th indiction, the year 6457. In this same city lies St. Pancratius, in the church of St. Stephen, which is in the middle of the city.[1]

The story presented first—of a people from Epidaurus (Pitaura, also Epidaurum, medieval Civita Vecchia, and more recently Cavtat) fleeing invaders and settling on a rather forbidding cliff—finds confirmation else-where,[2] but the date given for the event, circa A.D. 450, appears to be about two centuries too early.[3] This lack of precision may indicate that a tenth-century observer found the community's longevity impressive and there-fore receding into an ever more remote past.[4] With the date of the found-ing, however, the account lists refugees from Salona, a Roman town to the north of Ragusa, as the founders rather than the Greeks from Epidaurus with whom the account began.

This list of persons, some with families, purported to be the commu-nity's leading inhabitants and progenitors is interesting on its own account. Because the list was consequential enough to be included in this imperial bureaucratic report, it is perhaps possible to treat it as a consciously em-ployed rhetorical device, a historiographical list in which the composer signals to the reader to draw on a reservoir of shared knowledge about known persons, lineages, civic posts, and ecclesiastical offices in order to amplify context and meaning.[5] As such it was evocative, but unfortunately, only for the small literate Byzantine audience of officials and the wellborn living one thousand years ago. Victorinus, Gregory, Arsaphius, Vitalius, Valentine, the archdeacon, and Valentine, the father of Stephen, the Pro-tospatharius, were noted. These men held ecclesiastical office or civil titles and they bore both late Greek and Latin names. Although the context for interpreting this list has been lost, its existence provides a rare insight into early Ragusa's history. First, these persons were recognized by their civi-lized pursuits, and they passed down to their heirs the opportunity to continue that civilized tradition. It mattered little whether they had fled from Greek Epidaurus or Latin Salona: any new town founded on the division line between the Latin west and the Greek east was bound to attract a mixed population. It mattered more that earliest townsmen were willing to fill offices of church and state and could subsist on infrequent contacts with Constantinople. They kept alive the skills of urbanity of the late antique world, the chief of which was a bilingual literacy acquired through a traditional classical education.

For in early Ragusa, which prospered and expanded even before the tenth century, lay the opportunity for that modest success, survival really, which a Christian urban elite might achieve by adopting a "model of parity," that is, by submerging internal conflicts, indeed all competitive desires, in the interest of community survival.[6] In such a community the "elite tend to maintain a set of strong invisible boundaries, which mark firm upward limits to the aspirations of individuals, and to direct the aspirations of their members to forms of achievement that could potentially be shared by all other members in the peer group." In undergoing such an internal evolution Ragusa's citizens, those men recognized by officialdom in Constantinople, were creating the constitutional basis of urban survival in the aftermath of Antiquity. They became resources "to be spent not hoarded,"[7] when directed toward the difficult task of perpetuating civic traditions. On this account Porphyrogenitus relates a story of success, one to be noted because it was rare even on the relatively sheltered shores of the Adriatic Sea.

In these early centuries, Ragusan allegiance to Constantinople was measured by sporadic contact and occasional tribute, while Byzantine officials dealt in the only currencies available to them: recognition for the rare visiting delegate from this remote town, bestowal of honorary titles and offices, and identification in a list of valued functionaries. Recognition was a reward for those who, like Byzantium's other far-flung imperial servants, kept up their bilingual skills as a sign of their political allegiance. In Rome, steps had been taken as early as the sixth century to keep up Greek, which was fading from familiar parlance; the tenth century saw those efforts long exhausted. But a cohesive elite of families in Ragusa, and in a few other Adriatic and Sicilian cities loyal to Constantinople, managed to survive within the sphere of imperial tributary cities through the device of remaining literate in both Latin and Greek; this assured continued recognition from the *Romanoi*.[8]

Thus a literate elite, meeting together as *curiales,* are probably the persons we meet in Vitalius, Victorinus, Gregory, Arsaphius, and the two Valentines.[9] As a transposed enclave of city dwellers, with the good fortune of settling within a pre-existing building or monument,[10] their ancestors, the original inhabitants, had continued the *di-glossia* common to a late imperial city.

Wherever cities survived along the frontier between the Greek east and the Latin west, this *di-glossia* cut through the layers of urban society rather than dividing an elite which employed one language from a poorer substratum of townspeople that spoke another. Townspeople, organized in Latin-speaking or Greek-speaking households at Ragusa, may have been mutually incomprehensible to each other, but they shared a clear intent to succeed as a community. With inhibited communication, Latinphone and Grecophone households would find it necessary to refer their differences to the literate, and therefore bilingual, heads of leading households, so that the bilingual literate leaders truly constituted the community's backbone.[11] There is a plausible reason for the continued emphasis on the two characteristic features of late antique urban society in the new medieval Ragusa: separate constituencies based upon language grouping joined at the top of the social pyramid by a republican governing body. Perhaps both origin stories continued to be told side by side because those stories, at odds in their narratives, served different language constituencies. Only prolonged association would in time erode this reliance on two languages and establish the "vulgar usage" that the *De Administrando Imperio* found in use in Ragusa.

A Slavic account of the town's origins also exists; it differs in all particulars from the older, tenth-century account of the *De Administrando Imperio* but, strikingly, shares certain salient themes with it. About A.D. 950, the story relates, a Slavic king, Pavlimir, grandson of King Radoslav, debarked at the nearby harbor at Gravosa, or Gruž, from a long exile in Italy. With the aid of his entourage, which included both highborn Slavs and equally noble Italians, he founded a new town. This account is still taken seriously enough to find a place in the official histories of the city-state.[12] The story echoes familiar themes: it was an illustrious and royal group who founded the town. The community was clearly bilingual from the beginning, because King Pavlimir had both Slavs and Italians in his entourage. Again, the community was self-consciously organized in the sense that a group joined in devotion to the king's colonizing project founded Ragusa, not a migrating kindred or people speaking one tongue.

In the sixteenth century, when most traces of an early Greek inheritance had disappeared, noble Ragusan families resurrected claims for Greek antecedents by creating imaginative genealogies that linked existing families back through Epidaurus to the heroes of classical Greece. These origin stories that claimed Greek antecedents were reintroduced at a time when Ragusan bilingualism still existed but consisted of an Adriatic Italian dialect and a Slavic tongue rather than Greek and Latin. The myth of bilingual origins was evidently not to be allowed to fall into disuse. And these Renaissance genealogies were even more adamant about the illustrious status of the founders of the community than were the older, inherited origin stories.[13]

Through the sixteenth century and beyond, Ragusans remained quite consistent about the themes that they believed unique to their experience as an urban society, celebrating them in origin stories. A heritage as a community, divided into two language groups yet united in purpose, stood first among these features, and there is some early philological evidence that sustains this claim. Some early names employed at Ragusa—Alexius, Demetrius, and Nicephorus, for example—as well as the survival of many Greek terms and phrases, indicate that Greek had been known and used in the early community.[14] But there is philological evidence as well—names like Bonus, Calenda, Fuscus, Geninianus, Lamponius, Lampridius, Lupus, Maurus, Primus, Proculus, Sabinus, Sergius, Ursus, and Ursatius—that from early times a Latin language of late Roman origin predominated.[15]

Although the genealogies, which claimed grandiose classical Greek forebears, are among the more imposingly imagined Renaissance flights of fancy, they cannot, of course, be believed.[16] The truth behind even the finest noble Ragusan name was likely to have been Bosnian origins. Ragusa's prominent families were often the heirs of dispossessed Slavic nobles who had, periodically, been pushed out or moved to the coast, where they adopted an urban life along with allegiance to the town. This pattern of migration finds confirmation in the earliest preserved Ragusan charters where Slavic families may be found still entering the lists of noble town families as late as the thirteenth century.[17] It also figures as one of the reasons that Ragusa's history fails to fit within a *topos* of ethnicity, although ethnic difference features prominently in Yugoslav historiography of neighboring lands.

Faced with the unreliability of the surviving origin stories, historians have generally concluded that the early medieval centuries were Ragusa's "Latin" era. The thirteenth century, that is, the first substantially documented era of the town's history, when Slavic found its way into notarial charters, has been used as evidence for "slavization" of the community. This sequential mode of passage from Italian to Slavic neglects the evidence that medieval townspeople left us by respecting different origin stories and by insisting on a continued bilingualism as an integral feature of community life.[18] Ragusans acknowledged that Slavic and Italian could exist side by side in their story of King Pavlimir, while some preserved a belief that before Slavic and Italian were spoken Ragusans conversed in Greek and Latin. This conviction helped citizens account for qualities in which they invested great importance: ancient roots, noble origins, republican institutions, distinct but cooperating language groups willing to live peaceably together within the community, and high priority placed on bilingualism as the signature of citizenship.

The immediate advantages for defense represented by the limestone knoll to which the earliest inhabitants had fled were nearly outweighed by the long-term disadvantages of a barren and geologically unstable site. The entire Dalmatian coastline was, and continues to be, subject to sporadic seismic activity. One earthquake did enormous damage to Ragusa in 1520, and the earthquake of 1667 destroyed much of the town inside the walls, causing the death of perhaps two-thirds of the inhabitants in the quake itself and the fire that followed it.[19] This gives plausibility to the belief that the founders colonized the site knowing its inherent instability. Epidaurus, across the bay, Ragusa's forerunner, had suffered damage from tremors before it was attacked and destroyed by the invaders of the seventh century. Earthquake may have been viewed as the inevitable accompaniment of settlement on the Adriatic coastline and left in the hands of God.

A more immediate concern for the earliest townspeople was dealing with the barrenness of a site chosen for its inaccessability to marauders. The limestone knoll that the townspeople transformed for their use afforded protection from barbarian attack because a marshy trough separated it from Mt. Sergius (Mt. Srdj), a larger limestone projection that rises sharply from the coast to over four hundred meters. The minute new town sat on a peninsula that was almost an island with a mountain at its back. But the lack of a natural source of fresh spring water and inadequate soil for farming also describe this exposed site set in the sea.

The steep coast to the west of town was wooded, and after rounding a larger peninsula called Lapad, the shore indents again to form one very fine harbor at Gravosa or Gruž. Beyond that harbor the wooded coastal cliffs rise almost straight out of the sea to heights varying from three hundred to six hundred meters. The closest source of abundant fresh water runs in the short broad River Ombla, which appears only two kilometers inland from Gruž, and meets the sea in the most remote reaches of the sheltered harbor.

Early townspeople propelled small craft around the wooded peninsula of Lapad to this harbor for a sweet water source when water supplied by rainfall collected in cisterns inside the town failed to fill the needs of the little settlement.[20]

Although the northwesterly coast offered fresh water at not too great a distance, the southeasterly coast is slightly less steep and was then well covered with forest. This section of the Adriatic coast appeared green in the medieval centuries; it was very heavily wooded in places and pierced by deep fiords such as the Gulf of Catar (Kotor). On an axis between Ragusa and this gulf, and inland behind the sea cliffs, lay one long fertile valley known as Canali (Konavle) because of the ruins of an ancient viaduct that crossed it. The valley had been cultivated in ancient times and continued to produce grain. If Ragusa was to purchase foodstuffs from this or some of the other nearby fertile valleys and hillsides (Popovo and Travunia or Trebinje also lay nearby and were cultivated), amicable relations had to be maintained with the local population of farmers and their protectors.

"In this city not a single grain of wheat is eaten which does not have to be fetched from five hundred miles away," the Bishop of Dav told his royal French correspondent in 1572, and implied that it had always been so.[21] This was something of an exaggeration because fertile valleys near the town had always had some wheat to sell the townsmen but their harvests never came close to satisfying demand. Nevertheless, the bishop's words betrayed a fatal weakness: the townspeople could not subsist on local resources, nor from the small holdings of land it acquired over the centuries, sobering facts soon grasped by all Ragusa's would-be conquerors. Occupying Ragusa gave no access to rich resources, unless the ingenuity of town dwellers was counted as such.

Ragusa's harbor faced south, which distinguishes this seaport from the Adriatic ports prudently shielded from the full impact of the southern sirocco winds. This harbor, the only accessible moorage close to the settlement, had the advantage of protection from the fierce winter wind known as the bora because Mt. Srdj behind the town proved an effective barrier. But a south face left the town dangerously exposed to the sirocco's spring blasts. The barrier earthwork, or mole, constructed and reconstructed against the weather was a puny defense against a heavy sea. On the other hand, the largely beneficial mistral, which blows out of the northwest, reaching Ragusa obliquely, favored local shipping through the protected channels of the Dalmatian coast to the north and the west of the town. That wind could be expected to dominate in the summer and it guaranteed that the early inhabitants could continue to be a seafaring people. The summer season was held up, however, while the sirocco's period of spring dominance lasted. This postponed the onset of seasonal shipping with the inevitable effect of increasing the town's dependence for provisions on the neighboring countryside and the islands or on the townspeople's own efforts to provide adequate storage facilities for grain held over the winter.

Some of the immediate drawbacks of the town's site were balanced by the strategic location that the town occupied on both land and sea routes. The mountainous Bosnian karst (the limestone spine of the West Balkan chain of mountains) directly behind the town both shielded it from the harsh continental climate and provided accessible routes through a series of passes. Most of these routes connected up with the Via Egnatia, the ancient Roman road that began south of Ragusa at Duracchium (Durazzo, also Durres) and led across the Balkans to Constantinople. Three Balkan territories met behind Ragusa: Bosnia, its neighbor the Herzegovina or medieval Hlum, and Rascia, the original West Balkan homeland of the Serbs.

To the north and west of Ragusa the Dalmatian coast, with its sporadic but occasionally luxurious vegetation, was the traditional home of shepherds, the Vlachs, who practiced transhumance, favoring the highland pastures in the summer and the coast near Ragusa in the winter. South and east of the town shepherds practiced transhumance as well from the highlands of Montenegro to the shores of fiords and the coast. Supplies of animal products flowed into the early town.

Nearby islands of the Adriatic littoral were more essential as a source of marketable produce and manpower. A series of small islands lay to the east of the town in a chain with the most prominent, La Croma (Lokrum), visible from Ragusa's harbor. These islands could support a limited farming population, and their sheltered coves housed fishing fleets. Farther off the coast lay Lastovo, or Lagosta, and northwest of the town, beyond the island of Meleta, or Mjlet, lay the peninsula of Puncta Stagni, or Pelješać. It formed one pillar of the Korculan gate with the eastern tip of the island of that name. This island, much of whose history was spent as a possession of Venice, marked the beginning of the Adriatic shipping channel that wound along until it reached Istria. The islands were strategic for protection, as a source of food, and above all as a source of cooperating populations versed in the ways of the sea.

Perhaps Ragusa survived in a hostile world because of its natural fortification and because the nominal suzerainty of Constantinople dissuaded all but the most determined from attacks on the town. As time

Map 1. Republic of Ragusa, fifteenth century, at the height of territorial expansion.

progressed the Venetians, not the Moors, proved to be the most determined of all aggressors; at least they mounted the most serious threat to the
town's autonomy in its long history. When the Venetian Doge Pietro II
Orseolo's fleet swept down the Adriatic in A.D. 1000, to rid the region of
pirates, the Venetians recording the triumph listed Ragusa's name with its
island neighbors and raiders at the mouth of the Narenta (Neretva) River
among those who needed to be subdued to stop attacks on Venetian
shipping.[22] Ragusan accounts of the expedition differ substantially from
this opinion, as might be expected from a community that considered
piracy the crime of its enemies, not a term to be attached to its own
activity.[23] So the Ragusans insisted, not without reason, that Venice harbored imperial designs behind their rhetoric. Ragusa may have been occupied by the Venetians after this expedition; again, accounts differ.[24] For
the Venetians, meantime, and any other Christian seapower in the Adriatic,
this expedition opened the strategic *intra-culfum* upper Adriatic route, that
is, the route that lay among the coastal islands from Istria until it reached
the Korculan gates, to more pacific conditions and increased commercial
shipping.[25] Fortunate Ragusa became a port of call for the Venetian fleet
and began to build a merchant fleet of its own.[26]

In 1071 Ragusa was again attacked, this time from the south by the
Norman followers of Robert Guiscard.[27] The town may have been subject
to Norman occupation in 1071[28]; a century later it certainly did accept

Norman rule for a short period of time.[29] These Venetian and Norman visitations in the eleventh and twelfth centuries revealed how vulnerable might be a city that sat precariously perched on the frontier of the Venetian empire in the upper Adriatic and on the northwestern edge of the Norman sphere of influence, which dominated the south Adriatic waters.

Ragusa probably knew and therefore still feared Muslim raids on its ships and its people. Both Venice and the Normans promised defense against this threat, which suggests the town reached negotiated settlements with both powers regarding these periods of occupation. Constantinople was remote, often leaving the community to its own resources to secure its safety. Yet the link to Constantinople proved strong time and again. Ragusans returned to Byzantine protection after episodes of both Venetian and Norman control in the turbulent years of the eleventh and twelfth centuries.

Archaeological evidence suggests some modest urban growth occurred during this era. Constantine Porphyrogenitus believed the community had prospered and increased in size before the tenth century, but there is no surviving physical evidence that it had moved out beyond the protection of its limestone knoll until the eleventh century. In this period, two new districts were crowded in on top of the promontory, adding to the original district now known as Castellum; they were named St. Peter's and Pustijerna, respectively. These settlements extended the town toward the sea and were immediately surrounded by walls for protection.

It is, however, quite possible that the later chroniclers Resti and de Luccari were correct that Ragusa had been able to establish a fortified outpost on the coast across the marshy trough from the town as early as the late tenth century.[30] Nevertheless, the marsh itself was only slowly filled in, such that it could be turned into usable urban living space, over the next century. Ragusa had become a familiar name in Mediterranean life. In the eleventh century Benedictine monks traveled from Ragusa to Monte Cassino, where they left an inscription on the gate of the monastery. Then, in the middle of the twelfth century, the Arab geographer Idrisi counted Ragusa among the Christian Mediterranean ports and made a special note of the industriousness of its people.[31] These shreds of evidence from outside the community confirm a picture of a prospering port known abroad and counted among the Christian cities of the West (see Figure 4).

Unfortunately, the eleventh and twelfth centuries that brought expansion and prosperity to many Mediterranean ports failed to bring a spurt of growth to Ragusa. Instead, the community continued to contend with

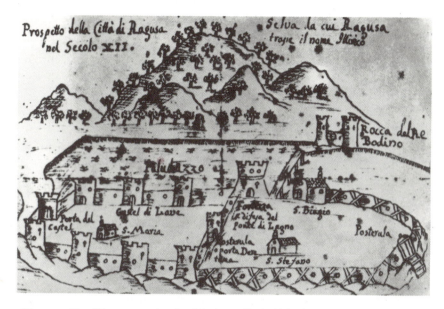

Figure 4. Twelfth-century sketch of Dubrovnik (held in the Franciscan Library at Dubrovnik). Reprinted in *Obnova Dubrovnika 1979–1989*, ed. Božo Letunić (Dubrovnik: Zavod za obnovu Dubrovnika, 1989).

Venice and at least briefly with the Normans for as autonomous a course as they could arrange in the complex politics of the Adriatic world. They were not always successful, but town leaders showed an increasing skill in diplomacy in the treaty arrangements that they drew up during the century, and which have survived. Treaties indicate that the controlling merchant elite wished to develop the same sort of maritime and inland trading network that allowed the port cities of Italy proper to expand in the era. In the last decades of the twelfth century, a treaty of friendship that encouraged trade was arranged with Count Tripon of nearby Catar (Kotor).[32] It was followed by a treaty of 1186 with Stephen, Strasimir, and Miroslav Nemanjić that opened the Serbian lands of the interior to trade with the coast.[33] Rascia, the original holding of the Nemanjić family and homeland of the Serbs, resisted reabsorption when the Comneni emperors reestablished their control over the West Balkan territories of Dioclea at Ragusa's doorstep. Over the following century the Nemanjić created a Serbian kingdom in these lands, and the Serbian-Ragusan trading alliance of 1186 marked the beginning of a long-term association between this landed realm of the interior and the coastal trading port of Ragusa. Almost immediately, Ragusan leaders followed up this success with a commercial treaty with Ban Kulin of Bosnia.[34] Rights of trade with the Balkan interior were secured in this fashion, and the future direction of Ragusan commercial ambitions were set by these initiatives.

In the last years of the twelfth century, after one of the periodic flare-ups in the town's troubled relations with the Venetians, Ragusans accepted the protection of the powerful King William II of Sicily. At least surviving documents reveal that in 1185 a Count Gervasius served as an agent of the Sicilian king with the title of Count of Ragusa, while Tasiligardus, the Sicilian king's *camerarius*, actively participated in the Ragusan treaty dealings with Rascia the following year, 1186.[35] This protection and, possibly, nominal occupation of the town, was short-lived because Ragusa appears to have returned to its traditional Byzantine alliance in 1187.

The Normans left their mark despite their brief tenure. The light ruling hand they employed at Ragusa suited the restricted resources the community afforded and for that reason, perhaps, differed from the exploitive Norman overlordship of the fertile and developed Apulian lands across the Adriatic Sea. Norman rule initiated a three-decade-long era of treaty making in which the Ragusans formed multiple alliances not only with the realms of the Balkan interior but with *altra sponda* Adriatic ports as well.[36] The aftermath of Norman rule apparently brought Norman influence to bear more strongly than the earlier political presence in a pattern that would be repeated after the later Venetian occupation; that is to say, Ragusans paid both their former occupiers the high compliment of imitation once they were physically free of them.

In the case of this twelfth-century occupation, it is quite possible that formative external influences, even those identifiably Byzantine in origin, were transmitted to Ragusa and neighboring Dalmatian cities through the agency of the Kingdom of Sicily. Local Benedictine monks had trekked to Monte Cassino in the eleventh century on the strength of its spiritual ascendency, and Ragusans gained critical insight into the complexities of twelfth-century politics through their contacts both with resident Sicilian royal agents and the Sicilian merchants with whom they traded. In matter of fact, neither Venice, which frequently took the credit, nor Constantinople, which has been awarded the honor, may properly claim the title of Ragusa's early window on the outside world. Norman Sicily may best deserve that title as Ragusa's close neighbor, a great power with whom city dwellers actively sought contact and a significant conduit for formative influences.

In 1199, Ragusan agents negotiated a commercial treaty with Fano directly across the Adriatic. This treaty stated that it formalized existing trading arrangements, rather than initiating new ones; possibly the merchants of Fano were the party who favored formal agreements.[37] That same year a commercial treaty was drawn up with Ancona, and in 1201 a trade agreement was negotiated with Monopoli.[38] Treaties with Bari, Termoli, Molfetta, and Bisceglie followed within the decade.[39] Soon after Ragusa received a visit from Pisan ambassadors and drew up a trading agreement with them.[40] Ragusans did not seek to open the Tyrrhenian Sea to Ragusan trade; their interests were restricted to gaining access to Pisan colonies in the eastern Mediterranean.

It is difficult to estimate how long it took to create the intricate trading network of which these early treaties gave promise. Ragusa's commercial success arrived much later than the twelfth century, and Venetian dominance obscured the earliest steps toward securing it. Treaties do, however, give a clear picture of Ragusan intentions in the last years of the twelfth century. In order for their port city to become a commercial carrier in the Mediterranean, the merchant citizenry relied on secured land routes into the newly established West Balkan realms at the town's doorstep to fill their ships. Port cities on the eastern coast of Italy or outside the Adriatic were then cultivated by treaty to accept goods brought on Ragusan ships. In the early thirteenth century, Ragusans had proceeded far enough along with this trading network so that they even brought wares to the island of Crete.[41] Local merchants managed to float this venture outside the protected waters of the Adriatic by making commercial partnerships with Venetian traders. There is evidence Ragusans traded outside the gulf in their own ships as well as aboard ships of the Venetian fleet, which had stopped at Ragusa for provisions or to take on extra business for the voyage out.[42]

The difficulty of assessing Ragusan autonomy in commercial ventures in these years stems from the controversies surrounding the impact of Ragusa's capitulation to Venice in the aftermath of the Fourth Crusade attack on the eastern Adriatic ports. Although Ragusa avoided the devastating attack on its walls that followed Zara's (Zadar's) resistance to the crusading armies, through the prompt dispatch of ambassadors to sue for conditions before the fleet moved further down the Adriatic, the treaty conditions that were granted in 1205 to Zara and to Ragusa were remarkably similar.[43] Ragusa avoided the razing of its walls, which Zara suffered, but it was bound to send two Ragusan ships to police the Adriatic whenever requested, as Zara was. In Adriatic trade, a limit of four commercial vessels carrying 280 *miliaria* of goods a year was set on Ragusan ships entering Venice. Since extant treaties with other Adriatic ports were not contravened and, in fact, were augmented by new Ragusan treaties drawn up over the following decade, it may be assumed that Venice did not immediately set limits on the capacity of Ragusans to compete with them in east-west Adriatic trade. Yet subsequent decades are full of incidents where, if not expressly forbidden, Ragusa's east-west trade was jeopardized. Venetian ambition kept pace with success: "Ogni merce che entra nell'Adriatico o esce dall'Adriatico deve toccar Venezia"[44] (all goods entering and leaving the Adriatic must pass through Venice) was not a policy goal that even the most adroit Dalmatian negotiators could forestall forever. Over the course of the thirteenth century, Venice attempted to regulate and limit Ragusan trade with its Apulian treaty ports in a bid to dominate east-west Adriatic trade as effectively as it controlled the north-south movement of trade goods. Ragusa's modest but critical achievement lay in preventing the full realization of this program.

Outside the Adriatic, Ragusans were more strictly prohibited from expansion. They were to pay the Venetians 5 percent on all goods imported from Romania; 20 percent on articles from Egypt, Tunis, and Barbary; and 2.5 percent on goods from Sicily. This, however, referred solely to goods brought by Ragusans to Venice. And even here an exception applied to Ragusan merchants (but not to the citizens of Zara) in regard to some imports: the Venetians waived the tax for goods brought from "Sclavonia" by Ragusan agents. This crucial waiver, in conjunction with the earlier Serbian treaty of 1186 and the Bosnian one that followed, shows the level of Ragusan expansion Venice was willing to tolerate in relation to its own markets and sphere of influence. The Venetian Senate was willing to allow the Ragusans to supply the market at Venice with goods from the Balkans, but they would not permit competition with their own interests in the eastern Mediterranean maritime trade. At least for the time being, they would also tolerate some east-west trade across the Adriatic to other Italian ports. This treaty of 1205 remained in force with periodic ratifications and small changes until Ragusa withdrew from Venetian overlordship in 1358. As late as 1340, the Venetians reminded the Ragusans of the weight limitations on the goods they brought to the Venetian port.[45] Although Venetian occupation at Ragusa followed the medieval or "light-handed" model of a sole executive officer called "count" (like the earlier Norman occupation, rather than an occupying army in local residence), patrol by the great

Venetian navy assured that the city of St. Mark became the single most influential external factor in communal development in the critical years of the thirteenth and much of the fourteenth centuries.

The years from 1204 until 1358 were also the first amply documented years at Ragusa.[46] Some fragmentary records survive from the earlier centuries in the collection known today as the *Acta Sanctae Mariae Maioris,* but both the major collection of statute law and the collections of fiscal records, minutes of Council, and charters filed in the chancellery office began only in the late thirteenth century.[47] Most of what is known of medieval Ragusa, its ancient constitution and its republican institutions, has been inferred from records of this and subsequent centuries.

## Religious Life

Medieval town chroniclers, writing much later, presented the early centuries as a prolonged crusade against the Muslims undertaken by a pious and beleaguered Christian citizenry.[48] The chroniclers viewed the ascendency of the Ragusan See to an archbishopric in the eleventh century as a sign of particular favor from Rome and a reward for withstanding the onslaught of Moors. Even the subsequent loss of Bar (Antivari) from the Ragusan archepiscopy when Bar gained its own bishop did not dispel local goodwill toward Rome, although it momentarily disturbed the equilibrium.[49] But since the loss of Bar and the favored position Ragusa subsequently enjoyed in the politics of the church stemmed from the same strategy—that of strengthening Rome's Adriatic outposts after the break with the Constantinople Patriarchate—there was more gained in ecclesiastical politics than lost in the eleventh century when Bar, with the neighboring southeastern territory, broke away.

A contentious religious environment gave license for Ragusan seamen to abscond with the relics of St. Blaise while in the east and to return in triumph to their home port. St. Blaise soon eclipsed relics mentioned in Constantine Porphyrogenitus's account—"the body of St. Pancratius lying in the Church of St. Stephen"—in local veneration. If Bari's seamen brought the ever popular St. Nicolas back home from their travels in the east, while Venetians returned with the bones of the Apostle Mark for the benefit of their lagoon city, Ragusa fared well enough with their plundered St. Blaise. How could a saint be more appropriate for a city? According to legend, he was a second-century bishop of a Mediterranean town, Sebaste, born of a wealthy noble family, and both kindly and generous in performing miracles for his townspeople. According to legend the Roman emperor ordered his death because he protected local Christians. St. Blasius or Blaise (Slavic St. Vlah) gained immediate and complete acceptance, nor did the Ragusan citizenry waver in their regard; he remained their saint throughout their long history as a city-state, and his relics may be found today preserved in the treasury. In numerous paintings and carvings, Blaise returned this affection by cradling a walled miniature of the town in his holy hands (see Figure 5).

Ragusan histories and chronicles coupled the themes of early republicanism and a militant Christianity in a manner familiar to anyone acquainted with the historiographical tradition of Venice or the other towns existing at the western edge of the Byzantine sphere of influence and the eastern edge of Rome's power. Chroniclers remained adamant on one matter: Ragusan Christians turned aside all threats with valor; they survived because their city won favor with God.

Townspeople kept alive a legend that the crusading English King Richard the Lionhearted was saved from shipwreck off Ragusa's walls in 1192, and in gratitude made a donation of 100,000 ducats for the erection of a church. By coming ashore on the island of La Croma (Lokrum), his votive church by rights should have been built there. Townsmen, however, convinced the king to erect his church within the walls rather than within the Benedictine monastery at Lokrum. All this was claimed in a letter of 20 February 1598, which town councilors sent to the Pope.[50] In remembrance of the monastery's acquiescence, it had been customary for the Benedictine Abbot from Lokrum to don the archbishop's mitre and crosier and offer a mass at Candlemass, the councillors insisted. They had done so for centuries. The Great Council wanted no papal meddling with this custom and, indeed, received none.

This incident speaks for remarkable tolerance and forbearance from Rome, but Ragusans would probably not have regarded it as such. Townspeople considered themselves to be devout and absolutely loyal to the Church at Rome, and thus worthy of maintaining their old customs. But standing outside the conflicts of the investiture controversy, they were not tested in their loyalties to the church as were believers across the Adriatic Sea. Because prolonged conflict between church and state had no place in Ragusan life, it applied no tests to local devotion. Although signs of devotion were omnipresent in the town's churches, many and rich relics, and in numerous monasteries, religious life lacked the polarizing capacity it

Figure 5. St. Blaise at Ploca. From Lukša Beritić, *Utvrđenja grada Dubrovnika* (Zagreb: JAZU, 1955).

often possessed elsewhere. Ragusa did not produce local saints for canonization or theologians of great note. Instead the community produced valued prelates for Rome who were well educated and unswervingly loyal. But these men found fame as able ecclesiastical statesmen or diplomats; that is, they proved to be not very different from their lay brothers and cousins who had stayed at home. Ragusans more than adequately proved their loyalty to Rome by undertaking diplomatic missions to the Turks and forbidding the erection of an Eastern Orthodox church within the town's walls.

The great monuments of local religious life were richly endowed for all eyes to see. Dominicans arrived in Ragusa in 1224 and began to build their great house at the sea gate in 1228. The Franciscans arrived in 1235 and erected their extensive buildings inside the town walls at the gate at Pile. The Poor Clares soon joined them across the *platea* or *stradun*. The Benedictines remained powerful, as did the town's convents, the oldest of which was the Convent of St. Thomas.

## The Constitution

In cultivating simultaneously a private sphere united by marriage and a public world governed by republican institutions, Ragusans trod a path that might have been appreciated in a much earlier age. Devolution of responsibility was not unique in the Mediterranean world, but it was rather remarkable in that it survived here into the early modern age. Deliberate care for their marriage alliances provided Ragusans a solidly cohesive circle to which they might refer all manner of divisive issues for resolution as one might consult, and rely on, an extended family. Through civic service, membership in the Great Council, and willingness to stand for elected office or accept appointment, noble Ragusan citizens maintained the machinery of a republican state and embarked on the secular path of patrician statecraft and governance.

The apportioning of private and public responsibilities holds out some hope for resolving the sometimes disputed problem of the codification of Ragusa's laws. Seven major books of statute law were codified in 1272 (an eighth book contains new laws), and a smaller body of customs law was recorded in 1277, while Ragusans governed their city under the watchful eye of a Venetian count. The count's role in this process is still a matter of dispute. The act of codification played usefully into the hands of the

Venetians who stood to benefit from the orderly exposition of local law and ancient custom. Codification is an act of sovereignty implying that the ruler's will and reason are superior to local and time-sanctioned customs. It may imply, to the jeopardy of local populations, that custom has the force of law only by permission of the ruler.[51] So Venice, its own laws uncodified, has been assumed by some to have dictated the law to Ragusa and to the other Dalmatian cities that collected their statute laws in this era, creating, in the words of Thomas Ashburner, the earliest full compendia of urban and maritime law in the medieval era.

It must be noted that Ashburner himself saw the Ragusan statute law's provenance as much older than Venetian influence in the thirteenth century. He fixed its origins in the ancient Rhodian sea law, but the tradition persists in Venetian historiography that Venice created small constitutional versions of its thirteenth-century self within the Adriatic cities it ruled.[52] Constantine Jireček, the Czech scholar who edited Ragusa's *Liber Statutorum* with Valtazar Bogišić at the beginning of the twentieth century, disagreed, noting that Ragusans respected the codified law as their own inheritance in 1272 and even after they separated themselves from Venice in 1358. The constitution was more ancient. The nobility had a first recorded mention in 1023 and, fifteen years before the Venetian-Ragusan treaty of 1205, the constitutional division of powers: "count, with judges, nobles, and the whole people . . . and the agreement of the Archbishop, appeared in the official correspondence of the Ragusan state."[53] When the law was codified in 1272, older laws governing private life were incorporated into the Statute Book; the phrase "according to the customs and usage of Ragusa" was invoked whenever new statutes were balloted as a tradition far older than the codification itself. Statute law was living law, according to Jireček and the emerging Slavic school of historiography, amended but respected for centuries before and after Ragusa freed itself from Venetian domination.

At Ragusa the Great Council, the assembled adult men of the noble circle, balloted all elected offices except a few reserved for the *cives de populo*. The method of election was cumbersome since an alternative to any nomination had to be introduced to allow for balloting.[54] The Great Council elected a senate of about forty members that oversaw foreign relations and diplomatic initiatives, and a Small Council, a legislative, judicial, and executive body that dealt with the Venetian count on a day-to-day basis until 1358.[55] When the citizenry felt confident enough to ease itself out from under Venetian control (aided by Venice's momentary embarrassments in warfare in the 1350s and the Ragusan Archbishop Saraca's secret negotiations with Hungary), the Great Council replaced the count with an elected triumvirate.[56] This mechanism soon proved awkward and was replaced by an elected rector whose executive power was effectively checked by his short term in office. In the first experiments after delivery from Venetian rule, the rectorship lasted only one month, so wary was the council of a strong executive office filled by one of their own number. This in turn proved unworkable, and a rectorship of six months was instituted, but no rector was to serve sequential terms in office. Structurally inefficient, time-consuming, and absorbing of energy, government responsibilities continued to fall to all noblemen, who learned and used "Old Ragusan," an Italian dialect increasingly distinct from contemporary vernacular speech. In council, they participated in a shared political exercise of discourse that affirmed the venerable nature of an ancient inherited political culture.

Fiscal policies provide apt illustrations of how Ragusans governed. The tax burden rested primarily on long-distance trade, augmented by occasional forced loans on privately held wealth. Those who paid were in most cases those who levied, that is, the merchant aristocracy who sat on the Great Council. Value-added taxes on consumption, like the widely exacted salt tax, existed, but customs bore the brunt of large expenditures. Out of collected revenues, the council paid tribute to great powers for protection or for the acquisition of territory. The oldest tribute, the *margarisium,* amounted to sixty *hyperperi* paid on St. Michael's Day (September 29) for the right to cultivate vineyards on the lands of the princes of Chelmo (the Hlum or the Herzegovina) and Travunia (Trebinje). A larger tribute of two thousand *hyperperi* was due on St. Demetrius Day in October for varied and extensive rights to lands in the Astarea. The Serbs received this tribute until the reign of the Bosnian ban, Tvrtko I (1353–91). His acquisition of territories in Travunia (Trebinje) and Canali (Konavle) gave him the right to collect the award.[57]

Ragusans gave a tribute for Stagno, or Ston, after 1333 when they gained rights to that strategic peninsula along the coast northwest of the town. There were two awards, one paid on the feast day of their beloved patron saint, Blasius or Vlah, to the Bosnian ban and one on Easter to the Serbian ruler. After separation from Venice in 1358, Ragusans paid a tribute of five hundred *hyperperi* to Hungary as a sign of allegiance. By the fifteenth century, diplomats had negotiated with the Turks to pay a tribute of 1500 ducats for lands in Canali (Konavle), as well as for peaceful travel and trade in the West Balkans. This rose to 15,000 ducats, a tenfold rise, over the

Figure 6. The Rector's Palace. Seat of government and rector's residence for term of office. From *Obnova Dubrovnika 1979–1989*, ed. Božo Letunić (Dubrovnik: Zavod za obnovu Dubrovnika, 1989).

decades, but in return Ragusans improved their trading rights significantly, particularly in the mining and minting centers. By 1481, adroit negotiators had reduced that tribute to 12,500 ducats.[58]

From 1205 until 1358, Ragusans owed the Venetians two armed vessels in times of war, as they had earlier given aid to Constantinople, then to the Normans, prior to the age of Venetian rule. After 1358, Ragusans transferred their obligation to supply two ships to the Hungarian monarch. Later still their alliance with Spain obligated the same levy of two ships in sixteenth-century battles with the Turks, which meant that Ragusans fought at Lepanto.[59] This levy of two ships defined Ragusan responsibility to police the *intra-culfum*, or Adriatic sea route, on which its own trade depended.

After fulfilling these less-than-onerous tribute obligations, the next most pressing issue of state was defense of the town proper and, as properties in the Astarea and the islands expanded, defense of the town's small territorial holdings. In the thirteenth century an extensive system of walls integrated existing fortifications to surround the entire six districts of the town. This decades-long building project represented a substantial capital outlay that increased in the fourteenth century with the purchase and fortification of Stagno or Ston and continued improvements in the town's defenses. As a matter of fact, defense was something of a local obsession. Nothing would do for the Great Council but the newest war machines and up-to-date technology, including an early cannon for the walls imported from Italy in the 1370s.[60] The Fortress of St. Lawrence (Lovran), the final jewel in the system of defense built to impress the Turks, guarded both Pile, the town's land gate, and the coastline with its vast bulk. The councils hired mercenary soldiers from Venice to command and organize town defenses, and they hired the best they could find because these knights served as advisors to council. For centuries, Great Councillors staffed the watch themselves, holding by election the post of Officer of the Night, which required them to leave their homes and remain on the walls entire nights. The harbor demanded fortification, constant upkeep, and repair. Ragusa outfitted a fleet when it was necessary to serve in policing the Adriatic.

These forbidding defenses stood ready but idle except for some clashes with the Slavs in the thirteenth and fourteenth centuries, and even then the senate did its best to placate their enemies in the interests of land trade. Was this a semblance of military pugnacity rather than genuine willingness to wage war? Ragusans had capitulated when threatened by Crusaders and the Venetian navy, often placated, and deferentially offered tribute money or tribute vessels; they seldom and only reluctantly fought. This reluctance combined with up-to-date arsenals provides a revealing glimpse of local political culture, since resolution of the apparent contradiction between aggressive and peaceful courses lay in an intention shared by the local patriciate to pursue an independent course in Mediterranean affairs. Apparently a balance between the two—placatory gestures and bristling defenses—was deemed the most promising course toward this goal, but only a high degree of determined concurrence could ensure the success of such an inherently divisive political stance.

So it comes as no surprise that councillors were lavish with the precious commodities of time and energy.[61] In 1301, the first surviving list of elected civic officials chosen by ballot included six judges of the Great Council, some to fill terms left vacant, and five advocates for the commune. Three judges for the Small Council and two advocates were balloted into office. A scribe was appointed, plus customs officials to oversee the collection of monies, and two procurators were elected to see to eleemosynary concerns; all were noble with the exception of the scribe. A group of officers to supervise fields and vineyards in lands outside the town walls and others to supervise the area enclosed within the town's walls were identified. Bakery inspectors, well inspectors, inspectors of salt pans, and special

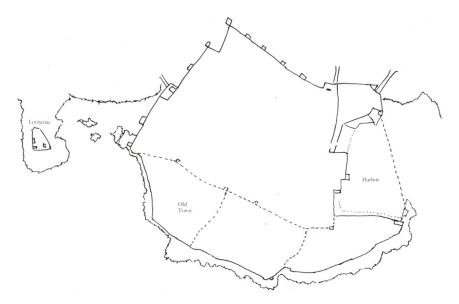

Map 2. Walled town with fortifications, 1351–1420.

authorities to oversee the island of Lokrum were appointed. Captains were chosen to oversee all the small villages under Ragusan jurisdiction, and counts were appointed to serve as representatives of the town government in the Astarea and on the islands. The harbor had its inspectors and other officials checked to keep Serbian coins from circulating in the town.[62] To these must be added the officers of the night and any diplomats currently on assignment to a foreign government as well as syndics sent to find skilled workers abroad. Some of the jobs, for example that of *salinarius*, were not onerous, and they may have served to train young noblemen of twenty (eighteen during the age of the plague) to fill more responsible positions later. Multiple office holding was unavoidable, and some names appear over and over again in responsible positions. This was particularly true for elders in the community who may have shouldered a disproportionate share of government to free younger men to pursue long-distance trade.

The much-consulted Mathias de Mence, active 1279 to 1315, member of a noble clan already divided into many branches when he served as judge in the late thirteenth century, provides an example of the uneven burdens and rewards tolerated within the patriciate. Mathias was the very model of the knowledgeable functionary who keeps the urban wheels turning. He was solicitous for the concerns of his noble peers and chose to devote most of his energies to governing his town. For Mathias that meant not only adjudicating cases but dealing patiently, on almost a daily basis, with Michael Morosini, the current Venetian-appointed foreign count. Through Small Council deliberations with the Venetian count, Ragusans made treaty right bearable; diplomacy applied to internal as well as foreign affairs. Mathias's name appeared regularly in the minutes of the Small Council, and he served so often as witness to his peer's notarized contracts that he might just as well have taken up residence at the chancellery. Clearly he was trusted to interpret the law within his circle. But Mathias was also a *pater familias,* with the marriages of ten offspring to negotiate. Increasingly brilliant matches, culminating in the marriage of his sixth son, Martinussius, to the orphaned heiress, Phylippa de Thoma, show how his career in poorly compensated government service eventually yielded prosperity for his heirs. There was more than one strategy to pursue for success in Ragusa.

Mathias's younger brother Lawrence chose to concentrate on his private fortune. He left four surviving children to divide his estate, so Lawrence's heirs were richer but not necessarily as politically advantaged as their cousins, Mathias's sons and daughters. A partition decree made after the death of Lawrence's intestate son, Michel, revealed significant personal wealth including a house and business establishment in Venice, the fruits of family business pursued in overseas trade.[63] In fact, the records of the more than a dozen noble de Mence households in Ragusa in 1300 reveal that members of that lineage differed substantially in levels of affluence. Blaise de Mence, blessed with the patron saint's name, gained further blessings. The dowry he accepted in 1282 when he wed Nicholetta de Volcassio amounted to six hundred *grossi* (fifty *hyperperi*) and one hundred *exagia* of gold. In drawing up the contract, notary Thomasini de Savere stated, "said kinsman [the bride's father, the silver-rich Pasque Volcassio] confirmed this amount [standing] before the statute in which it is written that no one may give or receive over 40 *hyperperi* in a dowry."[64] Young Blaise had secured an open-handed father-in-law and he prospered. Domagna, younger brother to Blaise, most likely joined Blaise in a *fraterna* to avoid dividing their father's estate, but he lacked Blaise's wealthy Volcassio contacts; furthermore, Domagna cut into time devoted to private business by more often filling civic posts, which his well-connected brother avoided.

Patrician society tolerated serious divergences in both wealth and vocation among brothers, cousins, and noble associates. Sometimes it even tolerated a genuine reprobate like Basilius de Basilio within its ranks. Basilio's actions, being of the worst sort, finally gained the attention of the generally tolerant Great Council after it was clear that youth had not drained away his penchant for trouble. He insulted his elders and freely abused women of all classes according to outraged testimony brought against him, two clearly reprehensible traits in a society that valued deference. Still he had carried on disgracefully at a safe distance from the town proper since the Great Council had in their wisdom made him count of the island territories.[65]

Noble merchants traveling out of town did not always escape political responsibility by relying on their more civic-minded brothers: nobles were continuously recruited as diplomats. The most trusted were regularly sent out from the town to negotiate with foreign powers or with Venice; typically they traveled in pairs. The senate provided them rich gifts to ease their access to the powerful, retinues of servants, sometimes the cost of a passage by ship, or pack animals for land travel. Such matters were thrashed out in senate meetings and duly recorded in the minutes, lending a deceptively pedestrian tone to matters of the highest political consequence for the city-state. All was negotiable when noble ambassadors received their missions from the senate, but often noblemen served without pay (*cum salario et sine salario*); private wealth was often expected to support the state's representative while abroad, so business of state accompanied and was nourished by private enterprise at Ragusa.[66]

In councils of state the privy nature of deliberations was dramatized by the survival of a unique early Adriatic dialect or Old Ragusan. For centuries this dialect's mastery signalled young men's coming of age; equipped with it they could understand deliberations of state and participate themselves, although notes of the councils were recorded in plain notarial Latin.[67] The Great Council's language for privileged discourse became a badge of office and class, placing a substantial burden of learning upon the young. Youth from noble families were expected to become literate in Latin under the instruction of a communally salaried schoolmaster. By the thirteenth century, most Ragusan households had become bilingual and employed an Italian common to Dalmatia (and understood in Venice) as well as a West Balkan Slavic dialect. As early as 1189 the Bosnian ban's treaty had referred to Ragusans by a Slavic name, that is, as *Dubravchane*. So there were four written or spoken languages for noble young men to master before they took their place in civic and business life: Italian, Slavic, Latin, and Old Ragusan.[68]

The demands placed on the capacities of the entire citizenry of noble birth called for training of more thorough nature than mere schooling in languages. The Great Council was itself a classroom, and before it the household had served as a preparatory school. Sober debates on matters of state, on marshalling and sharing out of communal resources, and on foreign policy and defense were serious concerns for men from their youth, when they entered the Great Council as full-fledged voting members, until their demise. Aphorisms counseling moderation, forbearance, and prudence came in handy here. Young men were likely to have accompanied fathers or other male relatives on ambassadorial journeys even before they entered the Great Council, since fathers brought sons into business ventures by having the young men accompany them, or other willing mentors, from the age of twelve or thirteen. Benedetto Cotrugli, a fulsome dispenser of locally esteemed aphorisms, clearly advocated care in training these valued scions of noble houses. It should be carefully noted that high expectations and early immersion in the demanding responsibilities of civic office without elevation above one's noble peers represented the ideal.[69]

If diplomacy verging on the heroic, as in the case of Archbishop Elias de Saraca (see Appendix 2), received no special gratitude, what civic acts did the old Ragusan republic reward with praise or monuments? Few, if any, beyond a brief note in the *Libri Reformationes,* and that record was unadorned by effusive praise. It did not even bring, in most instances, much mention of the individual benefactor. If Saraca's negotiations with the ruler of Hungary helped extricate Ragusa from the hated, long-standing disability of deferring to Venice, adroitly placing Ragusa under Hungarian protection when the Venetians were inhibited from any form of reprisal in 1358, how could the Great Council refuse the man accolade?[70] But the council did. No noble citizen in the Great Council had played as significant a role as Saraca in affairs of state, yet his fellow noble councillors, surely ingrates, reacted by requesting the pope to never again appoint a native son to the office of archbishop of Ragusa. Fear of unchecked power operating from the eminence of the archbishop's seat unsettled the noble circle to a point verging on paranoia.

Tellingly, one man alone, Miho Pracat, received a statue to his glory in medieval Ragusa, and he was a wealthy sea captain from the islands who left his considerable estate to the republic. Pracat was not a noble, nor enfranchised, and never sat in the Great Council. He was as much a benefactor of the city as any noble member of the Great Council and served his republic with as great a patriotism as any of them. In a sense, his very selection for a monument marked him as an outsider. In the spirit of an aristocracy in which no person or faction took precedence or exerted singular authority, the aristocrats of the Ragusan republic favored a rigid egalitarian code in parceling out honors among their own numbers and forbade the glorification of any single member.

Yet the smooth tenor of civic life was also a facade and a protection against the prying eyes of outsiders, which obscures the tumult of politics from our eyes as well. For instance, Ragusans may be glimpsed in belligerent acts only very rarely, but they were as subject to the stresses of occupation as any other polity under foreign dominion. In 1266 a group of men from the town accosted the Venetian count and his party outside the town walls. A member of the count's party was killed in armed scuffle, and when the count, Giovanni Quirino, attempted to prosecute, he was physically barred from the town. Quirino took flight to Venice, leaving his possessions behind; very possibly he fled for his own personal safety. Venetian authorities responded angrily but with considerable forebearance (that is, with words rather than acts of retaliation) and in time sent out another count to replace Quirino. The remonstrance Venice sent was addressed to *Universitati communitatis Ragusine,* the entire community of Ragusa.[71] In their wisdom, the Venetians saw the act against their appointed count as a concerted effort, not a random act of a few hostile individuals, and laid it at the door of the aristocratic Great Council. If the Venetian senate understood the issue correctly, the unruffled surface of civic life obscured—most likely intentionally—more violent reactions to occupying Venice; Ragusans were likely then to express their hostility in private acts undertaken outside the walls, trusting to the Great and Small Councils to provide a camouflage through their silence. This rare record of an attack hints at an entirely different political world of rancor and revenge because there is every possibility that the attackers were members of the noble circle itself, although the council never admitted this. It is also fairly obvious that the noble circle closed ranks to protect the individual perpetrators of the attack.

It is highly likely that at a deeper level Ragusan politics were contentious, divisive, and laden with anger and personal agendas, as was true in city-states elsewhere. Malfeasance and faction did exist. In the fifteenth century, councillors made a recorded attempt to stuff the ballot box, and in 1400 a short-lived rebellion involving four noblemen and some of the *cives de populo* disturbed the peace.[72] But over centuries of foreign occupation, Ragusans learned to resolve contentious issues privately while maintaining a unified outward appearance. Exchange of aphorisms, a code-like device, helped in this regard. Imperturbation was a mask put on at will, implying that the patriciate did not intend to make the outside world privy to their most difficult trials. Visible machinery of state carried a separate responsibility: to present to the world the picture Ragusa's noble citizens would have others see.

## Providing Communal Welfare

The machinery of state proved over time to be a useful instrument for securing important benefits to the noble circle and by extension to the rest of the community. Ragusan advocates of aristocratic republicanism learned how to make a pliant instrument of their governmental bureaucracy through facing a series of emergencies. In 1296, it was fire requiring reconstruction of much of the town. In 1319, it was economic crisis brought on by high grain prices and prolonged Mediterranean famine. On 3 November 1319, one part of the Great Council favored expelling *omnes Sclavos inutiles* (all nonemployed Slavs) from the town *propter famem* (because of famine), but they were resisted by the more moderate group who carried the day.[73] Fourteenth-century plague proved the greatest challenge of all, requiring the most energetic private and public strategies to ensure the survival of the noble class. Even above concern for defense, the community valued healthful living conditions; and this was, perhaps, a well-reasoned priority since disease was a more constant enemy than foreign armies.

If the integrity of the noble circle lay in the continuance of its lines from a limited circle of noblewomen, then survival was tied to salubrious conditions for their health and the health of their families. Noble Ragusans lived by tradition within their city walls. By the late fifteenth century, luxurious residences constructed by the most affluent families dotted the shoreline near the town, but they were intended primarily for use in the summer. Members of the Great Council were required to live at least a part of the year in the town proper. The vitality of urban life and good government were believed to rely on the actual presence of *nobili viri* on the town's streets and in its houses and places of business, with a very frequent show of noble wives and children as well. Philippus de Diversis described the appearance of noblewomen on the fifteenth-century streets as opulent, and while his words were often effusively complimentary he makes it very clear that Ragusans expected a display from their noble ladies similar to *le pompe* in Venice.[74] Under these circumstances, the Great Council had a vested interest in providing a reasonable level of safety to keep them living in town and pacing the streets and promenades.

From the earliest documented decades, there is evidence of communal efforts to create a fair town. This may be part of Ragusa's legacy from Constantinople, where public health measures were routinely instituted for the care of the urban populace. Sicilian agents may have served as a vehicle for transmission of these policies since Salerno became an early western center for the study of medicine, and Ragusans found some of their earliest physician consultants there. Sicilian towns had established sanitary laws and practices well before their more northern Italian neighbors.

Safety regulations (for fire, famine, *force majeure*) were another concern of the Great Council, and here again Ragusan programs showed a marked similarity to other cities within the Byzantine sphere of influence by instituting responses relatively early in the medieval centuries. When the community outran its cisterned water supply, forcing townspeople to rely more heavily on supplies brought by boat from a distance, an ambitious scheme was undertaken to divert water to the town from around the mountainous karst and the River Ombla. Council supported such a project, even handsomely as the Renaissance fountain near the town's land gate reveals, and hired the most highly recommended engineer from Italy to see the work done well; but a sober determination to receive value from the outlay meant that the Great Council oversaw the project very closely, much as they surveyed other bureaucratically conceived programs. As a result, an extensive record on communal projects can be found within the *Libri Reformationes*.[75]

So Ragusans shared with their Adriatic neighbors a heightened expectation for what civil agency should provide in the way of services, and health services figured prominently among these. They shared as well the disadvantage of remoteness from the Italian schools and universities, which produced professionally trained personnel who provided care. Ragusa was already served by doctors who had been brought from Italy by the initiative of the council in the late thirteenth century: 1295 provides an early example of a communal hiring.[76] By 1301, the procedure in use for hiring may be traced in the records: that year a syndic was deputized by Great Council to seek for and secure a surgeon for Ragusa from among those practicing in Venice.[77] As soon as three years later, another search had begun.[78] Searches continued in this fashion, and were not limited to Venice; Ragusan syndics might be sent to Zara to seek talent, or perhaps to Apulia.[79] Councillors showed some sophistication in distinguishing among qualifications for the surgeons they sought. Not barber surgeons but *medicus plagarum* (physician for wounds) were specified; that may indicate the council understood that trained surgeons formed their own guild at Venice and in other Italian cities.[80]

More intense efforts were invested in the steps to recruit university-trained physicians. In 1312, the Great Council issued a general order for the town's syndic to search throughout Italy for a physician.[81] In 1320, an agent was sent to scout out the university town of Bologna, in 1344 the university town of Padua. In the disastrous plague year of 1348, a town agent was sent, with little hope, to search wherever possible. In 1350 Ragusa was fortunate to find a physician in Padua, but another attempt was made the very next year to find a second one in Apulia. The plague lingered long in Ragusa, had the Paduan already succumbed to it? In 1359, two syndics were dispatched, the first to Venice and the next to Bologna, Padua, and Venice. Mantua was included in the cities visited in 1363. By this date the Great Council insisted that a "wise and excellent" physician be secured, registering their increased sophistication in matters medical. Early in the century, Ragusans had favored the matriculates of Salerno, and later in the century they recruited physicians trained at Padua; evidently they were aware of the migration of medical training from south to north in Italian universities.[82]

Minutes from the Great Council give a sense of what a satisfactory communal physician's duties might be, revealing a reasonably up-to-date knowledge of what constituted adequate medical care in the fourteenth century. Now and then minutes record the physician's return demands on the council.[83] The earliest civic contract with a physician, dating from 1301, allowed a two-year term, a residence, and a salary to a professor from Salerno. In return, he was required to counsel and treat the poor as well as the wealthy and refrain from conducting any private business with an agent in spices and aromatic unguents (that is, the pharmacist, who served the council under his own contract). The salary he received might be augmented by two *hyperperi* charged for care to patients. If, at the end of his term, this had not produced sufficient return, the council would offer partial recompense.[84] The syndic presented these negotiated terms to the council; evidently the physician would not make the trip by sea to Ragusa unless they were met. Most surgeons served townspeople free of charges, however, relying solely on their communal salaries, which was apparently more in keeping with what the council had in mind. There were times when the council provided the medicine and unguents necessary for treatment.[85]

One surgeon, Master Bonaventura, won a leave of absence to transact personal business, but because personal needs prompted his request he was required to find a replacement.[86]

Specificity of contracts increased with passing decades. A contract for a surgeon in 1323 stated that in return for a 240 *hyperperi* salary and a 20 *hyperperi* allowance for a residence, treatment must be supplied to the archbishop of Ragusa and his relatives, the count of Ragusa and his family, the clerk of chancellery and his family, and all those salaried by the communal government, present and future. He was also to treat the Franciscan and Dominican brothers in the town and the district of Ragusa. It was specified that the unguents, plasters, waters, and the other necessaries of the art of surgery were to be supplied to these persons without a charge. Fees were commonly charged to foreigners from nearby lands who came to identify the town as a source of care and even cures. From kings and foreign dignitaries, physicians and surgeons sometimes drew impressive fees, but the practitioner had to obtain leave of council to go to the king of Serbia to treat him when the case arose. A notarized contract often served for those who came to town for a cure. These specified high fees, in one instance eight *hyperperi* for a patient's ailment, which were, significantly, for a completed cure for that ailment, not merely for care provided.[87]

Close scrutiny of performance became accepted procedure in town, and if a communally paid practitioner did not appreciate it he soon left and moved elsewhere. When a Master Antonius was caught trafficking in drugs while drawing his communal salary, he was refused a renewal of his contract.[88] With a general rise in salaries over the fourteenth century, ranging from about one hundred to six hundred *hyperperi* for physicians and a less sharp curve in the rise of surgeons' salaries, communal health care employees were well paid by the Great Council, but bound to accept surveillance and respond to orders.[89]

The policy of paying well but monitoring care intensified with the plague in a variant on urban responses found elsewhere among Mediterranean city dwellers. Doctors may have been unable to supply any genuine relief for victims of the plague, but that did not deter communities from placing increased reliance on them, measured by the sums paid out in fees, salaries, and improved health facilities. Doctor's nostrums, inadequate as they might be, were better than consigning one's community to pestilence brought on by forces beyond human control. Ragusans bemoaned disease as an act of God as much as any other devout people, but they also listened to what their physicians advised them about contagion.

For an endogamous group that renewed itself through the fecundity of contracted marriages, the Black Plague was both unprecedented and devastating. One of the few surviving Ragusan *zibaldone* (it was written at a significantly later date than the plague) records the Black Plague as the worst calamity in the community's history. It stated that 110 councillors died from December 1347, when plague was first noted in the island villages, until late 1349, when it finally subsided. Ragusan citizens faced a further dilemma since as councillors they were expected not to leave their town while council met or in times of crisis. As the grim experience of other communities confirms, fleeing was the only sure defense against plague and it was closed to noble Ragusans.

A physician, Jacob of Padua, remained with the Great Council and served the sick during the worst early months of the plague's visit to the town (the first notice of plague at Ragusa came very early, in December 1347, when it was noted a sailor on shipboard in the harbor had died from it). Jacob of Padua appears to have advised the council to establish a place outside the walls for treatment of the ill and to treat those who came to town for a cure there rather than allow them within the town. Contagian theory, which a Paduan-trained physician learned as part of his third-year curriculum, favored separation of the well from the stricken. As the plague began to subside, the council voted for a hospice outside the walls to house all foreign travelers.[90] It was not a lazaretto, that is, an institution for the treatment of the seriously ill, but a hospice, introducing the principle of separation of foreigners from the citizenry within the town's walls. Isolation appears to have become an established notion by the waning months of the plague, and a hospice undoubtedly provided a defense.[91] The experience of the plague made the Ragusans value their physicians more than ever. After the sickness abated the Great Council recruited only those with reputations as "wise and excellent" and raised their salaries. Ragusans intensified their scrutiny of health care and turned their attention to measures that could prevent the return of the dread plague. They were not successful, of course; in fact some authorities rate the return of the plague in 1361–62 more devastating than the initial epidemic.[92] Mattei's *zibaldone* claimed, admittedly after the fact, that casualties to the plague were generally greater among women and children than they were among adult men.[93] Noble families may well have believed that they needed the intercession of council to challenge this devastating pestilence, which had mysteriously returned, if they were to survive.

In 1377, the Great Council took a more radical step in epidemic prevention by establishing a *trentino,* or thirty-day isolation period, for all ships' passengers and goods coming by sea to the town.[94] Undoubtedly it was one of the earliest programs of isolation to stem the plague, although some Apulian towns had already instituted measures to isolate visiting foreigners for an observation period. Ragusa appointed two new officials, *caza mortae* they termed them, to oversee the program, and designated two remote sites for terms of isolation for the affected. Civita Vecchia, or Cavtat, and the island of Mercana, or Mrkan, were chosen due to their remote, sparsely populated locations. The new law proved to be one of the more contested issues of the decade. It passed by a vote of only thirty-four in favor when sixty-three councillors were present, a narrow majority by Ragusan standards. A second measure and its balloting may reveal why the passage of the *trentino* aroused such controversy. A second proposal introduced the possibility of townspeople joining their loved ones or business associates at their site of isolation, at clear risk to their own health. This proposal stipulated that a visitor must share the entire term of isolation with the interned, but this seemed to mollify the *trentino*'s critics. This second ballot passed by a higher majority of forty-four votes. Evidently it found greater favor because it allowed for the resumption of normal life with the risk absorbed by business associates and kin. It lessened the personal cost of the *trentino,* always an important consideration among Ragusans, while it sharply limited responsibility for policing the measure (see Appendix 3).[95]

In 1397 the *trentino* was expanded. The new law forbade the import of wheat, fruit, and cloth (typical suspected articles in contagion theory) from locations known to harbor plague.[96] The period of isolation was extended to sixty days and supervision of ships was tightened.[97] As a result of the success of this legislation, sea-borne disease was successfully contained well before the Great Council found a response to land-borne epidemic. But in the fifteenth century, funds were found to build an elaborate lazaretto outside the town walls. This provided at least a partial answer to the problem of land-borne plague, but policing access to town by land trade routes was never to be as successful as policing vessels that arrived by sea.

The principle of separation for land travelers found expression as well in the Great Council's creation of a large *fondaco* near the sea gate of the town. In Italy, foreign quarters like the Venetian district of S. Silvestro (for Slavic traders) and the *fondacho dei Tedeschi* (for northerners, not merely Germans) were typically incorporated into the city proper. This had been the case earlier at Ragusa as well, where the streets near the harbor served as the foreign quarter. However the fifteenth century introduced a new atti-

tude toward foreign travelers at Ragusa, which resulted in effective measures to keep the *fondaco* isolated at a short distance outside the walls.
Reasons of health were acknowledged, but unacknowledged motives for
policing visitors may have operated as well.[98]

In time, a forty-day isolation period or *quarantino* for land travelers
became standard policy at Ragusa, as it was for visiting vessels. Sailors,
traders, and travelers from abroad came under increased surveillance, but
this was true in most other cities of the Mediterranean basin. On the other
hand, unlike health legislation in the Italian cities, policies at Ragusa do not
appear to have been aimed primarily at eliminating the poor and indigent
from the city streets. This did not mean that Ragusans were more compas-
sionate, but rather that it was unnecessary to resort to such indirect measures to exert control over the town's population of migrants, indigents,
and sources of unskilled intermittent labor. Quarantine served a simpler
purpose here in preserving the health and ensuring the survival of the noble
circle. Over the long term, this was perhaps the most sacred task entrusted
to the offices of government, and the direct simplicity of the plan accounted
for its effectiveness.

Was the devolution of responsibilities for urban welfare in practice in
Ragusa in any way unusual among the city-states of the Mediterranean
region? Efforts to preserve the health of an elite could produce civic measures that had the same beneficial consequences for other city dwellers as
they did for those they intended to benefit. Sweet water piped to town
benefitted everyone since it was available to everyone. That the Ragusan
Great Council's measures were intended primarily for their own families'
survival made them no less beneficial to those outside the noble circle. A
lazaretto, or a quarantine, might protect the health of an artisan or slave as
well as a noble.

Still the program adopted at Ragusa differs from those adopted in
Milan, Venice, Florence, and other cities in the more western reaches of the
Mediterranean basin. Noble Ragusans were treated by the "wise and famous" physician their Great Council brought from Italy at great expense,
willingly sharing the same caregiver who treated the poor. This was not so
in Milan where a hierarchy separating private and public physicians arose
within which those who could afford it disdained the use of a communally
salaried physician. Communally salaried doctors in most towns soon took
responsibility for the inspection and care of the poor only; the affluent
consulted their own private physicians. At Ragusa this was not the case.
Furthermore, most charitable bequests tended to be administered by civic

officials (like Miho Pracat's bequest to the Great Council for the benefit of the town). Whereas citizens of other towns often preferred privately organized confraternities, *scuole,* or religious houses to serve as their dispensers of charity, Ragusans trusted their civic authorities. In other towns, notaries established private practices in parishes and neighborhoods; at Ragusa notaries were recruited and salaried by the council and served in a centralized office of the chancellery. Those having business with a notary perforce traveled to that central office to transact business.

Over time, the variety of services civic agencies performed increased steadily at Ragusa. Although bureaucracy was carefully aimed at serving the citizenry by enhancing the chances for survival of members of the noble circle, foreign visitors, and later commentators, found here innovative departures in promoting urban welfare generally; that is to say, they read advanced or "modern" urban governance into Ragusan civil programs. In some part, Ragusa's reputation as a virtuous republic stemmed from a misapprehension about the intentions behind communal policies. The noble circle had every reason to show openhandedness to the town's residents. There was no need for them to distinguish themselves from non-noble town dwellers because that distinction was already absolute.

\*   \*   \*

In *Method for the Easy Comprehension of History,* Jean Bodin noted of Ragusans that theirs "was a government composed of *optimates.* Twenty-four families of very ancient nobility still remain, from whom the college of *optimates* is formed, . . . as with the Venetians, all serve at one time."[99] And, as with the Venetian officialdom, government served the interests of the noble circle. Ragusans passed with relative ease from private initiatives to public agency because the same persons dictated policy and administered programs in either case.[100] Unsalaried service to the republic represented sacred duty to the noble circle, and all who served had learned that from earliest childhood. Public office was an awkward avenue to private power and one seldom chosen by a noble citizen. Ragusa's "advanced" health programs, its communal services, and its admirably efficient and generally "incorruptible" bureaucracy served in the most traditional purpose of all: the continued survival of a small, highly coherent, and self-conscious ruling elite. Government, that is, public power, served effectively as an instrument of the noble circle in matters affecting all on which all concurred. The local "advanced" program for health care illustrates this well. As for deeper dissensions and rivalries in political life, an occasional glimpse of them establishes beyond doubt that they existed, but above all else medieval Ragusans concurred that it was necessary to shield them from prying eyes.[101]

## Notes

1. Constantine Porphyrogenitus, *De Administrando Imperio*, ed. Gy. Moravcsik, trans. R. J. H. Jenkins (Budapest: Pétar Tudományegyetani Görög Filológïaï Intezet, 1949), pp. 134–35.

2. See J. F. Roglić, "The Geographical Setting of Medieval Dubrovnik," in *Geographical Essays on Eastern Europe*, ed. N. Pounds (Bloomington: Indiana University Press, 1961), pp. 141–59; see also P. Skok "L'importance de Dubrovnik dans l'histoire des slaves," *Le Monde slave* 8 (1931): 161–71.

3. First mention of Ragusa may be found in *Ravenatis Anonymi Cosmographia*, ed. M. Pinder and G. Parthey (Berlin: F. Nicolai, 1860), p. 208. The date of this work is A.D. 667–70.

4. It may also be due to a mistaken copy of the correct date in a redaction of the manuscript.

5. On historiographical lists see J. J. Hexter, "The Rhetoric of History," in *Reappraisals in History* (Bloomington: Indiana University Press, 1971), pp. 62–66.

6. Peter Brown, *The World of Late Antiquity* (Cambridge, Mass.: Harvard University Press, 1978), p. 35.

7. Peter Brown, *The World of Late Antiquity*, p. 35.

8. Judith Herrin, *The Formation of Christendom* (Princeton, N.J.: Princeton University Press, 1985), p. 87.

9. See C. A. Ferguson, "Diglossia," in *Language in Culture and Society*, ed. Dell Hymes (New York: Harper and Row, 1964), pp. 429–39.

10. This was not unique on the Dalmatian coast. After the destruction of Salona in the seventh century, Diocletian's palace came to house a whole community, present-day Split. See I. Marović, "Archeolška istraživanja u okolici Dubrovnika," *Dubrovnik anali* 4 (1962): 9–30.

11. E. Haumant, "La Slavisation de la Dalmatie," *Revue historique* 124 (1917): 287–304; Viktor Novak, "The Slavonic-Latin Symbiosis in Dalmatia During the Middle Ages," *The Slavonic and East European Review* 32 (1954): 1–29; P. Skok, "L'importance de Dubrovnik," pp. 165–70.

12. "Dubrovnik," *Enciklopedija Jugoslavije*, vol. 3 (Zagreb, 1958), pp. 126–27.

13. Genealogies were incorporated into the chronicles. The major Ragusan chronicles are Junio Restić (Giunio Resti), *Chronica Ragusina*, ed. N. Nodilo (Zagreb, 1893); Giacomo Lukarević (di Luccari), *Copioso ristretto degli annali di Ragusa* (Vienna, 1605); *Annales Ragusini anonymi, item Nicolai de Ragnina*, ed. N. Nodilo (Zagreb: JAZU, 1883). The latter part of this work, or continuation of the *Anonymous Chronicle* by Nicolai de Ragnina, will be referred to henceforth as the *Annali di Ragusa di Nocolo di Ragnina*. Mauro Orbini, *Il Regno degli Slavi* (Pesaro:

Apresso Girolamo Concordia, 1604) also traces events in South Slav and Dalmatian history.

14. P. Skok, "Les Origines de Raguse," *Slavia časopis* 10 (Prague, 1931): 487. Skok claims Greek etymology for the following terms found in the notarial registers of Ragusa or medieval Dubrovnik:

| | |
|---|---|
| astarea | pedochia, pedotia |
| antimona | pelagus |
| entega-entegatus | per(a)chivium |
| aptagi | perperus |
| angaria | pivatus |
| pitropus, epitropus | protomagister |
| mandalia | protoplaustus |
| nauclerius | raco |
| oxamitum | teja |

15. Constantine Jireček, "Die Bedeutung von Ragusa in der Handelsge-schicte des Mittelalters" p. 372.

16. See Irmgard Mahnken, *Dubrovački patricijat u XIV veku* (Belgrade: SAN, 1960), p. 70.

17. On Ragusan claims to Greek antecedents see Fernand Braudel, *The Mediterranean*, trans. Siân Reynolds (New York: Harper, 1972), vol. 1, p. 132.

18. This represents current thinking. The problem has a long history in scholarship beginning with Daniel Farlati, *Illyricum Sacrum*, vol. 6: *Ecclesia Ragusina* (Venice: Sebastianum Coleti, 1800). The Illyrian movement increased interest and resulted in collection of sources on the question. See I. Kukuljević-Sakcinski, *Regesta documentorum Regni Croatiae, Slavoniae et Dalmatiae, Saeculi XIII, Starine*, 21, 22, 23, 24, 27, 28 (Zagreb: JAZU, 1889–96). The Yugoslav Academy produced two text series beginning in the last years of the nineteenth century, the *Monumenta historico-juridica slavorum meridionalium* and the *Monumenta historiam spectantia slavorum meridionalium*.

19. J. Mihailović, *Seizmički karakter i trusne katastrofe našeg južnog primorja* (Belgrade: SAN, 1947). Since seismic activity is intermittent, and it appears to have spared the thirteenth to fifteenth centuries from major disaster, it is also possible that Ragusa's earliest inhabitants were not troubled by major seismic disasters. The little evidence that does survive suggests the contrary, however. Pliny noted earthquake activity in this region in ancient times, and it appears to have been prolonged over the full span of the Roman era (J. Mihailović, *Seizmički karakter i trusne katastrofe našeg južnog primorja*). Aristides told of earthquakes in the eastern Mediterranean in the second century, and two hundred years later Zosimus tells in his *Historia Nova* of renewed activity throughout the Balkans and as far away as Crete (Pliny, *Natura Historiae*, Liber II, LXXXV; Zosimus, *Historia Nova*, IV, 8, quoted by Peter Brown in *The World of Late Antiquity*, pp. 49 and 52).

20. The peninsula that is now known as Lapad was considered part of Gravosa or Gruž, which reached almost to the town's gate in the medieval centuries. Josip Lučić, *Prošlost dubrovačke astareje* (Dubrovnik: Matica hrvatska, 1970), and

"Dubrovnik astareja," in *Beritičević zbornik* (Dubrovnik: Društvo prijatelja du-brovačke starine, 1960), pp. 45–55. The coastal lands under jurisdiction were known as the Astarea.

21. Ernest Charrier, *Négociations de la France dans le Levant. Collection des documents inédits sur l'histoire de France*, ser. 1, vol. 3 (Paris: Imprimerie nationale, 1840–60), p. 244.

22. A. Dandolo, *Chronicum Venetum*, ed. Ester Pastorello, 2nd ed., *Rerum Italicarum Scriptores* 12 (Bologna: Zanichelli, 1938–40), pp. 196–99, 277–81; see also D. Mandić, "Gregorio VII e l'occupazione Veneta della Dalmazia nell'anno 1076," *Venezia e il Levante fino al secolo XV*, in *Storia diritto economica*, ed. A. Pertusi (Florence and Venice: Olschki, 1972) I, pp. 453–71. On Venetian intentions in Dalmatia see Johannes Hoffman, "Venedig und die Narenter," *Studi veneziani* 11 (1969): 3–41.

23. Irene B. Katele, "Piracy and the Venetian State," *Speculum* 63, no. 4 (1988): 865–99. The author argues that in the years between 1261 and 1391, Venice continued raiding but distinguished between piracy and corsair activity.

24. For this view see Paul Pisani, *Num Ragusini ab omni jure Veneto a saec. X usque ad saec. XIV* (Paris: A. Picard, 1893), who states the case in the highly partisan language of the late-nineteenth-century controversy over the Latin/Slavic question.

25. See F. C. Lane, *Venice, a Maritime Republic* (Baltimore: Johns Hopkins University Press, 1973), pp. 26ff; D. Mandić, "Gregorio VII e l'occupazione Veneta della Dalmazia," pp. 453–71; Camillo Manfroni, *Storia della marina italiana dalle invasioni barbariche al trattato di Ninfeo* (Livorno: R. Accademia navale, 1899).

26. For Ragusa as a port of call on the route to the east see Bariša Krekić, *Dubrovnik et le Levant au moyen âge* (Paris: SEVPEN, 1961), pp. 13–24.

27. David Abulafia, "Dalmatian Ragusa and the Norman Kingdom of Sic-ily," *Slavonic and East European Review* 54 (1976): 419–28, provides a good review of the documentary evidence, concluding that the Ragusans joined Robert Guiscard perhaps under duress, but thereby gained some valuable protection against the growing power of Venice. He even affirms the chronicle of Junio Restić where it challenges Venice's claim to have taken Ragusa in 1171. See Junio Restić, *Chronica Ragusina*, p. 58. Abulafia ends his article: "The masters the Ragusans had were, by and large, the masters they wanted" (p. 428).

28. Ibid., p. 419.

29. J. Radonić, *Acta et Diplomata Ragusina* (Belgrade: Zbornik za IJK, 1934), I, pp. 10–11; T. Smičiklas, *Codex diplomaticus Croatiae, Dalmatiae et Slavoniae* (Za-greb: JAZU, 1904–34), vol. 2, p. 23. The latter is more widely available but there are errors in the text.

30. Restić, *Chronica Ragusina*, pp. 29–31; see also Lukarević (di Luccari), *Copioso ristretto degli annali di Rausa*, chapter 2. An early woodcut of Dubrovnik shows the twelfth-century community with a bridge over the marsh at the town's foot and a tower guarding access to the bridge on the shore (Dubrovnik: Franciscan Library). See Figure 4.

31. A. E. Lowe, *The Beneventan Script* (Oxford: Oxford University Press, 1914), pp. 60–63. On the Arab geographer Idrisi see W. Tomaschek, *Zur Kunde der Händemus-Halbinsel*, II, *Die Handelswege im 12 Jahrhunderte, nach den Erkundi-*

*gungen des Arabers Idrisi* (Sitzungsberichte der phil.-hist. Klasse der kais. Akademie, Band. 113, Vienna, 1886), p. 344.

32. T. Smičiklas, *Codex diplomaticus,* vol. 2, p. 177.

33. T. Smičiklas, *Codex diplomaticus,* vol. 2, pp. 201–2; V. Foretić, "Ugovor Dubrovnika sa srpskim velikim Zupanom Stefanom Nemanjom i stara dubrovačka djedina," *Rad, JAZU* 283 (1951): 51–118.

34. T. Smičiklas, *Codex diplomaticus,* vol. 2, p. 237.

35. David Abulafia, "Dalmatian Ragusa and the Norman Kingdom of Sicily," pp. 419–28.

36. *Altra sponda,* a term favored by the Venetians and others in the Adriatic, meant "other" or "opposite" shore.

37. J. Radonić, *Acta et Diplomata Ragusina,* I, pp. 12–13; T. Smičiklas, *Codex diplomaticus,* vol. 2, pp. 231–32.

38. J. Radonić, *Acta et Diplomata Ragusina,* I, pp. 14–15; T. Smičiklas, *Codex diplomaticus,* vol. 2, pp. 325–26; vol. 3, p. 1.

39. J. Radonić, *Acta et Diplomata Ragusina,* I, pp. 16–20; T. Smičiklas, *Codex diplomaticus,* vol. 3, pp. 29–30, 75–76, 107–8.

40. J. Radonić, *Acta et Diplomata Ragusina,* I, pp. 12–13; T. Smičiklas, *Codex diplomaticus,* vol. 3, pp. 75–76. On these treaties see Josip Lučić, "Pomorske-trgovačke veze Dubrovnika i Italije u XIII stoljeću," *Pomorskog-Zbornika* 5 (1967): 447–75.

41. Morrozzo della Rocca and A. Lombardo, *Documenti del Commercio Veneziano nel secoli XI–XIII* (Rome and Turin: Sede delli Istituto e Libraria italiana, 1940), vol. 1, pp. 85–86. A certain Laurencius Raguseus, apparently a resident of Ragusa, gave testimony in 1182 concerning a ship sailing from Alexandria; presumably he was involved in the venture. See also vol. 2, doc. 519, p. 59, and doc. 711, p. 242. Two more Ragusans doing business with Venetians, and possibly inhabitants of Venice as well, were involved in business with Constantinople and with Ancona respectively.

42. F. C. Lane, "Merchant Galleys, 1300–1344: Private and Communal Operation," in *Venice and History* (Baltimore: Johns Hopkins University Press, 1966), pp. 193–226; Constantine Jireček, "Die Bedeutung von Ragusa in der Handelsgeschichte des Mittelalters," *Almanach der Kais. Akademie der Wiss. in Wien* 49 (1899), pp. 365–452, is still reliable on Ragusan economic history and has not been replaced by more recent scholarship.

43. A useful review of the issue of the Fourth Crusade may be found in Donald Queller and Susan Stratton, "A Century of Controversy on the Fourth Crusade," *Studies in Medieval and Renaissance History* 6 (1969): 233–78. For the Venetian treaties with the Adriatic ports see S. Ljubić, *Listine ob odnošajih između južnoga slavenstva i mletačke republike* (Zagreb, 1868–93) I, pp. 46–49, 53, 82–85; T. Smičiklas, *Codex diplomaticus,* vol. 3, pp. 351–54; vol. 4, pp. 8–11.

44. Venetian State Archives (henceforth V. S. A.), *Cinque Savii,* vol. 9, f. 175.

45. *Libri Reformationes,* ed. Fr. Rački (Zagreb: JAZU, 1879–97), vols. 10, 13, 27, 28, and 29 of the series Monumenta spectantia historiam slavorum meridionalium, referred to sequentially as *Monumenta Ragusina* vols. 1–5 (henceforth cited as *MR*), vol. 5, p. 261. The 280 *miliaria* of goods would equal a little more than

ninety-three metric tons' burden, assuming Venice used its own measures, rather than the smaller *miliaria* of Ragusa. See Bruno Kisch, *Scales and Weights* (New Haven, Conn.: Yale University Press, 1961) for comparative weights and measures of Mediterranean city-states. See also F. C. Lane, "Tonnages, Medieval and Modern," *Economic History Review*, ser. 2, 17 (1964): 213–33, reprinted in F. C. Lane, *Venice and History* (Baltimore: Johns Hopkins University Press, 1966), pp. 345–70.

46. For statute law see V. Bogišić and C. Jireček, eds., *Liber statutorum civitatis Ragusii compositus anno 1272 cum legibus aetate posteriore insertis atque cum summariis, adnotationibus et scholiis a veteribus iuris consultis ragusinis additis*, Monumenta historico-juridica Slavorum meridionalium, vol. 10 (Zagreb: JAZU, 1904) (henceforth cited as *Liber Statutorum*); and M. Peterković, "Statut carinarnica grada Dubrovnika," in J. Radonić, *Leges et Ordines Ragusii, Fontes Rerum Slavorum Meridionalium*, ser. 5, Monumenta historico-juridica (Belgrade: SAN, 1936), pp. 385–477 (henceforth cited as *Liber statutorum doane*). The records of the town's council are incorporated in the *Libri Reformationes* and were edited by Rački; they are referred to as the *Monumenta Ragusina*, vols. 1–5. For archival holdings at Ragusa see G. Gelcich, "Dubrovački arhiv," *Glasnik zemaljskog muzeja u Bosni i Hercegovini*, Sarajevo, 22 (1910): 537–88. Some of the earliest notarial charters have been edited by Gregor Čremošnik and now reedited by Josip Lučić. They will be cited separately.

47. Besides certain very ancient fragments, the *Acta Sanctae Mariae Maioris* in the Dubrovnik State Archives is the earliest collection of surviving records from medieval Dubrovnik or Ragusa and pertain to the eleventh and twelfth centuries.

48. *Annali di Ragusa di Nocolo di Ragnina*, pp. 187–88.

49. See D. Farlati, *Illyricum Sacrum*, vol. 6, *Ecclesia Ragusina;* P. E. Fermendžin, *Acta Bosnae Potissimum Ecclesiastica* (Zagreb: JAZU, 1892). John Fine, *The Bosnian Church: A New Interpretation*, pp. 47–62, provides a recent survey of edited and unedited sources for church history in Dalmatia and the West Balkans.

50. Josip Lučić, *Dubrovnik's Relations with England, A Symposium* (Department of English, Faculty of Philosophy, University of Zagreb, 1977), p. 12.

51. On Ragusan statute law, beyond the introduction supplied by Bogišić and Jireček to the *Liber Statutorum*, see Walter Ashburner, *The Rhodian Sea Law* (London: Clarendon, 1909), p. ccix in particular. See also Constantine Jireček, *Die Romanen in den Städten Dalmatiens während des Mittelalters*, vols. 1 and 2, Denkenschriften der Kais. Akademie der Wiss. in Wien, Phil.-Hist. Klasse, Bd. 48, 49 (Vienna, 1901–3), as well as "Die Bedeutung von Ragusa in der Handelsgeschichte des Mittelalters," pp. 365–452. On possible Sicilian influences on Dalmatian development see E. A. Lowe, *The Beneventan Script* (Oxford: Oxford University Press, 1914), pp. 60ff. On the exercise of authority in codification of the law see J. G. A. Pocock, *The Ancient Constitution and the Feudal Law* (Cambridge: Cambridge University Press, 1957), p. 25.

52. Walter Ashburner, *The Rhodian Sea Law*, Introduction.

53. S. Ljubić, *Listine*, p. 14, and T. Smičiklas, *Codex diplomaticus*, vol. 2, p. 242. This was an agreement with the Cazichi (a powerful Dalmatian family) to end raids on shipping.

54. This presented few difficulties where law was concerned since "or not" or a similar phrase appended to the end of the proposal allowed for balloting an

alternative. Where offices were concerned, balloting caused difficulty because an alternate candidate had to be presented even if the office was undisputed or of little consequence.

55. David Rheubottom, "Hierarchy of Office in Fifteenth-Century Ragusa," *Bulletin of the John Rylands Society* 72, no. 3 (1990): 159. The Small Council held six elected councillors and five criminal justices. In its evolved fifteenth-century form the senate held five civil judges, members elected by the Great Council, 12 former rectors who served eleven months after their rectorships, and the Small Council.

56. Milorad Medini, *Dubrovnik Gučetića* (Belgrade: SAN, 1953) presents the story of Saraca's impressive diplomatic mission.

57. *Liber statutorum doane* gives a picture from 1277 of current customs taxes. A number of offices concerned supervisory and taxing functions. See David Rheubottom, "Hierarchy of Office in Fifteenth-Century Ragusa," pp. 162–63 for a list. See Bariša Krekić, "Developed Autonomy: The Patricians in Dubrovnik and Dalmatian Cities," in *The Urban Society of Eastern Europe in Premodern Times* (Berkeley: University of California Press, 1987), pp. 195–97. Miodrag Petrovich, "A Mediterranean City State: A Study of Dubrovnik Elites, 1592–1667" (Ph.D. diss., University of Chicago, 1973) and Ilija Mitić, *Dubrovačka država u medunarodnoj zajednici (od 1358 do 1815)* (Dubrovnik: JAZU, 1973) chapter 1, are useful as well.

58. Constantine Jireček, "Die Bedeutung von Ragusa," pp. 426–27. See also Ivan Božić, *Dubrovnik i Turska u XIV i XV veku* (Belgrade: SAN, 1952).

59. General histories of Ragusa and of Balkan history in English are in short supply. M. Dinić, "The Balkans," *Cambridge Medieval History* (Cambridge: Cambridge University Press, England), 2nd. ed., part 1, pp. 519–66, with bibliography, pp. 966–76, is useful. See also Vladimir Dedijer et al., *History of Yugoslavia* (New York: McGraw-Hill, 1974). Treaty galleys were grudgingly supplied although Venice demanded, and received, help from Ragusa against the Genoese at Chioggio.

60. Đurđica Petrović, *Dubrovačko oružje u XIV veku* (Belgrade: Vojni Muzej, 1976) chap. 3, pp. 127–32. The fourteenth-century town also used *machina*, that is, large and small trebuchets and other throwing devices to protect the walls.

61. On the Ragusan government in early modern times see Ilija Mitić, *Dubrovačka država u medunarodnoj zajednici (od 1358 do 1815)*. Homosexuality was considered a crime in Ragusa and most heinous among the patriciate. Bariša Krekić, *"Abominandum crimen:* Punishment of Homosexuals in Renaissance Dubrovnik," *Viator* 18 (1987): 337–45.

62. *MR*, vol. 5, pp. 7–10; 229.

63. Dubrovnik State Archives (henceforth DSA), *Diversa Cancellariae* 12, f. 315.

64. Gregor Čremošnik, *Spisi dubrovačke kancelarije, Knjiga I, Zapisi notara Thomazina de Savere* (Zagreb, 1951), doc. 919, p. 278.

65. Bariša Krekić, "Ser Basilius de Basilio," *Zbornik radova vizantološkog instituta SAN* 23 (1984): 172–82.

66. *MR* vol. 1, p. 79.

67. On the Ragusan chancellery and its development, the article by Gelcich cited in note 46 is still helpful. There are two works in western European languages available on the chancellery and its surviving collections. They are J. Tadić, "Les

Archives économiques de Raguse," *Annales, E.S.C.* 16 (1961): 1168–75, and C. Jire-ček, "Die Mittelalterliche Kanzlei der Ragusaner," *Archiv für Slav. Philologie* 16 (1904): 161–214. Vinko Foretić, "Dubrovački Arhiv u srednjem vijeku," *Dubrovnik anali* 6–7 (1957–59): 73–84, is valuable. For a review of the public registries or official collected acts of the town's councils and civic offices see A. Marinović, "I pubblici registri fondiari nella Repubblica di Dubrovnik nel medioevo," *Studi veneziani* 15 (1973): 135–76.

The early notaries hired by the communal government to oversee the chancellery were responsible for the organization of the archives. The most consequential figure among them was Thomasini de Savere, who saw to the preservation and organization of charters and whose notarial registers have been published. Other identifiable notaries followed him and contributed as well to the rationalization of procedures for preserving documents: Pascalis, 1276–1281; Diaconus Andreas de Benessa, 1313–1324; Marquadus, notarius, 1296–1303; Magister Richardus, 1301–1306; Franciscus de Farraria, cancellarius, 1303; Ubertinus de Flochis, 1311–1312; Magister Alterbinus de Cremona, 1312–1315; Ser Pone de Stamberto, 1318–1341; Joannes de Finnis, 1322; Soffredus Ser Parini de Pistorio, 1331–1365; Franciscus Bartholomei de Archol, 1342–1373; Simon filius Ser Chelli, 1342–1347; Joannes de Pergamo, 1348–1349; Franciscus de Placentia, 1359.

68. On language at Ragusa see Constantine Jireček, *Die Romanen in den Städten Dalmatiens,* pp. 45ff. See also P. Skok, "L'Importance de Dubrovnik dans l'histoire des slaves"; E. Haumant, "La Slavisation de la Dalmatie," *Revue historique* 124 (1917): 287–304; and, more recently, Viktor Novak, "The Slavonic-Latin Symbiosis in Dalmatia During the Middle Ages," *Slavonic and East European Review* 32 (1954): 1–29.

69. Cotrugli, Benedetto, *Della mercatura e del mercante perfetto* (Venice: Elefanta, 1583), f. 77; newly edited by Ugo Tucci as *Il Libro dell'arte di mercatura* (Venice: Arsenale, 1990), pp. 246–49.

70. Milorad Medini, *Dubrovnik Gučetića,* pp. 40–60.

71. T. Smičiklas, *Codex diplomaticus,* vol. 5, pp. 399–400.

72. On stuffing the ballot box see Zdravko Šundrica, "Skandal u velikom vijeću" in "Šetnja koz arhiv (2)," *Dubrovnik* 3 (1973): 114–15. On the brief fifteenth-century rebellion see Miodrag Petrovich, "A Mediterranean City-State: A Study of Dubrovnik Elites," Ph.D. diss., University of Chicago, 1973, p. 538.

73. *MR,* vol. 5, pp. 158–59.

74. Philippus de Diversis de Quartigianis de Lucca, *Situs aedificiorum, politiae, et laudabilium consuetudinum inclytae civitatis Ragusii,* ed. Brunelli (Zara, 1882), p. 67.

75. Lukša Beritić, "Dubrovački vodovod," *Dubrovnik anali* 8–9 (1960–61): 99–117. In the earlier period sweet water from Breno had been imported to augment the water captured in cisterns. Constantine Jireček, "Die Bedeutung von Ragusa," pp. 406–4. During the fourteenth century, the Great Council licensed and controlled the price of water transport (*MR,* vol. 2, pp. 202, 220, 292, 361; vol. 5, pp. 95, 237).

76. On the history of medicine at Ragusa see J. Tadić and R. Jeremić, *Prilozi za istoriju zdravstvene kulture starog Dubrovnika,* vol. 1, pp. 112–13; vol. 2, pp. 1–21,

116–17, 193. Giuseppi Gelcich, *Institutzioni maritime e sanitarie della Repubblica di Ragusa* (Trieste: Hermanstorfer, 1882), is still useful in some respects. More recently, see the publication in honor of the 650th founding of the Ragusan pharmacy, *Spomenica 650–godišnjice ljekarne »Male Braće« u Dubrovniku* (Zagreb, 1968); M. D. Grmek, "Quarantine," *CIBA Review* (1957): 30–31; Susan Stuard, "A Communal Program of Medical Care: Medieval Ragusa/Dubrovnik," *Journal of the History of Medicine and Allied Sciences* 28 (1973): 126–42; Bogumil Hrabak, "Kuga u balkanskim zemljama pod Turcima od 1450 do 1600 godine," *Istorijski glasnik* 1–2 (1957): 19–37; Bariša Krekić, "Pestes balkaniques des XV$^c$ et XVI$^c$ siècle," *Annales, E.S.C.* 18 (1963): 594–95.

77. Gregor Čremošnik, *Spisi, dubrovačke kancelarije, bk. 1: Zapisi notara Thomazina de Savere 1278–1282* (Zagreb: JAZU, 1951) (henceforth *Spisi Thomasini de Savere*), doc. 47, 128, 426, 468, 515. See also *MR*, vol. 5, p. 66. Recruiters or syndics served the town by providing communally salaried personnel of all sorts. In the fourteenth century recruiters brought glaziers from Venice to glass in windows of civic offices; Verena Han, *Tri veka dubrovačkog staklarstva* (Belgrade: SAN, 1981), pp. 11–19. In the fifteenth century Ragusa obtained a trumpeter from distant Bruges in the same fashion; Dušanka Dinić-Knežević, "Gradni briza u srednjovjekovnom Dubrovniku," *Dubrovnik anali* 22–23 (1985): 25–30.

78. *MR*, vol. 5, pp. 71–72.

79. *MR*, vol. 1, pp. 90, 111; *MR*. vol. 2, p. 269.

80. J. Tadić, *Dubrovnik portreti* (Belgrade: Srpska knjlzenvna zadruga, 1948) p. 351. Barbers may have served rural districts, however, and they did serve on board ships.

81. *MR*, vol. 5, p. 98.

82. *MR*, vol. 5, pp. 71, 319; *MR*, vol. 2, pp. 46, 319. J. Tadić, *Pisma i uputstva dubrovačke republicke* (Belgrade: Zbovnik za IJK, 1935), vol. 2, pp. 35, 117; M. Dinić, *Odluke veća dubrovačke republicke* (Belgrade: SAN, 1951), vol. 1, p. 224.

83. H. Rashdall, *The Universities of Europe in the Middle Ages,* ed. F. M. Powicke and A. B. Emden (Oxford: Clarendon Press, 1936), pp. 24–26; Vern Bullough, "Population and the Study and Practice of Medieval Medicine," *Bulletin of the History of Medicine* 36 (1962): 65; Anna Campbell, *The Black Death and Men of Learning* (New York: Columbia University Press, 1931); Carlo Cipolla, *Public Health and the Profession of Medicine in the Renaissance* (Cambridge: Cambridge University Press, 1976). On Venice and public health see B. Cechetti, "Medicina in Venezia nel 1300," *Archivio veneto* 25 (1883): 1–378, and more recently Guido Ruggiero, "The Co-operation of Physicians and the State," *Journal of the History of Medicine and Allied Sciences* 33 (1978) 156–66, and Ugo Stefanuti, *Documentazioni Cronolgiche per la storia della medicina, chirurgia e farmacia in Venezia dal 1258 al 1332* (Venice: F. Organia, 1961), and R. Mueller, "Aspetti sociali ed economici della peste al Venezia nel medioevo," in *Venezia e la Peste* (Venice: Marsilio, 1979).

84. *MR*, vol. 5, p. 6.

85. *MR*, vol. 5, p. 38.

86. *MR*, vol. 5, p. 192; *MR*, vol. 2, pp. 88, 91.

87. *MR*, vol. 1, p. 90; *MR*, vol. 2, p. 332; Gregor Čremošnik, "Nekoliko ljekarskih ugovora iz Dubrovinka," *Rešetarov zbornik*, pp. 43–45.

*[handwritten marginalia: "problem here"]*

88. *MR,* vol. 2, pp. 257, 258, 282, 306–7. "In minori consilio, in quo CVIII consiliarii, (captum), quod nullus medicus, tam physicus, salariatus communis possit exercere aliquas mercationes Ragusii, neque habere societatem cum aliquo spetiario" (*MR,* vol. 2, p. 332).

89. See J. Tadić and R. Jeremić, *Prilozi za istoriju zdravstvene kulture starog Dubrovnika,* vol. 2, pp. 1–20.

90. *Zibaldone, Memorie storiche su Ragusa racolte G. Mattei, Testamenta, 1348,* Ms. 434, biblioteca Male Brace, Dubrovnik, p. 661 (henceforth G. Mattei, *Zibaldone*).

91. *MR,* vol. 2, pp. 17, 31, 46, and 49.

92. M. Grmek, "Quarantine," pp. 30–33.

93. G. Mattei, *Zibaldone,* p. 661. Cf. David Herlihy and Christiane Klapisch-Zuber, *Les Toscans et leur familles* (Paris: SEVPEN, 1978), pp. 443–68. In 1424 in Florence, 604 of 874 deaths by plague were children (p. 463). Married women suffered heavily as well, although widows survived more often (p. 461).

94. D.S.A., *Liber Viridis,* cap. 49, f. 78, 27 June 1377. The text is quoted in Karl Lechner, *Das Grosse Sterben in Deutschland . . . in 1348–1351* (Innsbruck: Wagner, 1884), pp. 67–68. See Appendix 3.

95. On *caza mortae* see D.S.A. *Liber Viridis,* cap. 319, 15 January 1426.

96. D.S.A., *Liber Viridis,* cap. 91, 28 June 1397.

97. On quarantine and Mediterranean sea law see Walter Ashburner, *The Rhodian Sea Law,* p. cixix. If a sailor on ship falls ill on the sea and is put ashore, he is entitled to his share of profits, if they exist, and expenses and allowance for food. That right frequently affected his heirs, not him (*Liber Statutorum,* I. VII, c. 23).

98. On plague-era legislation in the Mediterranean see Cipolla, *Public Health,* cited above. See also L. Hirst, *The Conquest of Plague* (Oxford: Clarendon, 1953), pp. 380–81.

99. Jean Bodin, *Method for the Easy Comprehension of History,* trans. Beatrice Reynolds (New York: Columbia University Press, 1945), p. 245.

100. Frederic C. Lane claims a similar facility in passing from private organization to civic bureaucratic control in fourteenth-century Venice, and he claims a comparable facility and ease in returning an operation to private control. See Frederic Lane, "Operation of Merchant Galleys," in *Venice and History,* p. 216.

101. See Appendix 2 for a résumé of the later centuries of the republic of Ragusa.

# 3. The Noble Circle

Noble Ragusans had a great fondness for aphorisms. They wrote them into their records, chiseled them on buildings, and, if travelers' accounts are accurate, exchanged them when they met on street corners. Even in an age given to aphorizing, Ragusans drew notice for this marked tendency to reduce all responses to acceptable truths. Benedetto Cotrugli's merchant manual is the best surviving source for them: "Cover yourself with conditions against your enemy; with your friend be merely prudent," he solemnly advised. He repeated the oldest of sayings with enthusiasm—"Nurture your soul with virtue"—and took pride in aphorisms of classical venue: "Dice Theofrasto philosopho nel libro delle nozze; et disputò, che l'huomo che dee pigliare moglie, dee essere savio, ricco, sanno, & giovane" (Thephrastus contends in his book on marriage, that the man who takes a wife shall be wise, rich, healthy, and youthful). On fortune he cautioned that it only comes to the man who practices "measure and reason"; in fact, temperance, moderation, and careful deliberation were an aphoristic salve applied to each of life's difficulties. Where Italians indulged in aphorisms, Ragusans soaked them in through eyes and ears, perhaps, even through their fingertips. They practiced to the full their opportunity to generalize through a few manageable formulas the worrisome, sharply distinct exigencies of daily life.[1]

According to local wisdom Benedetto Cotrugli, born in 1410, paid deference to the noble circle by collecting together their aphorisms in his merchant manual. In all probability, this was so. Cotrugli, a commoner and citizen, gloried in the old Ragusan aristocratic values coded into aphorisms—as well he might, since he took as much pride in the noble, if illegitimate, blood that flowed in his veins as did noble councillors of legitimate lines. His original contribution lay in seeing the application to society at large of what passed at Ragusa for the wisdom of the *nobiles*, or *meliores* (nobles, the better sort), then explaining to that wider audience how one should go about assimilating "noble" ways.

Of an even more sober nature, ancient in spirit if not in provenance, were the maxims carved into buildings in the town. "Obliti privatorum, publica curate" (forget private concerns, tend to public welfare) was carved over the entry of the rector's palace (fifteenth century) and gravely greeted each newly elected rector, as he moved into residence for his term of office, as well as the daily traffic of councillors entering the palace to conduct the business of the city-state. The far arch of the customs house (fourteenth century) presented this grim inscription: "fallere notra vetant, et falli pondera meque pondero cum merces, ponderat ipse Deus" (weigh carefully, for as you weigh merchandise so will God weigh your soul). Ragusans received weighty charges when they regarded their public monuments.

Over the centuries such aphorisms became a cryptic language for the noble circle. As the distilled wisdom of experience, they supply brief texts that help explain some of the governing principles of political life. Proverbs, what Erasmus called brief and pregnant sayings, often tell us about the wisdom of commoners, but literate noble Ragusans preferred ancient aphorisms, short and pithy sentences, sometimes attributable to specific authors, at other times based on popular classical texts, that effectively marked off boundaries for human responses.[2] In exchanging aphorisms, Ragusans appear to have participated in a social exercise in counseling and moderating, that is, setting out boundaries for, each other.

Aphoristic messages such as "forget private affairs and tend to public welfare" remind us that procedures for governing the polity had never needed to be disentangled from customary family law, as was so often the case among Ragusa's more westerly neighbors. Here no socially divisive revival of Roman law was undertaken in the twelfth century because the governing sense of that legal tradition had never been lost. Even the Venetians adopted some local customary practices of family law from their land neighbors, but such influences, often Germanic in origin, stopped short of the Adriatic Sea.[3] Ragusans may have joined readily in *parlementum* with their Slavic neighbors and showed respect for the *vražda* of the Serbs, but within the town's walls an older and more purely Roman tradition prevailed.[4] The distinction between the law of persons and that of states laid down by late imperial Rome's great codifiers remained a largely unadulterated living tradition. That distinction, and a morality to buttress it, were expressed in aphoristic sayings and remained within the spirit of the law of the late antique world, as in like fashion the principles of ancient republicanism survived as an unwritten constitution. Both were reminders that private and public choices require prudence and forethought but differ from each other qualitatively; the wise person distinguishes between them carefully. Public matters and private concerns are not opposing poles of human existence that stand in mortal conflict with each other. Instead they represent complementary arenas of human endeavor. If this was a lesson many medieval Europeans had to relearn by reviving Roman law, Ragusans did not.

The phrase "According to the customs and usage of Ragusa," which appeared routinely in the minutes of the councils, possessed the character of an adage as well because it affirmed the ancient constitution of the community whenever it was spoken or noted.[5] The noble circle reaffirmed both their hereditary right and their political allegiance with the utterance of that phrase. In a certain sense the community, its walls and lands, laws, customs, riches, even its vista of mountainous coast and sea, were understood to be their own: a joint inheritance.

## Noble Status

When noble names first appear in some number in the documented thirteenth century, the noble circle had yet to harden its contours. Families from the interior were still being incorporated into the circle, and a few names identifiable in that day were never seen again in the councils' records, the families having died out, moved away, or simply been dropped from the governing circle. *Nobiles viri,* as members of the Great Council preferred to call themselves, are known from the cognomens employed in the records of the councils (*Libri Reformationes*). These records, derived from attendance taken at every session, form a sequential series from 1301 onward, and some records of council survive to trace names back over the two decades prior to 1301.

Constantine Jireček, relying on the minutes of council, counted over fifty noble lineage names, or cognate groups, in the thirteenth and early fourteenth centuries but reckoned that thirty-five disappeared in the Black Plague (1347–50).[6] Alexander Soloviev, employing the *Liber Rosso* of the mid-fifteenth century which parceled out land to nobles, estimated that only twenty-four names had survived. A more exhaustive recent study by Irmgard Mahnken undertook a longitudinal reconstruction, employing both private charters and council records, which resulted in genealogies for the families of *nobiles viri.*[7] Mahnken estimated that fifty-eight different lineages participated at one time or another in the noble circle from the thirteenth through the fifteenth centuries. After the first visit of the Black

Plague, the noble circle took somewhat more than a generation to replenish their numbers, but they were not as successful in preserving all the old cognate names. Perhaps because of the many offspring produced by noble families in the fifteenth century, a blessing duly recorded by the Great Council, new lineages were no longer attractive additions to the circle. No new lineage names were added, and the contours of the group hardened.[8]

The precise number of persons within this group varied dramatically over the centuries. The adult men of noble status, that is, the enfranchised citizenry, have been carefully counted. Mahnken estimated that for 1310, 300 men sat in the Great Council.[9] A century later that number, according to estimates, had reached 389 or 391, although the increase is deceptive: it covers a substantial loss in the Black Plague of 1347–50 (which was repeated in subsequent outbreaks), and a subsequent recovery that was followed by an increase at the turn of the fifteenth century.[10] By 1442 those sitting in Great Council had reached 553, a sharp increase of 40 percent in the adult male population.[11]

After this date, and without the incorporation of new names into the roster of those eligible for citizenship, the number of nobles declined gradually until the earthquake of 1667. The devastation of that event was so great that only eighty-four nobles remained to sit on the council and ten *civis de populo* families were admitted (the first few commoners had actually been admitted in 1662). In 1673, with the addition of five more commoner families, a new noble coterie had been created.[12] As a political expedient this succeeded, since it replenished the Great Council out of which major offices of state were filled, but it disturbed the congruity of the marrying circle or *prijateljstvo* with the enfranchised families. When the Salamanca coterie (old families) refused to make marriage alliances with the newly enfranchised families, members of an irreconcilably divided constituency faced each other in the councils of state for the first time in the recorded history of the city. The immediate impact of faction was muted by widespread concurrence among old and new noble citizens on measures to be taken to rebuild after the earthquake. Nevertheless, the presence of two marrying circles within the aristocracy produced an unfolding constitutional crisis of major dimensions.

Yugoslav historians have revived an old meaning of a familiar term to define the noble marrying circle: *prijateljstvo.* Today, the term translates generally as "circle of close friends," but originally it referred to the social group out of which one chose marriage partners in the West Balkan world.[13] Once in widespread use in West Balkan communities, *prijateljstvo* defines the noble circle tidily because that circle appears to have created an identity and its own entitlements on the criterion of marriage restricted to its slender ranks. Noble marriage established sons' birthright to sit in the Great Council. Not until the great earthquake of 1667 did the authority of statute law actually regulate membership in the Great Council.[14] Until then strict adherence to marriage within noble lines safeguarded noble privilege. This long reliance on the careful practice of marriage selection to identify members of the noble regime, and to create a foundation for a "model of parity" among themselves along the lines of what had existed in the ancient world, resulted in an extreme form of endogamy that was as strict as may be found among early European elites and to all appearances as carefully respected as Jean Bodin claimed it to be in the sixteenth century (see Chapter 8).

It was also a supple system, even one that hints at a collective patrician self-consciousness, at least during the medieval centuries. This supple quality helps account for the system's longevity and serviceability to the patriciate.[15] Until the middle of the fourteenth century, marriage strategies incorporated chosen persons from neighboring towns and lands into the noble circle, and marriages provided a few alliances with other commercial ports. As a strategy, endogamy relied on second, even third, marriages for both noblewomen and noblemen. Remarriages increased the likelihood of transgressing the church's prohibition of marriage within four degrees, but ecclesiastical authorities failed to investigate violations until quite late in Ragusa's history (see note 15). In the meantime, noble lines wove themselves into an intricate pattern of interrelation creating, and re-creating, conjugal families with great stability in values and conduct if not in membership. Few medieval city-states went to such lengths to secure remarriages, and some, like Genoa, actively discouraged women from remarrying when it lay within the interests of the deceased husband's lineage to retain her dowry and loyalty as the mother of heirs.

Long-lived marriages, fruitful in offspring who increased in numbers exponentially with the births and marriages of grandchildren and great-grandchildren stood as an ideal. Heeding Theophrastus on marriage with evident zeal, Ragusans drew precious time away from the vital concerns of business and politics to arrange their marital alliances, and they married for life—repeatedly in some cases. Unfortunate Rada de Bocignolo, a young woman of noble family who was born about 1282 and lived about twenty-five years, married several times after considerable match-making efforts among members of the patrician circle to which she belonged. As was customary, she was first wed soon after puberty to a young nobleman, Margaritus de Zanchino, but he died within three years, and she was left childless. Rada was married again within a short time to Jacobus de Lucha, who died the same year. Her third husband, whom she married after another brief widowhood, outlived her and remarried after her demise.

Possibly, the one offspring of his second marriage was the fortunate recipient of funds from Rada's dowry and inheritances from her first two husbands, as this lay within the possibilities of current inheritance law. But her nieces and nephews—the offspring of her siblings and those of the Ranina siblings of her third husband—numbered over thirty and had some claim as her heirs as well. Although Rada failed to produce heirs of her own body, her marriage alliances provided advantages of another sort to the noble circle, to whit: opportunity for the redistribution of her dowry and any inheritances received from her husbands to other eligible young noble-women and noblemen who would themselves marry and perpetuate the circle. Since elaborate negotiations were required on the part of her parents and a wider group of kin, as well as the kin groups of all three husbands, her marriages represented an intense but unrewarded effort over the relatively short span of eight or nine years to arrange a fruitful marriage.[16]

The marriages of Michael de Lucari, a true survivor who was born about 1350 to two noble parents, Anica and Nicola de Marco de Lucari, were arranged under the added pressure of the Black Plague, which returned devastatingly to Ragusa twice more after the initial onslaught in the fourteenth century. Michael and his younger brother both married three times. Michael contracted his first marriage to Slava de Zreva in the 1370s; this marriage produced four surviving children: two daughters and two sons. Slava de Zreva died, apparently from the effects of a return of the plague, and Michael de Lucari married a widow, Marussa de Babalio. Her first husband had been a prosperous man, and his two daughters had inherited the bulk of his estate, which would help supply them the dowries required for their future marriages. In the meantime their mother, Marussa de Babalio de Sorgo (now, de Lucari), and Michael de Lucari had five or six children together in the decade they remained married. Marussa then died, leaving eleven children: four stepchildren, two daughters from her first marriage, and five children surviving from her second marriage. Michael de Lucari then contracted a third marriage; this time the bride was a widow, but she brought no surviving children to the marriage. This meant that she entered the marriage with both her dowry from her first marriage, and, in all likelihood, some sort of inheritance from her first and childless husband.

warranted assumption?

This may have been welcome, because Michael de Lucari had the welfare of eleven children to consider, but not for long. Pervula de Gondola de Bona (now, de Lucari), as third wife, bore Michael de Lucari three children: one son and two daughters. These last two daughters appear to have died in childhood. All of the other daughters of Michael de Lucari wed with dowries. His stepdaughters did as well. The sons of this family married also, thus it may be assumed that they were provided for adequately through inheritance or expectation of inheritance. Regardless of their claims on parent or step-parent, all were provided with comparable portions. Dowries were largely standard, and the nobility respected the law of partible inheritance for sons; none of these sons or daughters entered religious orders.[17] The effort to treat offspring equally is as striking a feature of the pattern of remarriage as the serial marriages themselves.

A general set of expectations, regardless of order in family or descent from a first or later marriage, may be noted in the early fourteenth-century marriages contracted by five daughters of Vitalis de Bodacia from his sequential marriages to two noblewomen named Mira and Dea. There were seven children from these two marriages; the oldest daughter did not survive to marry, five younger sisters and a brother did marry. Four of the daughters wed into the noble circle, and a fifth married a nobleman from Bar (Antivari). Those who remained in town produced heirs, except for Anna, whose dowry may have disappeared in the financial ruin of her husband, one of the patrician Paborra brothers, whose business failure drew the attention of the council in 1319.[18] No *Liber Dotium* (chancellery book of dowry contracts) survives from the decade in which all four were wed, but evidence from the previous decades indicates that over 70 percent of dowries provided identical awards, not only in cash but in provision of a household slave and in the award of gold that would be used for jewelry.[19] Surely a dispersal of assets occasioned by the granting of dowries occurred with the marriages of five daughters. The marriage of one brother would not compensate the immediate family for this loss of capital. Apparently in this affluent town, most aristocratic youth expected to marry, and this was true even in cases where daughters outnumbered sons or children reached majority parentless. To all appearances the number of daughters to dower off or depend on step-parents did not substantially alter expectations for marriage within this system.[20]

Where were the honor-prompted agnatic concerns of which the painstakingly listed noble names in council records gave promise? To all appearances, the marriages noted here were not contracted "in the interest of the lineage," to quote Georges Duby's well-known phrase on western families, but rather in pursuit of renewed numerical strength within the patriciate.[21] Marriage strategies appear to be directed primarily toward perpetuation of a noble circle confronted with the dual threats of mortality and infertility. Among a limited population of noblewomen, who possessed the customary right to produce male heirs with the right to sit on the Great Council, childless marriage and early death loomed as mortal enemies. A study of the early modern European aristocracy by Litchfield indicates that fully 16 percent of noblemen who married could expect to produce no heirs.[22] Remarriage practiced routinely could reduce this figure, but neither in feudal Europe nor in Renaissance city-states was it a measure that lineage-minded elites easily extended to women. At Ragusa, marriage of virtually all eligible noble daughters clearly increased the instances of fertility; and remarriage for both men and women enhanced opportunities for a fertile union, but what of sons bearing the lineage name? They might see their natal family wealth dispersed widely through marriages of sisters. Yet even before the Black Plague of 1348–50 reduced the numerical strength of the patriciate, strategies for survival against the odds of mortality and infertility appear to have operated at Ragusa and they may, of course, be much older than the documented thirteenth century.[23]

A brief comparison of generational increase in two noble families, the Georgio, an immigrant noble family descended from Count Triphon, dominator Cattari, and the prolific Sorgo lineage, shows how both suffered loss in the era of the plague, which coincides with the first generation on the table. Through marriage and remarriage, however, the families slowly increased their numerical strength until the fifteenth century. The smaller number of known daughters in the first three listed generations in these families may be the result of accidents of reporting rather than skewed sex ratios within noble ranks. Georgio marriages produced about four children per family bearing that name over the generations, barring daughters' offspring who may be traced in the records under other lineage names. The stalwart progenitor of the Sorgo line, Vita de Dobroslavo (flourished 1253–1281) and his stalwart but unfortunately nameless wife produced seven surviving sons and at least two daughters, a record not matched in subsequent generations, when family size fluctuated between two and five surviving children per marriage. But this one early, fecund generation assured the survival of the family name while other noble cognate names disappeared in a maze of noble marriage and remarriage.

Generation Increase in the Georgio and Sorgo Families.[24]

| Generations from early 14th century | Georgio offspring | | | | Sorgo offspring | | | |
|---|---|---|---|---|---|---|---|---|
| | No. of marriages | Female offspring | Male offspring | Total | No. of marriages | Female offspring | Male offspring | Total |
| First | 4 | 1 | 4 | 5 | 1 | 2 | 7 | 9 |
| Second | 4 | 5 | 13 | 18 | 5 | 6 | 21 | 27 |
| Third | 9 | 10 | 16 | 26 | 12 | 11 | 23 | 34 |
| Fourth | 9 | 20 | 19 | 39 | 12 | 10 | 19 | 29 |
| Fifth | 10 | 23 | 25 | 48 | 11 | 13 | 28 | 41 |
| Sixth | 16 | 37 | 34 | 71 | 18 | 42 | 48 | 90 |

From the late fourteenth century onward, the Georgio were blessed with as many documented daughters as sons, but the Sorgo line continued to run to sons. Both lineages produced their high number of offspring through practicing remarriages, which suggests that the respective sixteen and eighteen families bearing these two noble names in the early years of the fifteenth century were more the result of successful reproductive strategies than of mere good fortune. The number of offspring remained notably high, at least when compared with the pattern among affluent urban elites in Italy, where the postplague years brought significant decreases in family size.[25]

The Volcassio, a silver-rich family, did not fare so well, although they made energetic efforts to follow the same strategies. The single family identifiable as Volcassio in the late thirteenth century produced five surviving heirs, all of whom married. Of these, two were sons bearing the lineage name who in turn produced families of five offspring each. One of these, a son, Junius, built a substantial fortune in mining and married three times in the course of his lifetime, but all his sons and grandsons died in the decades of the plague, as did his Volcassio uncles and nephews. Clearly a distributive system that practiced partible inheritance and relied on dowrying to encourage marriage could not preserve all cognate name groups, but this loss to the noble circle may be more apparent than real. The *prijateljstvo* continued with Volcassio descendants within its ranks who carried the family fortune with them.[26]

According to Cotrugli, *homo economicus* (that is, the noble aristocratic merchant) should be honest and follow venerable customs in his home because family life imparts good customs to the world.[27] Counseling each other to place general family interests before more self-centered preferences, Ragusans of the noble circle attempted to create the foundations of a just and good society within their own homes. From this stance, duty to the republic may be seen as a complement to duty to family. The welfare of the community and the perpetuation of the *prijateljstvo* were always closely entwined in men's minds. The town's three councils served to protect the noble circle in affairs where the *casa*, or household, could not serve. The constitution at Ragusa rested, then, on a deep-seated belief that a commonality of political interest united all members within the *prijateljstvo*. Ragusans practiced republican rule out of devotion to this idea and brought to council deliberations the same sort of expectations for general welfare that they brought to the conduct of their private lives.

The true test for the law's provenance may lie in the respect that continued to be paid in statute law to the inherited system of apportioning responsibility within the patriciate. Working for consensus in the private sphere exempted republican machinery of state from the burden of resolving factional disputes. This in turn allowed the ancient constitutional principles embodied in the *Liber Statutorum* to survive substantially unchanged.

Even such enlightened policies as those described in the previous chapter, the work of a "government of *optimates*" in Jean Bodin's phrase, skirted the edges of a more pressing issue: creating cohesion within noble ranks. Ragusans addressed this most critical political issue in private, in informal discussions among themselves; nobles deferred to each other most perfectly when they resolved their differences behind closed doors. In so doing they remanded the crucial issue of their identity as a body of citizens to the care and management of individual members in their private capacities. The range of maneuvers the patriciate could employ outside council was greater than the limited formal measures possible in council chambers under the eye of a foreign count.

The patriciate emerged in the earliest documented centuries as an intermarrying elite; that is to say, the kin network that served as a foundation for noble solidarity was well established by the last decades of the thirteenth century. It is possible then to analyze its financial underpinnings, which in turn help explain the constitutional significance of intermarriage for the noble citizenry, but the origins of the system remain something of a mystery.

Certainly marriages created occasions for promoting solidarity within the noble circle. By tracing marriage negotiations, one finds the values shared within the noble circle open to examination. Philippus de Diversis, a fifteenth-century schoolmaster who eulogized noble Ragusans and their town, was correct in a remarkable claim he made for the nobility. Insofar as it may be investigated within the surviving notarial charters, there were not in his day, nor had there been, examples of nobles marrying outside their noble circle, that is, into local *civis de populo* families.[28] And Jean Bodin was correct as well in his impression that these carefully restricted marriage practices provided the scaffolding for republican institutions.[29] Benedetto Cotrugli, also focusing on noble marriages, found three concerns paramount when a man planned marriage and chose a proper partner: first, a wife's character (that is, her honesty and virtue); second, her dowry and riches; and only third, her personal attractiveness, embodied in such qualities as beauty and a pleasant demeanor.[30] Of the three men, the native son, Cotrugli, supplies the key to the question of the centrality of marriage to individuals and society alike. Subordination of personal preference to the interests of status, wealth, and perpetuation of family line provided the most essential key to a successful life. So certain was Cotrugli that proper marriage occurred only within a closed circle that he found no need to mention class considerations at all.[31] And if aphorisms, homilies, advice, and the influence of families could train succeeding generations according to his prescription, then rewards, Cotrugli believed, were certain to follow.[32]

Cotrugli's second consideration, riches and a dowry, introduces us to the financial structures supporting the institution of marriage. Since dowries may be studied over successive decades for a span of centuries, they give a rare glimpse of how money came to be distributed among noble families, creating a kind of rough parity and tying all lineages together through the exchange of wealth. Among western Mediterranean city-states, Ragusa remained perhaps closest to Roman law on the issue of marriage prestations.[33] No Monday gift from groom to bride reciprocated the bride's family's *dos,* as was true in medieval Venice where some local customs of Germanic origin modified Roman law. As early as 1235 the sumptuary law that limited display at weddings made no mention of groom's gifts.[34] At Ragusa the distributive intent of late Roman law which respected the rights of all heirs, sisters and brothers alike, continued to be respected against the interests of passing on the patrimony intact.

The increasingly large dowries awarded at Ragusa signified, surely, an impressively generous distribution of an individual family's monies to others of noble status. True to Roman custom, *dos* was considered a daughter's Falcidian quarter, that is, her inheritance portion, but also her last legal claim on her patrimony; in theory at least, all residual family funds were to be divided among her surviving brothers.[35] Ragusans gained a network of interfamilial ties by awarding rich, often identical dowries. With remarriage, frequently, families with marriageable offspring might visit the chancellery once, twice, or three times to close negotiations for any one offspring's dowry or marriage settlement, introducing opportunities for numerous strategies into noble matrimonial business.

Ragusan parents went to exaggerated lengths to dower and marry off all daughters. Families dedicated few children, male or female, to the church. Similar or identical awards to three, four, or five daughters might be balanced by sons' wives' dotal gifts in large families. Still no single family could rely on a balanced number of daughters and sons to ensure parity, so more complex strategies were often a necessary recourse. Large families, in which all offspring married, appear to have represented a noble ideal, but the problems of infertility and early mortality jeopardized that ideal time and again.[36] In instances where the hoped-for large family balanced between daughters and sons was not achieved, auxiliary aid from kinsmen and kinswomen, godparents, even noble neighbors and friends, might be relied upon to swell a dotal award or initiate other corrective measures to balance wealth roughly so that all noble daughters who desired to do so might marry. Tutors watched over the fortunes of orphaned girls with as keen an eye as they employed over their own daughters' dowries.[37] Over a generation or two vast individual fortunes could be redistributed among noble households through various intermarriages. And over decades the town's total wealth increased, in a sense rewarding this dispersion of assets through the ever-renewing cycle of acquiring new kinship networks and, in turn, new wealth that initiated new fortunes, which were then redistributed.

Noble families registered dowries at the town chancellery and heeded norms for dotal, gifts, with the notary quick to remind a family if they overshot the mark, as attested by a statute law of 1235 limiting dowry awards and the notebooks of notary Thomasini de Savere from the years 1280 to 1282. Twenty-one noble dowries were registered with Savere at the chancellery over this span of months; of these 15 or 71 percent gave identical awards of four hundred *hyperperi* (two hundred ducats), fifty *exagia* of gold, and a personal slave to accompany the bride to her new home. Two noble assigns fell below this level; four rose above it despite Savere's reminders, three of those by a noteworthy 50 percent or more. Almost three-quarters of the noble dowries awarded complied with current custom, which thus effectively raised cash award limits on dowries to the sum of four hundred *hyperperi* plus gifts for display.[38]

Three observations shed light on this aspect of thirteenth-century noble marriage practice. First, there was a striking consistency in dowries awarded by noble families, which non-noble dowries in town came nowhere near matching; second, uniform grants were double what had been allowed by sumptuary law in 1235; and third, pressures to raise dowries fell on the cash award, not the accompanying "gifts" of gold and a slave. By law, a husband might invest the carefully monitored but still ballooning cash award, although he was expected to preserve the capital in case of his wife's future need, so, providentially, inflation in dowries fed only the portion destined for nonrisk at-home investment. Perforce a noble husband invested dowry safely, perhaps with the *massarii bladorum,* or grain office, that is, not in highly profitable but risk-ridden long-distance trade. In a real sense, the community benefitted, every time dowry was given, from a renewing supply of relatively cheap homebound investment capital. Each time customary limits on dowries rose in value, the community gained further. The town banked on it: dowry provided monies that remained in town for the support of communal projects.

Comparing the 1235 law codified into Ragusa's *Liber Statutorum* which limited the cash award of dowry to two hundred *hyperperi* to the 1280 awards reveals that dowries had doubled in half a century, that is, to four hundred *hyperperi.*[39] The middle years of the thirteenth century found Venice imposing the severest restrictions on Ragusans' overseas commercial ventures in its century and a half as overlord. Responsible interpretations stress that Venetian authorities successfully stifled economic expansion for the Adriatic communities under their rule through these policing measures.[40] But whatever the merits of that general premise, a doubling of dowries in a half-century, within a merchant aristocracy both increasing in numbers and favoring marriage for all its marriageable offspring, indicated some significant increase in private wealth, no matter what the Venetians attempted to do through their strict regulations.

The fourteenth century brought further economic expansion both in Balkan trade and on the high seas. The first volume of the *Libri Dotium,* the chancellery book of dowry contracts, allows a glimpse of one result of that expansion, from the decade of the first visit of the plague (1347–49). A small sample of recorded noble dowries reveals few dowry gifts at the old four hundred *hyperperi* level but seven at one thousand *hyperperi* and one at an outrageous two thousand *hyperperi,* or one thousand ducats, a *dos* which only the most affluent great families of Venice could match in that day. The value of gifts in jewelry and gold had increased, but slaves no longer figured in dotal awards.[41] In Ragusa, contract labor had supplanted slavery, and the cost of contract servants was so low that perhaps it now appeared a negligible expense to provide servants for the newly married couple. Half of the noble dowries awarded in the plague year were two-and-one-half times what they had been in 1280.[42] Later in the century dowries reached even more startling sums. By 1380 over half the dowries in a sample of thirty-two ranged between 1,000 and 1,500 *hyperperi*. Ten (over 30 percent of the total) amounted to more than 2,000 *hyperperi,* which suggests Ragusa's wealthiest nobles vied with the wealthiest nobles of Venice in offering dowry for daughters.[43]

Nonetheless, throughout this century a few dowries remained just at or slightly over the thirteenth-century norm of four hundred *hyperperi.* Apparently the law limiting dowries had not been revised, so probably four hundred *hyperperi* now served as a threshold below which noble dowries should not fall, that is, a reverse of the law's original intent. Significantly, those low awards still fetched noble husbands.[44] Is it possible that skyrocketing dotal awards were entirely unregulated and left to noble families to monitor themselves? Social pressures within the noble coterie tended to create clustering of awards at certain new figures: 1,000 *hyperperi,* 1,500 *hyperperi,* and 2,000 *hyperperi.* Dowries valued at five times the poorest awarded clearly created divisive pressures within noble ranks.

Pressures sustaining these great dowry increases are not difficult to find; wealthy fathers indulged in display before their noble peers when they dowered their daughters with splendid sums. In other instances, higher awards stemmed from the effects of plague mortality. Now whole family fortunes might be funneled into a dowry for a sole surviving daughter, a solution for heirs promoted by some tutors and condoned generally. Young and childless husbands left their widows entire estates, which were often added to the bride's natal family award when a young noblewoman entered a second marriage. Double assigns in a woman's second marriage might support a second groom's family of children from his first marriage.

Noble families contracted fewer marriages in this era, to an extent balancing greater awards. Noble dowries collected from the second volume of the *Libri Dotium* span a thirteen-year period (1380–93), whereas former samples represented two years or less. A pooling of capital occurred when larger awards accompanied fewer marriages, and this trend continued, if less dramatically, into the early fifteenth century. A sample from the fourth volume of the *Liber Dotium* recorded thirty-eight noble marriages in little over four years from 1412 to 1419.[45] By this era twenty-five awards, or 66 percent of the total awards, had escalated to over 2,000 *hyperperi*.

Through these decades that tested endogamy and traditional marriage strategies to the limit, noble Ragusans revealed certain priorities. First, as an entrenched elite, they had been willing to risk dangerous reduction of their numerical strength rather than attempt to make marriage alliances with non-nobles of the town; none of these noted marriages was contracted with a *civis de populo* family. Second, Ragusans had seen it expedient to burden dowry awards with inheritances out of respect for custom despite the clear divisive effects of creating a few highly advantageous marriage opportunities for a few noblemen. Heiresses became highly sought marriage partners. Customary limits were transcended and dowries increased five, six, even seven times their 1280 limit by the 1420s. Nevertheless, social controls were evidently at work throughout the century-and-a-half of greatest stress on the old dowry system. Each increment was matched by informal efforts to seek new ceilings on awards.

Even more noteworthy, throughout this period poorly dowered noble girls continued to find marriage partners among the most affluent citizens. In the 1380s, fifteen dowries below 1,000 *hyperperi* were offered, and noble grooms were found who would accept the low assign. In certain instances, a member of the Great Council accepted a small dowry from a second or third wife, allowing the bride's father to marry her honorably and perhaps appeasing the groom's fellow councillors, who may have resented a second or third generous dowry for another if they themselves remained bachelors. In the 1420s, ten noble awards stood at or near 2,000 *hyperperi,* and ten more between 2,300 and 2,500 *hyperperi*—over two-thirds of the sampled awards. A new scale of dowry awards had emerged, set and held in place by the force of social pressure.[46]

At this juncture (the 1420s)—a momentous one in terms of demographic recovery from the visitations of the plague—the Great Council intervened and again regulated dowries following the example, sometimes even the very arguments, of its former ruler, the Venetian Senate, which had passed its own sumptuary law limiting dowry in 1420. In 1423, the new Ragusan statute pegged awards at a more modest 1,600 *hyperperi*. (Venice had set cash awards at 1,600 ducats, an interesting mimicking of the number rather than the amount of the Venetian model.) The law set the worth of gold or silver and other jewels and finery that augmented the cash gift at a generous seven hundred *hyperperi*.[47] The law roundly condemned the inflationary trend in awards and echoed the plaints heard at Venice that awards had grown so high a father could no longer afford to dower his daughters, and that young women without a vocation for the religious life were entering convents. Since this was not currently the case in Ragusa, the law's rhetoric borrowed or anticipated trouble merely based on the example of what was happening across the Adriatic. In matter of fact, the poorly dowered noble daughter could still win a husband. Ragusa's few convents were small, held no more than a handful of women in most cases, and were incapable of absorbing numbers of dowerless noble daughters with no vocation for the religious life.[48] This appears to be an occasion when Ragusans chose to learn their social lessons from the experience of others (their Venetian neighbors in this case) rather than by recklessly forging ahead to learn from their own.

The year 1423 was a critical demographic moment nevertheless. By 1422 the numbers of the *prijateljstvo* had recovered from the great losses of the plague, and the adult males of the class numbered 389 in contrast to 300 in 1310.[49] In the next two decades they increased to 553—roughly 40 percent in twenty years.[50] The pressures for marrying all noble daughters to maintain the nobility's numerical strength had abated. Again Ragusan officials hint to us that they had only anticipated trouble in 1423 by choosing a relaxed, tolerant stance in enforcing the new dowry law: they relied entirely on voluntary compliance from the nobility. Dowries planned and promised before the passage of the law continued to be registered above the new limit for at least a decade. This lag in compliance, for compliance eventually came, provides an idea of the time period that family negotiations for a marriage with dowry required. Since daughters typically wed between the ages of fourteen and eighteen, the ten-year hiatus tolerated before dowries came in line with the law suggests marriage negotiations generally began for noble daughters when they had reached between four and eight years of age. The gravity of the task of arranging marriages may be measured by the years devoted to it by families; the care taken to honor agreements reenforced marriage's consequence.

By the 1440s, dowrying practices had come into line with the law of 1423. A sample of awards from that decade indicates that a full 85 percent of dowries stood at the prescribed 1,600 *hyperperi* limit.[51] Noble Ragusans had become again a statute-abiding people. The new limit, an eightfold increase over what had been set by the 1235 law, became the common dotal assign, signaling that the great era of dowry increase was over. The *prijateljstvo*, reduced now in lineages to fewer than forty, but reconstituted in numbers as the result of zealous if not frenzied marrying and childbearing, no longer needed to struggle so hard against demographic threats. Endogamy had survived the decades of increase, while noble authority went largely unchallenged at home and prospects for prosperity in trade were unprecedented. The new generation that came of age in the 1460s continued to heed the limits established by statute law, although this was a generation so much wealthier than those that had come before it that they could have continued the trend at no inconvenience to themselves.[52]

Standing at eight times the average award of two centuries earlier, the typical noble dowry of 1,600 *hyperperi* in no way approached the ideal of a daughter's fair share of the patrimony. Noble sons now inherited much vaster fortunes invested in ships, urban real estate, capital sums, outstanding loans, and, sometimes, cultivated lands. Nevertheless, a noble dowry could buy over fifty domestic slaves at fifteenth-century prices (see Chapters 6 and 7) or a quarter share in a trading vessel, or perhaps even ten modest town dwellings, which could be let out for rent (see Chapter 4). Cost of living remained so low at Ragusa that a dowry of 1,600 *hyperperi* could pay routine expenses for a noble family for years on end. Heaven forfend that it be squandered in that way; dowry was intended to be invested in "safe" ventures where it returned a modest dividend. Because the 1423 law prevented fortunes that fell to orphaned girls being awarded undivided in dowry, tutors of noble orphan girls had to find alternative means for investing large, inherited estates for their charges. Since women could own in their own right, this did not represent an unsurmountable hurdle but rather a new opportunity for deploying inherited private wealth into capital ventures.

Other channels for capital transmission had opened and proved attractive. Ragusans' familiarity with advanced banking investment procedures, drawn from their contacts with Florentine banking companies and Venetian investors, steadily opened attractive alternative avenues of investment.[53] And Ragusans began to show favor to more risk-prone ventures in the Mediterranean carrying trade, a sign of their new prosperity and increasing confidence.[54] In terms of the family, this meant that, when it came to the division of the patrimony, fathers began to sponsor generously the more risk-prone ventures of sons rather than merely to support the conservative investment opportunities represented by their daughters' generous dowries.

Relying on the fact that noble husbands had only the use (not ownership) of dotal awards, we can estimate conservatively that approximately

500 (out of a possible 550) married members of the Great Council who were alive and active in 1440 had 1,600 *hyperperi* in dowry each at their disposal; that is to say, they controlled approximately 800,000 *hyperperi* jointly (over 222,000 ducats at current rates of exchange).[55] Since by custom husbands wishing to risk dotal capital abroad had to ask special permission from the town's Small Council, it may be assumed that most of this large capital sum was invested safely at home: a comfortable cushion for all forty surviving noble lineages—for that matter for the community at large. In a sense communal life at Ragusa was financed out of dowry funds that served as a kind of privately invested "insurance," resting in this case on the wife's life span rather than on the husband's life.

The cash award given by a bride's natal family to the groom was not the only movement of wealth in marriage. Although cash awards had increased eightfold over the centuries, awards in gold and silver gifts to the bride had increased even more impressively. By the limits set in 1423 the worth of this portion of the dowry could not be greater than seven hundred *hyperperi*.[56] The bride's share now equaled almost half the value of the cash portion of the dowry, whereas in the thirteenth century the accompanying gift of gold had provided merely for a personal slave and a show of jewels suitable to a noble wife's station in life. Because jewels, gold, and silver stood only one step behind coin in liquidity, precious wares were sometimes used locally in transactions as a means of exchange. Married women had sole control over their increasingly large assets of gold, silver, and jewels exclusive of their husbands' intervention.[57] Thus these gifts accompanying dowry made noblewomen significant property holders with the effect of distributing liquid wealth very widely to individual members of the noble circle, that is, to both women and men of that class.

It is remarkable that noble fathers could continue to provide such ample gifts to their daughters while they embarked on ambitious capital investment schemes in their sons' interests. Evidently, Ragusans entered their golden century, the late fifteenth and sixteenth centuries, on the sound foundation of substantial private fortunes. These, in turn, had been distributed both at home for modest safe return and abroad at risk. Those monies invested at home promoted class solidarity because of the way in which they were awarded: as dowry within an endogamous group, unaccompanied by reciprocal groom's gifts, and with the possibility of parents' less complete authority over daughters' remarriages when dotal awards, in many cases, had grown greater than the original dotal assign.[58] In giving a generous dowry noble fathers assured themselves that their largesse fell into noble hands, but which noble hands those might be in the long term remained an open question. So dowry was often a means for the dispersal of noble wealth that moved beyond the control of the original grantor, the father of the bride. When the opportunity to enter the arena of the great maritime powers presented itself, Ragusans were able to participate buttressed by a cushion of dotal wealth, shared out widely, then invested safely at home. Within this intermarrying privileged group, wealth was by no means equally distributed, but in a real sense dowry provided a foundation so that even the poorest nobleman stood on some footing to make his fortune, provided he married and received a noble dowry.

Ragusans were not exclusively endogamous, however. They might marry outside their own circle as long as the alliance was noble. Consequently, marriage liaisons with the elite of other Adriatic towns, Catar (Kotor), Trau (Trogir), Spalato (Split), and Venice open perspectives on Ragusa's relations to sister cities. Ragusans intermarried with families from Dalmatian towns, and into Venice's patriciate. Dowries offered and accepted followed the same tendency to increase as dowries that were offered or accepted at home. In fact, dowries given or taken in exogamous matches fell within the norm in each decade examined. This suggests that some parity of awards existed in the Adriatic region, and measures to hold awards to agreed-upon limits existed in all these communities. A few marital exchanges among the Adriatic communities fostered valuable social as well as commercial contacts.[59]

Yet intermarrying with nobles from outside the town could have an entirely different outcome, as the case of the Ragusan marriages with a noble family from the commercial and mining community of nearby Catar (Kotor) affirm.

Thomas Dragonis was a wealthy and powerful figure in Ragusa's developing trade with Serbia. He was an inhabitant of Catar (Kotor) and father of four offspring. Two of his three sons married Ragusan noblewomen and received Ragusan dowries. An elder son married Tamara, daughter of the noble Sersius Clementis; a younger son married Phylippa, daughter of Andrea de Volcio. A law at least as old as the codification of 1272 forbade marriages to persons from Catar, and indeed a dispensation of that law for the marriage of Drago and Tamara is confirmed in the records. For the marriage of Paulus and Phylippa it is a strong possibility.[60] Drago's daughter also found a husband, Marinus de Bincola, among the Ragusan nobility. Drago's son had offspring who married into the Ragusan noble circle; in fact, with one exception, all marriages of Thomas Dragonis's

Incorporation of the Thoma from Catar (Kotor).

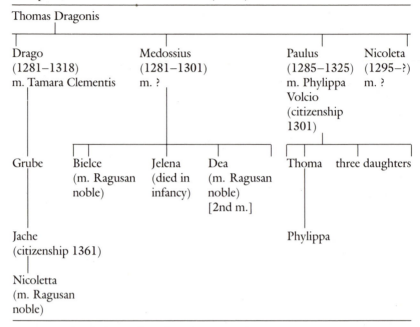

Thomas Dragonis

| Drago | Medossius | Paulus | Nicoleta |
|-------|-----------|--------|----------|
| (1281–1318) | (1281–1301) | (1285–1325) | (1295–?) |
| m. Tamara Clementis | m. ? | m. Phylippa | m. ? |
| | | Volcio | |
| | | (citizenship | |
| | | 1301) | |

| Grube | Bielce | Jelena | Dea | Thoma | three daughters |
|-------|--------|--------|-----|-------|-----------------|
| | (m. Ragusan | (died in | (m. Ragusan | | |
| | noble) | infancy) | noble) | | |
| | | | [2nd m.] | | |

Jache                                Phylippa
(citizenship 1361)

Nicoletta
(m. Ragusan
noble)

From Irmgard Mahnken, *Dubrovački patricijat,* Genealogy LXX.[61]

grandchildren were contracted with Ragusans. Marriages serving to incorporate individual members of this family into the *prijateljstvo* spread over three generations, but the order of events tells more of the story: after contracting his marriage, Paulus de Thoma then applied to the Great Council for citizenship. In the instances where sufficient information is available to reach conclusions, the Thoma timed their entry into the Great Council after their marriages to noble women. Apparently their legal incorporation alone did not transmit citizen status to subsequent generations; their sons sat on the Great Council because they were born of the marriage of a member of council and a noble Ragusan woman. Incorporation into the noble circle and admission to council were thus distinct processes: one private, the other public and legal. Of the two, the private took precedence.

The Thoma's smooth entry into noble ranks reveals the political purposes to which noble marriage strategies were directed, since it required a number of steps in which different families within the Ragusan noble circle wed their daughters and sons to the heirs of Thomas Dragonis for that lineage to join the *prijateljstvo*. Marriage negotiations may have been initiated by the Thoma, but noble Ragusan families clearly accepted their suit.

Optimistically, and at moments rather recklessly, Ragusans arranged marriages to serve diverse goals at once: Dowries accompanying marriage clearly served as a system of inheritance, introducing potentially divisive distinctions in wealth during the years of plague; marriages were used to incorporate foreign lineages into the noble circle; moreover, remarriages stabilized truncated families after the death of a spouse, and they encouraged fecundity. Noble marriages further served to redistribute capital accumulated in one generation more broadly in following generations. And Ragusans also expected their negotiations to result in marriages for all willing members of noble families. To cap it all, citizens sometimes used marriage to make links with great noble merchant families in other Adriatic towns.

Against our expectations, which are often based on the discouraging marital experiences of Italian urban elites who overloaded their marriage strategies with many aims, Ragusans confound us by faring quite well with their many-faceted agendas. Not only did the noble circle preserve its numbers and its customary contours over time but the group grew wealthier as a whole, and as wealth accumulated it was distributed into numerous hands. Great fortunes spread outward: in the fifteenth century cash awards in dowries had grown to eight times what they had been two centuries earlier.[62] And there is substantial evidence that this was a shrinking segment of accumulated family wealth since other conduits for capital had opened and channeled acquired capital into other areas.[63] Because this newfound wealth made the majority of men of the noble circle at least moderately prosperous, many favored marriage practices that had become, by this date, unique among Mediterranean city-states because they worked well.[64]

Testaments or wills, which civic authorities advocated for all persons with property, tell a similar story of building noble solidarity on the foundation of exchanged wealth. A study of noble wills drawn up through the painful years of the first visitation of the Black Plague reveal that wills, like dowries, were expected to serve complex purposes. Ragusan noblemen could, of course, trust to the statutes of inheritance law and neglect writing their own wills if they so desired. Partible inheritance law saw to their sons' futures, while their wives, if aged widows, could easily live on the return of their dowries. Daughters were likely to have received their dowries from the patrimony, and even charitable gifts might have been given during a lifetime rather than as a last bequest. For these reasons, will-writing, even in the plague years was done under exceptional circumstances, as the following list indicates:

RAGUSAN NOBLEMEN: REASONS FOR WILL-MAKING.[65]

| | |
|---|---:|
| In orders (no legitimate issue) | 9 |
| Propertied male (no legitimate issue at time of composition of will) | 38 |
| Married, with issue, some underage | 24 |
| Married, one or more daughters undowered | 15 |
| Married, heirs by more than one wife | 12 |
| Reasons for will-writing unknown | 7 |
| Decima (granting ⅒ of assets to charity) | 2 |
| Total | 107 |

Ninety-nine wills were included in this study, which means there was some duplication of stated reasons for going to the bother and expense of registering a will at the central chancellery. These included writing a will when children were underage, some daughters were unmarried, or, possibly, if there were children from two or three marriages. Fear of the plague's devastation speaks loudly through all these testaments. Perhaps the most interesting will-makers were those propertied men without issue who were compelled to draw up their wills. A noble youth, Andreas de Bona, promised both his home and his money to his young wife in his testament. If she remarried, as she most likely would, she would carry that wealth into a second marriage as part of her dowry.[66] Affluent Peter de Mence wrote his will in his wife's favor, then outlived her and wed another.[67] Peter de Benessa, on the other hand, made his wife his major legatee in his will, but he left a house to his nephew Symon.[68] With the exception of this gift of a house, all three of these bequests were made in full recognition that wealth would not revert to the lineage but would be dispersed to others within the noble circle.

If gifts to childless wives were common, they were not the only choices open to noblemen. The noble and single Michel de Crossio left a house to his niece for her use during her lifetime.[69] Johannes de Petrana had the distinction of being one of ten children, and when he wrote his will he ignored his married brothers' offspring and left his fortune to his mother and to a sister who had entered religious orders and become the abbess of her convent.[70] Andrea Nicola de Mence, ill from the plague, wrote his will from his sickbed. He left a bequest to Maria, the daughter of Mathias de Petragna, who was not his near kin nor designated *filiola* (goddaughter); in the labyrinthine interrelation of noble Ragusans she may well have been kin to him in some degree, but she appears to have been merely an unmarried noblewoman. Was she a friend, a near neighbor, or possibly his intended bride in a marriage that was never to be celebrated?[71] Ties of affection, association, or kinship, which affirmed ties to maternal kin and in-laws as well as paternal kin, came into play when disposing of wealth. This may be in some part due to conscience-stricken behavior in plague years, but it echoes preferences revealed generally in noble bequests and in efforts to promote noble welfare through civic legislation.

Care provided for noble orphans tells a comparable story. By law, two tutors were appointed by council for a newly orphaned noble child; generally they were both a man and a woman if the orphan was a girl or still an infant. In some instances, a fatherless child found his or her mother appointed as tutor. Dowries for orphaned girls were deposited in the *thesaurus de St. Maria* or invested by tutors as directed in the deceased parents' wills.

For sons, a somewhat more complicated system was instituted. In 1351, the two (male) tutors of impetuous young Matico, the orphaned son of a nobleman, Pasce de Resti, requested that the Small Council approve a grant from the young man's estate so he might invest in trade (*ad faciendum mercationes*). Misadventure, apparently, dogged young Matico's footsteps, so while the Small Council initially agreed to the grant, a year later it returned Matico to the authority of his tutors "in all matters, as he might be subject to his father."[72] Apparently he had squandered the advance on his inheritance. In 1366, an affluent heir named Juncho, son of Marino de Sorgo, having reached the age of twenty years, was granted sums held in security for him by the communal government according to the terms of his father's will.[73] Juncho had the full attention of the council, that is, many fathers instead of just one to judge his maturity. Tutors even took responsibility for illegitimate children. Goce de Poce served as tutor and procurator of the dowry of Magdalena, an illegitimate daughter of his noble friend, Michael de Bona.[74]

Noblewomen's bequests show as pronounced a tendency to distribute wealth broadly as do the bequests of their male kin. Noblewomen tended to distribute small sums widely if their wills were drawn up near the end of their lives, their children married, and their own wants cared for:

RAGUSAN NOBLEWOMEN: REASONS FOR WILL-MAKING.[75]

| | |
|---|---|
| Major bequest to husband, small bequests to others | 2 |
| Decima (charitable gifts to others than offspring) | 11 |
| Bequests of one-quarter of dowry (as law proscribed) | 10 |
| Gifted away her entire dowry (disregarded law) | 2 |
| Total | 25 |

Women wrote fewer wills than men, but in the years of the plague there was often reason to draw up a will; some of these wills were clearly made in the last hours of life, at the deathbed rather than in the offices of the chancellery. Of two noblewomen who disposed of their entire dowries, one, young Tomasina de Tudisio, clearly childless, gave two religious orders one hundred *hyperperi* each, her three surviving brothers one hundred *hyperperi* each, and her married and unmarried sisters comparable shares. She left only three hundred *hyperperi* to her husband, so she not only distributed her estate, probably composed of little more than her dowry, but favored her natal family with it.[76] Maria de Paborra gave gifts of one hundred and 138 *hyperperi* to two women who were her friends, and other gifts to her servants.[77] This looks very much like distribution to her small circle of intimates. Young Agnes de Crossio divided her estate among her sisters, while Rada de Sorgo gave her jewels and the residual of her dowry to the daughter of her husband's brother.[78] Tisa de Sorento, who had married a nobleman from Trau, gave one hundred fifty *hyperperi* to her husband, fifty to her brother, and one hundred to her mother, plus smaller bequests to servants.[79] Francha, the wife of Marino de Goce, favored her sons when she divided the quarter of her dowry at her disposal. She left a gift to the illegitimate daughter of one of her sons as well.[80] Anna de Martinussio did not give money to her surviving sons; her will contained bequests to be distributed among her brother's children. This family had eleven offspring, and they would welcome her generosity.[81] One noble mother's will made a daughter executor; that daughter did not inherit but her mother's bequests clearly had won her approval.[82]

Nonetheless when death came to a bride before any children were born to her, she usually willed her dowry to her husband, the sole matrimonial promise within her failing powers to keep. In late 1348, such bequests came under the rule of a statute law that required a childless bride to return her dowry to her natal family except for one-quarter, which she might dispose of as she wished.[83] Not all wills immediately conformed to this statute; in fact, piteous death-bed bequests of an entire dowry to a new spouse continued to occur, but general acceptance of the principle that brides' families warranted a return of their outlay helped preserve the dispersive system that encouraged noble marriages. It ensured that inherited dowry did not swell a husband's patrimony to the bride's family's loss.

This 1348 law stood as one among a number of strategies that prevented the amassing of capital that could be passed on undivided—in other words, the concentration of family wealth into single fortunes or patrimonies. The distinction appears quite clear: making great personal fortunes was encouraged, inheriting them intact was not. In the fourteenth century, statute law had become a means of occasional intercession in the interests of the distributive intent of Ragusa's ancient law. Business or contract law worked toward this same goal. While other city-states adopted a *collegantia* formula, granting three-quarters profit to an investing sedentary partner, with the traveling junior partner receiving only one-quarter of profits, Ragusa favored its patrician sons, or junior partners, with a *collegantia* granting them a more generous one-third of profits made on the contract.[84] Moreover, both custom and statute law sustained the principle of partible inheritance among sons. Dowry law itself dispersed wealth by increasing the property noble daughters owned unencumbered.

Why was there not a surrender to that alternative possibility in the distribution of family monies, a cash-driven reordering of family values, and in time of society at large, through favoring an inheriting head of household as the chief, even sole, controller of familial wealth? Why was this latter alternative—a widespread tendency in contemporary Italian cities—not adopted in Ragusa? Even Venice was not exempt from these pressures to concentrate wealth in the hands of a few men. The potentially divisive effects of attempts to concentrate and control wealth appear to have been present at Ragusa as well as in Italy. Is some claim to be made that Ragusa remained an aristocratic society, even a society of orders where wealth was monopolized by the privileged class but those within it shared quite equally in the control of that wealth, while this condition gave way in Italy proper to new rankings based on affluence and the strategies only the very affluent head of a household could execute?

Yet Ragusa was not an ideal aristocratic world even by the standards of Renaissance utopian thought. Self-serving individual strategies pursued by affluent persons were mounted, and sometimes they succeeded. In fact, two stories, this time of noblewomen rather than noblemen, may make that clear. The first story involved an heiress, Phylippa de Mence (1331–83), the widow of Martinussius de Mence. Phylippa represented the fourth generation of the noble Thoma family who had come to live in Ragusa, and she was the sole surviving daughter of the only male Thoma of the preceding generation. She became, at age two, an heiress of great means because her father had left his entire estate to her. Her husband, however, was not equally wealthy; Martinussius de Mence, the sixth son of that prolific Small Council regular, Mathias de Mence, won a great prize with his marriage to Phylippa, secured perhaps by his father's service to, and prestige within, the noble circle. In fact Mathias de Mence's greatest political feat likely lay in marrying the heiress Phylippa to his own son. Phylippa bore three children to Martinussius, who soon left her a widow with young children. But Phylippa did not choose to follow a typical noblewoman's life course from that moment onward. She had been designated the chief heir of her father, Drago de Thoma, and now became her husband's heir as well. Drago had left her large holdings in the interior. His will required three folio pages to record his holdings at a time when most wills, even noble ones, ran to little more than a folio's length.[85] As his sole survivor Phylippa had a right secured through testamentary bequest to her father's estate, but nevertheless it was unusual to leave such substantial holdings to one child, especially a daughter.[86] Phylippa proved to be independent in her management of her estate; she avoided making a second marriage after the death of Martinussius de Mence and thereafter involved herself in an ambitious investment program using her inherited wealth as a base.

This story would be so commonplace in a more western European setting in the late medieval centuries that it may seem unnecessary to examine it: widows who controlled their own fortunes often wielded considerable power when they acted incisively. But while a Phylippa would occasion little or no surprise in other city-states and realms, in Ragusa her independence and the aggressive investment policy she initiated were both irregular and a matter of concern to the Great Council. Phylippa was one of five members of the noble circle who began construction of great homes outside the walls of the town, causing some consternation to civic authorities.[87] Her "palace" was a visible act of ostentation and signified an ambition to live substantially above her peers. As her daughter Margarita neared marriageable age, Phylippa displayed even more alarming ambitions by opening negotiations with Ludovico Correr of Venice, son of the most affluent Venetian noble family of that day.[88] The marriage was celebrated in 1359; the new bride traveled to Venice in state by a rowed vessel, with twenty rowers to a tier, all by order of Ragusa's Great Council.[89] Phylippa's actions continued to call forth comments from council, but she appears to have been sufficiently civic-minded in her investment policies that she came to be seen as a community benefactor rather than as a dangerously headstrong advocate of her children's advancement over others. Council records referred to her as "Domina" Phylippa, while more egalitarian addresses were in general use for noblewomen.[90] And "domina" she was—willfully defiant in the face of the more egalitarian attitudes found around her. Yet she was neither shunned nor directly censured; in fact, the communal government chose to celebrate rather than condemn her daughter's brilliant marriage match to a Venetian magnate.[91]

The combination of a private fortune swollen by gifts from family members who were victims of plague, and a resolute and independent personality put the councils and the noble circle at the mercy of another woman's program for disposing of her personal wealth. Nicoletta de Goce, through the workings of fortune, was the last family legatee of the great silver merchant Junius Volcassio. Nicoletta survived the visitations of the plague, but she and her mother became in time the sole survivors in a devastated family. Her father died of plague, making her his universal heir, then her husband, sole surviving heir of Junius Volcassio, died, leaving her that great estate; her children all died, in turn depriving her of the opportunity to pass her great wealth to descendants in the direct line. Nicoletta dutifully remarried once. Her second husband was the nobleman Jacho de Sorgo. She was soon left his universal heir and a still childless widow.[92] Nicoletta never wed again, although she was an heiress still capable of bearing children who was likely courted and urged to wed. She resolutely administered her own wealth, a good part of which was invested in land in the Astarea. She let out her land for assarting and cultivation, particularly favoring viticulture, which had become an important export-supporting industry in the local coastal lands.[93] Having lost so many close kin, she either underwent a conversion to very strict piety or became more preoccupied with her devotions in her second widowhood. Her future intentions of favoring one convent with all her wealth at her death evidently became widely known and resented. In response the Small Council actually admitted a suit challenging the legality of her inheritance from her second husband, Jacho de Sorgo, and her planned disposition of her estate.

Nicoletta was charged and brought to trial. She was found guilty, imprisoned in the town and only allowed visits by her mother and a few close friends. In time, when she refused to repudiate her second husband's estate or change her own will, she was exiled and only halfheartedly rehabilitated in the later years of her life. This case investigated before the

Small Council lacked precedent, and the measures undertaken by council to change Nicoletta's mind appear to be more in the line of coercion than just deserts for breaking statutory prohibitions.

Nicoletta's troubles apparently began when her kinsman by marriage, Francho Basilio, accused her of falsifying the will of her second husband, Jacho de Sorgo.[94] Francho Basilio was Jacho de Sorgo's sister's child. He came from a large family, married twice, and produced a large family of his own; his expectations seem very clear. He and his siblings and offspring expected some of Nicoletta's fortune to be shared among them. Following local custom, if not law, they had every right to expect that at least Jacho de Sorgo's portion of the estate would be theirs if Nicoletta did not remarry and produce heirs herself.

While this notorious and highly public case dragged on, Nicoletta resolutely maintained her innocence, supported by the testimony of her mother, her few friends, and the nuns who were to receive her great fortune. She was offered a pardon in 1392 while still in exile but proudly refused it. Only in 1396 did she return to her native town. The contested will of Jacho de Sorgo has survived; it differs in form from other late-fourteenth-century wills, but that is not evidence that Nicoletta was guilty of falsification, nor in fact was she ever proved to be. Her apparent crime lay in her independence of action, and in her wholly incomprehensible failure to follow custom and take care of needy close kin in the planned settling of her estate before she gave her wealth to a convent.

Nicoletta de Goce might have been spared harassment and censure had she lived elsewhere in Christian Europe. Her life was spent in careful administration of her wealth, while her pious hope lay in rewards in heaven: this was wholly unremarkable behavior in a religious age. Secular concerns, such as her second husband's nephew's expectations, do not appear to have been important to her. Devout, consumed by her preoccupation with death, and perhaps puzzled by why she was spared when all her loved ones had died around her, Nicoletta's willingness to leave her wealth to one order of nuns might have even been accepted at Ragusa if she had seen to her kin's needs first or if she had planned a more equitable distribution of her wealth to the various religious orders within the community. This was the general pattern of charitable bequests among members of the noble circle; in fact, it was so commonly repeated it probably existed in formula at the chancellery. But her behavior, probably little more than independent and idiosyncratic in other contexts, was viewed as irresponsible and suspiciously criminal at Ragusa. She was the exception, and her censure shows us customary expectations at work in the noble community.

Both Phylippa's and Nicoletta's behavior lay outside the ordinary network of concern and care for future noble generations so common among Ragusans. Both women were independent and self-motivated, thus suspect by their noble circle of kin and associates. The Great Council had highly effective methods for policing noble sons who fell out of line with accepted norms. Short of ostracism or exile, there was assignment to Puncta Stagno and the settlement at Ston. There the salt pans bred malaria, and a term in office often meant a death sentence. There were other, milder forms of remonstrance administered publicly before the assembled Great Council. But for women the lifelong assimilation of class values was the chief means for assuring conformity. This proved insufficient for Phylippa and Nicoletta, whose lives therefore portray the divisive pressures of great wealth working to fragment the solidarity of the marrying circle.[95]

In point of fact the entire edifice of concern for rough parity within the noble circle was maintained imperfectly. Perhaps this was necessarily so: for at the very time Ragusans wished to preserve parity within their ranks they sincerely encouraged townsmen to accumulate great personal wealth. In the 1330s when relations with Bosnia worsened for a time, Ragusan traders had only to state in council debate that they had 30,000 *hyperperi* invested in trade with that region to spur efforts to end the troubles.[96] Diplomatic missions routinely accompanied private commerce in defense of private property. Prosperity was fed by great personal fortunes and continued to be expanded by the same means.

Clear distinctions in wealth were evident to foreigners by the fifteenth century at least. Philippus de Diversis divided the nobility of Ragusa into three groups based on appearance and reputation. He noted the *supremi,* or great families, of the long-distance merchants who traded in precious metals, silk, spices, and other luxury wares. He spoke next of a middling level of merchant who traded in more pedestrian and local wares and, finally, the lowest rank, or those whom de Diversis characterized as "hens and eggs" nobility.[97] The last group traded what they could from the produce of their lands in the islands and the Astarea. If his observations were accurate rather than merely formula based on truisms from his native north Italy, the noble circle had split into three layers according to income, creating substantial inequality within the merchant aristocracy.[98]

Yet the evidence from wills and dowries does not corroborate the division of the nobility into three ranks. The great Thoma and Volcassio fortunes made in inland mining and trade had been redistributed by the middle of the fourteenth century; new fortunes based on land and sea trade had begun to grow in turn. Households bearing the same noble name differed greatly in personal wealth; great fortunes could be gained in one lifetime and distributed in the next. Proven means for redistributing fortunes meant daughters from some poor lineages that were dying out married into wealthy lineages that survived. And private fortunes accumulated in one generation were not the sole significant determinants of wealth in subsequent generations.[99] A relatively poor but respected Small Council member like Mathias de Mence could secure an heiress for his son through adroit political maneuvering. The power of the *prijateljstvo* was such that persons did not drop out of the noble circle merely because they were less affluent than others; opportunities were made for them. "A model of parity" was an ideal never perfectly realized.

Attempts at evenhandedness may be seen even in the charters that distributed private gifts to local charitable and religious orders. In 1281 the abbesses of St. Thomas, St. Peter Minor, St. Maria de Castello, St. Andreas de Castello, St. Bartholomeus, St. Symeon, and St. Nicolaus acknowledged gifts from two noble estates. The *procuratores* of the Monastery of Lacroma, of Meleta, the abbot of St. Jacob de Visinica, the founder of St. Savini de Dasa, the guardian of the Franciscans, and the prior of the Dominicans each stood for their gifts as well. Gifts were apparently proportioned to size in a complex formula reflected in the order in which they were listed; then each of eighteen individually listed *reclusa* of neighborhood parishes received small but similar bequests.[100] The power of the chancellery to regularize behavior may be seen here as well as in the drawing up dowries and wills. Since most religious orders drew their members from noble families, evenhanded gift giving had the same equalizing effect here as with bequests exchanged among the lay citizenry. But custom reigned here too, and no one, apparently, could prevent a Nicoletta de Goce from violating custom in charitable gift giving. Still, in numerous instances—enough, apparently to tip the balance—private initiatives were informed by a firm sense of class identity and commonly shared responsibilities to the group.

\*   \*   \*

If Ragusa remained a community based on a traditional social order, then this was so because noble class solidarity prevailed against the power-

ful pressures subverting it. The chief of these was wealth, the very accumulation of large private fortunes which, it should be noted in the interests of
accuracy, the noble circle actively promoted despite the divisive potential of
unequal wealth. Triumphing over individual or narrow lineage-prompted
concerns, solidarity in the private sphere of noble life led to a united stance
against both foreign powers and other residents within their city-state,
whom noble Ragusans tolerated as their non-noble neighbors.

*Notes*

1. Benedetto Cotrugli, *Della mercatura e del mercante perfetto,* f. 106, 14, 91,
23. (These are paraphrased; for a modern edition see *Il Libro dell'arte di mercatura,*
ed. Ugo Tucci [Venice: Arsenale, 1990].) Ugo Tucci, "The Psychology of the
Merchant in the Sixteenth Century," in *Renaissance Venice,* ed. John Hale, (Totawa,
N.J.: Rowam and Littlefield, 1973), pp. 346–78, provided the paraphrase of the first
aphorism. Tucci contends that Cotrugli's outlook aptly illustrates the mentality of a
Venetian merchant in the sixteenth century.
    Cotrugli's reference to Theophrastus is to the now lost work on marriage, *De
Nuptiis,* which he may have known through St. Jerome's *Adversus Iovinianum.* See
Suzanne Treggiari, *"Digna Condicio:* Betrothals in the Roman Upper Class," *Echo
du monde classique,* n.s. 3 (1984): 419–51.
    2. Cotrugli claims to have followed the career of a merchant and consul only
after leaving "the sweet pursuit of learning," where he obtained a number of his
learned maxims. On proverbs and aphorisms marking language see Kenneth Burke,
*Philosophy of Literary Form* (Baton Rouge: Louisiana State University Press, 1941),
pp. 293–304; Eileen Keenan, "Norm Makers, Norm Breakers," in *Explorations in the
Ethnography of Speaking,* ed. Richard Bauman and Joel Sherzer (New York: Cambridge University Press, 1974), pp. 125–43; Natalie Davis, "Proverbial Wisdom and
Popular Errors," in *Society and Culture in Early Modern France* (Stanford: Stanford
University Press, 1975), pp. 227–67.
    3. Venetians gave a "Monday gift" at marriage that corresponded to the
German *morgengabe,* for example. See Giorgio Zordan, "I rari aspetti della communione familiare di beni nella Venezia dei secoli XI–XII," *Studi veneziani* 8 (1966):
127–94.
    4. The *parlementum* was a meeting for resolving conflict among neighbor-
ing powers in Balkans. Only vestiges of it remained in documented centuries. Both
Bogišić and Jireček have commented on it. The *vražda,* a longstanding agreement
between Ragusans and Serbs, required payment of five hundred *hyperperi* for
murder, rather than the death penalty. Venice censured the Ragusan government
for respecting this Serbian policy in the fourteenth century. Bariša Krekić, "Developed Autonomy: The Patricians in Dubrovnik and Dalmatian Cities" in Bariša
Krekić, ed., *The Urban Society of Eastern Europe in Premodern Times* (Berkeley:
University of California Press, 1987), p. 191.
    5. These questions are addressed in V. Bogišić and C. Jireček's introduction

to the statute law of Ragusa in the Monumenta historico-juridica Slavorum meridionalium edition of the *Liber Statutorum civitatis Ragusii.*

6. Constantine Jireček, *Die Romanen in den Städten Dalmatiens während des
Mittelalters* (Vienna, 1903), I, p. 99.

7. D.S.A., *Liber Rosso,* f. 302v–461. A. Soloviev, "Le Patriciat de Raguse au
XV^e siècle," in *Rešetarov zbornik iz dubrovačke prošlosti,* ed. M. Vidoević and J. Tadić
(Dubrovnik: Matica hrvatska, 1931), pp. 59–66.

8. I. Mahnken, *Dubrovački patricijat u XIV veku,* (Belgrade: SAN, 1961),
pp. 62–75. On this genealogical study see Josip Lučić, "O dubrovačkom patricijatu u
XIV stoljecu," *Istorijski zbornik* 37 (1964): 393–411. Mahnken provides fifty-eight
genealogies in part 2, while Lučić notes fifty-three lineages surviving until 1366
(pp. 404–5). On the numbers of the patriciate see also Bariša Krekić, "Developed
Autonomy: The Patricians in Dubrovnik and Dalmatian Cities," pp. 197–98.

9. I. Mahnken, *Dubrovački patricijat,* pp. 14–16.

10. A. Soloviev, "Le Patriciat de Raguse," p. 65; B. Krekić, *Dubrovnik in the
Fourteenth and Fifteenth Centuries* (Norman: University of Oklahoma Press, 1972),
p. 33.

11. Philippus de Diversis, *Situs aedificorium, politae et laudabilium consuetudinum inclytae civitatis Ragusii,* ed. Brunelli (Zara, 1882), p. 67. On de Diversis see Ivan
Božić, "Dve Beleške o Filipu de Diversisu," *Zbornik filoz. fakulteta, Belgrade* 11
(1970): 313–29.

12. Radovan Samardžić, *Borba Dubrovnika za Opstanak posle velikog zemljotresa 1667* (Belgrade: SAN, 1960), doc. 5, pp. 33–35, lists the nobles who died in the
earthquake. Gregor Novak, "Dubrovački potres 1667, i Mletci," *Dubrovnik anali* 12
(1970): 9–25.

13. Josip Lučić, "O dubrovačkom patricijatu u XIV stoljeću," pp. 393–411.

14. Citizenship was defined in the fifteenth century. D.S.A., *Liber Viridis,* c.
428 (1449), quoted in Miodrag Petrovich, "A Mediterranean City-State: A Study of
Dubrovnik Elites, 1592–1667" (Ph.D. diss., University of Chicago, 1973), pp. 45–46.

15. Practices were carried out within civil and ecclesiastical limits, which
added further restrictions. In the thirteenth century, intermarriage with Catar
(Kotor) was forbidden, but the law was transgressed in the case of marriages with
the noble Thoma and Basilio families. In 1362 Hungary requested that noble
Ragusans wed only into families under Hungarian protection when they married
nobility outside the republic. By the fifteenth century families respected the church's
laws on incest, in regard to blood, affinity and conpaternity. See Dušanka Dinić-
Knežević, *Položaj žena u Dubrovniku u XIII i XIV veku* (Belgrade: SAN, 1974),
pp. 61–92, 203–4.

The period for greatest restriction on the choice of marriage partners occurred
after the thirteenth century, when the noble families ceased incorporating new
lineages into their circle. The principle of incest law—*in quartu gradu affinitatis*—
was strictly observed, but it is unlikely that noble marriage practices could have
withstood the sharp glare of ecclesiastical surveillance brought to bear elsewhere,
particularly on the elites of Italy and feudal France. Duplicating in godparentage the
degrees in blood relation was criticized elsewhere, but Ragusans practiced it. Uncles
and aunts were chosen as godparents, and members of orders without heirs (and

hopefully few siblings with heirs) were frequently chosen as well. More contrary to the letter of canon law on incest were violations of the degree of affinity created through step-parentage. Here, clearly, fourteenth-century noble Ragusans violated canon law. The offspring of a parent who remarried did not exclude all kin to the fourth degree of his or her step-parent (or step-parents because that, too, occurred). Clerical surveillance of marriage practices increased in the fifteenth century but then, too, the incidences of remarriage, which created such difficulty, decreased as the plague abated. Ten marriages of noble Ragusans who bore the same last names—Sorga (three), de Mence (four), and Goce (three)—were investigated to arrive at these conclusions. Genealogies indicate that these marriages scrupulously respected blood affinity but transgressed incest restrictions on step-parentage. Compare Georges Duby, *Medieval Marriage: Two Models from Twelfth-Century France* (Baltimore: Johns Hopkins University Press, 1978).

16. I. Mahnken, *Dubrovački patricijat,* Genealogy IX and pp. 137–40.

17. I. Mahnken, *Dubrovački patricijat,* Genealogy XLI and pp. 300–301. I cannot locate the Sorgo daughters' dowries, but they would likely be somewhat larger than their stepsisters' since both were heirs of their father, with their inheritance protected by tutors. Under the stress of plague these decades saw greater "spread" in dotal awards.

18. *MR,* vol. 5, p. 593.

19. Susan Stuard, "Dowries and Increments in Wealth in Medieval Ragusa (Dubrovnik)," *Journal of Economic History* 41 (1981): 795–811.

20. I. Mahnken, *Dubrovački patricijat,* Genealogy X, and pp. 140–44. The Sorgo daughters would have had their interests ensured by tutors. Mothers often served as tutors for their unwed daughters along with a nobleman who might or might not be a sibling of the deceased father. This system secured the future rights of orphaned children when remarriage occurred.

21. Georges Duby, *Medieval Marriage: Two Models.* See also Marc Bloch, *Feudal Society,* trans. L. A. Manyon (Chicago: University of Chicago Press, 1964), vol. 1, pp. 123–44.

22. R. Litchfield, "Demographic Characteristics of Florentine Patrician Families," *Journal of Economic History* 19 (1969): 197. See also P. Cooper, "Inheritance and Settlement by Great Landowners," in *Family and Inheritance,* ed. Jack Goody, Joan Thirsk, and E. P. Thompson (Cambridge: Cambridge University Press, 1976), p. 287 (Table A), and Benedetto Cotrugli, *Della mercatura e del mercante perfetto,* f. 100 (Tucci ed., p. 247). Cotrugli notes that men may produce offspring until they are eighty, women until they are fifty, which is a generous definition of fertility even among medieval and Renaissance thinkers. Such opinions would prove convenient among a circle of persons who advocated remarriage.

23. The claims for longevity of Ragusan marital practices were made by the Ragusan chroniclers, Luccari, Nicola Ranina, the Anonymous Chronicle, and by Philippus de Diversis in *Situs aedificiorum,* and by Luigi Beccadelli, Archbishop of Ragusa (see Chapter 8). Remarriage was practiced among aristocratic Venetians. See Stanley Chojnacki, "The Power of Love: Wives and Husbands in Late Medieval Venice," in *Women and Power in the Middle Ages,* ed. Mary Erler and Maryanne Kowaleski (Athens: University of Georgia Press, 1988), p. 126. In Florence, lineages

were often loathe to see a widow remarry and leave with her dowry, while a widow's brothers might well urge just such a choice. Christiane Klapisch-Zuber, "The 'Cruel Mother': Maternity, Widowhood, and Dowry in Florence in the Fourteenth and Fifteenth Centuries," in *Women, Family, and Ritual in Renaissance Italy,* trans. Lydia G. Cochrane (Chicago: University of Chicago Press, 1985), pp. 117–64.

24. I. Mahnken, *Dubrovački patricijat,* Genealogies XXXVII and LXVII and pp. 201–27, 407–24.

25. R. Litchfield, "Demographic Characteristics of Florentine Patrician Families," pp. 191–97.

26. I. Mahnken, *Dubrovački patricijat,* Genealogies LXXIII and pp. 441–43. D.S.A., *Testamenta* III, f. 55–57 v. See also Dušanka Dinić-Knežević, *Položaj žena u Dubrovniku u XIII i XIV veku,* pp. 49–52. See Chapter 7 on fortunes for the importance of mining to the Ragusan economy and more generally for the growth of the medieval Balkan economy. Speros Vryonis, "The Question of the Byzantine Mines," *Speculum* 37, no. 1 (1962): 1–17, provides a good introduction to the issue for the western reader.

27. B. Cotrugli, *Della mercatura,* f. 87 (Tucci ed., p. 230).

28. Philippus de Diversus, *Situs aedificiorum,* p. 67. Ragusan nobility made some alliances with other noble urban families in Adriatic towns.

29. Jean Bodin, *Six Bookes of a Commonweale,* trans. Kenneth D. McRae (rpt., Cambridge, Mass.: Harvard University Press, 1979), p. 235.

30. Benedetto Cotrugli, *Della mercatura,* f. 92 (Tucci ed., p. 237).

31. Cotrugli's lost essay on the family may have given consideration to class issues, however.

32. David Rheubottom, "'Sisters First': Betrothal Order and Age at Marriage in Fifteenth Century Ragusa," *Journal of Family History* 13, no. 4 (1988): 359–76, shows the marriage pattern of the Ragusan patriciate in its fully realized fifteenth-century form.

33. However, the lower Adriatic cities share this trait with Ragusa. See André Guillou, "Il matrimonio nell'Italia bizantina nei secoli X et XI," in *Matrimonio nella società alto-medievale* (Spoleto, 1970), vol. 2, pp. 569–86.

34. *Ordo de dotibus,* 1235; *Liber Statutorum,* p. xiv.

35. In practice married daughters might inherit from their fathers; in fact, a partition of the estate of Michel de Mence, who died intestate, gave his substantial holdings to the husbands of his two surviving daughters in an awkward accommodation to inheritance in the direct line (both daughters had offspring and would presumably inherit from their fathers) that the law did not provide (D.S.A., *Diversa Cancellariae,* 12, f. 315).

36. Remarriages of women were unusual in some Italian cities. The most common argument against them was that they were not in the interest of the first husband's lineage. See Enrico Besta, *La famiglia nella storia del diritto Italiano* (Padua: A. Milani, 1933); Francesco Ercole, "L'istituto dotale nella pratica e nella legislazione statutaria dell'Italia superiore," *Revista italiana per le scienze giuridiche* 65 (1908): 191–302, 66 (1910): 167–257; Stanley Chojnacki, "Dowries and Kinsmen in Early Renaissance Venice," in *Women in Medieval Society,* ed. Susan Mosher Stuard (Philadelphia: University of Pennsylvania Press, 1976), pp. 177–99; Carol L. Lan-

sing, *The Florentine Magnates: Lineage and Faction in a Medieval Commune* (Princeton, N.J.: Princeton University Press, 1991); F. W. Kent, *Household and Lineage in Renaissance Florence* (Princeton, N.J.: Princeton University Press, 1977); Gene Brucker, *Renaissance Florence* (New York: Wiley, 1969); David Herlihy and Christiane Klapisch-Zuber, *Les Toscans et leurs familles*, (Paris: SEVPEN, 1978); Julius Kirshner and Anthony Mohlo, "The Dowry Fund and the Marriage Market in Early Quattrocento Florence," *Journal of Modern History* 50 (1978): 403–38. On church law and the remarriage of women, see G. Buckler, "Women in Byzantine Law," *Byzantion* 11 (1936): 406–8, and A. Rosembert, *La Veuve en droit canonique jusqu'à XVIᵉ siècle* (Paris, 1923).

37. See *Liber Statutorum*, VIII, c. 42, for laws governing tutors' behavior. Tutors for the orphaned daughters of Lucas de Baraba made distinguished marriages for the girls despite a poor inheritance. D.S.A., *Liber Dotium*, II, f. 153, 154v. The orphaned daughters of Symon de Benessa did very well with dowries of 2,200 and 2,500 *hyperperi* in the early fifteenth century. The difference in the awards for Coletta and Lucia probably represented growth in their jointly invested estate over a few months, apparently, or a gift to the latter. D.S.A., *Liber Dotium*, IV, f. 13, 19.

The *hyperperi* was the money of account in use in Ragusa in the medieval centuries. The silver *grosso* was the major circulating coin; twelve *grossi* equaled one *hyperperi*. The *hyperperi* diminished steadily in relation to the ducat, and tables in this study reflect that progression:

early fourteenth century, 2 *hyperperi* = 1 ducat
late fourteenth century, 2.5 *hyperperi* = 1 ducat
fifteenth century, 3 *hyperperi* = 1 ducat

38. Dowries awarded noble daughters, 1280–82:

| | Cash (hyperperi) | Jewelry | Other | Percent of Sample |
|---|---|---|---|---|
| 2 dowries | 400 | none listed | none listed | 10 |
| | 319 | none listed | none listed | |
| 15 dowries | 400 | 50 *exagia auri* | clothes, slave | 71 |
| 4 dowries | 470 | 50 *exagia auri* | clothes, slave | 19 |
| | 600 | 100 *exagia auri* | clothes, slave | |
| | 650 | 50 *exagia auri* | clothes, slave | |
| | 750 | silver, gold, jewels | | |

Source: Gregor Čremošnik, *Spisi . . . Thomazina de Savere*, doc. 375, 387, 391, 395, 424, 430, 432, 541, 582, 610, 622, 677, 697, 714, 722a, 742, 743, 902, 919.

39. *Liber Statutorum*, p. xiv, *Ordo de dotibus*, 1235.
40. See Chapter 2.

41. *Liber Dotium,* I, 1348–49:

| Cash (hyperperi) | | Jewelry | Percent of Sample |
|---|---|---|---|
| 4 dowries | 400–800 | 25–100 *exagia auri* | 29 |
| 7 dowries | 1,000* | 100 *exagia auri* (one 70 *exagia auri*) | 50 |
| 2 dowries | 1,400 | 100 *exagia auri* | 14 |
| 1 dowry | 2,000 | 100 *exagia auri* | 7 |

*One dowry listed a house of stone beyond the gold for jewels and the 1,000-*hyperperi* cash bequest.
Source: D.S.A., *Liber Dotium,* I, f. iv, 2v, 3v, 7, 5v, 9, 9v, 10v (bis) 12, 13v.

42. Accounting, however, for inflation in the *grossi.* See note 35 above.

43. D.S.A., *Liber Dotium,* II, 1380–93:

| Cash (hyperperi) | | Jewelry | Percent of Sample |
|---|---|---|---|
| 5 dowries | 400–600 | varied gifts | 16 |
| 10 dowries | 900–1,000 | 100 *exagia auri* plus jewels | 31 |
| 7 dowries | 1,500 | 100 *exagia auri* | 21.5 |
| 8 dowries | 2,000–2,400 | 100 *exagia auri* | 25 |
| 2 dowries | 3,000 | 100 *exagia auri* | 6.5 |

Source: D.S.A., *Liber Dotium,* II, f. 85v. 96v, 97, 98, 101v, 105, 105v, 106, 106v, 109, 112v–113, 114v, 125, 126, 127, 132, 137, 138, 138v, 139, 139v, 143, 144v, 148, 151v, 153, 154v.

44. Junius Volcassio, a very wealthy silver merchant wed the much poorer Cathe Bubagna, his second of three wives. Her family had ties with Montenegro; it produced some ecclesiastics and disappeared after 1348 (I. Mahnken, *Dubrovačke patricijat,* Genealogy XIII). Before the Catena and Celipa lineages died out completely in the fourteenth century, daughters of both lines married into the Tudisio lineage: Nicoleta became the second wife of Zive de Tudisio; Rade Celipa married Martolus de Tudisio. See I. Mahnken, *Dubrovački patricijat,* Genealogy XIII, XIX, LXXI. When Caterina, daughter of Paul de Martinussio, wed Nicolas de Zavernico in 1348, she brought a small dowry of 600 *hyperperi.* In a second marriage during the outbreak of the plague, it may have been less important to Nicolas to gain a larger sum. D.S.A., *Liber Dotium* I, f. 7v.

45. D.S.A., *Liber Dotium,* IV, 1412–19:

|  | Cash (hyperperi) | Percent of Sample |
|---|---|---|
| 1 dowry | possessions | 3 |
| 2 dowries | 400–600 | 5 |
| 3 dowries | 1,000–1,300 | 8 |
| 7 dowries | 1,400–1,900 | 18 |
| 10 dowries | 2,000–2,250 | 26 |
| 14 dowries | 2,500 | 37 |
|  | 3,000 | 3 |

Source: *Liber Dotium*, IV, f. 5, 8v, 10v, 11, 11v, 12v, 13, 15, 17, 18, 18v, 19, 24, 24v, 25, 26, 28, 32, 33, 35, 38v, 39v, 44, 45, 46v, 48, 49, 49v, 51, 51v, 52, 53v, 54, 55, 55v, 56v.

46. D.S.A., *Liber Dotium*, V, 1420–26:

|  | Cash (hyperperi) | Percent of Sample |
|---|---|---|
| 3 dowries | property | 10 |
| 1 dowry | 600 | 3 |
| 5 dowries | 1,100–1,500 | 17 |
| 10 dowries | 1,600–2,000 | 33 |
| 10 dowries | 2,300–2,500 | 33 |
| 1 dowry | 2,800 | 3 |

Source: *Liber Dotium*, V, f. 1v, 2, 3v, 6, 6v, 8, 11–14, 17, 17v, 18, 18v, 19v, 23, 25, 28–30, 30v, 31v, 37, 38v.

Life-long noble bachelors who never found a wife became a much more serious problem in the fifteenth century. This was another source of friction within the patriciate where some men married twice or three times. See David Rheubottom, "'Sisters First': Betrothal Order and Age at Marriage in Fifteenth Century Ragusa," p. 363.

47. D.S.A., *Liber Viridis*, C. 180, f. 140v. See reconfirmations, C. 371, f. 234–35; and C. 478, f. 296v. Venice had passed its own law limiting dowries in 1420. It placed cash awards at 1,600 ducats. See Stanley Chojnacki, "Dowries and Kinsmen," pp. 177–99 and Reinhold Mueller, "The Procurators of San Marco," *Studi veneziani* 13 (1971): 206ff.

48. In the late thirteenth century, there were six convents in the city proper and at least eighteen *reclusa* living singly or in pairs in parish churches in the city. In the fourteenth century, the Poor Clares established an order near the Franciscan monastery. These orders were small and in most cases held only ten or twelve women. Gregor Čremošnik, *Zapisi notara Thomasina de Savere*, doc. 486, pp. 144–46.

49. See discussion of the size of the noble circle in Chapter 2. I. Mahnken, *Dubrovački patricijat*, pp. 14–16.

50. A. Soloviev, "Le Patriciat de Raguse," p. 65.

51. D.S.A., *Liber Dotium*, VI, 1440–43:

|         | Cash (hyperperi)      | Percent of Sample |
|---------|-----------------------|-------------------|
| 1 dowry    | 1,250              | 4  |
| 24 dowries | 1,600*             | 85 |
| 2 dowries  | 1,900–2,100        | 7  |
| 1 dowry    | possessions (a home) | 4  |

*One 1,600 *hyperpera* dowry listed the bequest of a home as well, making it significantly larger. In *exagia* of gold, 150 to 200 became the common bequest, although there continued to be a range of gifts, as well as substitutions of specific jewels that appear to be heirlooms.
Source: D.S.A., *Liber Dotium*, VI, f. 2v, 4, 4v, 7, 8v, 11, 12, 15v, 18v, 21v, 27, 30v, 34, 34v, 35, 36v, 37v, 38, 38v, 39, 40v, 42, 47v, 49v.

52. D.S.A., *Liber Dotium*, VII, 1460–65:

|            | Cash (hyperperi)                                 | Percent of Sample |
|------------|--------------------------------------------------|-------------------|
| 4 dowries  | 1,300                                            | 14 |
| 23 dowries | 1,600                                            | 82 |
| 1 dowry    | possessions (houses in Castellum, possibly rents) | 4  |

Source: *Liber Dotium*, VII, f. 4, 7v, 9, 11, 11v, 12v, 14, 21, 22, 23v, 32, 34, 34v, 37v, 38v, 39, 42, 42v, 47v, 49v, 50v, 52v, 53, 54v.

53. Bariša Krekić, "Foreigners in Dubrovnik," *Viator* 8 (1978): 67–75; idem., "Four Florentine Commercial Companies in Dubrovnik," in *The Medieval City*, ed. Harry Miskimin, David Herlihy, and Benjamin Kedar (New Haven, Conn.: Yale University Press, 1977), pp. 25–41. D. Dinić-Knežević, "Trgovina žitom u Dubrovniku," *Godišnjak filoz. fakulteta, Novi Sad* 10 (1967): 79–131. On Venetian banking procedures see Reinhold Mueller, "The Role of Bank Money in Venice, 1300–1500," *Studi veneziani*, n.s. 3 (1979): 47–96. See also Frederic C. Lane and Reinhold Mueller, *Money and Banking in Medieval and Renaissance Venice*, vol. 1 (Baltimore: Johns Hopkins University Press, 1985).

54. See Jorjo Tadić, *Dubrovnik portreti* (Belgrade: SAN, 1948); idem., "Le Port de Raguse au moyen âge." Le navire et l'économie maritime du moyen âge au XVIIIᵉ siècle, in *Travaux du second colloque international d'histoire maritime* (Paris: SEVPEN, 1959), pp. 1–21. See also Fernand Braudel, *The Mediterranean*, vol. 1, pp. 340ff.

55. For laws governing dowries see *Liber Statutorum*, IV, c. 4, 5, 7–9, 24, 26–43, 53, 54. The laws governing the deposition of dowries if a woman were without heirs at her death was amended in the year of the plague (*Liber Statutorum*, VIII, c. 94) to favor a woman's natal family with the return of three-quarters of her dowry cash award.

56. D.S.A., *Liber Viridis*, c. 180, f. 140v.

57. Susan Mosher Stuard, "The Adriatic Trade in Silver, c. 1300," *Studi veneziani* 17–18 (1975–76): 95–143.

58. Wills, bequests, and gifts to religious institutions reflect the same attitudes. See discussion later in this chapter.

59. D.S.A., *Liber Dotium*, II, f. 7v. Lucas de Gambe accepted Marie de Catar
as a second wife in 1348 with a 1,000 *hyperperi* dowry. See also D.S.A., *Liber Dotium*,
II, f. 9 and 12 for 1,000 awards given and accepted from Catar spouses. See also
D.S.A., *Liber Dotium*, II, f. 85v (Catar); f. 148 (Spalato or Split); D.S.A., *Liber
Dotium*, IV, f. 8 (Spalato or Split); f. 65v (Zara or Zadar); f. 122 (Trau or Trogir);
D.S.A., *Liber Dotium*, VI, f. 39 (Catar). These provide examples of dowries given in
exogamous marriages with awards typical for noble dowries of the decade. See also
I. Mahnken, *Dubrovački patricijat*, p. 334, for the marriage of Philippa, daughter of
Phylippa de Thoma and Martinussius de Mence, to Lodovico Correr of Venice. The
amount of this dowry is not known, but there is reason to believe it far outstripped
typical awards of the day.

60. *MR*, vol. 5, p. 90.

61. Marriage before incorporation has been figured through the marriage
age of offspring. For example, three of the children of Paulus and Phylippa (two
daughters and one son) were wed in 1311 and 1312. This suggests birth before 1300,
whereas their father gained his citizenship in 1301.

62. Susan Mosher Stuard, "Dowry Increase and Increments in Wealth in
Medieval Ragusa (Dubrovnik)," *Journal of Economic History* 41 (1981): 795–811.
Kirshner and Mohlo note that round figures of 100, 250, 500, and 1,000 florins were
favored by investors in the Monte ("The Dowry Fund," p. 418). In Genoa, families
attempted to keep inflating dowry awards within lines; see Diane Owen Hughes,
"Domestic Ideals and Social Behavior," in *The Family in History*, ed. Charles Rosen-
berg (Philadelphia: University of Pennsylvania Press, 1975), pp. 114–44; idem.,
"From Brideprice to Dowry in Mediterranean Europe," *Journal of Family History* 3
(1978): 278–85; idem., "Urban Growth and Family Structure in Medieval Genoa,"
*Past and Present* 66 (1975): 3–28.

63. Shares in new vessels for the fleet became important alternative investments. See S. Vekarić, "Vrste i tipovi dubrovačkih brodova XIV stoljeća," *Dubrovnik anali* 10–11 (1966–67): 19–42; idem., "Dubrovačka trgovačka flota, 1599 godine," *Dubrovnik anali* 13 (1974): 427–32. See also Josip Luetić, *O pomorstvu dubrovačke republike u XVIII stoljeću* (Dubrovnik: Pomorski muzej, 1959).

64. There is evidence that the Albergo in Genoa underwent a comparable
narrowing of the circle of acceptable marriage partners in the late fourteenth and
fifteenth centuries. Diane Owen Hughes, "Domestic Ideals and Social Behavior,"
pp. 114–44. On Florence, see Carol L. Lansing, *The Florentine Magnates: Lineage
and Faction in a Medieval Commune* (Princeton, N.J.: Princeton University Press,
1991). At Venice, marriage choices stratified the aristocracy in the same era. See
Stanley Chojnacki, "Dowries and Kinsmen," pp. 173–99; J. C. Davis, *The Decline of
the Venetian Nobility as a Ruling Class* (Baltimore: Johns Hopkins University Press,
1962); P. J. Cooper, "Inheritance and Settlement by Great Landowners," pp. 192–
312; and R. Litchfield, "Demographic Characteristics of Florentine Patrician Families," p. 191.

65. D.S.A., *Testamenta*, V, inclusive. Noble wills: 144, of which 77 were
drawn up for men and 67 for women. There were as well 454 other wills for non-

noble residents of the town, people who lived in the Astarea or the islands and foreigners who came to town to register their wills, and for foreigners who took advantage of the town's chancellery to draw up a legal and binding testament. Of these, 263 were drawn up for men and 191 for women. On laws governing inheritance, see *Liber Statutorum,* L. IV, c. 13ff. The law provided for minors and unmarried daughters first, then divided all goods into movable and immovable possessions. These were divided into equal shares for all sons. The oldest son chose the first portion of immovable goods and so on, the youngest son the first portion of movable goods and so on, to insure equality.

66. D.S.A., *Testamenta,* IV, f. 32.

67. D.S.A., *Testamenta,* III, f. 60.

68. D.S.A., *Testamenta,* I, f. 12.

69. D.S.A., *Testamenta,* II, f. 13v.

70. D.S.A., *Testamenta,* III, f. 17v.

71. D.S.A., *Testamenta,* III, f. 50.

72. *MR,* vol. 2, pp. 124, 141.

73. *MR,* vol. 4, p. 59. A widowed mother had the right to serve as tutor for her dependent children by statute law. *Liber Statutorum,* L. VIII, c. 42:6.

74. D.S.A., *Liber Dotium,* V, f. 4v. Dowries for noble and illegitimate daughters might be left in the keeping of the Thesaurius de St. Maria. See, for example, D.S.A., *Liber Dotium,* V, f. 108.

75. See notes 49 through 54 for references. See also *Liber Statutorum,* VIII, c. 95, for a 1348 law that stipulated the return of three quarters of a woman's dowry to her family if she died childless, distributing only the remaining one quarter by testament.

76. D.S.A., *Testamenta,* V, f. 51v.

77. D.S.A., *Testamenta,* V, f. 53–53v.

78. D.S.A., *Testamenta,* V, f. 57–57v.

79. D.S.A., *Testamenta,* V, f. 13–13v.

80. D.S.A., *Testamenta,* V, f. 41v.

81. D.S.A., *Testamenta,* V, f. 45.

82. D.S.A., *Testamenta,* V, f. 40v–41.

83. *Liber Statutorum,* VIII, c. 95.

84. *Liber Statutorum,* III, c. 13, 46; L. VII, c. 50, 51.

85. D.S.A., *Testamenta,* III, f. 40–41v, and 75v, for the wills of her father, Drago de Thoma, and of her husband, Martinussius de Mence. See also the discussion in I. Mahnken, *Dubrovački patricijat,* pp. 333–34, and in Dušanka Dinić-Knežević, *Položaj žena u Dubrovniku,* pp. 53–60.

86. Single male heirs inherited their father's estate. A sole daughter's rights to inherit required a will or deposition.

87. The entry for 1378 locates the residence near the bridge that led to the Dominican monastery; it forms a part of the fortification of the town. *MR,* vol. 4, p. 157.

88. *MR,* vol. 3, pp. 67, 77, 84.

89. "Consilio Rogatorum ball. xxiii, prima pars est de faciendo dirui duas conduras que sunt prope menia civitatis extra, ante pontem predicatorum, et

domum quondam Junii de Georgio et domum domine Philippe que sunt prope menia civitatis." *MR*, vol. 4, p. 157.

90. *MR*, vol. 3, pp. 170, 172. However, the link with the Venetian Correr proved profitable to the town because Ludovico Correr invested in Balkan trade in subsequent years. See T. Smičiklas, *Codex diplomaticus*, vol. 13, p. 567.

91. D. Dinić-Knežević, *Položaj žena u Dubrovniku*, pp. 48–53.

92. I. Mahnken, *Dubrovački patricijat*, p. 423. D.S.A., *Libri Reformationes*, XXXIX, f. 158; XXVIII, f. 47, 48, 49v, 50.

93. D.S.A., *Diversa Cancellariae*, XXXI, f. 181v. See discussion in D. Dinić-Knežević, *Položaj žena u Dubrovniku*, pp. 48–53.

94. D.S.A., *Libri Reformationes*, XXXIX, f. 158.

95. D.S.A., *Diversa Notariae* III, f. 114v, published in full in D. Dinić-Knežević, *Položaj žena u Dubrovniku*, pp. 201–2. Heaven protect a woman seeking separation from her husband on the grounds of abuse, as Anna de Gondola petitioned the justices of the Small Council in 1319. Despite her plea and evidence she was remanded to family to resolve the problem rather than granted a separation allowable under statute law.

96. Desanka Kovačević, "Zore Bokšić, dubrovački trgovac i protovestijar bosanskih Kraljeva," *Godišnjak društvo istoričara Bosne i Herčegovine* 13 (1962): 289–310.

97. Philippus de Diversis, *Situs aedificiorum*, p. 56. Bariša Krekić, translating into English from the Serbo-Croation translation of Diversis's Latin (Ivan Božić, "Filip de Diversis *Opis Dubrovniku*," *Časopis "Dubrovnik"* [1983] pp. 23–24), provides a version more ambiguous on whether "hens and eggs" merchants were indeed noble. The manuscript of Diversis's work in the Dubrovnik archives suggests the issue is a matter of punctuation, with Božić supplying a full break in his translation. Compare Bariša Krekić, "Developed Autonomy: The Patricians in Dubrovnik and Dalmatian Cities," pp. 189–90.

98. See James Cushman Davis, *The Decline of the Venetian Nobility as a Ruling Class* (Baltimore: Johns Hopkins University Press, 1962), for information on ultimogeniture, which was adopted in Venice in the early modern centuries.

99. One of the significant determinants of wealth was the favor of elders of the community. Undertaking arduous ambassadorial missions as part of a long-distance trade venture, and promoting communal welfare through helping to recruit notaries, physicians, and other communally salaried functionaries helped promote business successes. Charitable gifts appear to have impressed elder councillors in a position to direct business toward an ambitious young merchant of the noble class. Miodrag Petrovich, in "A Mediterranean City-State: A Study of Dubrovnik Elites," suggests that Ragusans sought forgiveness in their pious bequests for any inadvertent sin against their government with the same fervor that other medieval people sought forgiveness for the sin of usury against the church.

100. Gregor Čremošnik, *Spisi Thomasina de Savere*, doc. 486, pp. 144–46 (1281).

# 4. Women in Ragusa

"If [men] were less self-absorbed and more rational, they would realize that our sex is as much perfect as the male in its own kind, all of which would make it impossible to state that one sex is more worthy than the other," wrote Maria de Gondola in a spirited defense of women's equality that challenged the notion of Aristotelian authority. (Her remarks prefaced her husband's sixteenth-century Slavic translation of the philosopher's work.)[1] But how could this Ragusan Renaissance woman show such surprise at natural inequality arguments when they had been the governing ideas on gender in scholastic discourse in western European lands for a good three centuries?

It has been alleged that the city-state of Ragusa failed to undergo the dynamic development of more western societies in the emerging modern world. The woman question gives the lie to that *topos* by turning it on its head. That women here were not systematically deprived of rights in a bourgeois culture that based its ideological justifications on the authority of Ancients like Aristotle served to give women continuing opportunities to participate in civil, intellectual, and economic life. Women followed a separate, at times opposite, course from women in westward-lying European lands in the late medieval centuries, raising the question as to why some flexibility was introduced into their condition during the very time when systems of gender grew more rigid in societies farther west.

To begin with an example from social life, Ragusa had remained true to a Roman law tradition that relegated women to the status of minors for a lifetime: they did not appear in court without a male advocate; they passed from their father's authority into that of their husbands', symbolized by the pledge of their Falcidian quarter, or *dos* (that is, their dowry and inheritance from their natal families), which their husbands administered or controlled.[2] Referred to as the *tutela,* the cluster of provisions placing women in the status of legal minors in relation to their inheritance limited women's participation in public life.[3] However, the endogamous Ragusan patriciate confronted a pressing difficulty in the later Middle Ages, that of sustaining their numerical strength in the face of plague-induced mortality. This problem was met by remarriage, for a second and even a third time for both noblewomen and noblemen, but this did not suffice to provide guardians for all orphaned heirs. So the Small Council introduced the expedient measure of creating tutors to oversee orphans—among them women.[4] The outcome was clear, if unforeseen: by allowing women to serve as tutors it became difficult to enforce the *tutela* over them. The law was not jettisoned, but it had been stretched. This is not to say that women in Italian cities could not stretch the law as well, but men of their families did not see the same utility in women's civic acts. In the endogamous society of Ragusa, sisters and wives fulfilled some functions that the magnates of Italian towns offered to "new men" who joined their ranks.

In Ragusa, certain women appear in court with a male *advocatus*, but others transacted their own business before civil authorities. With her children full grown, the widow Boni de Mence set her affairs in order by disposing of her dowry; no man stood in for her, but her own son served as *advocatus* for the wife of his business partner.[5] The *tutela* was relaxed for some rather than repealed.

This suggests that Roman law, which held such local weight as a joint inheritance defining both polity and aristocratic privilege, also constituted a living tradition to be adapted and reinterpreted rather than unquestioningly obeyed. This was often made clear where the rights of women were at stake. And by the same token, Ragusa's experience differed from that of her city-state neighbors across the Adriatic in Italy proper. With the mid-twelfth-century revival of Roman law, which led to revision of statutes in cities like Genoa, Siena, and Pisa, Roman dowry and the *tutela* had taken on quite an exaggerated importance. In the effort to win people over from traditional practices, town consuls in twelfth-century Siena attempted "vivere lege romana cum tota civitate" (to live according to Roman law in all aspects of city life).[6] This meant that while a Sienese wife owned her dowry as her natal inheritance, it was to be managed by her husband because of her "legal incapacity." Late Roman law had spoken little about woman's incapacity, but when Roman law was revived in twelfth-century Italy, it became a principle firmly welded to it.

The arguments of the Bolognese canon lawyer Gratian, who influenced all three cities' statutes, were quite clear on the matter: "Woman should be subject to her husband's rule, and has no authority, either to teach, to bear witness, to give surety, or to judge."[7] This took the old institution of the *tutela* to absurd lengths because, as Thomas Kuehn relates, it sometimes led to the rights of guardianship being passed over a mother to a minor male heir on the death of his father, producing the absurdity of an infant son with a *tutela* over his mother. In time in Florence, to cite one instance, the *tutela* was supplanted by a new sort of guardianship called the *mundium*, which placed all women under the guardianship of adult males. In order to secure disinterested guardians for women, the *mundualdus* was to be exercised by a male who was not kin and would not benefit from a woman's estate.[8] This innovation strengthened the general perception in Italy that women were not to exercise political or civil, that is, public, rights in their own person.

When such protective procedures were instituted, Roman law precedents, as interpreted in medieval canon law, provided justification to civilian lawyers in Italy's cities. At the moment when elasticity was introduced into law in Ragusa, women came under more rigid restrictions that curtailed their rights in Italian city life. Women might be seen in civic courts but they were not heard, and they were not as likely to exercise authority over others delegated to them by political agencies.

By contrast, the more relaxed attitude toward the *tutela* found in Ragusa provided women definite advantages. Women from all classes participated in business life. Statute law would, at first glance, appear to preclude this possibility because the law specifically stated a woman could not incur a debt of more than fifteen *hyperperi* (about seven ducats in the fourteenth century).[9] But wealthy widows pursued business interests: the noble widow "Domina" Phylippa de Thoma invested in urban property, the affluent heiress Nicoletta de Goce in rural property. The *civis de populi* widow of Zore Bokšić, Maria by name, continued the family's highly lucrative trade with Bosnia after her husband's death and became a power in her own right.[10] Now, strictly speaking, all three were creditors, not debtors, so they did not transgress the statute limiting indebtedness, but what of women from the popular classes who owned taverns near the harbor? They also lent money, but most likely had seen credit extended to them at one time or another in order to set up in business, through informal arrangements if not through contracts drawn up by a notary at the chancellery.[11] Women bought and sold from the produce market to the high-figure transactions of long-distance trade. In a sense, the community doubled its pool of commercial personnel by admitting women to business life. In a community that monitored urban immigration carefully, avoiding the population expansion common in Italian towns, this participation of urban women permitted expansion of commerce without making room for a mass migration of foreign personnel.

So the role of women in judicial and business life gives some indication of communal preferences for business associates among leading citizens of cities. By limiting their wives' and daughters' rights ever more strictly, affluent Italian men had made it feasible to open doors to lower-ranked bourgeois men who joined them in business ventures. Furthermore, entrenched elites encouraged immigration into their towns and permitted a few new men to ascend the ladder to the highest levels of civic life, which on occasion led to a challenge or overthrow of an old elite by a new one, much to the former's chagrin. Aristocratic Ragusans made a different choice: to open opportunity to some women of their own families instead, and to encourage women generally to augment their male kin in pursuing family business interests. A relaxed attitude toward the strictures of statute law, which enforced the *tutela*, made this possible. Through this means, the patriciate helped insulate themselves against a massed popular challenge from new men eager to work their way into power and, perhaps, mount some challenge to the ruling noble elite.

Clearly, not all women entered business nor were they encouraged to do so; nevertheless, as the town prospered women gained generally in control over wealth. In all walks of life, they grew richer measured by the size of their dowries, or share of natal family wealth provided to them at the time of marriage. As Chapter 6 notes, *civis de populo* dowries started lower and rose less precipitously than noble dowries, but on a rare occasion, as with the 2,500-*hyperperi* dowry recorded in 1439 for the second marriage of Anusla de Caboga, these overreached noble dotal awards as well as the law.[12] Even unskilled laborers registered dowries for their daughters at the chancellery, and these also increased substantially over time.

There was less slighting of statute law involved in the increased value of married women's wealth during the late medieval centuries. Husbands continued to control their wives' cash awards, which were generally invested in low-risk ventures, since husbands were responsible for the entire *dos* should their wives have need of it in their widowhood or otherwise to "support the burdens of matrimony."[13] But dowry was not the only movement of wealth in marriage. Noble women had received a chattel slave and gold for jewelry from their natal families when they married in thirteenth-century Ragusa, a "gift" sometimes called the *donaro*. By the fourteenth century, slavery had largely died out, but this award of gold and jewels to new brides had increased in value.[14] By the fifteenth century, when dowries settled at eight times what they had been in the middle of the thirteenth century (1,600 *hyperperi* versus 200 *hyperperi* in 1235), the accompanying *donaro* for the bride was stipulated at almost half the value of the *dos,* that is, it was worth seven hundred *hyperperi.* A statute law passed in 1423 specified that women controlled this wealth absolutely. They consulted no one, not even their husbands, about the disposal of this personal wealth in gold or jewels.[15]

Ragusa's reputation as a walking showcase of women's jewels owes much to this increased wealth. That display of wealth reached far down through the strata of urban society because most women, even servants, owned and wore silver and jewels. These possessions appear in women's wills, where they range from the noble woman's finest crown to the servant woman's silver bangle.

Recently, Stanley Chojnacki has argued that there was a comparable increase in the share of family wealth that aristocratic women controlled in Venice.[16] And he has also pointed out that aristocratic women sometimes disposed of their wealth in a manner different from their male kin, follow-ing agendas they set themselves.[17] This suggests that aristocratic city-states sometimes favored women of their own families with wealth that served to increase the aristocracy's control of communal resources vis-à-vis the un-enfranchised. But in Venice, there were institutions with the power, and the stated purpose, of overseeing wealthy women's property and administering it for them: the increasingly powerful *Procuratoria* of San Marco for one.[18] It is possible that wealth might descend in noble families through women without necessarily increasing women's participatory rights in commerce or in political life.

Traveling again to Florence for a comparison, the deviation from Adriatic social values grows pronounced. Although women received ac-companying gifts from their families at marriage (*paraphernalia*), and also received a *donaro,* or gift, from their husbands, this did not generally lead to an increased ability to dispose of wealth as women wished. Take, for example, the conclusions to which Christiane Klapisch was brought. She suggested in "The Griselda Complex: Dowry and Marriage Gifts in the Quattrocento"[19] that when men gave wedding gifts, they and their lineages expected to get them back. These rich gifts were loans, often heirloom pieces of jewelry known to belong to a lineage and within its authority, whereas a woman gave over her dowry until she became a widow, and even then she might have to sue her in-laws to get it back.[20]

"In Florence, men *were* and *made* the 'houses,'" Klapisch has asserted, and a young widow who remarried often left her children behind in the house of their father.[21] An affluent woman in Genoa seldom ever enjoyed the opportunity to remarry even if she was a young, wealthy widow and inclined to remarry.[22] In the interests of deceased husbands' lineage, the family into which a woman married sometimes exercised their rights of authority and guardianship over her for the full course of her life, leading historians to assert, quite properly, that in Italy the greatest restrictions on women's rights were imposed first among the wealthy and came to affect others through imitation of the practices of the most affluent families.[23] Since widows generally enjoyed the greatest freedom of all women in medieval life, it would appear that by the quattrocento, some Italian cities had successfully curtailed even this avenue toward autonomy afforded by the death of a husband.

Another force in late medieval Italian society stood between women and a full exercise of their rights of possession, namely sumptuary law. According to Diane Owen Hughes, the thirteenth century began a series of sumptuary laws in Italian cities that had swollen to at least eighty-three separate pieces of legislation by the fifteenth century.[24] All personal display was limited, but one matter is clear: women's behavior came under surveillance and restriction far more often than men's. Now women's increasing wealth in the form of dowry and of gold, silver, and jewelry has little worth if it cannot be displayed. And in truth, whether it was natal wealth or lineage jewelry, Italian women appear to have gone to great lengths to wear their jewels as signs of status. Like Ragusan women, they valued display as an assertion of property right. The increase in attention to fashion associated with the fourteenth and fifteenth centuries favored this display as well as a willingness on the part of the wealthy to start a new cycle of fashions through commissions to *aurifici*, or goldsmiths.[25] Women in Italy insisted on being the consumers and exhibitors of wealth even if they were largely barred from trading and investing wealth. Since even mere display discomforted city fathers, who legislated against it repeatedly in sumptuary law, a likely conclusion is that public manifestations of women's ownership of wealth were found unsettling and suspect. Dowry increase, in particular, came under the censure of sumptuary law.

The private woman had made her debut in European culture in the courts and statutes of Italy's cities, and because Italy served so often as a model for change north of the Alps, this phenomenon of a new private, restricted status, justified often by incapacity arguments, spread as Italian

Renaissance manners and morals were adopted. The Roman *dos* was a particularly powerful vehicle for transmission of the new notions of gender. Through the Renaissance centuries, Roman *dos* moved northward, eradicating older customs of marital gift giving. The French *dot* and the English portion or settlement came to dominate affluent levels of northern society, and, apparently, by early modern times there were few regions in Europe where wealthy families escaped being drawn into this custom of dowry giving with all the accompanying conditions of legal incapacity for the married woman.

Meanwhile in Ragusa, the patriciate in particular appear to have been bent on moving in a different direction. Sumptuary law was not unknown in this community, in fact the 1235 law preserved with the *Liber Statutorum* limiting dowry grants to two hundred *hyperperi* stands as one of the oldest instances of known sumptuary law in the medieval era.[26] But from that date until 1423, Ragusans were content to avoid further sumptuary legislation and to allow noble families to police their own grants of dowry. Only then, in 1423, did the Great Council reassert its control over dotal awards, and still councillors in their wisdom allowed a good decade for gifts to come into conformance with the law.[27] Furthermore, town fathers made no effort to limit display of luxuries for women when they passed this law. After all, Ragusa was known for its production and export of articles in silver and gold; some of them, like *cercellis sclavonescha* (Slavic earrings), *frontali* (forehead ornaments), *corona* (crowns), *maspellis* (buttons), *cinctura* (belts), rings, bracelets, and necklaces were destined to be worn by women. It seems quite clear then that Ragusan women fully possessed their own treasures of jewels and the goldsmith's art. And women wore their wealth in the streets in such a fine display that Philippus de Diversis, resident schoolmaster and eulogist, praised their bearing and style to the sky.[28]

Because gold and silver wares were traded overseas, where they fed fashions—especially to Venice, the leading market for luxury wares in all of Europe by the fourteenth century—they possessed a liquidity second only to coins. So women in Ragusa were allowed to wear their jewels and parade them around; and they could, entirely on their own, trade them, since they owned them unencumbered. Their display provided a stimulus to the market in what had become a lucrative export industry; silver and some gold from inland Balkan mines were fashioned into a wide variety of wares in Ragusa. Foreign traders could view the full display on women from the noble class down through the ranks to servants, who owned their own bangles, earrings, and *frontali*, albeit made from "white" silver, which was full of lead. This walking showcase had its effect. Italy craved fashions from the east and adopted styles *sclavonescha*. As arbiters of taste for the rest of Europe, Italian town dwellers in turn stimulated Europe-wide consumption patterns through purchasing and wearing imported jewelry, even when their behavior ran counter to sumptuary law.

At home, trend-setting Ragusan women commissioned works they willingly displayed to the overall benefit of the local economy. The so-called minor arts they encouraged in the late medieval centuries appear as anything but minor in a giant *ladica* (ship) for the table, that is, a great saltcellar produced from ten pounds or more of pure Balkan silver.[29] Nor were crowns and belts in silver embellished with gold trifles by any stretch of the imagination. Through their taste and imagination, the women of Ragusa could influence consumption and cultural preference elsewhere and apparently they took this responsibility seriously. Reading the lists of commissioned and owned goods is like reading the records of hordes, but with the sure knowledge that these personally owned treasures were traded and reproduced in exportable quantities.[30] Patronage meant the power of choice, and women in Ragusa could exert patronage because they controlled significant personal wealth.

In Ragusa a secure aristocratic society granted women the right to consume, display, and trade wealth with little fear that exhibited wealth threatened the social order. Women's social, civil, and economic participation helps account for the difference between Maria de Gondola expressing outrage over Aristotle's arguments about women's inequality—arguments she had perhaps not encountered before and found distasteful—and Nicolosa Sanuti's sadder acknowledgment about Italian life:

> Magistracies are not conceded to women; they do not strive for priesthoods, triumphs, the spoils of war, because these are considered the spoils of men. Ornament and apparel, because they are our insignia of worth, we cannot suffer to be taken from us.[31]

Nicolosa fully understood that Aristotle's arguments about natural inferiority held weight in her society and deprived women of opportunity for all but ornament and apparel, and sumptuary laws increasingly closed off that avenue of expression.

More importantly, what stands between these two women's perceptions were very different notions of gender that operated in their communities of Ragusa and Bologna respectively. For Sanuti, Aristotle's doctrine of natural inequality was old hat: its arguments of polar opposition to define woman had been in circulation as long as Roman law itself, that is, for Bologna, from the twelfth century. Since then those arguments had leapt over the boundary of canon law to be introduced into both scholastic theology and urban statute law; in all three instances usage confirmed the system of polar opposition of "woman" to "man."[32] Man's very capacities—in Gratian's words "to teach, to bear witness, to give surety or to judge"—precluded woman's possessing those capacities in a polarity of privation.[33] Ironically, Ragusans who had respected Roman law with its own assumptions about inequality embedded in the *tutela* from the foundation of their community, had in their wisdom bent the law so as to modify those assumptions by the late medieval centuries.[34] Women and men came to occupy corresponding rather than opposed gender categories qualified, it must be noted, by the clear political discrimination that women could not sit on Great Council, nor were they enfranchised.[35]

Nonetheless, Ragusan women might feel entitled to participate in literary circles and scholarly activities, as had Maria de Gondola, because she descended from a long line of women who owned books, and apparently had learned to read them through private instruction.[36] Pasqua de Volcassio willed books as part of her estate as early as 1282; many aristocratic women followed her lead. For the most part religious in nature, books willed by laywomen hint at a literate culture that they shared with their few patrician sisters who had entered Ragusa's convents.[37]

Furthermore, political matters were frequently resolved in private discourse at Ragusa, a device that abetted patrician control because noblemen could then present a united front to the community at public convocations. This predisposition to resolve political questions in private benefitted patrician women. Unlike their peers elsewhere, women did not see a withdrawal of significant power from the private or domestic sphere that was then vested in formal public assemblies from which they were barred by sex. In matter of fact, the very understanding of patrician status in Ragusa stemmed from affirming women's noble status, since sons of noblewomen alone sat by right on the Great Council. Rather than denying this fundamental constitutional principle, Ragusan noblemen were prone to affirm it.[38]

Perhaps the extent of women's power will remain an unanswered question figuring among the best kept secrets of old Ragusa. When, in the late thirteenth century, Phylippa Volcio wed Paul de Thoma, thereby securing his membership in the noble circle and paving the way for his incorporation into the Great Council, did she exercise her own free choice, or merely fulfill the terms of a plan conceived by her father and other male kin? (See Chapter 3.) Her constitutional right to incorporate a husband into the noble circle was absolute and exclusive to the women who shared noble birth with her. Records reveal nothing about Phylippa Volcio's exercise of her own will in this matter, yet her willful granddaughter and namesake, Phylippa de Thoma, modeled her headstrong behavior on some impressive woman figure out of her past.

The anthropological investigations of David Rheubottom may provide some answers about women's political role within the patriciate. Using available fifteenth-century documentation, he can map noble Ragusan families' marriage strategies in some detail. In thirty-three selected noble families, daughters' right to marry led to their betrothals years before their brothers wed. Men married at more advanced ages than their sisters, and some never married at all. Within the political sphere, sons-in-law might be drawn into political alliance with their inlaws. "It is the receiving of a woman in marriage that marks the recipient as one who owes respect and deference," Rheubottom finds. Through tracing alliance systems based on marriage patterns, Rheubottom may be able to determine whether noblewomen figured powerfully in influencing alliance-making, a process that lay at the heart of Ragusa's consensual politics.[39]

A tradition of civil rights for all women inhabitants of the town is suggested by some evidence in a preserved record of civil complaints, the *Lamenta de Intus et de Foris*. In 1373, a servant girl named Draysa accused Matcus de Georgio, a young nobleman and scion of a great family, of a rape, at night, at the town gate of Pile.[40] There are other comparable charges on the books, one brought by a noble head of household against a fellow nobleman because he attacked women servants.[41] Now these recorded complaints represent rare fissures in the wall of aristocratic solidarity, so while the outcome of the first-mentioned judicial process absolved Matcus de Georgio, in a certain sense the thorough investigation of the charge signified a censure and enforcement of servant women's rights to walk abroad in town free from fear of assault. Although Guido Ruggiero's study of Venice would lead us to believe that noblemen got off very easily when charges of crimes against servant women were brought against them,[42] Ragusa was a society where norms were frequently enforced by informal means rather than through civilly mandated punishments. The noble circle sometimes sent the reprobates in their midst to Stagno (Ston) to serve the republic and, while there, to be infected with malaria from the salt pans. No judicial condemnation occurred in such cases, but justice was nonetheless retributive, and swift. The very fact that the aristocratic Small Council heard and then fully investigated a servant girl's complaint argues for a willingness to censure their own members in an effort to prevent and punish attacks in public places. This served as some enforcement of civil rights for women of the town.[43]

But Ragusa was not a utopia for women. Aristocratic women never held a public office more significant than the office of *salanarius* (inspector of salt works). Literacy for noblewomen stood at the will of their parents, unlike men who were educated at communal expense. When Anna de Gondola sought separation from her noble but abusive husband in 1319, it was not granted.[44] Servant women soon learned that they might be protected from assault in the streets but not in the household. If a man assumed financial responsibility for the welfare of a servant or any other non-noble woman, and her offspring resulting from their sexual union, he was free to do as he wished. Moreover, acknowledging illegitimate offspring had become so institutionalized in the town by the late medieval era that it figured as a significant factor in the composition of non-noble ranks of society (see Chapters 5 and 6). Social status, rather than arguments about woman's incapacity, governed women's sexuality in this town with its sure sense of ranking and social order.

If no utopia for women, Ragusa was nonetheless a city of women. In pursuit of commerce, Ragusan men often traveled inland or abroad, leaving women in preponderance through much of the year. More importantly, women figured prominently in the town's permanent work force, particularly in production. Women servants outnumbered serving men in significant numbers, carrying much of the responsibility for the low-skilled labor necessary for community life. When the Great Council initiated major textile production in the fifteenth century, it did so by importing the newest Italian expertise in the person of Peter Pantella, who supervised textile production. As for the necessary labor, the council adopted one of the oldest economic institutions of the Mediterranean world, the *gynaeceum*, or women's workshop. It was staffed by women brought from the interior who were housed together and worked together. David Herlihy has noted that the *gynaeceum* disappeared in western Europe in the fifteenth century, domesticating production of cloth to the household in a new pattern of production.[45]

Apparently a large, successful *gynaeceum* survived at Ragusa, with women hired and housed together outside the household. Without the new notions of gender that had gained ascendency in western Europe, older production structures remained practicable. By such means, the patriciate enriched themselves and ensured their ability to pursue their own unique course: at one turn introducing the most up-to-date urban manufacture, at the next turn employing a genuinely ancient institution like the *gynaeceum* to support it. Both possibilities derived from the same source, the stubborn reliance on a self-conscious idea of a properly ordered world.

\* \* \*

As the anthropologist Ernestine Friedl has argued, in egalitarian societies where men compete for political or ritual power over a lifetime, women find themselves at a clear disadvantage, in contrast to systems wherein acquisition through inheritance of political or ritual rank sustain at least a few women in powerful roles.[46] In the subtle politics of consensus that characterized rule at Ragusa, some noblewomen may have played such significant roles. A politics of reconciliation and delay based on only the most reluctant use of armed aggression may possibly be laid to women's counsel in the private exchanges that characterized Ragusan political life. But this is a story the records will not easily tell. That women were afforded more economic opportunities and civil rights than those enjoyed by women in cities across the Adriatic appears quite clear, however.

In their Ragusan Renaissance, women were contributors less impeded by the damaging notion of "natural" inequality that marginalized women to the status of a mute audience in humanist circles in Italy and other western-lying European lands. Exhibiting the same enthusiasm to immerse themselves in poetry, music, learning, and the arts as women across the Adriatic, Ragusan women failed to encounter a rationale that enforced a disabling gender code on their lives. This was a legacy they left to later generations.

*Notes*

1. Maria de Gondola, preface dedicated to her friend, Donna Fiore Zuzori, in the published treatise of her husband, Nicolo de Gondola, *Discorsi sopra la metheora d'Aristotele* (Venice, 1584). The idea owes a debt to Joan Kelly, "Did Women Have a Renaissance?" in *Women, History, and Theory* (Chicago: University of Chicago Press, 1985), pp. 19–50. This essay first appeared in *Becoming Visible*, ed. Renate Bridenthal and Claudia Koonz (Boston: Houghton Mifflin, 1976). On Yugoslav women writers see Zdenka Marković, *Pjesnikinje starog Dubrovnika* (Zagreb: JAZU, 1970), pp. 43–46.

2. *Liber Statutorum,* pp. lxiv, 59–60, 67–70, 88.

3. See Gigliola Villata di Renzo, *La tutela: Indagini sulla scuola dei glossatori* (Milan: Giuffre, 1975). See also Manlio Bellomo, *La condizione giuridica della donna in Italia: vicende antiche e moderne* (Turin: Giuffre, 1970), pp. 26–28.

4. D.S.A., *Reformationes,* XXIX, f. 8, Martolus de Goce and Milsa Radili were appointed joint tutors for an orphan girl in 1391. In the city of Siena in Italy, the same measure was introduced in the era of the plague, but to what effect on the *tutela* it is unknown. Edward English, "The Status of Noble Women in Late Medieval Siena: Patrimonies and Adversity," talk presented at the Centre for Medieval Studies, University of Toronto, February 24, 1990.

5. D.S.A., *Diversa Cancellariae,* VIII, fol. 4. Domagna de Mence served as an *advocatus* for the wife of a business associate. However, his own mother transacted business with the chancellery without one, D.S.A., *Diversa Cancellariae,* IX, fol. 21, f. 95.

6. Eleanor Sabina Riemer, "Women in the Medieval City: Sources and Uses of Wealth by Sienese Women in the Thirteenth Century" (Ph.D. diss., New York University, 1975). Stated by Consuls of the Commune in 1176.

7. Gratian, *Decretum, Questio* V, c. 33. *Corpus Juris Canonici,* ed. Emil Freidberg (Graz: Bernard Tauchnitz, 1911), volume I, col. 1254–1255. "Mulierem constat subiectam dominio viri esse, et nullam auctoritatem habere; nec docere potest, nec testis esse, neque fidem dare, nec iudicare."

8. Thomas Kuehn, "*Cum consensu mundualdi*: Legal Guardianship of Women in Quattrocento Florence," *Viator:* 13 (1982): 309–33.

9. *Liber Statutorum,* 4, cap. 20, p. 90.

10. Dušanka Dinić-Knežević, *Položaj žena u Dubrovniku u XIII i XIV veku* (Belgrade: SAN, 1974), pp. 44–60.

11. J. Tadić and R. Jeremić, *Prilozi za istoriju zdravstvene kulture starog Dubrovnika* (Belgrade, 1966) notes that prostitution was practiced out of the taverns at the harbor. In Ragusa this was a woman-dominated business, allowing free women and some immigrants opportunity.

12. D.S.A., *Liber Dotium,* V. f. 161.

13. Julius Kirshner, "Wives' Claims Against Insolvent Husbands," in *Women of the Medieval World,* ed. Julius Kirshner and Suzanne Wemple (London: Basil Blackwell, 1985), pp. 256–303.

14. Susan Mosher Stuard, "Urban Domestic Slavery in Medieval Ragusa," *Journal of Medieval History* 9 (1983): 155–71.

15. For more on increase in dowry grants see Susan Mosher Stuard, "Dowries and Increments in Wealth in Medieval Ragusa (Dubrovnik)," pp. 795–811. See also I. Mahnken, *Dubrovački patricijat.* For the dowry law see D.S.A., *Liber Viridis,* C. 180, f. 140.

16. Stanley Chojnacki, "The Power of Love: Wives and Husbands in Late Medieval Venice" in *Women and Power in the Middle Ages,* ed. Mary Erler and Maryanne Kowaleski (Athens: University of Georgia Press, 1988), pp. 126–48.

17. Stanley Chojnacki, "Dowries and Kinsmen in Early Renaissance Venice," in *Women in Medieval Society,* ed. Susan Mosher Stuard (Philadelphia: University of Pennsylvania Press, 1976), pp. 199–208.

18. Reinhold Mueller, "The Procurators of San Marco," *Studi veneziani* 13 (1971), pp. 105–220.

19. Translated by Lydia Cochrane, in *Women, Family, and Ritual in Renaissance Italy* (Chicago: University of Chicago Press, 1985), pp. 213–48.

20. Donald E. Queller and Thomas F. Madden, in "Father of the Bride: Fathers, Daughters, and Dowries in Late Medieval and Early Renaissance Venice" (unpublished ms.), paint a more positive picture of women's status in the fourteenth and fifteenth centuries in Venice.

21. Christiane Klapisch, "The 'Cruel Mother': Maternity, Widowhood, and Dowry in Florence in the Fourteenth and Fifteenth Centuries," in *Women, Family, and Ritual in Renaissance Italy*, p. 117.

22. Diane Owen Hughes, "Domestic Ideals and Social Behavior: Evidence from Medieval Genoa," in *The Family in History*, ed. Charles Rosenberg (Philadelphia: University of Pennsylvania Press, 1975), pp. 115–43. See also Jacques Heers, *Le clan familial au moyen âge* (Paris, 1974).

23. See opinions of Bellomo, Klapisch, and Hughes cited above.

24. Diane Owen Hughes, "Sumptuary Law and Social Relations in Renaissance Italy," in *Disputes and Settlements*, ed. John Bossy (Cambridge: Cambridge University Press, 1983), p. 71.

25. See N. Margaret Newett, "The Sumptuary Laws of Venice," in *Historical Essays by Members of Owen's College, Manchester*, ed. T. F. Tout and James Tait (London: Longmans, Green, 1902), pp. 235–78; and G. Bistort, *Il Magistrato alle pompe nella repubblica di Venezia* (Venice, 1912).

26. *Liber Statutorum*, p. lxiv.

27. D.S.A., *Liber Viridis*, c. 180, f. 140v; see Stuard, "Dowry and Increments in Wealth," pp. 803–5. On the size of dowry in the era after the passage of the 1423 law, see David Rheubottom, " 'Sisters First': Betrothal Order and Age at Marriage in Fifteenth-Century Ragusa," *Journal of Family History* 13, no. 4 (1988), pp. 359–406.

28. Philippus de Diversis, *Situs aedificiorum*, p. 67. On goldsmiths, see C. Fisković, "Dubrovački zlatari od XIII do XVII stoljeća," pp. 143–249.

29. These were numerous in Ragusa. D.S.A., *Diversa Cancellariae*, IX, f. 179, 211; XII, f. 212v, 238, 240v, 285; XIII, f. 81v; XIV, f. 41v, 68, 131; XVI, f. 56v; XVII, f. 53v; XVIII, f.31v, 105v, 112.

30. Susan Mosher Stuard, "The Adriatic Trade in Silver," pp. 95–143.

31. As cited in Hughes, "Sumptuary Law," p. 87.

32. See in particular, Ruth Kelso, *Doctrine for a Lady of the Renaissance* (Urbana: University of Illinois Press, 1956), pp. 5–37; also Ian MacLean, *The Renaissance Notion of Woman* (Cambridge: Cambridge University Press, 1981); and Joan Kelly, "Did Women Have a Renaissance?" in *Becoming Visible*, ed. Renate Bridenthal and Claudia Koonz (Boston: Houghton Mifflin, 1976), pp. 135–65.

33. Gratian, *Decretum, Questio* V, c. 33 *Corpus iuris canonici*, vol. 1, col. 1254–1255.

34. On the ancient origins of Ragusan law see Walter Ashburner, *The Rhodian Sea Law* (London: Clarendon, 1909), introduction.

35. Dinic-Knežević, *Položaj žena u Dubrovniku*, pp. 121–34. They did occupy the largely honorific appointed of *salinarius*, inspector of salt works.

36. See Susan Groag Bell, "Medieval Women Book Owners: Arbiters of Lay Piety and Ambassadors of Culture," *SIGNS: Journal of Women in Culture and Society* 7 (1982): 742–68. See G. Čremošnik, ed., *Kancelarijski i notarski spisi 1278–1301* (Belgrade: Zbornik za IJK, 1932), vol. 3, sec. III, bk. 1, pp. 229–30, doc. 731.

37. *Spisi Thomasina de Savere,* doc. 731.

38. Jean Bodin was well aware of this and noted it in *Six Bookes of a Commonweale,* p. 10. See also Mirko Deanović, *Anciens contacts entre la France et Raguse* (Zagreb: Institut Français de Zagreb, 1950).

39. David Rheubottom, "'Sisters First': Betrothal Order and Age at Marriage in Fifteenth-Century Ragusa," pp. 259–76.

40. D.S.A., *Lamenta de Intus et de Foris,* I, 3/5/1373, fol. 115. The case is a complicated one that the judges pursued over the month of March. Testimony from two fellow servants did not support the charge brought by Draysa on 5 March 1373. Matcus testified he was elsewhere at the time and presented a witness to support his testimony. He was absolved of the charge. Nonetheless, considerable effort had been made to investigate the charge. Judges did not hesitate to imprison citizens on sexual charges; see Bariša Krekić, "*Abominandum Crimen:* Punishment of Homosexuals in Renaissance Dubrovnik," pp. 337–45.

41. D.S.A., *Lamenta de Intus et de Foris,* I, 311/27/1373, f. 229.

42. Guido Ruggiero, *The Boundary of Eros* (New York: Oxford University Press, 1985).

43. This is not an argument for equality before the law for all urban women, but rather for the assurance of some civil rights to women living in the town. Within noble households a different code prevailed. Servant and slave women bore noblemen illegitimate children who were frequently acknowledged by the household and provided for within it.

44. D.S.A., *Diversa Notariae,* III f. 114v. See discussion in Chapter 3.

45. David Herlihy, *Opera Muliebria* (Philadelphia: Temple University Press, 1989), pp. 187–91. See also Dušanka Dinić-Knežević, *Tkanine u privredi srednjovekovnog Dubrovnika* (Belgrade: SAN, 1982).

46. Ernestine Friedl, *Women and Men* (New York: Holt, 1975), pp. 62–63. She applies the generalization to contemporary life (pp. 138–39).

# 5. Ragusan Households

From early times the old nobility of Ragusa had divided itself into a number of shifting households. In fact, "household" is a more easily applied concept in the Ragusan context than "family," which at any given moment might mean both the entire kinship network of a noble person and an immediate descent group of parents and offspring. At one time, all noble households had clustered together in Castellum, in a real sense comprising the town. Porphyrogenitus noted that the town prospered and grew, bringing in time noble settlement to the two new districts of St. Peter and Pustijerna. With the incorporation of the flatland at the foot of town, and later the coastal hillside, noble families again spread their residences to new sites.

Some families came to be associated with a district of the walled town—the de Mences with the tower bearing their name that guarded the coastal heights, for one, but the de Mences were a group of many families by the thirteenth century and spread their households all over the town. By the fourteenth century, one branch, the descendants of Martinussius de Mence and Phylippa de Thoma, even possessed a "palace" outside the gates. The Goce of the Platea were a branch of a noble lineage fortunate enough to have a great residence (and soon small homes besides) on the main concourse and business street of town. The wide contours of the *platea* (*stradun*) ran from the land gate of Pile to the harbor, where all major civic buildings—the palace, customs house, mint, and harbor sheds—gave easy access to each other.[1] The *platea* was a prized spot, as accessible to the three new *sexteria* being constructed on the coastal hill as to the three old town districts. Still, the Goce had grown so numerous by the fourteenth century that they lived all over the city and never monopolized the *platea*. The Gondola moved out as well, although their great house near the rector's palace stood as a visible monument to their fortunes.

Ragusan architecture was the result of tearing down and rebuilding as family needs required; this gives a haphazard appearance to the oldest districts, but it also provides convincing testimony that Ragusans built residences as functional palaces, combining domestic and commercial features that were easily adapted as the times dictated. Since all nobles lived in town, at least for the winter season, the town grew dense, crowded with business and domestic establishments housed together, and focused inward toward the *platea* by the huge walls that shut out most vistas. By the thirteenth century, town walls marked what was to be the final spatial limit of the community.[2] Ragusa never expanded farther, and even its suburbs were largely composed of summer palaces built on pleasant coastal sites, a sparse settlement by the standards of other city-states.

In town, Ragusans lived with perpetual pressure on their living space and accommodated to it. It was perfectly acceptable to make a dower house part of a marriage settlement, but it was not a common practice, probably because separate housing was not always available for newly wed couples.[3] Young people might gain a home from the gift of a relative; it might be large or small, an outright grant or merely for use during a lifetime. All these solutions may be found in noble testamentary bequests.[4]

Neighboring noble houses were sometimes joined when a marriage was contracted between two families. Sometimes this meant constructing a room over the street that connected two facing houses. Although most of these accommodations to house new noble families were condoned, breaking out walls and joining households was forbidden after 1296. On 16 August 1296, fire broke out and carried from street to street through a warren of interconnected houses and passageways. Only cistern water, depleted after the dry months of summer, remained to fight the fire, so much of the town was destroyed. Ragusans learned from this disaster. Henceforth, connecting residences was prohibited, but the law was difficult to enforce.[5] New ways to accommodate the marriages so essential to the noble circle had to be devised.

In the next century, the first noble residences outside the town's walls appeared on the shoreline, stone-built, spacious, and expensive.[6] This was not typical noble housing, however, for those who still lived in town did so more modestly. A young nobleman named Stephen de Luccari purchased his house of wood in town for 120 *hyperperi* in 1382.[7] It amounted to four times the price of a dwelling for a neighboring tavern keeper, who purchased his residence for a mere thirty *hyperperi*.[8] These noble and artisan dwellings may well have stood side by side. Gladoslava, whose husband was a stone worker, possessed a house worth fifty *hyperperi* in Castellum, the old district of the town. It stood right next to the much more grand stone house of a nobleman, Peter de Saracha.[9] In the new *sexterium* of St. Blaise across town, near the harbor, a small wooden house worth only twenty-eight *hyperperi* stood between the great houses of two noblemen, Jura de Caboga and Vita de Goce.[10] When the newer *sexteriae* developed on the landward slope during the fourteenth century, they attracted both noble inhabitants and much humbler families. Young Johannes, son of the nobleman Jacob de Gondola, built a fine home of *maceria* or wood and clay construction in that part of town.[11] But in comparison to the first houses built outside the walls by "Domina" Phylippa de Mence and four wealthy noblemen, Pervo de Sorgo, Marino de Mence, Iello de Sorento, and Pervo de Goce (the possessors of the greatest personal fortunes of their generation), noble residences in town fitted modestly into mixed neighborhoods supporting commerce and housing.[12]

Such mixed districts provide a clue to the social composition of Ragusa in the late medieval centuries. Noble houses accommodated family and commerce. Houses might be crowded, but they expanded up and out to give room to large families and, significantly, large numbers of servants employed in commercial as well as domestic tasks. Young couples waited for an available house, living perhaps in connecting quarters of their parents' homes until their children caused too great crowding of available space. Even if young couples moved to separate quarters, remarriages could occasion future moves on the death of either spouse. Adult brothers, joined by *fraterna,* continued to live together only to separate in later decades of life. Traders kept second homes abroad. Noble Ragusans shuttled in and out of residences over a lifetime according to complex family plans, business pressures, promised gifts, and bequests in wills, or they constructed new homes in the town's new districts after they exhausted the available housing stock.

Cheek by jowl with the grand, and all about them, were very modest homes inhabited by artisans and former servants. Neighborhoods provided a locus for people related by business endeavors and a focal point for a society linked by diverse ties to the households of the great. For the nonnoble, that is, *civis de populo* families, foreign artisans come to town to make a living, former servants of a noble household, and others fortunate enough to gain status as *habitatores* in town, noble neighbors were the key to a patronage system. Only nobles petitioned council for privileges, so access to business opportunity and, in many cases, assurances of a chance to remain in town flowed outward from noble households. Much later, artisans developed a degree of unity by clustering together on streets named for their craft, but the pattern of settlement through the fourteenth century found artisans located for the convenience of the noble houses that had sought their migration in the first place. And artisans trickled into town at a pace determined by decisions set by the commercial elite.

The Ragusan Great Council practiced a strict immigration policy, which becomes clear from an examination of the minutes of the town's councils, the *Reformationes,* beginning with the earliest recording in 1301. A person who obtained the right to remain in Ragusa when granted a form of citizenship which came in time to be known as *civis de populo,* or, if he was registered, as *habitator.* The Small Council awarded both privileges at the request of noblemen, so private needs of commercial households prompted formal action for the most part. Between 1301 and 1350, eighty-three persons, six with their families or male heirs carefully enumerated, were admitted into the town as non-noble citizens or as residents.[13] Of these, 18 percent were described as skilled artisans or men with a profession. The majority were immigrants from abroad; in fact, 55.4 percent had emigrated from overseas. Only 24 percent were identified as immigrants from nearby islands, coastal lands, or the Balkan hinterland. Another 14.5 percent bore identifiable Slavic names, which suggests birth in near-lying lands. Among Slavic immigrants, the Small Council plainly favored those with a trade or skill; significantly, almost the entire Slavic migration to town occurred between 1348 and 1350, when the council had a pressing need to replace skilled workers who had died as a result of plague.

Even strict immigration allowed a certain degree of urban expansion, however, and the newly built thirteenth-century *sexteria* were settled in the course of the next century. This expansion, so clearly selective, gave a high priority to crafts that expanded current commercial ventures: gold and silversmithing, for example. Cvito Fiskovič counted sixty-six goldsmiths active in the community in the first half of the fourteenth century; from their names it is evident that a number of them were recent immigrants to the town.[14] From 1281 to 1301, by contrast, Josip Lučić located only thirty-five goldsmiths active in the community. A few of those survived long enough to be included in the group Fiskovič identified.[15]

The steady trickle of skilled *aurifici* into town suggests that goldsmiths were sought out, very possibly actively recruited to move to town much like physicians and barber surgeons, and at rates determined by those noble commercial houses that followed the trade in precious metals. Frequently, the new arrivals were young, single men intent on making their personal fortunes in a few years then moving on or returning home. This left to a future date the decision to settle at Ragusa or return home. Immigrant goldsmiths initially achieved only a tenuous footing in the community. This gained solidity considerably later for a few who had obtained approval from their Ragusan hosts and were willing to trust their futures to the town.

Each new household, of noble, artisan, or unskilled worker composition, represented new mouths to feed and a drain on short supplies of precious sweet water. Grain, the staple of urban life, was apportioned by ticket in an ancient system based on the Roman *anona,* so what the walls and gates could not do by way of enforcing strict immigration the issuing of tickets for grain allotment could control.[16] This system appears to be as ancient as the town itself. The late medieval community increased at a slow pace, and the walls did not hold the indigent or even the temporarily unemployed for very long: at a time of famine like 1319 the Great Council could and did consider expelling all "useless" mouths. Yet each accretion in the size of the noble circle, and any new artisan household that passed muster, placed in turn higher demands on the local supply of unskilled labor, which always stood in high ratio to skilled labor for achieving even a small degree of expansion in a medieval community. The Balkan highlands that gave so little access to urban centers had always supplied the unskilled in abundance, so the town had long experience with admitting laborers on its own terms, that is, as *servi* and *ancillae,* or chattel slaves, rather than wage workers.

Demands for unskilled labor were seldom handled directly by government decree, while slavery remained a time-sanctioned institution in which households managed their own labor needs through the private initiative of purchasing their own workers. In fact, backed by strict immigration policy, the centuries-old Dalmatian slave trade, coupled with the economic role assumed by Ragusan noble households in the community's commercial life, conspired to make slavery a simple and convenient method for delivering nonspecialized labor to this urban community. In fact, labor supplied by slaves or contract workers from the interior provides one important key to the success of households.

Slavery was an old, well-established institution in Dalmatia by the thirteenth century. Earlier in the century the mouth of the Narenta (Neretva), north of Ragusa, served as a major slave market for traders from across the Adriatic.[17] In 985, Prince Crnomir of Bosnia deplored the conditions that prevailed in rural Bosnia, where people had no defense against foreign traders capturing and enslaving them.[18] He addressed his complaint to the Ragusans, so there is little doubt about whom he held responsible. Nor can local slave traders be exonerated on the grounds that they merely fulfilled papal directives in enslaving known heretics.[19] There is no evidence that Ragusans bothered to baptize their newly imported slaves as did Florentines and some Venetians. This is a telling sign that they, devout Catholics, found slaves' religious practices close enough to their own Christian ways to be acceptable. It seems clear that the entire region condoned the institution of slavery: a late thirteenth-century ban of Bosnia kept at least a few slaves in his own court.[20]

The neighboring Serbs did a more effective job of protecting their rural populations. The Code of Dusan, composed in the fourteenth century, warned that any person selling a Christian to unbelievers or heretics would have his hands cut off and his tongue cut out on being caught. The true faith was of course orthodoxy, and the fearsome slave vendor a Catholic from the coast.[21] The code expressed what had long been practice for the Nemanjić dynasty: the princes protected their subjects and regulated trade with the foreigners from the Dalmatian ports, controlling both articles of trade and marketing practice.[22]

Domestic slavery, as it was practiced in Ragusa, intersected at a number of points with the Adriatic trade in slaves yet remained a distinct, possibly a unique, urban system for supplying labor to a commercial economy. Surviving thirteenth-century charters allow a glimpse of how it functioned and permit a more thorough analysis of the reasons for dismantling and replacing the system soon after. The number of slave sales and contracts remaining from the late thirteenth century are impressive, given the community's size. In the sixteenth century, at the height of its expansion, Ragusa housed seven thousand or so persons within the town's walls.[23] In the late thirteenth century, the town's population was, perhaps, half that great.[24] In those early documented years, specifically between November 1280 and January 1284, 236 slaves changed hands. Most of these, almost 90 percent, were women. Another series of contracts, which began in August 1299 and ended in May 1301, included thirty-five records of slave sales, augmented by twenty-one charters that registered a slave at the chancellery.[25] Almost 300 slaves entered, lived in, or passed through Ragusa in the last two decades of the century, and only eight of those years are accounted for.[26] By year and sex the charters present the following picture:[27]

Sales of Slaves and Registered Slaves.

| | Sales | | | Registered | | |
|---|---|---|---|---|---|---|
| | M | F | Total | M | F | Subtotal |
| 1280 | 1 | 21 | 22 | | 1 | 1 |
| 1281 | 8 | 81 | 89 | 3 | | 3 |
| 1283 | 7 | 35 | 42 | | | |
| 1284 | | 2 | 2 | | | |
| 1299 | | 5 | 5 | | 5 | 5 |
| 1300 | 2 | 18 | 20 | 2 | 10 | 12 |
| 1301 | 1 | 9 | 10 | 5 | 20 | 25 |
| Total | 28 | 243 | 271 | 10 | 36 | 46 |
| | Females = 87.9% | | | Males = 12.1% | | |

The first series, that is, from 1280 to 1284, is useful for analysis. In that period, thirty-nine months in all, 154 or 64.7 percent of slave sales were concluded among Ragusans, or with Ragusans as the purchasing party. In these instances, we may be fairly certain that the town was serving not merely as an entrepôt for trading ventures between inland suppliers and overseas purchasers but as a consumer of slave labor itself. In the other 35.3 percent of the sales, Bosnian traders or other foreign slave vendors sold slaves directly to foreigners who, in most instances, transported the slave out of the community and overseas. The first figure then, provides some idea of the local market for slaves, that is to say, Ragusans accounted for a market twice the size of that for exported slaves. A wide variety of townspeople bought and sold slaves; Charles Verlinden, an eminent authority on the Mediterranean trade in slaves, believed he could identify a few Ragusans who specialized in slave trading.[28] Yugoslav scholars who have studied slave contracts are less certain. Most merchants trading with the interior maintained a diversified trade, and slaving appeared to be no more than a part-time interest in their diverse commerce, although a few noble traders were frequent suppliers to foreign traders and appear to have had no compunction about selling Balkan inhabitants into life-long servitude overseas.

A certain number of women may be found among the vendors and purchasers of slaves. Numerous artisans and persons with a professional calling, in all, a wide diversity of persons, bought and sold slaves, so slave charters suggest a brisk internal market for slaves, a high turnover if judged by the rate of sales—154 sales in a thirty-nine-month period in a town with a population of only about three thousand, and a relatively high slave density.

Sale charters were brief, terse documents, but they do reveal something about the nature of the institution of urban slavery. In the late summer of 1281, Jacobo Guillelmo of Venice was visiting Ragusa and interested in purchasing a slave. He bought one named Dabrica from a noblewoman, Slava, the wife of Marino de Bincola.[29] The purchase price was ten *hyperperi*, a typical price for an *ancilla* in that decade. The former owner turned around the next day and purchased a new household slave named Dragosti. She was a newly arrived slave from Bosnia and the price was exactly what the noblewoman had received for the slave she had sold to the Venetian. While the ages of the two slaves are not given, the likelihood is that Slava de Bincola had traded a trained slave who was older for an untrained rural girl from Bosnia with a longer, productive life ahead. Whether as a sideline or an intentional vocation, Slava de Bincola, a noblewoman, was involved in training slaves for the export market. Many variants of this story may be found in the charters.

Residents of Italian towns who sought newly imported slaves complained frequently about the deplorable habits and outlandish language and customs of slaves imported from the area north and east of the Black Sea. Slaves who had served in Ragusan households increased in value when they had shed their country ways and become somewhat familiar with the demands of an urban domestic establishment and knew at least a few Italian words. Urban households were, of course, labor intensive, especially when they combined residence and business functions. A Ragusan slave, once trained in such a household, was a much more valuable commodity on the Italian market, where slavery had become an acceptable source of labor for the heaviest domestic tasks; in this light Slava de Bincola's transaction makes commercial sense.[30]

A woman sold into chattel slavery in a Ragusan household could expect some further specialized training, if she adjusted to life there and satisfied her owners. The *Liber Statutorum* mentioned the *ancilla babica* by name, that is, the mammy or wet nurse of the Ragusan household. By law she was to be rewarded with manumission on the death of her owners, although her offspring remained slaves of the household.[31] She was senior in the household to many other unfree persons. Ragusans referred to their servants and chattel slaves by a bewildering series of terms, which, in sum, suggest varying gradations according to rank, free or unfree status, function in the household, and probably favoritism. *Servus* and *ancilla*, the proper legal terms for male and female slaves in Roman law, were in use, but certain persons called *nutrix* (nurse) and *baiula* (governess) might also be slaves or manumitted slaves. *Homo,* in the sense of *Bogdan, homo Mergnani,* signified a heterogeneous category of dependent male servants, both free or unfree. Others, again both free or unfree, men or women, were simply called *servientes,* while a further group "waited on" citizens of the town, in the sense of *dedi me ad serviendum* or *ad standum.* In the fourteenth century, the terms *famuli* and *famulae* came to be preferred. Women in particular were referred to frequently as *famulae,* implying a degree of intimacy with their mistresses and masters. Servants who were *famulae* followed after their mistresses in house changes over a lifetime and provided a degree of continuity in relationships that otherwise might be lacking among a people who remarried and moved frequently. In the late thirteenth century, a bride still listed a slave with her dowry when she entered a marriage. In other instances *pueri* and *puellae* were employed as words to describe servitors and household dependents. These two terms, particularly the former, were used in the traditional sense of persons in dependence rather than as a classification by age.[32] A "boy" or "girl" did as bid for a lifetime.

This rather bewildering variety of terms for household servants connoted more than an acquired level of skills or economic function. Servile nomenclature illustrates a complex ranking in the household, based on incentives and punishments paid out by the householder. Highly personal in nature, and effective for that reason, the complex hierarchy of the household fostered an environment where a semblance of deference gained tangible rewards and resistance swift punishment. First came the family with its offspring; then came the servants most closely associated with them, personal servants, wet nurses, and possibly business agents. Even the highest ranked individuals might be slaves, or they might be salaried servants, or manumitted servants whose continued presence in the household had been secured by the promise of a major bequest in a will or testament.

That rank disregarded the distinction between free and unfree only strengthened the hand of the householder. With the critical distinction of free and servile blurred, current behavior alone secured future reward, both monetary rewards and the prized right to remain in town. By employing the entire gradation of terms for those in service, a householder avoided the stark mention of *servus* and *ancilla,* in a sense obliterating the harsh truth of the unfree condition from the day-to-day conduct of household business. *Famula,* as a term of favor, rewarded the compliant servant through intimation of closeness with the owners. Certainly the evidence of frequent manumissions suggest that slaves lived companionably in households, winning approval and rewards from their owners. In that sense, manumission served to emphasize that dependence on the noble household extended beyond the condition of slavery itself; all unskilled servitors who obtained a future right to remain in town did so only when they pleased their noble masters.

Ragusans overwhelmingly favored women as slaves. Nearly 90 percent of the surviving slave charters record sales of women. The mountainous land above the Dalmatian coast had suffered levies on its manpower from Roman times, when Dalmatia first grew famous for its army recruits, through the era of Turkish domination, when the Janissary army, captured while young from Balkan villages, struck fear into hearts at the mere mention of its name. This thirteenth-century levy differed from the others only in that it drew more heavily on the women of the region than on men. These highland women, known to be large-boned and robust, suggested by their great numbers that urban domestic slavery seemed to Ragusans to be women's work. Living as members of a household, they stood under the authority of the *ancilla babica, nutrix,* and *bauila.* Slave women were thought to be more docile and tractable than men, and, deprived of a family network of their own, probably proved to be so in day-to-day life. The needs of a domestic household meshed comfortably with those of the commercial establishment attached to it. The enslaved mountain women could lift bales, clean, wrap, sort, and process exportable wax, skins, and other goods using the same skills they acquired for domestic service. To their loss, *ancillae* were equal to the work, they appeared to be more docile than men, and they could be moved to work through rewards and punishments.

Fortuitously, for Ragusans at any rate, scholastic theology and Renaissance utopian visions, particularly the idealized *città felice,* uninformed as yet by egalitarian notions, accepted slavery and other forms of bondage as proper; if these systems rose to the level of consideration at all, they provided the underpinning for utopian life in beautiful and appropriate settings. How fitting for Ragusa with its great physical beauty, its good-humored, confidant, and elegant patriciate. Above all, contemporary literature saw bondage as inevitable, part of the nature of inequality, and therefore immutable.[33] Ragusans exercised whatever moral scruples they possessed in believing their practices more humane than those of foreigners who came to buy slaves on their markets, hence the initiative to outlaw the export of slaves in 1416.[34] Human suffering of the enslaved speaks from the documents nevertheless: the child of a slave sold away, a countryman come to town to find his wife who had been carried off by merchants, the misery of overwork, dogged efforts to flee.

And townspeople manifested a long-standing anxiety in the policing of slavery and spent considerable effort in council to secure the return of fugitive or runaway slaves. A fine on the return of the purchase price, if a slave ran away, figured in the text of numerous contracts.[35] Statute law provided elaborate measures to guarantee an owner's right to pursue a runaway slave, and to punish any who might harbor or abet a fugitive.[36]

But slaves did run away and proclamations of recent escapes were common occurrences. From July 1322 until March 1323, thirteen fugitives were reported to the count and Small Council: two were *servi* or male slaves, all others were *famulae* or *famuli,* family servants, who might have been household slaves or contracted servants.[37] One was the runaway daughter of the slave of an artisan, herself a slave as well by terms of the law.[38] Roughly half the fugitives reported in this nine-month period were males, although men comprised little more than one tenth of the slaves listed for sale; Ragusans had some reason then for their apprehension over the wisdom of relying on *servi*. Clearly women posed less of a fugitive problem for householders—once housed within the town, that is. *Servi*, enslaved men, were employed in traditional male-identified pursuits: in retinues for ambassadorial missions, in caravans for traders, on shipboard—in other words, in situations that offered some opportunity to flee.[39] Women slaves, domiciled with other dependents in households in the town, sometimes encumbered by offspring or tied to the household through promised rewards, were more easily controlled, less able to flee, and therefore a preferred source of labor.

The citizens of the town remained apprehensive about their large servile population nevertheless. The town's Great Council was dismayed by the possibility of gangs or groups of servants entering the homes of nobles and the *cives de populo* and doing harm. The council forbade public assembly to male servants: "Considerantes quod per fragilitatem et maliciam servitialium multa enormia pericula accidere possunt," (very great danger can exist from the frailty and mischief of servants).[40] And Ragusan slave owners kept no more males as slaves than was absolutely necessary. Even female slaves were forbidden from congregating at the sites of fires or other urban disturbances. A tractable, preferably invisible, corps of hardworking persons housed in scattered households represented an urban ideal.

The noble families of the town had secured such a functional source of nonskilled labor through the institution of slavery that it seems remarkable that they dismantled the system in the early fourteenth century. They did so in response to a problem posed by the market rather than in response to problems created by their own slaves. Noble householders had never been the sole market in town for valuable imported slaves. Trading slaves to foreigners cut into local supplies, and Ragusans also allowed their recruited skilled artisanal population to acquire slaves of their own, which created further scarcity. Among known slave owners in the late thirteenth-century charters were a barber, a stone mason, four tailors, the wife of a dock superintendent, a notary, his wife, a master of the arsenal, a physician, an officer of the town militia, and four goldsmiths.[41] Six other purchasers were titled "Magister" in the charters; they were evidently professional men employed in the community.[42] Such a diversity of *civis de populo* and foreign *habitator* slave-owners would cut into the available supply of slaves, however slavery suited Ragusa's household economy so well that the noble circle appears to have been ready to allow free non-noble residents of the town to secure their own domestic slaves.

Many skilled artisans, even some of the professional class, and certainly the foreign traders who arrived in Ragusa for only brief visits, were unaccompanied by families. Female slaves provided these bachelors with a domestic establishment, often a sexual life and companionship. In other words, slaves helped keep the resident bachelor population settled and quiescent. The traveling years, when a young Italian made his fortune abroad in a prospering town like Ragusa, were being lengthened in the thirteenth and fourteenth centuries. Ragusa relied heavily on single men—its goldsmiths and stone masons, for example, often came to work for only a few years. A temporary household with a resident female slave accommodated an artisan without requiring any concern on the part of civil authorities or particular attention from the Small Council or noble householders. Francho Sacchetti, popular Florentine author and the son of a merchant banker who lived and worked in Ragusa in the early decades of the fourteenth century, in all likelihood had a slave girl named Maria for a mother. Francho's birth predated his father's marriage to a suitable, well-dowered Italian girl by a considerable number of years. He was accepted as a member of his father's later established married household, nonetheless. Such arrangements occur within slave systems, particularly where slavery is a domestic institution,[43] yet few offspring of such liaisons fared as well as this future teller of tales, whose father, Bencius del Bono, had acknowledged him.

The pressure of demand for slaves drove prices higher. The practice of sharing with non-noble households scarce, newly enslaved rural workers did not alone account for the strain within the system of domestic slavery. It did, however, add its own pressure by constantly nudging the prices of scarce slaves upward. Slaves more than doubled in price after the turn into the fourteenth century. Yet in this era, the greater pressure for noble Ragusans lay in accommodating the long-distance merchants from Italy who frequented the port, increasingly demanding more and more slaves for export. Over a period of years, Ragusans' success in utilizing domestic slaves in a wide variety of tasks produced an interesting dilemma: incentives steadily multiplied to sell household slaves to foreigners at attractive prices, as Slava de Bincola had sold Dabrica. Each domestic slave sold abroad left a slot to fill, nudging prices upward and forcing householders to scour the highlands for replacements. Noble households, then, found it increasingly necessary to balance the advantage of a quick profit in a slave sale against the need to purchase a new and untrained slave.

Slaves, by certain comparative standards, were expensive to purchase in the late thirteenth century. The average price for a female slave was a little less than ten *hyperperi* (five ducats, in Venetian currency). In 1284, a towns-man could purchase a cow for two *hyperperi*.[44] Also in this decade a youthful citizen wishing to live outside his father's home after his father's remarriage could demand out of that household's accounts twelve *hyperperi* for a year's expenses and another six *hyperperi* to provide for a servant of his own.[45] This figure may provide a baseline for what it cost to maintain a bachelor in Ragusa. A slave's average price, then, amounted to over three-quarters of a year's expenses for a young man living alone, or five times the price of a cow. Around 1300, a Ragusan could purchase a hut or modest dwelling for six *hyperperi*.[46] A female slave was more expensive than a simple residence for artisans and other wage earners. Thus slaves appeared expensive because other routine urban expenses were low; however, if slave prices are compared to communally paid wages, a different picture emerges. The *Pro-tomagister arsenatus* was hired by the commune for 100 *hyperperi* in 1333, 160 *hyperperi* in 1347, and 240 *hyperperi* in 1357.[47] Even allowing for a steady rise in slave prices in the fourteenth century, slaves were comfortably affordable for men earning such high communal wages. Young noblewomen who married in the late thirteenth century typically brought a slave and four hundred *hyperperi*, or two hundred ducats, as a cash allotment in dowry. The price of a dotal slave amounted to a mere one-fortieth of dowry wealth.[48] Slaves were both expensive, if the cost of living at Ragusa is used as a comparison, and relatively inexpensive, if communal salaries and the private wealth of the noble families are applied as measuring rods.

Prices did increase over the decade, however, and it is this increment in price that appears to have convinced Ragusan householders that change was in order. The increment may be understood by observing seasonal variations in prices in the best documented years, that is, 1281, 1282, and 1283. In all three seasons, activity in trading slaves intensified in the last six weeks of summer. In 1281, 32 percent of the total year's sales took place in this six-week period; in 1282, the figure reached 35.8 percent. During the late summer, most sales were made to foreign purchasers, which proved opposite to circumstances during the rest of the year.[49] Traders from Venice were frequent purchasers, but traders from Apulia and other Adriatic communities attended the market. Buyers from eastern lands, particularly from Crete, suggest that the Venetian fleet was in port with some Levantine passengers. Prices rose; in 1281 the average price paid for a slave showed a slight increase during this late summer period. The mean price paid from 1280 to 1284 was 9.5 *hyperperi;* the price in this six-week period reached 9.8 *hyperperi.*[50] In 1282, the price paid for a slave in the same six-week period jumped to 11.7 *hyperperi.* A smaller and less reliable sample of charters for the late summer of 1283 saw the price reach an inflationary 13 *hyperperi* on average.[51]

During these periods of heightened activity in the slave trade, direct sales of newly acquired Bosnian slaves to foreigners do not appear to have sufficed to meet demand from abroad. Foreign merchants also bought directly from noble Ragusan households whenever possible: they purchased slaves from noblewomen, possibly slaves who were dowry slaves; they even purchased the occasional domestic slave of an artisan who owned at most one or two chattel slaves. Even at this early date, slavery had begun to price itself too high to be a cheap and convenient method for supplying nonskilled labor to the community. Because of a limited and possibly decreasing supply of slaves from the interior, and because of an increasing demand from overseas traders, slavery grew increasingly less practical at home.

During these decades women enslaved at Ragusa, then trained and sold to foreigners, unwillingly pioneered the large-scale sea-borne migration of unskilled and unfree laborers that became such a striking feature of early modern trade on the high seas. Slaves were eagerly sought after, and their prices bid up, by affluent householders and long-distance traders from Italy's great cities. Frequently, these traders merely sought a single domestic slave for their own households, but that meant that any foreign trader visiting town might be in the market for a slave.

Meanwhile in Italian cities, trained slaves from abroad who were able to accommodate to domestic slavery became attractive commodities. Thus, by the close of the thirteenth century, the price of women slaves trained at Ragusa rose in price generally in Mediterranean trade. Verlinden's studies of the Mediterranean slave trade reveal that these women often commanded substantially higher prices than those offered for untrained slaves from the Black Sea region.[52] *Schiava* from the West Balkans became an accustomed sight in the cities of Italy proper. Was Ragusa's own success with domestic slavery its own undoing? In the increasing popularity of domestic slavery, did they produce a drain on sources of slaves?

By the turn of the fourteenth century, the number of recorded slave sales had diminished at Ragusa. This may be a result of less systematic records for 1299 to 1301, but other evidence suggests that it reflects a genuine decline. In these years, sales of slaves were being replaced by contracts for labor arranged with the rural peasantry of Bosnia, the Herzegovina, and other nearby territories.[53] These contracts required an initial payment of money to an individual (or the parents of that individual) in return for a stipulated period of work. Such contracts had been in use for decades, but they experienced a sudden rise in popularity. The person who supplied the labor, or more frequently the parents or guardians of that person, received the sum in full or in part, the remainder on fulfilling the contract. The contract might or might not contain a number of provisos: conditions if the laborer ran away; stipulations about the lodging, feeding, and clothing of the worker; clauses promising the worker the opportunity to learn a skill (for male workers primarily); and the conditions under which the contract would become null and void.[54] By 1310, these contracts predominate over sales of slaves registered at the Ragusan chancellery. This represents a significant reorganization in the mode of supply for labor to Ragusan households but, as events would have it, little substantial change in actual conditions for laborers supplying that need.[55]

One obvious difference lay in a term of labor being supplied to the household. Since contract laborers were not legally chattel slaves, they worked for a term after which they were free; they could not be resold, or, significantly, exported overseas. A foreigner could, of course, make a contract with a rural person for labor, and it would be understood that she or he would accompany the foreigner overseas, but laborers recruited by Ragusans to work in Ragusa would remain there by force of law.[56] The council confirmed this distinction by requiring all slaves transported abroad to be accompanied by a charter stating that they were the legal chattels of their owners. A contract laborer was protected from being passed off as a slave because no such contract could be produced.[57] In the subsequent decades, neither the slave trade from the Balkan region nor the use of slaves in town was actually abolished, but overseas traders found that most available laborers stood under long-term contract rather than enslavement in town. Whether the contract labor was in any way a more humane system, particularly for the women supplying unskilled work to the household, is another matter entirely.

It is important to re-emphasize at this point that the distinction between the chattel slave and the legally free but dependent servant of the household had always been unclear. Chattel slaves had realistic expectations that they would be manumitted during their lifetimes if they remained in the same household. Noble wills and last testaments freed not only dower slaves and the *ancilla babica* of the household but whole groups of slaves. Noblewomen were fond of dowering their former slaves and servants as an act of private piety, acts that fit well into the system of incentives for industrious, docile behavior and in effect populated the town over decades. One noblewoman went farther than to grant a dowry for her manumitted slave, instead of dowrying the slave she had freed, she offered a grant to a freedman of the town if he would marry her servant.[58] Traditionally, slaves of the household were not treated in ways distinct from other servants; they might not even be called by terms that distinguished them from manumitted dependents or even from wage-earning servants. Distinctions among servants were further blurred by opportunities that Ragusan slave owners occasionally provided for slaves to purchase their own freedom, or replace themselves as slaves of the household.[59] One slave won her manumission by finding a fellow countrywoman to be enslaved in her place.[60] She then turned around and contracted out her own labor, on what might be considered a marginal upward step toward free wage-earning status. Masters and slaves dickered and negotiated, a dialogue that may possibly have humanized the institution for the slaves themselves, but one that placed enormous power in the hands of slave owners. An elaborate system of incentives and rewards lay at the disposal of noble masters.

The elimination of chattel slavery from the variety of conditions of dependence represented little substantial change for the workers themselves or for that matter the complexion of the commercial household. Households that had contained slaves in earlier decades had assumed a legal obligation to provide for a slave's old age, either in the form of manumission with gifts or with a living supplied for those who had grown enfeebled. Contracts with young persons allowed the urban householder to make the best of the servitor's vigorous and productive years. Contracts were often made with persons under fifteen and they allowed for terms of five, ten, or even twenty years, with, of course, no provision for care of the worker at the end of that period. An unmotivated contract worker could be returned to the countryside after a term of labor with nothing to show for her or his prolonged stay in town except memories. A hardworking contract laborer who had won the esteem of others in the household was rewarded through the same system of promised rewards and incentives that had proved effective for chattel slaves. The contract system could in fact be cheaper than slavery for the householder because it limited the responsibility for workers to the years of service.

In 1348, the year of the plague, the Great Council legitimated the household's authority over the bewildering variety of free, quasi-free, and wage laborers of the household. Council asserted that the rights of surveillance over *servi* and *ancillae*, that is, persons legally bound in chattel slavery, were extended henceforth to all *serviciales* of the household, a devastating initiative that went into effect without recorded incident or protest.[61] This law, and its successor drawn up in 1366, ensured civil tranquility in the fearful months while the plague raged, but ultimately they sanctioned the householders' control over all laborers well after the tumult of the plague years lay behind. A contract worker now acquired a legal status distinct from chattel slavery but an actual expectation that differed only from enslavement in some certainty of freedom after the contract was fulfilled.

Numerous factors combined to assist noble householders in consolidating their authority over all their servants in this fashion. Few opportunities existed for the unskilled outside the orbit of the noble household. Moreover, freed servants were restricted in their opportunity to establish their own autonomous households in the town, even if this merely meant they were restricted, not prohibited. The favor of the noble household remained the key to successful integration into the urban community. In sponsoring a new laboring family, nobles provided bequests to set up a separate household, access to urban services, influence in obtaining training in a skill, and opportunity for wage-earning work. All these benefits descended from the noble household and no other sources could be tapped, in fact they did not exist.

So for the noble householders of the fourteenth century, reliance on contract labor did not mean a less deferential corps of servile laborers, but rather a less expensive alternative to chattel slavery. A rural peasant contracted for service for a twenty-year term, all for ten or eleven *hyperperi* in 1310.[62] The price of a slave had just about doubled over the preceding twenty years, consequently the contractor was receiving twenty years of labor in 1310 for just a little over half the current price of a slave. This was a bargain in an urban labor market unmatched by the price for unskilled labor in Italian city-states overseas. Some bargains in labor challenge credulity: two country women contracted for periods of twenty years each for two *hyperperi* and five *hyperperi*, respectively, at Ragusa in 1310. This was an almost unimaginably low cost for labor, particularly when it is gauged against the owner's responsibility to provide only food, clothes, and lodging, with no obligation to see to the servant's declining years.[63] For certain young rural women, whose parents received the initial sum for the contract, and who served twenty years at rates below ten *hyperperi*, the fourteenth-century contract may have been a more exploitive system for rendering their labor to the urban economy than slavery itself.

The economic consequences of slavery as a method of delivering nonskilled labor to the urban community (both chattel slavery and its successor the labor contract system) enhanced the competitive position of merchant householders in the pursuit of long-distance trade. Four factors, in particular, warrant emphasis. The price of slaves was low in terms of noble wealth in the late thirteenth century, with the result that a brake was placed on the rising costs of urban living. This would encourage capital accumulation and provide a competitive edge over towns where the price of labor was substantially higher. When prices of slaves spiraled, slaves were replaced by an even cheaper mode of supply, the labor contract. If Ragusans were not as badly caught in the urban "price scissors" of the late medieval economy as the inhabitants of Italy's cities, they may owe it in part to the critical timing of this transition, the early decades of the fourteenth century.[64] Even when slavery was finally outlawed in Ragusa in the fifteenth century, on the expressed grounds that it was inhuman and against nature, only the export of slaves was prohibited.[65] Clearly noble householders in this "città felice" never contemplated the thought that their household dependents were treated in an inhuman fashion. The borderline between slavery and other forms of domestic service continued to be imprecise, to the overwhelming advantage of the noble householder.[66] As the center of an orbit of dependents and former dependents now living in quarters near the household, noble Ragusans found the labor they needed at a very small cost. Skilled artisans settling in town followed this noble model as far as their resources permitted.

The demands for unskilled labor never forced the Great Council into an expanded, and expensive, program for monitoring and accommodating a free wage-earning but unskilled population who gained and lost employment in rhythm with the community's commercial fortunes. The merchant aristocracy willingly shouldered many communal expenditures: medical care for all, a subsidized grain supply, and a central chancellery, but it never needed to provide expensive policing for entire neighborhoods of restless wage workers or, for that matter, services for the indigent or unemployed. Private households assumed full responsibility for their respective labor needs. Householders purchased slaves as needed, contracted for laborers as needed, and provided care, surveillance, and future opportunities for the favored among them who continued to live in town. Civil government intervened as little as possible in this matter where the household remained both paramount and adequate.

A corollary was a placid, smoothly functioning community, conducive to fostering trade. Foreign visitors marveled at the pleasant, even "jolly" inhabitants industriously going about their work (see Chapter 8). Everywhere visitors noted a semblance of deference from the laboring classes. Ragusan crowds were not prone to assemble in the streets, nor did they terrorize worthy councillors and prosperous artisans; riots were largely unknown. How were visitors to know that most outlets for hostility were precluded by individual households negotiating privately for laborers who were chosen for their tractable, compliant behavior? Through clever manipulation of the power at their disposal, the nobility left few choices to those who worked in town but to improve their lives through striving for the incentives and rewards noble households offered.

Last, blurring the distinction between the unfree and the free but dependent domestic servant was possible and practical as long as the commercial and residential functions of noble households continued to be closely associated. Eventually the attitudes learned in these households colored the social values of the entire community. Strong ties forged over decades, gifts, preferential favors, continued association with great neighbors, and continued support from noble households, all conspired to keep disenfranchised town residents within the orbit of noble influence. As a result, working-class households, when they were formed, were substantially more heedful of noble preferences and purposes than they might have been had they begun their urban life as free wage laborers.

In the fourteenth century, transitions from chattel slavery to contract labor principles for the absorption of neighboring peoples into the Ragusan work force were established. In one sense or another, the contract system came to influence other arenas of community life. New lands turned to viticulture by noble families were assarted and cultivated by contract labor. By the fifteenth century, even the local peasantry worked under a similar system. Augmented by household servants who, when they were not fully employed in the town could be sent out to country residences to help in the endless tasks of agricultural production, the countryside began to mirror the town. Within the town itself, the contract remained dominant through the fifteenth century, and in matter of fact, Ragusans could now rely even more confidently on a supply of rural laborers because the Turks had conquered the Balkan lands. For many country people, the only way to leave the Turkish-dominated hinterland was to escape to Ragusa and accept whatever conditions town life offered. When, in the fifteenth century, an industry for weaving exportable rough cloth was introduced into town, it bore resemblances to the old contracting system. Women were recruited from the countryside to staff a workshop, and they were housed together in supervised group quarters in the town. This textile "workshop" differed very little in organization from the noble household that served as its model, except that the workshop housed a substantially larger aggregation of low-skilled workers.[67] So when the *gynaeceum* was disappearing from Italy and western Europe in the fifteenth century, it remained a working system at Ragusa.[68]

As for skilled artisans recruited from abroad to work in Ragusa, the community into which they settled resembled the Italian cities they left behind only superficially. No religious revivals swept through town in which the skilled and unskilled found a common voice; higher orders among the skilled craftsmen could not raise an eager following among the unemployed and discontented, as the Ciompi leaders had done so successfully in Florence in 1361. Settling themselves within the orbits of noble households, artisans also faced a restricted set of choices. To all appearances these restricted circumstances were happenstance, but in fact they resulted from adroit, long-term management from above, a form of cooperative social planning not practiced in other late medieval cities.

\*   \*   \*

From the point of view of the modern reader, it may be difficult to see any plan or rationality in the narrow warren of streets and noble residences that have survived from old Ragusa. But it is arguable that these households were highly effective users of unskilled labor—that they were substantially more cost-efficient than labor systems in other cities which relied more completely on wage labor. Ragusan households were well served by their *sclavi*, the term that was used as a synonym for *servi* and *ancillae* as early as 1272, although Ragusans did not reserve it exclusively for denoting chattels.[69] Ragusa prospered because it remained the sum of its noble households, and those households learned how to deploy labor in a highly productive fashion.

*Notes*

1. On the residences in Ragusa/Dubrovnik see Jorjo Tadić, *Dubrovnik portreti*.

2. On the town plan and fortifications and walls see L. Beritić, *Utvrđenja grada Dubrovnika* (Zagreb: JAZU, 1955).

3. Possessions as part of a dowry settlement occurred in the Black Plague era as exceptional events when an orphan and heir married. In the early fifteenth century they became somewhat more common, but in the dowries sampled in Chapter 3, only six noble dowries consisted of all or part possessions. "*Domus in Castellum*" was given as an award in D.S.A., *Liber Dotium*, VI (1439–50), but it was an exception (see Chapter 3).

4. D.S.A., *Testamenta*, I, f. 112 for the gift of a house to Symon de Benessa in his uncle's will.

5. *Liber Statutorum*, L. VIII, 57.

6. *MR*, vol. 3, p. 67. The six persons noted, including Domina Phylippa de Mence, were investing large personal fortunes, some of which had been accumulated in a lifetime, but for this post-plague building in stone, they may just as well represent inherited fortunes. On noble summer residences in the fifteenth and sixteenth centuries, see Ivan Zdravković, *Dubrovački dvorci* (Belgrade: SAN, 1951).

7. D.S.A., *Liber Dotium*, II, *venditiones*, f. 10v.

8. D.S.A., *Liber Dotium*, II, *venditiones*, f. 10v–11.

9. D.S.A., *Liber Dotium*, I, *venditiones*, f. 1.

10. D.S.A., *Liber Dotium*, II, *venditiones*, f. 2.

11. D.S.A., *Liber Dotium*, V, *venditiones*, f. 20v.

12. *MR*, vol. 3, p. 67.

13. I. Mahnken, *Dubrovački patricijat*, pp. 91–102.

14. C. Fisković, "Dubrovački zlatari od XIII do XVII stoljeća," *Starohrvatska prosvjeta,* ser. 1, 3 (1949): 143–249.

15. J. Lučić, *Obrti i usluge u Dubrovniku,* pp. 67–70.

16. Dušanka Dinić-Knežević, "Trgovina žitom u Dubrovniku," pp. 79–131.

17. On slavery in the Balkans see Gregor Čremošnik, "Izvori za istoriju roblja i servicijalnih odnosa u našim zemljama sr. vijeka," *Istorijski-pravni zbornik* 1 (1949): 146–62; idem., "Pravni položaj našeg roblja u sredjem vijeku," *Sarajevo zemaljski muzej u Bosni i Hercegovini, glasnik,* n.s., 2 (1947): 69–73; idem., *Kancelarijski i notarski spisi, 1278–1301,* henceforth referred to as G. Cremošnik, *Spisi, 1278–1301;* Vuk Vinaver, "Trgovina Bosanskim robljem tokom XIV veka u Dubrovniku," *Dubrovnik anali* 2 (1953): 125–47; M. Dinić, *Iz dubrovačkog arhiva* I (Belgrade: SAN, 1967), contained documents pertinent to the slave trade for the period after 1301. More recently, see J. Lučić, *Obrti i usluge u Dubrovniku,* pp. 135–59, which provides a comparative scale of service occupations for the household, including slavery.

18. D.S.A., fr. 985, *Pismo Kneza Crnomira Knezu i Općini Dubrovačkoj;* L. Stojanović, *Acta srpske povelje i pisma* (Belgrade: Zbornik za IJK, 1929), doc. 25, pp. 23–24.

19. For a recent interpretation see John Fine, *The Bosnian Church: A New Interpretation.*

20. Gregor Čremošnik, *Spisi, 1278–1301,* doc. 10, p. 22, and doc. 101, p. 58. One woman slave in the fourteenth century presented her case before the court asserting that she was orthodox in her beliefs, not a heretic, and therefore deserved to be freed. She won her case. M. Dinić, *Iz dubrovačkog arhiva* I, doc. 161, p. 63; see C. Truhelka, "Još o testamentu gosta Radina i patarenima," *Glasnik zemaljskog muzeja, Sarajevo* 25 (1913): 380–81.

21. Malcolm Burr, "The Code of Stefan Dušan," *Slavonic and East European Review* 28 (1949–50): 202.

22. Serbs as well as Greeks were enslaved, however, and reached the Mediterranean slave markets in the fourteenth and fifteenth centuries. C. Verlinden, "Orthodoxie et esclavage au bas moyen âge," *Melanges Eugene Tiserant, studi e testi* 235 (1964): 427–56, and "Le Recruitment des esclaves à Venise aux XIV et XV siècles," *Institut historique belge de Rome* 39 (1968): 83–202.

23. J. Tadić, "Le Port de Raguse au moyen âge. Le Navire et l'économie maritime du moyen âge au XVIIIᵉᵐᵉ siècle," p. 18.

24. *MR,* vol. 5, p. 393. In 1330 city householders were allowed from two to twenty *ster* of grain to last one-third of a year. Two *ster* were estimated by the council to be sufficient to feed two persons (the smallest allotment) for that length of time. Larger households could draw up to twenty *ster.* In all, two thousand *ster* were allotted. At the most, one thousand could draw two *ster* each. Assuming a woman and child for each male, the population would have been approximately three thousand persons. Dušanka Dinić-Knežević, "Trgovina žitom u Dubrovniku," pp. 128–29, bases an estimate of population, which is somewhat higher than this figure for the early fourteenth century, on the imported grain purchased. Her work notes, however, an estimated rise in grain consumption by the late fourteenth century from ten thousand *ster* of grain to twenty thousand *ster.* If this represents real increase, substantial population growth occurred after the Black Plague. The

author does admit that private persons purchased grain on their own initiative to augment supplies obtained by the *massarii bladorum* throughout the century. For this reason both the estimate given above and Tadić's estimate may be low. The issue of population reveals a difference of opinion among historians of Ragusa. A "small" population school exists, which follows the general opinion of Tadić that the town grew to no more than seven thousand people in its greatest period of prosperity. Others follow the opinion of Philippus de Diversis, *Situs aedificiorum,* that Ragusa possessed a significantly larger population, but the man was prone to exaggeration in his attempt to flatter.

25. The table is based on charters from two sources, Gregor Čremošnik, *Spisi, 1278–1301* and *Spisi, Thomasina de Savere.*

26. For comparison see Charles Verlinden, *L'Esclavage dans l'Europe médiévale,* vol. 2 (Ghent, 1977), pp. 743–64. The figures in this table agree almost completely with Verlinden's findings, and they are both considerably lower than those published by Yugoslav historians such as Čremošnik and Vinaver.

27. The registrations of slaves at the chancellery present a difficulty. Slaves presented themselves, consenting and willing, to be the chattels of their owners, hence the tendency on the part of historians to refer to these as "self-enslavings." What they appear to represent are periodic checks on the slave population of the town. When no sales contract was available to verify a person's enslavement, the civil government insisted on a notarized statement in order to distinguish between the free and the unfree.

28. See Charles Verlinden, "Le Recruitment des esclaves à Venise aux XIV et XV siècles," and *L'Esclavage dans l'Europe médiévale,* vol. 2, pp. 750–59. He identifies certain Ragusans like Bogdanus Volcassio as long-distance slave traders, and he provides evidence that Ragusans persisted in the Mediterranean slave trade after it was outlawed in the fifteenth century.

29. Gregor Čremošnik, *Spisi, 1278–1301,* docs. 127 and 128. Dominus Jacobus Guillelmus from Venice had purchased another slave named Radosclava on 21 August 1281; *ibid.,* doc. 126.

30. Iris Origo, "The Domestic Enemy: Eastern Slaves in Tuscany in the Fourteenth and Fifteenth Centuries," *Speculum* 30 (1955): 321–99.

31. *Liber Statutorum,* L. VI, c. 51.

32. J. Lučić, *Obrti i usluge u Dubrovniku,* pp. 136–60.

33. Frank Manuel and Fritzie Manuel, *Utopian Thought in the Western World,* p. 166.

34. *Liber Statutorum* VII, c. 93; VI, c. 33 (4).

35. Gregor Čremošnik, *Spisi, 1278–1301,* doc. 190.

36. Gregor Čremošnik, *Spisi, 1278–1301,* doc. 288, doc. 342.

37. *MR,* vol. 1, p. 122–27.

38. *Liber Statutorum,* L. VI, c. 51.

39. On slaves in caravans see M. Dinić, "Dubrovačka srednjevekovna karavanska trgovina," *Jugoslavenski istorijski časopis* 3 (1937): 119–46. On slaves aboard Ragusan ships see *Liber Statutorum,* L. VII, c. 19. On slaves used for hauling goods to town see *Liber Statutorum,* L. IV, c. 47; and on *famuli* in retinues see *MR,* vol. 3, pp. 40–41.

40. *Liber Statutorum,* L. VI, c. 33:4.

41. Gregor Čremošnik, *Spisi, 1278–1301,* doc. 41, 46, 58, 160, 169, 179, 186, 217, 224, 255, 276, 300, 323, 337, 342, 431, 463, 469.

42. Gregor Čremošnik, *Spisi, 1278–1301,* doc. 71, 164, 173, 241, 345, 445.

43. Ignacij Voje, "Bencius del Buono," *Istorijski časopis* 18 (1971): 189–99.

44. Gregor Čremošnik, *Spisi, 1278–1301,* doc. 363. A horse cost about the same as a slave, and inflation in price kept pace with inflation in prices for slaves. M. Dinić, *Iz dubrovačkog arhiva* 3, doc. 65, p. 27.

45. *Liber Statutorum,* L. IV, c. 9.

46. D.S.A., *Diversa cancellariae,* IV, f. 20.

47. *MR,* vol. 5, p. 328; vol. 1, p. 254; vol. 2, p. 179.

48. It has been assumed a dowry slave stayed with the bride for a lifetime, becoming nurse to her children, but the dowry slave died out as a custom by the fourteenth century. See Chapter 3.

49. In 1281, thirty-five out of 106 slave sales; in 1282, twenty-nine out of 81 slave sales.

50. The mean average price in 1281 was 9.5 *hyperperi;* thirty-five late summer sales produced a mean average price of 9.8 *hyperperi.* There were twenty-nine summer sales in 1282 with a mean average price of 11.7 *hyperperi.*

51. There were only seven late summer sales in 1283, yielding a mean average price of 13.3 *hyperperi.*

52. Along with the works of Charles Verlinden already cited see "La Crête, débouché et plague tournante de la traité des esclaves aux XIV^e et XV^e siècles," *Studi in onore Amintore Fanfani* (Milan: Guiffre, 1962), pp. 594–669. See also A. Teja, "La schiavitu domestica ed il traffico degli schiavi," *Revista Dalmatica* 22 (1941): 33–44; A. Tenenti, "Gli schiavi di Venezia alla fine de cinquecento," *Rivista storica italiana* 67 (1955): 52–69. Wilhelm Heyd first noted that the traffic in slaves in medieval trade moved from east to west; *Histoire du commerce du Levant au moyen-âge,* 6th ed. 2 vols., supplement (Amsterdam: O. Harrassawit, 1855), pp. 555–63. More recently, see Pierre Dockes, *Medieval Slavery and Liberation,* trans. Arthur Goldhammer (Chicago: University of Chicago Press, 1982).

53. Gregor Čremošnik, "Izvori za istoriju roblja i servicijalnih," pp. 151–62; and Vuk Vinaver, "Trgovina Bosanskim robljem tokom XIV veka u Dubrovniku," p. 141.

54. Based on volume 1, D.S.A., *Diversa Notariae,* G. Čremošnik produced the following table ("Izvori za istoriju roblja i servicijalnih," pp. 151–62):

| Charters | Contracts for labor | Slaves |
| --- | --- | --- |
| 1310 | 128 | 10 |
| 1312 | 203 | 6 |
| 1322 | 198 | 9 |

55. For example, Radoanus was to serve Nicola, the tailor, for a term of ten years. He would receive his food and clothes and would learn "arnisia artis, que dantur secundum usum Ragusii" (Gregor Čremošnik, *Spisi, 1278–1301,* doc. 41). By

contrast a nonspecialized contract for a woman worker contained the following conditions: Stana, a laborer from the mining site of Rudnik contracted to work three years; two-thirds of one *hyperperus* would be given to her mother, and one and a third more would be given to her mother at the end of the daughter's term. The mother was responsible if the daughter ran away (Gregor Čremošnik, *Spisi, 1278–1301,* doc. 79). Terms of service lengthened substantially in the fourteenth century.

56. R. Samardžić, "Podmladak dubrovačkih trgovaca i zanatlija u XVI veku," *Zbornik studentiskih stručnih radova* (1948): 64–78. Persons from abroad could, and did, contract with families from the interior whom they then transported to Apulia or elsewhere for the duration of a term of service; this was done, apparently, in full knowledge that the contract for labor would be served abroad rather than in Ragusa. For an example, see D.S.A., *Diversa Notariae,* V, f. 35v.

57. Vuk Vinaver, "Trgovina Bosanskim robljem tokom XIV veka," p. 133.

58. D.S.A., *Testamenta,* V, f. 13–13v.

59. See Gregor Čremošnik, *Spisi, 1278–1301,* doc. 154 for an example of wages for domestic servants.

60. Gregor Čremošnik, *Spisi, 1278–1301,* doc. 193 and 193a.

61. *Liber Statutorum,* L. VII, c. 93; L. VI, c. 33:4.

62. D.S.A., *Diversa Notariae,* I, f. 2.

63. D.S.A., *Diversa Notariae,* I, f. 2v.

64. On cost of living in Italian cities see Gino Luzzatto, "Il costa della vita a venezia nel trecento," in *Studi di storia economica veneziana* (Padua: CEDAM, 1954), pp. 285–87; Jacques Heers, *L'Occident aux XIV<sup>e</sup>–XV<sup>e</sup> siècles: Aspects économiques et sociaux* (Paris: Presses Universitaires de France, 1966); and more recently, Richard Goldthwaite, *Building Trades in Fifteenth Century Florence* (Baltimore: Johns Hopkins University Press, 1982); idem., "Il prezzo del grano a Firenze dal XIV al XV secolo," *Quaderni storici* 28 (1975): 3–36. See also Charles M. de la Roncière, *Prix et salaires à Florence au XIV<sup>e</sup> siècle, 1280–1380* (Rome: Ecole français de Rome, 1982).

65. Vuk Vinaver, "Trgovina Bosanskim robljem tokom XIV veka," p. 142.

66. In the past few years attitudes toward domestic servants has received attention in the scholarly literature. See in particular Cissy Fairchilds, *Domestic Enemies: Servants and Their Masters in Old Regime France* (Baltimore: Johns Hopkins University Press, 1983), and Sara C. Maza, *Servants and Masters in Eighteenth Century France,* (Princeton, N.J.: Princeton University Press, 1983).

67. Dušanka Dinić-Knežević, "Petar Pantella, trgovac i suknar u Dubrovniku," *Godišnak filoz. fakulteta, Novi Sad* 13, no. 1 (1970): 87–144.

68. David Herlihy, *Opera Muliebria* (Philadelphia: Temple University Press, 1989); see in particular the final chapter.

69. *Liber Statutorum,* L. I, c. 14.

# 6. Community

## Links Through Descent

A prosopographer generally seeks out a group within a community and then investigates the lives of its members for what they tell about the whole; those lives serve as representative illustrations of a greater unknown group of persons. In Ragusa, it is unwise to assume that untold faceless masses of persons existed outside of those identified in the process of studying households. The exact contours of the *prijateljstvo* have been documented; the households of artisans such as goldsmiths, masons, and tailors are less perfectly known, but both the number and composition of artisan households may be estimated with some accuracy. The group understood least well in most urban centers—nonskilled workers, the poor, those who performed seasonal work—are not necessarily an unknown quantity in this community either, largely because those who remained in town had some traceable link to the Ragusan merchant aristocracy. And intimate ties—those of blood and descent—tracked outward from noble households to the houses of increasingly prosperous *civis de populo* families, to artisan households, and even to the very modest dwellings of former servants and slaves.

An internal connective tissue of blood and descent, quite apart from formal ties of community life, was rendered unusually potent because Ragusa was a remote town and remained small in numbers. Benedetto Cotrugli understood this dimension of local society thoroughly. Since he was prone to divide all his many topics into four categories in the *Perfect Merchant,* as a matter of course he placed descendants into four *modi* for his reader's instruction. First he listed legitimate offspring born in wedlock. Next, significantly, in a deviation from the Italian tradition of giving second place to those with legal claims on the family, Cotrugli mentioned offspring born out of wedlock—*de soluti et de soluta,* an abbreviated phrase from Roman law signifying that the parents were free to marry when that child was born but for their own reasons had not done so. By canon law the children of such unions qualified for future legitimation. Only third did he place adopted offspring or children, like wards, for whom one assumed care by legal acts. In his last category he placed bastards, that is, offspring of unlawful unions such as adultery or incest.[1] His careful distinctions among those born out of wedlock resonated strongly within an elite bounded by the demand to wed strictly among a finite set of lineages. Cotrugli reminded them here that prescriptions of canon law framed a much larger social space for marriage than local custom. As a matter of fact, noble citizens had already moved assuredly into that space between local marrying custom and canon law, creating secondary households of illegitimate lines endowed with wealth and their lineage names—in short, many of the advantages enjoyed by their noble kin save noble status, coats of arms, and the right to sit in the Great Council. Perhaps this occurred at Ragusa, as Georges Duby has claimed it did elsewhere, from the drive of powerful men to perpetuate their blood lines, but there were a host of other practical reasons for acknowledging and supporting some illegitimate offspring in a community like Ragusa, with its strict practice of endogamy.[2] They will be considered in this chapter. By Cotrugli's generation, it would seem, noble Ragusan citizens had embarked on a social experiment wherein they practiced a religiously and socially sanctioned monogamy accompanied by an unusually frank form of polygyny.[3] Since *civis de populo* families required no special act of incorporation by the Small Council if they were acknowledged offspring of noblemen, these new urban families in a sense formed an outer circle around the nobility, filling many of the roles that fell to an industrious bourgeoisie in other towns.

Benedetto Cotrugli had reason to understand this social wrinkle in all its complexity because his own ancestors were related to the noble circle through the link of acknowledged illegitimate offspring. In 1383 his Montenegrin ancestors, residents from Catar (Kotor), had been offered non-noble citizenship by the Ragusan Small Council; the entire Cotrugli family was tendered the grant of the condition that they all take up residence in Ragusa. The Cotrugli and their descendants became *cives de populo* by this act, eligible for the benefits and rights of citizenship short of enfranchisement and seats on the Great Council.[4] They were also eligible for certain non-noble civic offices: Cotrugli himself served in the critical post of consul in Naples, where he found time to compose his merchant manual.[5] As this immigrant family prospered by tying their fortunes to Ragusa, they soon found it necessary to find marriage partners for their own children. The best matches available to them lay with acknowledged illegitimate families bearing noble names. The Cotruglis married one daughter to the prosperous son of the noble Givche Dersa. Membership in the Great Council eluded Dersa's son because his mother, a widow, was not a noblewoman. This natural son had come up short before the hard realization that the noble circle excluded him from Great Council as ineligible on grounds of his illegitimacy, which they easily accomplished since tradition so perfectly enforced noble mothers' right to determine their sons' status. Another of the immigrant Cotrugli married into the clan of the Goce *de populo,* a branch of that lineage prosperous and large on the scale of their noble cousins, yet ineligible to marry with them because it was an illegitimate line. Both these proud *civis de populo* lineages had little choice but to wed with the "new families" of the expanding fourteenth-century town like the Cotrugli. Acknowledged children found their marriage partners among foreign traders, Italians who had moved to Ragusa and accepted residence status, or skilled artisans. It comes as no surprise that they preferred marriages to others who, like them, bore names of noble houses.

Cotrugli did not question the fact that in a properly arranged society the rights of offspring extended beyond rights afforded to legitimate heirs, and he saw those rights as integral to family interests understood in their broadest sense. He expressed no misgivings about the morality of a man fathering two families, and he echoed local sentiment when he viewed as proper the fair provision for acknowledged illegitimate offspring. But if his morality echoed that of his day, its utility to noble families still remains noteworthy, even exceptional, as it worked out in Ragusa.

Behind his acceptance of prosperous illegitimate descent lines whose fathers were noble but whose mothers were not (and it was these persons and their descendants who inhabited a second or outer circle around the core of the nobility at Ragusa) stood generations of legacies to illegitimate heirs who had themselves intermarried, grown prosperous, and carved out their own social space within the community. The *Liber Statutorum* carefully delineated the rights of illegitimate offspring in 1272, but it was not this law, nor canon law, that prescribed the web of ties to the nobility devised over the next two centuries. The *Liber Statutorum* specified very clearly that a father might provide for illegitimate heirs in his will with modest bequests; in no way should these challenge the right of legitimate heirs, whether direct or adoptive.[6]

As for the ecclesiastical laws of marriage, Ragusans were seldom disturbed by probing into their behavior any more than they were bothered by priestly prying for incest violations. The church was remarkably tolerant of social mores in this Christian outpost set up against the land of the infidel Turks. (See discussion later in this chapter.) The pope spared the town much of the surveillance lavished on the marriages and morals of the powerful in more western-lying lands, at least through the critical decades of the fourteenth century. Often assisted by their noble kin, Ragusan fathers who sired illegitimate children devised complex programs for securing those children's futures—and future loyalty. In time, these bonds created a circle of families who encountered far more latitude in arranging their own marriage alliances than the noble circle itself. That is to say, their exogamous marriages partially compensated for the nobility's own strict endogamy by enlarging the possible framework of the advantageous family alliances Ragusa's trading community could forge.

On a less generous plane, when noble houses were served by chattel slaves, liaisons between noble sons and *ancillae* were also acknowledged by bequests, manumissions of the mother and her offspring, and outright gifts of money. Following Roman law precedent, the offspring from these liaisons were unfree until manumitted, but if the father was unencumbered by marriage, the mother's servile status did not prevent the parents from qualifying *de soluti et de soluta*.[7] Once freed, the offspring of such a union found little opprobrium attached to their condition. They could inherit, learn a trade, even take their father's name; moreover, their ties to a noble household enhanced their future chances of marrying. Pasque de Goce had an illegitimate child from a union with a household slave, and his noble mother, rather than he, left that child a bequest in her will.[8] Illegitimate offspring who were acknowledged and manumitted received even greater social acceptance when they were the sole heirs of an otherwise childless nobleman. In fact, those children born to noble youth, noble lifelong bachelors, and noble churchmen tended to gain the most advantageous settlements from their noble fathers. Numerous illegitimate offspring who were recognized and supported may be traced in charters in the decades while slavery was still practiced.

Other circumstances might also encourage the recognition of children born out of wedlock.[9] Some were the favored children of a second household in the interior at a trading center; a whole range of future options opened up for such children. One son of a noble trader and a local woman of the interior was trained as a craftsman and remained where he was born. Two natural daughters received cash dowries, just as if they were towns-women, and were married off to traders: one of those traders was specifi-cally identified as a Bosnian merchant, clearly a man of local standing. An illegitimate son of a slave owned by Peter de Mence and presumably fathered by him was wed to the free daughter of a family from the interior, and that family provided a modest dowry to seal the match.[10] From the point of view of a family outside the territorial jurisdiction of Ragusa, an illegitimate son of a slave was sufficiently attractive as a marriage partner to win their daughter with a dowry, provided, of course, that he had some future expectations for support from a noble father who would continue to acknowledge him. In other instances, nobly acknowledged children of servants and slaves married in town and settled there, which may mark the pinnacle of success to which illegitimate offspring of unions with slaves or servants might aspire. The noble household remained the primary source of opportunity for these illegitimate offspring and, possibly, the source of further patronage.[11]

    In the thirteenth century, it had been a simple act of piety to free all slaves in one's will. Pasqua de Volcassio freed all hers in her last will and gave them the expected one *hyperperus* a year to provide for their futures.[12] The sum would allow a servant a scant living or a minimum dowry. Maria, wife of Leucii Nichole, freed not only her house slave but one she had owned who had run away.[13] The noble ecclesiastic Savini Gataldi, founder of St. Savini de Dasa, freed all his *servi* and *ancillae* in his will with their clothes, belongings, and one *hyperperus* each.[14]

    Still, slavery encumbered the fluid working of a system of rewards and benefits to favored servants and their illegitimate offspring. The contract labor system that replaced it cast fewer legal impediments in the paths of noble family members who were inclined to keep servants and their off-spring within their definition of kin and descendants. An early fourteenth-century will mentioned a contract servant who was freed from service and given five *hyperperi* under the condition that she marry.[15] Another noble-woman more deviously paid a groom ten *hyperperi* directly if he would marry her servant.[16] In the days when contract workers could be dismissed after their term of work with no further consideration and householders no longer had a responsibility to see to their servants' old age, rewards of supporting gifts had the effect of sponsoring new working-class families in town. As the century progressed, gifts in wills for household servants became even more handsome endowments.

Dowries Provided *Famulae* by Ragusan Householders.[17]

| Date | Servant | Spouse | Amount |
|------|---------|--------|--------|
| 1348 | Boni, *famula* Michael de Bincola | Dobre | 30 *hyperperi* |
| 1348 | Tuerdive, *famula* Crize de Beho | Rusin | 70 *hyperperi** |
| 1348 | Budra, *famula* | Draso, famulus | 20 *hyperperi* |
| 1348 | Ullizza, *famula* Rade Volcassio | Drupse | house of wood |
| 1380 | Miloslava, *famula* | Obrada | 50 *hyperperi** |
| 1386 | Dobra, *famula* Mathie Georgio | Milas Obromich | 50 *hyperperi** |
| 1386 | Dichna, *famula* Domina Pana Abbatissa St. Clara | Nicolas | 60 *hyperperi* |
| 1394 | Climpna, *famula* Maroe Sorgo | Petchus | 20 *hyperperi* |
| 1394 | Perussa, *famula* Janius Sorgo | Michoe Tuarnich | 40 *hyperperi* |

*An award of gold or jewelry accompanied the cash award

The *famula* or domestic servants entering marriage with bequests greater than twenty *hyperperi* had begun their ascent into the ranks of wage-earning householders, the petty bourgeoisie. Since grain tickets to draw from the *rupe* were based on residence in town, these servants secured the right to draw on urban resources through the patronage these legacies represented. Sponsorship to live in town provided a key to all further resources. Increases in the size of bequests to children born to servant women and noble fathers tell the same story. The noble Andreas de Sorgo provided his natural daughter Marcussa with a dowry of forty *hyperperi*;[18] Vloachus de Palmota gave his illegitimate daughter Rade a very generous three hundred-*hyperperi* dowry in 1348, a considerably firmer boost up the social ladder.[19] In 1380, Radula, a daughter of noble Mathias de Georgio, received two hundred *hyperperi*, and in 1386 Rigussa, daughter of Andreas de Babalio, received one hundred seventy *hyperperi*.[20] In 1393, Radoslava received one hundred *hyperperi* in dowry from her noble father, Pervulo de Gondola, and married Juecho, the pelter.[21] Dowry increase was not as consistent for illegitimate daughters as for noble ones through the century because so many conditions applied here—whether the young women or their mothers continued to live in the noble household or receive support, how comely they were, how well they pleased—but gifts still rose substantially. These handsome dowries far outshone those bequests left to single *famulae;* a servant might easily conclude that producing a child while serving a noble household would serve her and hers far better than waiting until the death of a mistress or master in hopes of receiving a small legacy.

Servant girls from the countryside did not need long to acquaint themselves with the best strategies to secure a future as a Ragusan resident. A liaison out of wedlock was attractive if the man acknowledged any resulting children. But the community did not tolerate abandoned children or, for that matter, any sexual liaison that might result in the abandoning or orphaning of dependent children. A servant girl would also soon learn that men's sexual assaults on servile women were reported and punished in town, even if a servant girl was assaulted or raped by a noble citizen. And, if servants did not report crimes committed against them, their masters reported in their place. The noble councillor Marino Ranina brought charges of assault against his fellow noble, Marino de Getaldi. In anger, Ranina accused Getaldi of assaulting two of his servant girls when they were working in his vineyard outside the town.[22] Draysa, a servant girl, brought her own charge against a young nobleman, Mathias de Georgio, accusing him of a rape committed at night just inside the town gates.[23] Velna, the servant of a noblewoman, complained that she had been attacked in the mountainous territory of Jonchetta.[24] Even the remoteness of the site did not deter her from seeking justice in the town. Servile women evidently expected the same protection in public places as the free women of the town.

If this appears at first inconsistent with the latitude permitted noblemen to gain sexual access to serving girls housed in their own noble establishments, it is an inconsistency easily explained. The morality of the household and of public places followed separate codes because households readily assumed responsibility for their illegitimate offspring, which was in truth all the polity demanded. Sexual assaults on the streets brought reprisal not because a servant girl necessarily held a respected position in the community but in order to discourage any sexual union for which the man did not accept his responsibility. Ragusans did not outrun the limits of this expedient solution until the community developed a more diverse social complexion in the late fifteenth century. Not until then did the anonymity of an orphanage provided at the expense of the commune excuse men of the town from responsibility for their out-of-wedlock offspring. Situated between the street of the goldsmiths and the *platea*, Ragusa's orphanage offered a double-doored passage near its street entrance where newborns could be left anonymously. Until that time, and even after in numerous cases, households provided for their own.

Serving women who had been attached to noble households by service or birth found husbands with reasonably bright prospects in the decades of urban expansion. Earlier, in the late thirteenth century, manumitted slaves had either left town or married each other and set up housekeeping in the shadow of a noble household. They might not have gained even this right on a one-*hyperperus* bequest, which meant they never left the confines of a great noble household over a lifetime. In the fourteenth century, by contrast, certain contract servants transformed themselves into wage earners once they had learned a skill and completed their terms of contract, although the least favored still never rose above the level of household dependents.

A few generous awards to *famulae,* and the more handsome dowries provided daughters born to servants by noble fathers, opened new prospects of marriage and social mobility for the fortunate few. They married up, and occasionally a family gained a style of life rivaling that of the nobility itself.[25]

This was possible because the prosperity of the fourteenth century brought increased diversity in manufactures and trades into the community, which in turn increased the need for skilled artisans. What had begun as a trickle of immigrant workers in the early part of the century increased substantially in the latter decades. Losses of working men to the plague accounted for some of this new migration, but a greater diversity of trades practiced in town, and the need to provision those trades, brought others.

From 1351 to 1399, the Ragusan Council gave 120 grants to immigrants of *civis de populo* status.[26] Sometimes conditional clauses were appended to the grants. The most frequent stipulation demanded that the person granted citizenship become a permanent resident of the community and that he transfer his entire family to Ragusa, as the Small Council had required of the immigrant Cotrugli. Of these extant 120 grants, eleven specifically stated this demand. For the most part then, residence grants were offered to traders or artisans whose special skill won them the council's interest. The council could, and did, take the time to screen immigrant *cives de populo* for suitability, and the criteria were a composite of considerations in which the skills figured but compliant behavior, steadiness, responsibility, and possibly the suitability of the migrant's heirs, figured as well.

The other 109 grants designated only individuals; they went to bachelors, although ten grants provided rights for men who were related as father and adult sons or brothers—men who most likely worked in business together and may have been accompanied by women of their family. These men were selected by the noble citizenry out of the stream of skilled artisans and businessmen who passed through the town in their search to build private fortunes. The few chosen were allowed to make a commitment to the community, that is, to settle in town. In certain instances, men assured civil authorities that they would pursue their current occupations once they lived in the community. In all ways, they came to inhabit a special category of chosen persons: they provided services and skills in a few highly selective areas of production, and they settled in neighborhoods dominated by the nobility's great commercial households. Most important perhaps, they or their children wed the former servants or the illegitimate issue of noble houses as the most eligible single women the community offered, after which new immigrant working class households slid easily into the orbits of the great commercial establishments. While the husband's link to the merchant aristocracy lay in his selection by the council, his Ragusan bride's eligibility likely rested on her wealth stemming at some remove from a noble master or mistress. Former household servants, once dowered, wed artisans; acknowledged illegitimate daughters wed foreign merchants who had become residents or *cives de populo* in an emerging gradation of status based as much upon the strength of the link to noble householders' wealth and patronage as on a man's occupation.

Lorino Rici, a Florentine merchant who had married, settled, and raised a family in Ragusa, opened marriage negotiations with the noble Marino Dersa when his own daughter reached marriageable age. Marino Dersa had an illegitimate son on whom he lavished considerable attention and wealth. Wedding this son-out-of-wedlock to his daughter was a wise strategy for a wealthy *civis de populo* merchant like Rici, for he did business daily with the aristocracy, lived on scale similar to theirs, but was cut out of the opportunity to marry into their legitimate families because of the Ragusan code of strict endogamy.[27]

As a matter of fact, Lorino Rici de Flora was one of the most prominent of the new fourteenth-century non-noble merchants who had settled in town. He had begun life as a young trader sent out from his native city of Florence to make his fortune, which he quickly did by attaching himself to resident Florentines with established trading networks in Dalmatia and points east. Lorino Rici had the good fortune to work with that genial, ever-popular Bencius del Buono de Flora, who tickled his Ragusan hosts with his good humor and deft hand at easing Ragusan silver and gold into the most lucrative pathways of international trade (see Chapter 7). Every important Florentine merchant banking company operating on the eastern shore of the Adriatic had business of one sort or another with these two outgoing men.[28] In enterprising fashion, they staffed the courier route across the Balkans to Constantinople, and they speculated in grain transport, issued letters of exchange to Venice, and transported precious metals to the Venetian marketplace.[29] On a wave of good will, Lorino Rici, like Bencius before him, was granted first the status of *habitator,* then offered citizenship. Unlike Bencius del Buono, whose ambition was set on a triumphal return to Florence after he had grown sufficiently rich, Rici settled for non-noble Ragusan citizenship perhaps because he had fallen in love with a local girl and wished to contract a marriage in Ragusa. But when Rici married his native Ragusan bride and accepted the proffered citizenship, he gave up the geographic and social mobility, and ambitions, that still lay open to his more senior business partner, whose own companion in town was a slave girl who bore him a son out of wedlock.[30] And, by settling in town, Rici destined his own offspring to the dubious future of marrying outside the highest levels of society within which he and Bencius traveled comfortably. Thus while he could afford to dower his daughter Nicoletta at the handsome level of one thousand *hyperperi* in 1382, she wed outside the *prijateljstvo.* Although members of the noble circle clearly intended to maintain the closest ties with Rici, they might do so only through family marriage alliances with one of the illegitimate lines descending from the nobility.

Lorino Rici's own children, the children of the small community of wealthy immigrant merchants and of communal salaried officials, and illegitimate heirs of noble families who had been acknowledged and were major legatees in their fathers' wills, came to form a new circle closely paralleling the nobility in prosperity and business success. They were not invited into the Great Council (until 1667 and the great earthquake), nor were they chosen as marriage partners by members of the noble circle, which severely curtailed their choices of suitably affluent partners in such a small community. They might inherit from the nobility, they increasingly lived on a scale commensurate with the nobility, they often shared with them the most venerable of noble names, but they could not bear noble coats of arms nor enter council.

How simple it would be to read conscious intent into this creation, through the link of descent, of an affluent circle of non-noble citizens outside the inner one. In fact, noble Ragusans did not father illegitimate children with the conscious purpose of tying valued business associates to their noble houses. This outer circle was a haphazard creation, the sum of expedient solutions, which in true Ragusan fashion satisfied simultaneously the promptings of conscience, ties of affection, and hard business sense. Noblemen who were childless widowers or noble bachelors who could not find a suitable match among the much-marrying *prijateljstvo* brought to their out-of-wedlock families the same responsible attitudes that their noble peers brought to their noble families. A nobleman stationed in the interior who fathered a "second family," whom he rarely visited, might treat his offspring less generously than his counterpart with no competing family ties who fathered a natural child in town.[31] A nobleman in orders, whose servant bore him illegitimate issue, might be a bit more generous to his offspring than any of his peers. And in keeping with canon law, if both the noble father and non-noble mother were free to marry in the eyes of the church (*de soluti et de soluta*), the heir's birth was not considered the same as the outcome of an adulterous union but rather the product of a union of free, consenting partners. Generally these children fared best. Although the noble *prijateljstvo* was sufficiently powerful to exclude the issue of such liaisons from their own circle, they lacked the power and, perhaps, the desire, to disinherit these children if the father was inclined to acknowledge them. Ragusans merely followed conventional morality. Their non-noble heirs and the "new men" brought to town as business partners, a group allowed to prosper as the wealth of the nobility increased, enjoyed greater freedom and wed less restrictively. Thus they expanded the community's potential range of business alliances and smoothed the community's entry into the heady world of family alliances in the interests of long-distance trade and high finance.

So marriage among the *civis de populo* families took on a consequence almost as great as marriage among those within the noble circle. Dowries awarded by non-noble families reflected a care and concern as great as that lavished on noble brides, and the cash and jewels challenged noble gifts. In the fifteenth century, the marital assigns awarded to daughters who bore noble names but were not themselves noble increased significantly even while they continued to reflect important gradations of social status and a range of wealth and marital expectations. By the late fourteenth century, the best dowered of these women were already the legitimate children and grandchildren of *civis de populo* families derived two or more generations back from a noble line. An occasional large dowry awarded among them suggests that certain affluent *civis de populo* families had amassed great trading fortunes in partnership with their noble cousins. But other women led more modest lives measured by the dowries provided for them. Taken together these women bearing the great noble names, and their grooms, inhabited the entire spectrum of Ragusan society from the level of the noble circle itself down to the artisanal level, as the following table indicates.

Fifteenth-Century Dowries for Non-Noble Daughters[32] with Noble Lineage Names.

| Date | Dowered daughter | Spouse | Amount of dowry |
|---|---|---|---|
| 1418 | Clara de Goce | Georgius Luchacich | 150 *hyperperi* |
| 1424 | Pasqua, f. Pauluscus de Bonda | Nicola | 150 *hyperperi*\* |
| 1425 | Ancula, f. Andreas de Sorgo | Nicola, f. nat. Thoma de Spalato | 222 *hyperperi* |
| 1433 | Mirussa, f. Luce de Caboga | Martolus Davisini | 1,100 *hyperperi*\* |
| 1433 | Anusla, f. Luce de Caboga | Antonius | 1,100 *hyperperi*\* |
| 1434 | Lucia, f. Michael de Sorgo | Petar, f. Laurencius de Sorgo | 500 *hyperperi* |
| 1435 | Radula, f. Ruschi de Poca | Pasque, f. Clemens de Bodacia | 450 *hyperperi*\* |
| 1436 | Slaussa, f. Johannes de Georgio | Givchus, *manipulus murator* | 20 *hyperperi*\* |
| 1438 | Floria, f. Luce de Caboga | Blassius de Voldopia | 1,100 *hyperperi*\* |
| 1439 | Anusla, f. Luce de Caboga | Jacobus de Radulno | 2,500 *hyperperi*\* |
| 1462 | Parile, f. Rosini de Volcigno | Marinus, f. Pasque de Goce | 680 *hyperperi*\* |
| 1462 | Nicoletta, f. Martolus de Goce | Nicolaus, f. Johannes | 1,000 *hyperperi*\* |

Italics indicate a name shared with a noble lineage.
\*Indicates a gift of gold, silver, or jewelry accompanying the cash award.

Slaussa, illegitimate daughter of Johannes de Georgio, had some claim on her father and his noble household, but as the child of the servant it gave her merely the opportunity to wed a stonemason; her future in the community would be as the wife of an artisan with restricted expectations of wealth and status. Pasqua de Goce, on the other hand, was born a generation away from her noble antecedents because her father was the bastard son of the noble Ilco de Goce who had produced no legitimate issue with his wife, Boni de Mence, so he treated his illegitimate son generously. Pasqua, and others dowered at more than one hundred *hyperperi* with some gold and jewels for display, inhabited a higher rank than Slaussa, qualifying for marriage among the more prosperous *civis de populo* families. By contrast, the three daughters of Luce de Caboga (Anusla appears twice since she married twice in six years) inhabited the highest rank of non-noble families. Actually the prosperous but non-noble Luce de Caboga provided dowries for six daughters out of his estate, and generous bequests for his son as well. Luce, a son of his father's late years, had a legitimate half-brother, nevertheless his father acknowledged and supported him. To all appearances he was the bright ambitious son his father would have wished to follow him into the Great Council, but that was not to be. Nevertheless, Luce prospered on a scale to make his noble half-brother envious, and he spent a lifetime in trade in partnership with noble merchants. In turn, the dowries he provided for his own daughters were very generous. Anusla, who added to hers through inheriting from a first husband, possessed a dowry beyond the capacity of all but the most affluent among her cousins within the noble circle. Anusla's second dowry was in truth illegal—by offering it she defied the 1,600 *hyperperi* limit set by sumptuary law in 1423. In the highly visible act of generously dowrying his offspring, Caboga mounted a challenge of sorts to the *prijateljstvo*. Such a defiant gesture of conspicuous display was rarely seen among the "new families" of the *cives de populo,* but on occasion a family like the non-noble but prosperous Caboga showed the nobility that they could match or better their style.

Regardless of the social rung on which these new families found themselves, whether they were artisan wage earners or *cives de populo,* they acknowledged their debt to noble houses. Tales of business successes, advantages in making marriage alliances, and securing official posts related back in one way or another to the patronage of the nobility. If Luce de Caboga's daughter outdid noble women in the splendor of her second dowry, the challenge to noble hegemony was muted. In most instances, *civis de populo* families deferred to the noble circle from whom those favors flowed. They knew their place. The she-goat may dissemble but the horns will tell, an old Dalmatian maxim scornfully stated.[33] Constant reminders reached Anusla and her sisters that they were just such nanny goats unable to mix with the purebred lines of noble Ragusan daughters. The nobility kept up their own impenetrable social barrier against the *cives de populo,* bestowing generous favors on them but refusing marriage with their daughters and sons. Nothing—wealth, display in the streets, a grand household or dowry—broke in on these closed ranks.

The numbers of new, affluent *civis de populo* families never overwhelmed the noble circle by sheer size, so in a sense this group never achieved the critical mass to sustain an all-out challenge to noble prerogative. By the fifteenth century, centuries after the church had gone to some trouble to drive home the message in western Europe, both marrying circles warned that their marriages might defy incest restrictions in canon law, and some sought dispensation from the pope if their marriages violated the law.[34] Ironically, the non-noble often stood at more risk than the noble, because of their small numbers and because the marriages of their own noble ancestors restricted their current choices. Certain ancient noble lines, by contrast, had existed so long, were so cognizant of their lines of descent, and now contained so many branches, that when noble persons bearing the same name married—Sorgo to Sorgo for example—their union was more likely to pass examination than many a *civis de populo* match. The noble Sorgo intermarrying were more immune from violation, since two scions of that noble line might be related only through a remote thirteenth-century common forebear. So the links within non-noble branches of old lineages, complicated by the remarriage of parents or grandparents, and god-parentage, actually held more potential for producing incest violations. By the fifteenth century, both noble and non-noble groups carefully consulted genealogies as part of premarital negotiations.[35] The most prudent learned to choose close relatives as godparents for their children. *Civis de populo* families wisely chose members of the nobility as godparents for their children, that is, persons whose direct descendants were not available to them as marriage partners.[36]

*Civis de populo* youth and their dowered sisters, finding restricted opportunity to wed in town, were likely to marry outsiders or immigrants, or they married outside the town proper. In the villages on the coast or on the islands under Ragusan jurisdiction, *civis de populo* families found attractive marriage partners. These communities, many blessed with the productive combination of ploughed fields, vineyards, orchards, market gardens, fishing fleets, and seagoing inhabitants, grew and prospered. As Ragusa launched long-distance fleets, town traders drew increasingly on those from outside the city walls to man ships, offering opportunity to rise to captain and build private fortunes. Here lay an opportunity to create an increasingly heterogeneous non-noble class loyal to the republic.

But the Ragusan *cives de populo* failed to overwhelm the nobility. Geographically diffuse, less concentrated within the walled town, and sometimes more tightly bound to the nobility than to each other by descent and inheritance, *civis de populo* families remained for the most part a politically enfeebled group.

## Political Identity

*Cives de populo* could join together in fraternal organizations, however. In 1349, the confraternity of St. Anthony was founded; only non-noble merchants were eligible for membership. Soon after, the confraternity of St. Lazarus was established, and in time the Antonini came to be known as the "old merchants" and the Lazarini as the "new." The most powerful members of both confraternities were the merchants, traders, and sea captains of the island towns and the small communities on the coast who built their fortunes on sea trade. One Antonini, Zore Bocza (Bokšić) amassed a fortune on a level with the greatest noble fortunes of the fourteenth century and did so pursuing the inland trade. On the strength of his virtual monopoly of commerce with Bosnia, the ban made him *protovestiar*, and at the end of his life he left a substantial fortune of ten thousand ducats in his will.[37] Nevertheless, his enormous success did not translate into enhanced political power in town for himself or for his confraternity. Neither the Antonini nor the Lazarini directly challenged the noble citizenry of Ragusa or their councils of state; indeed, their members patriotically accepted assignments from the senate or Great Council when so honored. Confraternities composed of affluent merchants from the Astarea or the islands developed a stronger base of political power. The confraternity of St. Ivan, from the Primorje (coast), played an active role in the government of its local region, but the Antonini and Lazarini, concentrated in the town proper, understood their roles in economic rather than in political terms.[38]

The lack of direct challenge to the prerogatives of the noble citizenry has remained a puzzling question in the historiography of the community. The social composition of the *civis de populo* families, who had the wealth to mount a direct challenge to aristocratic rule but neither the numbers nor apparently the will to do so, goes some distance toward explaining this puzzle. As a result, the nobility created an alternative to a "closing" of their ranks quite unlike the Venetian *serrata* of the 1290s, which closed noble ranks against an upwardly mobile Venetian bourgeoisie. In Ragusa, endogamy sufficed to preserve the solidarity of the noble class. An unwritten code of behavior maintained through private means rather than council's statutory acts underlay political cohesion.

In the fourteenth century, when closure of a sort occurred for the patriciate, that is, by the political acts of the Great Council, it took the curious form of the exclusion of its own members (*nobilis vir*) from certain activities: *fecit becarrias* (butchering) stood as the first recorded prohibition. By explicitly excluding their own numbers from some occupations, the Great Council acknowledged a precise political or legal demarcation between the patriciate and other townsmen. The first of these statutes was passed in 1325, and others followed over the next two decades; together these measures amounted to a statutory definition of aristocratic status.[39]

This initiative prompted an expedient bookkeeping device of listing noble men and their antecedents, Miodrag Petrovich asserts.[40] This remained only an implicit "closing" however, since no direct challenge to the group's prerogatives had been mounted that might have forced a more precise definition of who sat by law in Great Council and by what criteria. Because the Great Council also enacted specific measures that defined a role for the *cives de populo* by opening some political functions to them and by providing them continuing rights within a variety of occupations, closing proceeded along a directly opposite course from that which had occurred earlier at Venice.[41]

The diametrically opposed paths by which a "closing" occurred, that is, the protective Venetian closing of patrician ranks as opposed to this public assertion of limits on patrician behavior at Ragusa, continued to be made manifest by contrasting developments over the course of the subsequent century. While noble Venetians received political recognition of their status and entitlements about 1300, it took another century for noble families to separate themselves from the more affluent bourgeoisie in regard to their political identity and, more significantly, their marriages. A century passed before aristocratic families married on an exclusive basis, according to the work of Stanley Chojnacki.[42] While others have argued a more traditional line, that the *serrata* was largely accomplished by about 1300, both sides concur that Venetians enacted legislation to protect their privileges, and thus constituted themselves an identifiable patrician class safeguarded from incursions from upcoming bourgeois families.[43] Ragusans signaled their patrician status on wholly different grounds that did not include drawing away from the bourgeoisie in the course of the fourteenth century.

As a matter of fact, certain civic offices were opened to men of Ragusan *civis de populo* families to make room for their political participation. The most important was that of consul in a foreign port, but members of prosperous non-noble trading families soon assumed more general diplomatic responsibilities. These posts grew in importance as Ragusa's overseas commerce increased, and as that happened leading *civis de populo* families came to resemble the nobility, augmenting their limited numbers, following the same careers, and representing their community abroad in the best possible light.[44] Under the press of commercial expansion, the wealthy outer circle of families held an increasingly wide variety of offices in which they served as faithfully and responsibly as any noble citizen might.

However, the Ragusan chronicles told a very different story about the social composition of the community. The sixteenth-century *Anonymous Chronicle,* which related the early history of the community, stated that in very early times a division had been made among the people of the town. The richest of the inhabitants were chosen as governors, and each of the families of these governors chose a patron saint. When more people came to join the urban ranks, further division had been made between nobles and their servants. The Great Council, for convenience, divided the people into three groups: nobles or gentlemen, townsmen, and servants. The chronicle emphasized that the division was received peacefully, and that non-noble townsmen and servants acquiesced in the rectitude of the choices.[45] Sixteenth-century patricians found this narration about their elevation convincing, and it became accepted wisdom, finding echoes in other later histories. But on the patriciate's establishment of a place, a job, and a status for the non-noble inhabitant of the commune, the chronicles are silent. No medieval narrative tradition recorded the ways in which council made conscious and informed decisions when they offered immigrants residence in the community or the inheritable right of non-noble citizenship to newcomers.

Yet as Ragusa prospered, nobles lived in contact with their former servants and townspeople, with whom they shared their proud names. If Ragusans proved to be a tractable lot it was not, as the *Anonymous Chronicle* observed, that they had historically assented to the principle of rule by their betters, but rather that their own status was so completely derived from the will of the *prijateljstvo* that to challenge their authority was practically unthinkable.

## Cost of Living

There were, on the other hand, substantial rewards for people who grasped the chance to live and work in Ragusa. A prudent course, open to all regardless of social rank, lay in seizing the abundant economic opportunities for getting rich in Ragusa, investing incomes, or by some other means taking advantage of the increasing differential between wages and the cost of living in this prosperous community. This chance to get rich assured the loyalty of many persons who were content to let the nobility rule as long as they prospered.

At Ragusa daily expenses were kept in bounds; in fact, the cost of living was low by urban standards. Stated in terms of what statute law reckoned to be a reasonable living allowance, a single person could live on twelve *hyperperi* a year in 1272 (see Chapter 5). One hundred years later, that cost had risen but twelve *hyperperi* could still apparently feed one person for a year. In 1378, the senate ordered three *hyperperi* to feed a small family (two or three persons) on a month's voyage across the Adriatic. By municipal regulation, the cost of a shipboard diet was kept in line with prices in the town, so it may be assumed that a small family could be fed on about three *hyperperi* a month or thirty-six *hyperperi* a year.[46] A barber, whom the commune employed at eighty *hyperperi* in wages a year, would then feed a small family on less than half his wage.[47] A physician earning one thousand *hyperperi* would allocate less than 1/20 of his wage to food for a small family.[48] Coupled with equally inexpensive housing in the new *sexteria* of the community (thirty to fifty *hyperperi* for modest quarters), even a barber was likely to be left with discretionary income after providing food and lodging for his family, while a physician could accumulate substantial savings for investment after paying for living expenses.

The grain staple supervised by the venerable *massarii bladorum* was the lynchpin in the communal provisioning system. From earliest times, grain had been imported to Ragusa; the community never outgrew the means to feed itself from the lands under its jurisdiction, because those lands had never adequately sustained the urban population. But overseas grain shipments from Apulia and Sicily sufficed to feed the walled town for centuries, at least through the late thirteenth century. It is an indication of how well population growth in the community was kept in bounds that these supplies from grain-producing areas such as Sicily, a short sea journey away, continued to suffice even through many years in the fourteenth century.[49] Grain from Levantine sources began to augment this supply during the decades of expansion, but Ragusa became dependent on Levantine grain only in the very last years of the century.

By long tradition, grain purchased abroad was stored and distributed in town under communal supervision with the office of the *massarii bladorum,* one of the most important posts balloted in the Great Council. Low-risk capital ventures such as the capital in estates of orphans and the promised or awarded dowries of noble and *civis de populo* women were frequently invested in the grain office; over the years wise management gained that office a reputation for steady return while grain prices set in town exhibited an impressive stability from 1300 onward. In January 1304, one *ster* of grain cost sixteen *grossi* (one and one-third *hyperperi*).[50] The price ranged between sixteen and twenty-four *grossi* a *ster* until mid-century, and then with the Black Plague it rose precipitously but soon fell back again. A bit earlier in the time of famine after the disastrous Mediterranean harvests of 1319, the grain office noted in its minutes that it could and would sell its stored supplies of grain to the community at a loss.[51] The office had the financial stability to take this loss and cushion the town's inhabitants from the worst of the disaster. In the second half of the fourteenth century, when grain purchases abroad increased in volume, prices fluctuated between twenty-four and forty-five *grossi* a *ster* with the most frequent range between twenty-four and thirty-six *grossi*.[52]

Against this doubling in price over the course of the century, the salary earned by a textile worker had quadrupled under the stimulation of increased production for export.[53] Like these textile workers' wages, most other urban wages were rising. The *protomagister arsenatus,* chief of the arsenal, was hired from Venice for a salary of 100 *hyperperi* in 1333, 160 *hyperperi* in 1347, and 240 *hyperperi* in 1357.[54] Before the Black Plague, salaries paid to surgeons rose from 100 *hyperperi* (even less in some cases) to over 200 *hyperperi,* and they continued to rise through the rest of the century. In the early fourteenth century, physicians were paid only slightly higher salaries than surgeons, but salaries reached 1,000 *hyperperi* for some of those specially recruited "wise and famous" physicians brought to town in the last decades of the century, far outrunning what any surgeon could earn.[55] Salaries and wages in all occupations increased, sometimes quadrupling, while the price of grain set by the commune only doubled.

The ancient system of provisioning of grain set the norm for food-stuffs. Councils regulated the price of wine in the community.[56] Cheese was subject to price limits.[57] Prices for perishable foodstuffs brought to town from the Astarea by small-time producers and from more remote locations by farmers and gardeners were monitored and regulated in clear favor to the town-dwelling consumer. The sale of meat within town marketplaces was monitored with particular care. The price set for mutton, a traditional source of red meat in the diet of the West Balkan region, suggests retail prices were maintained at an artificially low level. Like prices for grain, the price for mutton little more than doubled during the century, while urban demand for the product increased sharply.[58] Townsmen paid only a few pennies, or *follari,* for fresh supplies of meat, so almost anyone living in town could afford to buy it.

Set Market Prices for Meat.

| 1302 | carnes de montono castrato | follaros 3 pro libro |
|------|-----------------------------|----------------------|
| 1303 | carnes de castrato | follaros 5 pro libro |
| 1357 | carnes castratine | follaros 6 pro libro |
| 1363 | carnes castratine | follaros 6 pro libro |
| 1364 | carnes mutonine castrate | follaros 7 pro libro |
| 1367 | carnes castratine | follaros 6 pro libro |
| 1367 | libra carnium mutolinarum castratinarum | follaros 8 pro libro |

12 follari = 1 grosso
12 grossi = 1 hyperperus

Price-setting and official surveillance of town marketplaces secured food at artificially low prices, but the Balkans did not undergo the inflation in prices for foodstuffs that occurred in western Europe. A traveler to Serbia noted that huge amounts of fish could be bought for a few thaler as late as the sixteenth century. Here, as in procuring servants, the town dictated terms to the countryside because so few other urban centers offered better, competitive alternatives. The rule of the Turks only fixed this relation; it had already existed prior to their invasion of the West Balkans in the last years of the fourteenth century.

In the midst of its deliberations about great matters of state, the Small Council returned again and again to the mundane questions of provisioning and setting prices for fuel or foodstuffs. In 1300, the council interrupted its deliberations on great matters to order that no person transport food, cheese, oil, or firewood away from the town proper.[59] Policy clearly favored supplying the local urban market over the exports of foodstuffs. All varieties of meat from lowly mutton to more succulent cuts from younger animals were listed among the foodstuffs available for consumption, and virtually all comestibles came under regulation for quality and price.[60] Although prices for the general run of foodstuffs rose, they seldom more than doubled in the course of the fourteenth century, so their increase fell significantly short of increases in townspeople's incomes.

Urban housing was a bargain as well. In the fourteenth century a semi-skilled worker earning a wage of forty hyperperi could purchase a modest residence in town for as little as twenty-five or thirty hyperperi, that is, between two-thirds and three-quarters of his yearly wage. Housing matched other costs in failing to rise steeply over the century. Taken together, these various components of the community's cost of living afforded a pleasant standard of living for employed persons.

Low-cost food, fuel, and housing provided even greater bargains from the standpoint of the merchant aristocracy who made their living from long-distance trade. They were the individuals who demanded, and received, good quality and low prices, and they were first to benefit from the town's plentifully supplied markets. As the health care program of the commune guarded their health, price regulation guarded noble pocketbooks. But neither health care nor price fixing was narrowly construed to benefit only the nobility, and anyone who had residence in town prospered at the expense of rural suppliers.

One effect of regulation was to allow wage earners to accumulate capital for investment in long-distance trade. Non-noble investors returned a favor to the merchant aristocracy in the form of investments in their enterprises, most particularly in building and furnishing the merchant marine. According to Jorjo Tadić, at the height of Ragusan expansion on the seas, over half the income from moving freight went to ship's crews, the rest to shareholders in the vessel. Shareholders could contract for a quarter or an eighth of a vessel, allowing any resident with capital to invest in trade.

Although rural suppliers absorbed much of the cost for provisioning Ragusa cheaply, the policy also affected the incomes of the merchant aristocracy. Ragusa and the territories over which it ruled represented a small zone true to the silver standard in a Mediterranean economy, which by the 1350s was dominated by gold.[61] Neighboring Dalmatian towns and Adriatic ports which were still under Venetian rule, and which still relied on silver coins provided them by the Venetian mint, also clung to silver, but after the 1320s the coin supplied them by Venice was a much reduced *soldino* or *mezzanino,* and it was suitable only for local commerce because it had a low value in foreign exchange. Not so the full-weight Ragusan *grosso,* which the Ragusan government began minting on its own initiative as soon as Venice began producing debased silver coins like the *soldino* for its colonial empire.[62] The full-weight Ragusan *grosso* might have been undervalued against gold in foreign exchange from time to time, but it was still a good silver coin, and it was attractive to foreign merchants who came to Ragusa for business purposes. The Great Council risked a potential loss of its own coined silver to both east and west whenever the ratio of silver to gold improved. Apparently they took this risk out of a sincere belief in the wisdom of using a sound silver coin for local exchange and local wages. Furthermore, Balkan silver permitted pursuing a silver standard.

From the 1330s, when the government first established its own mint and began supporting its own silver coinage by collecting a tenth of all bulk silver imported to town by local silver merchants, townspeople enjoyed the solid advantages of a sound silver currency. As Villani stated, in most Italian cities by the fourteenth century, great merchants paid wages in debased silver or copper coin while they bought and sold imported wares in good gold currency.[63] Ragusan monetary policy did not victimize wage earners in that way. Workers continued to enjoy the advantages of good silver coin, while Italian town dwellers adjusted to making exchanges either with the prohibitively dear gold ducat or florin as the means of exchange, or with a debased silver coin or even copper.[64]

Stated in terms of the cost of living for townspeople of Ragusa, the silver *grosso* provided a sound currency with liquidity for wages and commerce. This *grosso,* supported by its copper divisibles, or *follari,* circulated briskly in Ragusan business centers, neighborhood markets, and industrial workshops. It promoted exchange within the town and satisfied the needs of persons whose demands for currency were better filled by good small denomination silver coin than by gold coins. But, as an undervalued currency in relation to gold, silver coin lost purchasing power abroad through most of the century.[65] In the late thirteenth century, twenty-four *grossi* equaled one ducat in international exchange.[66] That ratio to the Venetian ducat increased to thirty *grossi* by the turn of the fifteenth century. Purchasing power of the *grosso* abroad had been reduced by half in the same period during which communal salaries paid by the merchant aristocracy in silver (and out of revenues on foreign trade) rose from four- to tenfold. The same merchant aristocracy, through its Small Council, regulated prices for foodstuffs in the community through regulation. Those prices, stated in terms of the silver *grosso,* only doubled in this period. Yet if costs to the community were to be stated in terms of the gold ducat, that is, in terms of foreign exchange, which determined the fortunes of long-distance merchants, then the price of foodstuffs was even less incremental, rising by only about a quarter. By the same token the communal wages paid to salaried employees of the commune cost 50 percent more to the merchant aristocracy, who paid them out of their customs duties on foreign trade by the turn of the fifteenth century. By clinging to a full-weight silver *grosso,* the merchant aristocracy subsidized the urban standard of living for artisans and wage laborers living in town. Their own *grosso* bought consistently less abroad, even though it remained a stable currency at home. The benefits of this policy were enjoyed by all who lived in the community, including at times, of course, the members of the nobility themselves. Yet a relatively more pronounced advantage accrued to artisans and wage earners than to great

Figure 7. Sponza Palace, constructed in the fourteenth century, with Renaissance façade. Site of the fourteenth-century customs house and mint. From *Obnova Dubrovnika 1979–1989,* ed. Božo Letunić (Dubrovnik: Zavod za obnovu Dubrovnika, 1989).

merchants because the former did not confront the diminishing value of the silver *grosso* in foreign exchange, which the latter did whenever they traded abroad.

Good wages and the attendant opportunity for capital accumulation were to this extent underwritten by the merchant aristocracy. Merchants who dealt in foreign exchange were cognizant of the cost they assumed in erecting a silver standard within a Mediterranean economy gone over to gold. It is important to note in this regard that Ragusans enjoyed nearly exclusive access to mined Balkan silver and could support their expensive monetary policy out of newly mined silver.

## A Diversified Economy

From the late thirteenth century until the "golden age" of the late fifteenth and sixteenth centuries, Ragusans profited from a growing diversity in trades, manufactures, and services. Ragusans experimented in production as a response to market conditions abroad or compensated at home for occasional scarcities of imported manufactured goods from the West. In the fifteenth century, during one period of scarcity in the rough textile imports traded to the Balkan interior, the council hired an Italian manager, Peter Pantella, to organize a local manufacture of cheap cloth for the market in the interior. Weaving of cheap cloth for export inland was set up in a specially constructed workshop with a large force of semiskilled rural women who wove, and were housed, under the jurisdiction of the master—in other words, in a large-scale *gynaeceum*. The production was great for a few years, and to all appearances this was a successful venture; nevertheless, it was dismantled when supplies of cheap cloth from abroad again became available.[67] As an endeavor, its swift construction, which resulted in almost immediate large production and its equally swift dismantling, illustrate that a supple system of industrial production underlay commerce. Industries were introduced into the community in response to the expressed priorities of noble traders who understood their markets and the vicissitudes of the carrying trade. Manufactures were eliminated as rapidly as they were built. The selective development of critical trades continued through the late medieval centuries. Some, like the manufacture of cheap cloth, were short-lived; others, like goldsmithing, survived. The most successful ventures were those that made minimum demands on the expansion of the work force and produced an exportable product of great value. The luxury trades, which produced exportable, light, high-priced commodities like jewelry were most prominent among these (see Chapter 7).

Workers and all that they produced in services and wares were regulated by the councils, and the minutes of the Small Council supply numerous references to emerging industries. The number of times a manufacture was mentioned in the *Libri Reformationes* can supply some idea of the trade's relative importance in the home economy. In his study of laborers in Ragusa at the turn of the fourteenth century, Josip Lučić found that thirteen separate trades were noted in the minutes of the council in a single year (1300–1301), with varying frequencies.

Skilled Artisans Noted in Council Minutes 1300–1301.[68]

| Title | Latin term | Number of times mentioned |
|---|---|---|
| *Leather worker | Calegarius | 20 |
| *Goldsmith | Aurifex | 17 |
| Mason | Petrarius, talapetra | 14 |
| Carpenter, woodworker | Marangonus | 9 |
| Blacksmith, ironworker | Faber, ferrarius | 7 |
| *Tailor, in special fur garments | Zupparius | 6 |
| *Tanner, furrier | Pelliparius, pilicarius | 4 |
| Tailor | Sartor | 4 |
| Caulker | Calafatus | 3 |
| Cooper | Botarius | 2 |
| Hatmaker(?) | Clubucarius | 2 |
| Refiner of ores | Grebener, cudellarius, etc. | 2 |
| Coppersmith | Calderarius | 1 |

*Luxury trade manufactures.

This list is far from exhaustive. In years when the work on fortifications or the waterworks were at their height, *manipulus murator* and *murator* or *murarius* (stonemasons, builders, and stone workers) were present in significant numbers and received mention in the council's minutes. A fuller list would certainly include sack makers and a few weapons makers, even glaziers (some hired by the communal council to supply glass for civic buildings).[69] But the frequency of pelters, goldsmiths, tailors of diverse sorts, tanners, and furriers testifies to involvement in the production of exportable high-value clothing, which could be produced locally or found in the Balkan interior. Fur-trimmed robes and jewels had become fashionable in Italy by the fourteenth century, and Ragusans launched into these manufactures, importing foreign workers with the requisite skills to produce goods Italians would buy. These export-oriented trades accounted for a substantial portion of the artisans offered the opportunity to become permanent residents in the community.

\*   \*   \*

In conclusion, the noble circle often enjoyed the opportunity to choose the non-noble inhabitants of the community. They distinguished carefully among those who would visit there to work only a brief time and those who would settle as permanent residents in town. Residence in Ragusa became one of the attractive alternatives for men seeking to build a fortune in the Mediterranean world in the fourteenth century. For Italians who possessed a skill or trade, the town provided a viable alternative to sometimes depressed job markets nearer home. When the Ragusan syndics in search of skilled artisans traveled to Italy, they encountered little difficulty finding talented persons willing to migrate across the Adriatic Sea; new manufactures were swiftly staffed by immigrant labor. Securing workers from the Slavic lands near or in Ragusan territory was never difficult. The Ragusan councils maintained a strict immigration policy to keep out unwanted seekers after unskilled jobs and selected only those workers it wished to incorporate, through chattel slavery in the earliest documented decades, then through a system of contract labor in the later medieval centuries. Within workshops and the constellation of noble Ragusan households, there were sufficient skilled and unskilled laborers to accomplish the diversification of trades required to promote commercial expansion and to staff necessary urban trades and services. Many of those supplying labor, both skilled or unskilled, were attached to noble households by personal ties. And many non-noble households held former servants wed to immigrant artisans.

A prosopography of medieval Ragusa presents a cityscape of intimately related, industrious, and highly cooperative people wherein a semblance of deference at least was generally paid to the noble citizenry. The community's reputation was fostered by stories about the wealth of its inhabitants and the pacific and pleasant routines of their daily lives. "Fortune commonly supports those who are prudent," the old adage said, and Ragusans were very prudent indeed.

*Notes*

1. Benedetto Cotrugli, *Della mercatura,* f. 100; (Tucci ed., p. 247).
2. F. W. Kent, *Household and Lineage in Renaissance Florence* (Princeton, N.J.: Princeton University Press, 1977); Georges Duby, "Lineage, Nobility and Chivalry," in *Family and Society,* trans. Elborg Forster and Patricia Ranum (Baltimore: Johns Hopkins University Press, 1972), pp. 16–40.

3. Compare Bartolomé Clavero, *Mayorazgo propriedad feudal en Castilla* (Madrid: Siglo Veintiuno Editores, 1974), p. 98; P. J. Cooper, "Inheritance and Settlement by Great Landowners," p. 296; Benjamin Kedar, "Genoese Notaries of 1382," in *The Medieval City*, ed. Harry Miskimin et al. (New Haven, Conn.: Yale University Press, 1975), pp. 73–94.

4. I. Mahnken, *Dubrovački patricijat*, pp. 79–80.

5. M. Dinić, *Odluke veća dubrovačke republike*, vol. 1, p. 354; I. Mahnken, *Dubrovački patricijat*, p. 95.

6. *Liber Statutorum*, L. IV, c. 71, "parvam quantitatem de bonis suis." L. IV, c. 72 establishes as well that a father may censure and punish his illegitimate offspring if he had acknowledged them; thus acknowledgment represented the imposition of authority over these offspring as well as legitimate offspring. On the rights of legitimate heirs, see Jenny Teichman, *Illegitimacy, An Examination of Bastardy* (Ithaca, N.Y.: Cornell University Press, 1982), especially chapter 3. See also Peter Laslett, Karla Oosterveen, and Richard M. Smith, eds., *Bastardy and Its Comparative History* (Cambridge, Mass.: Harvard University Press, 1980). Adoption, a legal possibility, was not practiced as, for example, Florentines employed it.

7. *Liber Statutorum*, L. VI, c. 53.

8. D.S.A., *Testamenta*, V, f. 41v.

9. I. Mahnken, *Dubrovački patricijat*, part II, Genealogies, X/2, XII, XV/1, XXXI, XXXIV/6, XXXVI/1, XLII, XLIII, XLVII/3, LII, LIII, LIV, LV/1, LVII, LVIII, LXI, LXV, LXXII/1, LXXIII. Mahnken traced illegitimate heirs mentioned in noble wills wherever possible. Her work is the source for the examples in this paragraph.

10. The son of a former slave belonging to the noble de Mence family was married to the daughter of a family from Popovo, and that family provided the couple with a suitable dowry bequest. Gregor Čremošnik, *Spisi, 1278–1301*, doc. 188.

11. That was true until the middle of the fifteenth century, when an orphanage for illegitimate and homeless children was established. D.S.A., *Liber Viridis*, CCLII, f. 103v. See J. Tadić and R. Jeremić, *Prilozi za istoriju zdravstvene kulture starog Dubrovnika*, vol. 2 (Belgrade: SAN, 1939), pp. 199–216. Until that time most illegitimate children of noblemen appear to have been raised in noble households and settled near them in their adult years. Dušanka Dinić-Knežević, *Položaj žena u Dubrovniku*, pp. 138ff.

12. Gregor Čremošnik, *Spisi, 1278–1301*, doc. 731, pp. 229–30.

13. Gregor Čremošnik, *Spisi, 1278–1301*, doc. 982, p. 294.

14. Gregor Čremošnik, *Spisi, 1278–1301*, doc. 513, pp. 156–57.

15. D.S.A., *Testamenta*, III, f. 8v–9, "quod Yuana famula mea sit libera et absoluta in perpetuum ab omni servitute domus mee et habeat ypp. V pro sua maritatione."

16. D.S.A., *Testamenta*, V, f. 86.

17. D.S.A., *Liber Dotium*, I, f. 2, 6, 11v, 12v; *Liber Dotium*, II, f. 85, 122, 123, 130, 153; *Liber Dotium*, IV, f. 53v; *Liber Dotium*, V, f. 140. Based on a study of seventy-two early fourteenth-century dowries, the average bequest made in a non-noble dowry was 74.9 *hyperperi*. This assumes that a dower house would be worth about thirty *hyperperi*. It was more difficult to set a value on the jewels that accompanied

bequests. The spread of awards among the seventy-two dowries was 20 *hyperperi* to 230 *hyperperi*. D.S.A., *Liber Dotium*, I, f. 1–14v.

18. D.S.A., *Liber Dotium*, I, f. 11.

19. D.S.A., *Liber Dotium*, I, f. 6.

20. D.S.A., *Liber Dotium*, II, f. 85, 124.

21. D.S.A., *Liber Dotium*, II, f. 149v. Pelters dressed skins and pelts.

22. D.S.A., *Lamenta de Intus*, 1404–1407, 4/15/1406, f. 181.

23. D.S.A., *Lamenta de Intus et de Foris*, 1, 3/5/1373, f. 115.

24. D.S.A., *Lamenta de Intus et de Foris*, 1, 11/27/1373, f. 229.

25. An illegitimate child of a noble father need not be the child of a household servant. In fact, the strict endogamy of the patriciate may best be understood by reference to the following case: The nobleman Nicola de Mate de Grade accepted a dowry from a non-noble woman of the town. She was not a household servant; the offspring were acknowledged by their noble father. These two factors suggest a marriage had been contracted that was recognized by the church. However, de Grade's children were not included within the noble circle. D.S.A., *Liber Dotium*, V, f. 60v.

26. I. Mahnken, *Dubrovački patricijat*, pp. 91–96, has listed all the grants from the *Libri Reformationes*.

27. D.S.A., *Liber Dotium*, II, f. 98.

28. I. Voje, "Bencius del Buono," *Istorijski časopis* 18 (1971): 189–91.

29. On Florentines in the Balkans see B. Krekić, "Kurirski saobracaj Dubrovnika sa carigradom i solunom u provoj polovini XIV veka," *Zbornik radova Vizantoloskog Instituta* 1 (1952): 113–20; idem., "Four Florentine Banking Companies in Dubrovnik," pp. 29–30. Jireček first commented on the courier route across the Balkans staffed by Florentines, C. Jireček, "Die Bedeutung von Ragusa," p. 396. See Chapter 7 on the roles of Bencius del Buono and Lorini Rici in transporting precious metals to Venice.

30. Lorino Rici was offered citizenship in 1344; *MR*, vol. 1, p. 155. In 1351 he purchased a house in Ragusa; D.S.A., *Diversa Cancellariae*, XVII, f. 19.

31. Town liaisons grew in importance in the fifteenth century, when the nobility contained a substantial group of life-long bachelors who could not find a wife. David Rheubottom, "'Sisters First': Betrothal Order and Age at Marriage," pp. 359–76.

32. D.S.A., *Liber Dotium*, IV, f. 54; *Liber Dotium*, V, f. 36, 95, 96, 99, 124v, 138, 161 (bis), 165v, 167v; *Liber Dotium*, VII, f. 19, 24v.

33. Benedetto Cotrugli, *Della mercatura*, f. 88, "che dice bene' proverbio di Dalmatia, Se la capra si denegasse, le corna la manifestariano" (Tucci ed., p. 233).

34. D.S.A., *Pacta Matrimonialia*, II, f. 9v reproduced in Dušanka Dinić-Knežević, *Položaj žena u Dubrovniku*, pp. 203–4.

35. D.S.A., *Pacta Matrimonialia*, I, 10, 12, 13, 21. See discussion in Dinić-Knežević, *Položaj žena u Dubrovniku*, pp. 71–72.

36. The children and grandchildren of Givco Dersa and Nicoletta Rici married the Goce de populo, and Fiffa, another non-noble lineage descending from the Goce. The offspring of Luce de Caboga married non-noble Goce and the offspring

of a Dersa. I. Mahnken, *Dubrovački patricijat,* part II, Genealogies, XV/1, XXVIII, XXXIV/6 and XXXIV/8.

37. Dešanka Kovačević, "Zore Bokšić, Dubrovački trgovac i protovestijar bosanskih Kraljeva," *Godišnjak društvo istoričara Bosne i Hercegovine* 13 (1962): 295–97.

38. Dragan Roller, *Dubrovački zanati u XV i XVI stoljeću* (Zagreb: Jugoslavenska Akademija građa za gospodarsku povijest Hvratske, 2, 1951); Vinko Foretić, "Dubrovačke bratovštine," *Časopis za hrvatsku povijest* (Zagreb: JAZU, 1943). See also Ante Marinović, "Prilog poznavanju dubrovačkih bratovština," *Dubrovnik anali* 1 (1952): 233–45; idem., "Local Autonomies in the Ancient Republic of Ragusa," in *Actes du IIᵉ congrès international des études du sud-est européen* 2 (Athens, 1972), pp. 499–511. Nobles did not join merchant confraternities.

39. *MR,* vol. 5, pp. 176, 231, 349; *MR,* vol. 1, p. 268. Fr. Rački translated *beccarias* as Italian *maccelum* or butchering, *MR,* II, p. 107. I. Mahnken, *Dubrovačke patricijat,* pp. 28–29. Bariša Krekić has written on the closing in English in his various studies of Dubrovnik.

40. Miodrag Petrovich, "A Mediterranean City-State: A Study of Dubrovnik Elites," p. 560. This list has not survived. See also Branco Nedeljković, "Nekoliko karakteristike i opaske o dubrovačkom pravu i drzavi XIV i XV stoljeća (1348–1460)" *Istorijski časopis* 18 (1971): 95–106.

41. The poverty of some members of the Great Council, an issue discussed in Chapter 4 in regard to poor noble dowries, appears to lie behind this "closing." As with the poorly endowed, a solution appears to be found by maintaining the impoverished within noble ranks rather than allowing them to sink into lower social orders. See Chapter 3.

42. Stanley Chojnacki, "In Search of the Venetian Patriciate," pp. 47–60; see also Stanley Chojnacki, "Marriage Legislation and Patrician Society in Early Fifteenth-century Venice," in *Law, Custom, and the Social Fabric in Medieval Europe,* ed. Bernard S. Bachrach, and David Nicholas (in press).

43. For the other side of the debate see Guido Ruggiero, "Modernization and the Mythic State in Early Renaissance Venice: The Serrata Revisited," *Viator* 10 (1979): 245–56.

44. *MR,* vol. 5, pp. 176, 231, 349; vol. 1, p. 268. The earliest of these reads, "quod nullus nobilis de Raugio audeat vel presumet modo aliquo vel ingenio facere becchariam hinc ad unum annum proximum sub pena X yperp. qui contrafecerit et qualibet vice. . . ."

45. N. Nodilo, ed., *Annales Ragusini anonymi item Nicolai de Ragnina,* pp. 8–9. The chronicles claim further that the people gave their assent to rule through public acclamation in the streets. The *laudo populi* may have been found in surviving thirteenth-century laws and treaties but soon died out. Josip Lučić, *L'Histoire de Dubrovnik,* pp. 64–66.

46. *MR,* vol. 4, p. 161.

47. *MR,* vol. 4, p. 105.

48. *MR,* vol. 3, pp. 39–40, 78.

49. Bariša Krekić, *Dubrovnik et le Levant au moyen âge,* pp. 89–94. Dušanka Dinić-Knežević, "Trgovina žitom u Dubrovniku," pp. 121–24. On the grain trade

with Apulia, see Mariana Popović-Radenković, "Le relazioni commerciali fra Dubrovnik (Raguse) e la Puglia nel periodo angioino (1266–1442)," *Archivio storico per le province napoletane*, n.s., 37–38 (1957–58).

50. *MR*, vol. 5, p. 71.

51. *MR*, vol. 5, p. 165. The council noted that the government was selling grain in the community at the price of eighteen *grossi*, while it had purchased grain abroad for 17½ *grossi*, to which would be added costs for shipping and storage. The minute cites the scarcity and high cost of grain as the reason for the decision, and the question was likely raised in council because the grain office traditionally made a profit on investment.

52. Bariša Krekić, *Dubrovnik et le Levant*, p. 94. Dušanka Dinić-Knežević, "Trgovina žitom u Dubrovniku," pp. 121–24. On the grain trade with Apulia see Mariana Popović-Radenković, "Le relazioni commerciali fra Dubrovnik (Raguse) e la Puglia nel periodo angioino (1266–1442)." For comparison see Richard Goldthwaite, "Il prezzo del grano a Firenze dal XIV al XVI secolo," *Quaderni storici* 28 (1975): 3–36, particularly pp. 8–9, for comparative prices. See also G. Luzzatto, "Il costo della vita," in *Studi di storia economica veneziana* (Padua: CEDAM, 1954), pp. 285–87. In the fifteenth century the town dug huge pits called *rupe* out of the limestone in the oldest and highest district of the town.

53. *MR*, vol. 5, pp. 308, 405.

54. *MR*, vol. 5, 328; *MR*, vol. 1, p. 254; *MR*, vol. 2, p. 179.

55. Susan Stuard, "A Communal Program of Medical Care: Medieval Ragusa/Dubrovnik," pp. 131–38.

56. Dušanka Dinić-Knežević, "Trgovina vinom u Dubrovniku," *Godišnjak filoz. fakulteta, Novi Sad* 9 (1966): 39–55.

57. The amount of cheese one could keep on hand was regulated; *MR*, vol. 2, pp. 200–201.

58. *MR*, vol. 5, pp. 30, 49; *MR*, vol. 2, p. 187; *MR*, vol. 3, p. 278; *MR*, vol. 4, pp. 96, 100.

59. *MR*, vol. 1, p. 1.

60. A number of different cuts of meat and types of animals were differentiated in the minutes of council. According to the information supplied in the preceding table, in 1367 a family could obtain six light pounds (328 grams) of mutton a week for four *grossi*. See note 51 above.

61. Milan Rešetar, *Dubrovačka numizmatika* 2 vols. (Belgrade, 1924), unfortunately misunderstands the role of the *hyperperus* as a money of account but is valuable in other ways. See more recently, V. Vinaver, "Prilozi istoriji plemenitih metala, cena i nadnica srednjevekovni Dubrovnik," *Istorijski glasnik* 1–2 (1960): 51–94; B. Saria, "O težini najstarijih dubrovačkih dinara," *Rešetarov zbornik iz Dubrovačke prošlosti* (Dubrovnik, 1931), pp. 40–41. Michael Metcalf, *Coinage of the Balkans 620–1355* (Chicago: University of Chicago Press, 1965), pp. 253–58, and plates XIII and XIV, provide an introduction to Serbian coinage. See also M. Dinić, "Krstati groševi," *Zbornik radova vizantološkog instituta* 1 (1950): 86–112; idem., *Za istoriju rudarstva u srednjevekovnoj Srbiji i Bosni*, vol. 1 (Belgrade: SAN, 1955). On Venetian monetary policy and coinage see N. Papadopoli, *Le monete di Venezia*

(Venice, 1893), and Roberto Cessi, *Problemi monetari veneziani, R. Academia dei Liincei,* ser. 4, vol. 1 (Padua: PAN, 1937). See further discussion in Chapter 7.

62. Vuk Vinaver, "Der Venezianische Goldzechin in der Republik Ragusa," *Bollettino dell'Istituto di storia della società e dello stato veneziano* 4 (1962): 116–21. See also G. Luzzatto, "Il costo della vita," pp. 285–87.

63. Carlo Cipolla, *Storia moneta,* vol. 1 (Florence, 1976), pp. 121–23.

64. Frederic Lane, "Le vecchie monete di conto veneziane ed il ritorno all'oro," *Atti dell'Instituto Veneto di Scienze, Lettere ed Arti, Cl. scienze morali e lettere* 117 (1958–59); R. Cessi, *Problemi monetari veneziani,* see introduction.

65. I. Mahnken, *Dubrovački patricijat,* p. 106.

66. By the same comparison a salary paid in silver to a communally salaried employee at Ragusa decreased in purchasing power when the term of service was completed and the employee returned to Italy proper in the late fourteenth and fifteenth centuries.

67. Dušanka Dinić-Knežević, "Petar Pantella, trgovac i suknar u Dubrovniku," pp. 87–144.

68. Josip Lučić, *Obrti i usluge u Dubrovniku,* pp. 23–100. Benedetto Cotrugli, *Della mercatura,* f. 24; (Tucci ed., p. 164).

69. On glass making, see Verena Han, *Tri veka dubrovačkog staklarstva, XIV–XVI* (Belgrade: SAN, 1981). On weapons and weapons makers see Đurđica Petrović, *Dubrovačko oružje u XIV veku* (Belgrade: Vojni Muzej, 1976).

# 7. Fortunes

Old Ragusa might be dismissed as a mere curiosity surviving into early modern times but for the fact that its social configurations were cost efficient, giving townspeople an edge in the highly competitive capitalist trading networks of the Mediterranean basin. If Ragusans had been a more forthcoming people who left diaries, *ricordi,* and *zibaldone* for posterity, it would be much easier to assess their rise to prominence in the trade with the Balkans and the carrying trade in the Mediterranean. Since Ragusans guarded their formulas for economic success rather closely, modern evaluators can appreciate their successes only through reconstruction. Yugoslav historians of the past two generations have carried on this project with considerable success.

Because the economy of the community corresponds more closely than polity and society to the Italian city-state model, Ragusa's late-blooming prosperity holds fewer surprises. Ragusa's trading relations with other ports and with the Balkan interior have been carefully explored and are now well understood.[1] But how Ragusans found a way to open the rich markets of the more developed Italian cities to their products in the late thirteenth and fourteenth centuries remains something of a mystery. Ragusans achieved their fortunes late in comparison with city-states that underwent expansion in the eleventh, twelfth, and early thirteenth centuries. Cutting into markets that already had closer suppliers required careful reading of those markets and some sense of which articles of trade would capture the interest of the buying public. As a latecomer, Ragusa's success as a trading power did not necessarily lie in repeating the initiatives of those trading powers who already possessed secure positions in the Mediterranean carrying trade and shares of urban markets. Ragusans needed their own wedge.

To Ragusa's great advantage, late medieval Italy was fast becoming a consumer society. Because of the long-term cumulative advantage of a favorable balance of payments in European trade, great wealth came to be concentrated in its cities. Since wealth was distributed rather widely, both socially and geographically, and fluidity within both the political and the ecclesiastical hierarchies assured a constant renewal of powerful groups with new demands for goods, luxury markets constantly renewed themselves. Still, urban Italians had lost their desire for imported goods for the most part, generally preferring what they produced or manufactured themselves. Of these luxury markets, Venice was not only the greatest but, from a Ragusan standpoint, the most convenient. It had been Venetian policy from 1205 onward to channel Ragusans into bringing to the city only goods from Sclavonia (the Balkan interior). Generally, these were goods like lumber, furs, or precious metals which Venice could not obtain easily from closer sources on the Italian peninsula.[2] Ragusans needed to transcend Venetian restrictions on the scale of this trade if they were to expand into luxury markets in a major way. So for the crucial years 1205 to 1358, this channeling of their efforts into importing only Balkan products stood as an impediment they must circumvent or translate into an advantage. The way out was to foster trade in the few imported goods Venetians would buy that originated in the Balkans; this created a very small window of opportunity.

An acute awareness of market conditions in Venice and other cities was the key to solving this problem. And ultimately Ragusans did solve it; so well so that they financed a great mercantile navy that, in Braudel's words, "snatched loads" right out from under the eyes of the Genoese and Venetians, and in their very own harbors.[3] This level of success occurred in the late fifteenth and sixteenth centuries. In earlier years, beginning as early as the thirteenth century, the Ragusans began their rise to prosperity through the much slower process of learning to assess the Italian buying public's preferences. Their major contribution to European economic development probably lay in their acquired skill in assessing buyer preferences and changes in consumer fashions, then learning to stimulate consumption patterns to their own advantage.

By the late thirteenth century, for which sufficient documentation is available, Ragusan home industries were producing luxury goods for shipment abroad. Ragusan merchants had permanent residences in Venice, near the Rialto, where they had ample opportunity to study consumers. The *contrata s. Silvestro* was the recognized Slavic quarter of Venice by that date. A special *curia slavorum* provided both surveillance and arbitration for disputes arising from the business of foreigners who, like the Ragusans and other inhabitants of Dalmatia and Sclavonia, frequented the city's busy markets. The earliest extant Venetian *Grazie* (literally, *Pardons,* but the *Grazie* contain much more than that) included references to many Ragusans in S. Silvestro in transitory or more permanent roles: sailors, petty traders, brokers, and long-distance merchants.[4] The Slavic quarter lay obliquely opposite the Grand Canal from the *fondacho dei tedeschi*, and was connected with it by the Rialto; but unlike the quarters for foreign merchants from the north, this Slavic quarter was integrated into the community and Ragusans actually owned houses there. The nobleman Vita de Goce lived in Venice in his own home for much of his career.[5] He was designated *honoris vir* by the Venetians for his services in trading between the foreign "Slavic" suppliers and local traders.[6] Michael de Mence counted a residence in Venice among his many foreign commercial properties, although most of his other real estate lay in the Balkan interior near producing mining sites.[7]

Day-to-day trade between Ragusa and Venice was regulated by the treaty of 1205, which was reissued and subject to slight modifications as need arose. The deliberations of 1319 were particularly momentous and may have even enhanced conditions for commerce in some articles of trade such as precious wares, although generally Venice proved unresponsive to Ragusa's overtures for improved conditions for imports during these decades.[8] Even after Ragusans declared their independence, the doge's orders continued to affect Ragusan merchants' access to the Rialto. But before or after 1358, whenever the Ragusan senate even suspected that their Venetian trade was in some jeopardy, they immediately dispatched negotiators to meet with the doge and his councils. Trade in goods from Sclavonia to Venice received every consideration diplomacy conferred.[9]

With time, patience, and luck, Ragusan traders found some products that met Venetian restrictions and still found buyers in the luxury market. Marketable great coats, that is, garments designed for men, along with certain other luxurious fur-trimmed jackets, coats, and capes, were local Balkan commodities with a long tradition behind them that fit this bill. Processing fur pelts from domestic herds or from wild animals and weaving heavy wool textiles had been established crafts and manufactures in the Dalmatian coastal region since ancient times. Shepherds practicing transhumance led their flocks from the high mountain valleys in the summer to the coast close to the Dalmatian towns where they sold wool and pelts to local traders in winter. The *dalmatica*, which became a staple of ecclesiastical costume very early in the history of the Christian church, attests to the ancient origins of this manufacture. The variety of skilled artisans practicing the cloth trades in Ragusa by 1300 attests to the evolution of this traditional manufacture and its diversification through the intervening centuries. Among the most-mentioned occupations in the Small Council's minutes of 1300 were pelterers and *zuparii,* that is, tailors who specialized in making fur-lined and fur-banded garments.[10] Also mentioned were tanners, furriers, hatmakers, regular tailors (*sartori*), and a variety of other skilled workers in textiles (see Chapter 6). Diversification in the manufacture of garments had occurred well before 1300 to reach this level of complexity. Both the number of leather workers (they were mentioned at least twenty times in council regulations in 1300–1301) and the communal government's interest in supervising their output suggests a brisk business on a scale greater than necessary to serve only the needs of local consumption.

And in matter of fact, great coats appealing to men of wealth and status had grown fashionable and appeared on the market in Italian cities by 1300. These coats attracted only the most affluent consumers, that is, those who could afford warm, heavy garments, a fur lining, and fur trim for display. This was not a large market— at least Ragusans did not have a large share in it, as Pisans did in the early Renaissance—but fur was one imported luxury article Italians would buy.[11] The Ragusan supplier was less worried about volume of trade; he needed to see goods obtained from Sclavonia traded at Venice. And great coats were high-priced items that could be turned out by a small work force of highly skilled specialists who catered to market preferences.

This exploration of the Venetian market, which stood as the richest and the most diverse of all Italy's markets for luxury goods in the thirteenth century, provided Ragusan suppliers an unparalleled opportunity to assess Italian tastes. Since Venetian policy allowed Ragusans unfettered access to the Rialto and other markets in the city, and Ragusans understood and spoke Adriatic dialects and shared common understandings of commerce and the rules of trade, market conditions were ripe for expansion. There had never been a policy of isolating Ragusans in a special *fondacho,* such as that assigned to foreign speakers like the Germans from the north, because Ragusans were not viewed as particularly foreign.

All these factors encouraged trade in luxury apparel. A surviving inventory of Marco Polo's belongings drawn up at his death contained a great coat of significant value which, like most luxury garments, was to be passed on as part of the estate.[12] By the turn of the fourteenth century, portraits, paintings, and frescos presented Venetian gentlemen attired in great coats that were banded with fur as a mark of wealth and ostentation.[13] Alert to opportunity, Ragusan long-distance merchants had found one important luxury trade they might enter. In fact, as suppliers of luxury wares, they may have even helped promote growth for this fashion. Clothing, according to contemporary commentators, led the list of wares that had begun to follow fashion. Ragusans had everything to gain by promoting this trend.[14]

This initial sally into a market where whim or sudden changes in preference for a particular cut or fur trim could affect sales may have inspired the more daring initiatives in marketing that followed. Some Ragusan merchants turned their attention to the high-risk venture of marketing the output of silver and gold bullion of Sclavonia in the first decades of the fourteenth century. The risk represented by this marketing endeavor was much higher than in the garment trade, because of the intrinsic value of the precious ore and the complications of bringing newly mined silver and gold to Venice for sale on the open market. Since entry into this new market occurred relatively late (about 1310), documentation for the venture is fairly ample, so both the gamble for a major role in supplying the luxury trade and the attendant risks may be known in fairly great detail.

Precious ore from newly opened Balkan mines which was transported to the coast, then carried to Venice by Ragusan traders and brokers, had not reached the luxury market to any marked extent in the thirteenth century, although the Balkan mines had been in production since mid-century. When the producing silver mines first opened at Brescova (Brskovo) and later at Rudnica (Rudnik), the bulk of the silver was mined into a Serbian *grosso*, intended to increase the purchasing power of the Nemanjić rulers of Rascia or Serbia who had embarked on a program of expansion. As coin, it reached the coast, and as coin, it traveled to Venice. Yet changes in Venetian minting policies undervalued this new silver as the century progressed, and there lay the frustration for the Ragusan merchant, and possibly the motive for doing more with the Balkan silver production than merely conveying it to the mint at Venice.

This problem of undervaluing the supply of new precious ore highlights the difficulties inherent in Ragusa's subordinate position as a Venetian trading partner. As early as 1280 the Venetians had succeeded in commanding Balkan silver on their own terms. They had accomplished this by condemning the silver coin issue of the king of Serbia as a falsification of their own prized *grossi*.[15] Dante, from his excellent vantage point in exile at Ravenna, noted this and recorded it when he composed the *Purgatorio*.[16] And the law was enforced: there were special officials stationed at the waterfront in Venice, with the significant title of *super denariis grossi de Brescova*, who confiscated all Serbian coins and took them to the Venetian mint, where they were reminted into Venetian *grossi*.[17] In these years, Venice pursued a bi-metallic policy, continuing to mint their full-weight silver *grossi* while they also minted a gold ducat. An influx of Balkan coin was quite necessary because it could be cheaply obtained by condemnation, which in turn allowed the bi-metallic standard to survive. The major cost of this policy was borne by suppliers whose silver coins were seriously undervalued by government-set ratios; thus silver was not allowed to seek its own market value after it entered Venice. Venetians themselves did not suffer the consequences of this policy, but apparently the Germans, who brought silver from Goslar, suffered, as did the Ragusans, because the Venetian authorities forced them to accept whatever price the mint offered.

For the Ragusans, the implications of the 1280 policy were serious indeed because the Venetians had the capacity to order and enforce a surveillance at Ragusa similar to that which they maintained at home. The Serbian *grosso* was not allowed to circulate at Ragusa; in fact, Small Council–appointed officials, also called *super denarii*, oversaw Ragusan streets and markets and confiscated all illegally circulating Serbian coins.[18] The Venetian-appointed count could of course demand this surveillance, although in truth the integrity of Venetian coinage was not actually threatened, as Venetians sometimes claimed, by Serbian "falsifying," or by the circulation of Balkan silver coin in the Ragusan marketplace. The Serbian coins were differently marked—some showed a figure holding a recognizable pennant in contrast to the seated figure on Venetian *grossi*—and they were similar but not identical in weight to the Venetian *grosso*.[19] Since little threat to the integrity of Venetian currency actually existed, the twin condemnations of coin at Ragusa and at Venice fulfilled another and very likely deliberate purpose of shunting Serbian coin through both towns and both ports to speed it on its way to the mint, where it could be cheaply reminted to maintain Venice's unique bi-metallic currency system.

Escaping this tightly controlled and only marginally profitable exchange required some ingenuity on the part of the Ragusans. The open market for silver at Venice provided such an opportunity, in part at least, because of the mint's tax of only one-fifth on imported silver that was destined to be sold publicly on the open market—a policy that was in operation by the early fourteenth century.[20] By 1310, Ragusans were busy producing silver wares for the open market and paying their fifth on it once they reached Venice. By the 1330s, their fabrication and export of silver wares had reached substantial proportions. By this decade, silver merchants had learned how to augment their exports of fabricated wares with exports of bulk silver for the open market. Thus a third and highly lucrative mode for merchandising Balkan silver came into being.[21] Significantly, however, silver wares, not silver bars or ingots, reoriented the terms of trade in the favor of the suppliers. Long-distance Ragusan merchants who were intimately involved in the market understood the importance of silver wares, and they initiated negotiations with Venice whenever they saw their trading privileges jeopardized (see note 8). In fabricated wares they had evidently found articles with sufficient appeal to consumers to rise above the constraints that mint policy and trading in the goods of Sclavonia had previously imposed on their expansion into trade on Italy's luxury markets.

In the Venetian *Grazie,* which among other matters record petty crimes, Ragusans may be glimpsed learning lessons about doing business at Venice. It was a sign of their habitual presence on that market that they appeared quite often in the *Grazie* and an indication of their familiarity with Venetian policies and procedures that they won pardons. In the *Grazie,* a number of Ragusan inhabitants may be found as early as the first decade of· the fourteenth century. Marinus de Goce, whose close relative, Vita, was a long-term resident of Venice; Jacobo de Domino de Ragusio; and Pantaleoni de Ragusio all received pardons for petty crimes committed in the conduct of their trade.[22] Their compatriots, Marino de Volcassio de Ragusio and Nicoletto de Laurencio de Ragusio, whose names also appeared in the *Grazie,* were involved in transactions critical to merchandising silver. The former, Marino de Volcassio, probably the brother of one of the most affluent of Ragusa's silver merchants, Junio de Volcassio, owed twenty *grossi* for marks of silver traded on the Venetian market in 1334.[23] Nicoletto de Laurencio, very possibly a member of the numerous noble de Mence family that traded at both the mining centers in the Balkan interior and Venice, was similarly fined for failure to pay his fifth on four pounds of silver.[24] A more complex pardon involved a Venetian, Peter Reynaldo, who had been found guilty for not paying a fifth for belts (*zonas*) of Ragusan silver supplied to him by Florentine agents active in trade on the Venetian market.[25] Likewise Catarino Quintavallo (whose family had long-standing commercial ties with Ragusa, where they had, on occasion, purchased silver belts) was fined for failing to pay his fifth when trading his silver belts at Venice.[26] Another Venetian merchant banker whose family did business regularly at Ragusa, Marco Stornado, was accused and found guilty, then pardoned for the same offense.[27] These pardons, which provide a glimpse of transactions involving identifiable Venetian merchant bankers, Ragusan long-distance merchants, and, on occasion, their Florentine agents, all trading silver belts, provide some idea of the nature of the new trade in silver wares. If charters from both Venetian and Ragusan collections are collated, this trade in silver wares and exchange of bulk silver may be reconstructed in surprisingly full detail.

To begin at Ragusa, the place of fabrication, Ragusan merchants brought Balkan silver to town from the interior then commissioned local or newly immigrant *aurifici* to produce an array of goods from it.[28] These commissions reflected the merchant's own assessment of what would sell readily on the open market as well as his estimate of his chosen *aurifici*'s skills and specialties. Once the silver was returned to him as finished goods (frequently with a bag of unworked silver that may have been the weighed fifth to be sent to the mint once the silver reached Venice),[29] the merchant might choose an agent to take his silver overseas, or he could secure a vessel and take it to Venice himself. By the early 1330s, Ragusans were as likely to trust their silver to Florentine factors and agents as they were to accompany it to Venice themselves. If they entrusted the silver to a Florentine, they specified the weight of silver to be sold at Venice, the period of time after reaching Venice within which the sale should be transacted, and the minimum price to be accepted for the silver.[30] To shift now to the Venetian marketplace, if Peter Reynaldo of Venice purchased silver belts from Ragusa through a Florentine agent (as the *Grazie* recorded), he was answering the terms of trade arranged months or weeks before at Ragusa by a silver merchant. In this manner, fabricated wares were presented beguilingly on the open market both to Venetian consumers and to foreign visitors who had been attracted to Venice because it was the most famous market for luxury wares in all of Europe.

Florentine agents and Ragusan silver merchants had visible proof that their silver, particularly ponderous belts of silver, were not only purchased at Venice but worn there as well. The shift to fashion in the fourteenth-century cities of Italy provided a powerful stimulus for consumption of precious ores. Contemporary observers suggested that men's fashions in those very years had changed from a traditional form of dress and become distinct in cut and more visually masculine in both cut and contour.[31] Italian men of letters Franco Sacchetti and Giovanni Villani swore that new fashions had swept towns and obliterated most traditional articles of local costume, to the amusement and the consternation of the inhabitants themselves. Villani attributed French origins to the new styles current in his native Florence, and others had commented as well that new Italian urban clothes imitated the costume of French knights. To the satirical novelist

Sacchetti style was the height of foolishness. He recounted the story of a man who, returning for his dinner wearing his fashionable gorget, dribbled hot soup under it and burned himself since he couldn't extricate himself from its embraces.[32] Dante Allighieri recalled a better time, that of his ancestor Cacciaguida, when "there was no necklace, no coronal, no embroidered gowns, no girdle that was more to be looked at than the person."[33] For men, style dictated hose or tight trousers that revealed the shape of the leg and a short, padded doublet whose exaggerated shoulders, arms, and chest girth were cloth-padded in approximation of a breastplate or body armor. A large, linked belt, often with a dagger or knife attached, cinched the doublet at the hips, providing shape and securing the garment. Despite contemporary derision, this trousered costume was not completely unfamiliar. Tight trousers or hose were a traditional component of affluent urban men's wardrobes, and short doublets and cloaks had existed in earlier decades when they were worn under fur-trimmed great coats.[34] But style had become manifestly more important by the fourteenth century, and styles were both more body revealing and more conducive to the display of wealth than was true in earlier decades.

First, cutting costly material to produce tight trousers or hose and a short doublet was a wasteful, consequently more lavish, use of rich fabric than the traditional long, one-piece garment of uncut fabric which both men and women had worn previously. And the new style lent itself to the display of precious metal. If the *S. Giorgio* produced in the workshop of Paolo Veneziano in the 1340s is any indication, the use of a wide metal or leather belt came into fashion in the early decades of the century.[35] There a kneeling figure is adorned with a prominently displayed, intricately ornamented belt. A silver reliquary from the Treasury of St. Mark's in the form of a gesturing male figure confirms this trend (Figure 8).[36] In this small figure, the full costume is displayed: the great silver belt has a purse attached to it, and the figure sports a full display of silver buttons on coat and sleeves. A miniature by Donatore Inginocchiato from a little later in the century shows a kneeling male figure with a large linked metal belt, probably of silver (Figure 9).[37] His costume is completed by a large medallion hanging from a heavy linked chain about the neck and numerous rings on his fingers. In genre art, visual display of wealth as a badge of status had become an important consideration, and silver lent itself well to expressing this message (see Figure 10).

Inginocchiato's miniatures and Villani's and Sacchetti's comments provide a context for understanding the bewildering array of manufactured

Figure 8. Silver reliquary from the Treasury of St. Mark, Venice. From
Rosita Levi-Pisetzky, *Storia del costume* (Venice: Alfieri, 1964), vol. 2.

Figure 9. Detail from miniature, "Donatore Inginocchiato." From Rosita
Levi-Pisetzky, *Storia del costume* (Venice: Alfieri, 1964), vol. 2.

Figure 10. Miniature from "Lancelot du Lac." From Rosita Levi-Pisetzky, *Storia del costume* (Venice: Alfieri, 1964), vol. 2.

and exported silver articles described in the folios of the Ragusan notarial charters that recorded the orders or commissions to goldsmiths. Silver bracelets, silver cups, plaited necklaces, necklaces of pearl (possibly false pearls of silver), gold bracelets and rings, and white buttons with fine silver on them for trim appear in one fourteenth-century order.[38] Later, in 1330, a bag of engraved silver, a silver ship (*nef* or Slavic, *ladica*), a "jewel" (brooch) of pearls, a silver saltcellar, and bracelets and bags of silver were ordered together.[39] Silver crowns, four *frontali* (head ornaments), and fifteen silver bracelets worked in gold appeared in another order;[40] eight pairs of *cercellis schlavoneschis* (Slavic bangles) in yet another.[41] If articles were destined to be women's apparel, they were as likely to be gold as silver. In neither instance did they consume large quantities of precious metal, although precious and semi-precious stones and skilled craftsmanship could make them into high-priced commodities.

In contrast to those for women's jewelry, an order for fourteen pounds of silver to be fabricated into fashionable belts for men arrests the eye.[42] Other single items, usually wares for domestic uses (cups, *aquavariae*, a silver *nef*), could consume large quantities of silver, but as household items they were likely destined to be protected by the walls of their future possessors. By contrast men's belts were exhibited for the eyes of all in the marketplace, and they were not destined to be purchased by kings and princes only. There is also no guarantee that the aforementioned fourteen pounds of silver for belts would produce many belts at small weight; quite the contrary, weights and prices, when noted, suggest a diversity of weight and value from light and cheap to ponderous and very expensive for the numerous belts mentioned in the charters. And the weight and value of the most magnificent increased over the decades.

One king, at least, commissioned such a belt. Early in his reign Dušan, the great Serbian warrior king (later emperor), commissioned one belt and a *nef,* or saltcellar in the shape of a ship, to be fashioned from thirteen pounds, five ounces, of silver, early in his reign.[43] A bit later, one raised-work belt alone, commissioned in 1335 and meant not for a king but for an Italian merchant, required eleven pounds of silver.[44] A belt commissioned as early as 1313 weighed eleven pounds and cost 143 *hyperperi,* while another ordered a few months later at ninety-eight *hyperperi* would have weighed only about one-third less, if it was also of fine silver.[45] The largest, recorded in 1334, warrants quoting because it stretches credibility: "a silver belt worked in gold weighing thirty-one pounds and eight ounces."[46] Even with the 328-gram, or light, Roman pound in use at Ragusa, this represented a huge weight to carry on the body; armor might better define it. A Florentine factor visiting Ragusa purchased one silver belt at the high price of thirty ducats; it was smaller than the most impressive silver belts, but since gold currency commanded substantial weight in silver by the date of purchase (1333), Duccio Pucci, factor of the Acciaiuoli, had found a memento of his travels to Dalmatia guaranteed to dazzle his fellow Florentines.[47]

At the other end of the scale, eleven belts could be fabricated from twelve pounds, less three ounces, of silver,[48] while a middling belt in silver might have some gold work and still cost only twenty *hyperperi.*[49] A belt, not of silver but white metal "furnished with silver," cost a mere six *hyperperi* and one *grosso*.[50] A silver belt worth thirty *hyperperi*, one worth sixty *hyperperi*, one worth ninety *hyperperi*, and three worth one hundred fifty *hyperperi* together were more typical of the trade.[51] Belts were engraved, trimmed with filament or raised work, embellished in gold, or made of "white metal" (silver with a very high content of lead) and trimmed with silver of a greater fineness.[52]

This range in quality suited the Balkan production of ores as ingeniously as it suited Europe's increasingly sophisticated market for consumer goods. Balkan silver varied greatly in quality, probably a good deal more than the German production, which had been imported into Venice early in the thirteenth century and had once sustained its silver currency. The best Balkan ore was gold laden and came from Nova Brdo in the fourteenth century; it was always scarce, but was likely responsible for two belts trimmed in gold weighing 20 pounds, 8½ ounces together, which cost a steep 511 *hyperperi*.[53] Two other worked belts of silver trimmed with gold cost only 178 *hyperperi* in 1340; they must have been smaller and less lavishly decked with gold.[54] All these outshone a meaner belt sporting its bit of gold trim worth only ten *hyperperi*.[55]

By contrast with these gold-trimmed items, a simple silver belt could cost as little as two and one-half *hyperperi*; here "silver" was little more than a euphemism.[56] This belt probably contained only an inferior amalgam. Ragusan merchants had been unable to disguise such inferior ores when they exported their ore to Venice's mint.[57] Mint standards precluded adulterating silver or passing off poorer quality ores mixed with lead, while fabricated wares for the market actually profited from the availability of a wide range in the fineness of ores. Consumers chose belts according to finely shaded distinctions in purchasing power, and the less affluent were pleased to obliterate those distinctions as completely as possible through the illusion of the *aurifici*'s art. Thus the luxury market could absorb the entire range of Balkan ores. The resulting emphasis on visual display of wealth indicates that appearance had achieved new social consequence and the market was steadily diversifying, while silver, from the finest to the most base, was seen as fit to convey status to the viewing public.

Ragusan merchants cultivated this new market for display with considerable skill given their rather marginal position in the Mediterranean basin, and they adapted with alacrity to changes in the gold-silver ratio when Venice lessened its efforts to maintain its bi-metallic standard in the fourteenth century. This change in policy led to the gradual introduction of the gold standard and with it a sharp decrease in demand for silver. All this was first introduced over a few short months in 1310, with the result that silver was suddenly cheapened in relation to gold and, consequently, silver brought by Ragusan merchants to Venice in the form of Serbian *grossi* brought an even lower return. It was now clearly more profitable to trade silver wares on the open market and to allot only the required one-fifth to the mint. After the Venetian "defense of the *grossi*" (that is, the attempt to create a bi-metallic standard and maintain the traditional silver coinage) ended altogether in the 1330s, Ragusan production for the open market increased substantially. Both the export and fabrication of silver were highly sensitive to marketing conditions and to mint policy in Venice. That appears to be true through the entire first half of the fourteenth century; after that; when the new trade in fabricated silver articles had become well established, the Ragusan-fed demand for these wares and for bulk lots of silver expanded irrespective of mint policy. Ragusan silver merchants had captured a lucrative overseas trade, and since it fed consumer tastes it now expanded according to its own rhythms.

In these decades, the painting and fresco work that celebrated great donor families displayed silver accessories with increased frequency. Even the minor arts, manuscript illustration and genre art in particular, showed Venetians wearing the new styles.[58] The painstaking portraiture of Altichiero de Zevio established beyond a doubt that a large, linked silver belt with a long silver dagger attached was a central feature of the new styles for men.[59] The artist, who probably belonged to the *aurifici* or goldsmith guild himself, painted the members of the family of Lupi di Soragna presenting gifts to the Virgin in a typical donor portrait sometime between 1379 and 1384. This work, now at S. Affresio in Padua, showed seven kneeling male heirs who figured as donors. All of them wear linked silver belts. This line of linked belts provided horizontal reiteration that held the long, rectangular group portrait together. In the crowded scene, each belt was painstakingly individuated by drawing attention to its particular raised work and design. Left-handed daggers broke up the horizontal line created by the seven belts, angling at the same degree for each figure.

In the early 1300s men who had formerly dressed soberly were suddenly appearing everywhere in cities clad in enough silver around their waists to constitute a small fortune. This was particularly true for great merchants of leading urban families, which suggests this newly fashionable belt could convey important messages about the affluent, "grave," or mature men who wore them.[60] But it is a puzzle that while literary, notarial, and artistic evidence suggests that belts of great weight, price, and ostentation were being worn by leading citizens of Venice and other great cities as well, there was little mention of the new expensive style in sumptuary legislation. Venice presents a most striking example of this omission. Belts, to be sure, were regulated. In fact, the sumptuary law of 1360, written when the new fashion in belts was on the rise, indicated that no woman might wear a belt worth more than twenty ducats, but it ignored men's apparel entirely.[61] Certainly among the belts fabricated by Ragusan *aurifici* and exported to Venice to be sold on the market there were some of moderate value that might fall under this regulation for women's wear, but the great belts known to consume vast quantities of silver and valued at two to ten times this twenty-ducat limit appear to have escaped all civic regulation. Since it is clear that they were bought, sold, and worn at Venice, it is possible that the most dazzling display of wealth on the city's street and squares was actually exempt from the sumptuary law. Perhaps in regulating the consumption of silver, gold, jewels, and rich fabrics worn by women, children, and youth, as well as members of the lower social ranks, the Venetian senate aimed sumptuary legislation at curtailing the imitation of the new fashion they themselves had adopted. That is, if only great men could wear great belts, they would serve their intended visual purpose.

The availability of numerous belts that aped those of the best quality with cheaper metal indicates that the market for belts had deepened and imitation of the styles worn by the most grand men was indeed possible. In numerous instances, cheaper articles were exported by Ragusans to Venice, where they could be sold in the same market as the most expensive silver belts. This cheap imitation of status apparel may very well have confused visual signals, to the frustration and disgust of Venice's merchant aristocracy. For in adopting the new, expensive fashions, sober men of standing may have sought a visual sign of their own status. And if this was so, sumptuary legislation might well exempt the original trend setters, thereby laying open one critical feature of the late medieval market that introduced fashion to Europe. Initial adoption of a new style could serve the visual purpose of distinguishing the privileged and wealthy from others; through imitation, and a proliferating demand for less expensive versions, the symbol could be robbed of its original meaning. Of course, this would please Ragusan merchants who supplied silver articles to the market. They had the capacity to produce belts at all prices, and increase in the depth of the market would be particularly attractive to them since Balkan mines produced ores of varied quality.[62] Ragusans profited best, perhaps, from what most distressed the designers of sumptuary legislation.

New tastes and the new social purposes that fashion served required the supplier to know his consumer intimately and to be sensitive to his changing preferences. In earlier decades, great merchants of consequence from Italian cities had stood apart from others because of the rich display of fabric in their long coats or tunics and the fat, silver-filled purses they wore at their waists. The fat purse was fast becoming an anachronism in a fourteenth-century world, as leading commercial cities ceased to mint any large silver coins for use in long-distance trade. In the more sophisticated world of international trade, a letter of exchange drawn on a Florentine merchant banking company was less risky and more convenient than carrying large quantities of coin. Letters of exchange might be employed conveniently in trade wherever Florentines were active. In the Adriatic and at Venice, Florentines had become ubiquitous; in fact, their trading network stretched to Constantinople and numerous other eastern and southern Mediterranean ports.[63] By the 1330s, when the Venetian *grossi* had been allowed to fall into disuse and the mint continued to produce only fractional-weight silver coins for its eastern colonies, a fat purse no longer connoted a rich merchant. Gold coin, which had replaced the silver currency in international trade, was so valuable that even if a merchant could afford to display it on his person he was risking his fortune if he did so.

Yet no coin or currency conveyed messages about a great merchant's status and capacity to do business quite so eloquently as the old silver *grossi*. Venice had minted a large silver coin for a much longer period than other city-states because it clung to this notion; and in wearing fabricated silver after their great silver coins had finally disappeared, Venetians continued to exhibit their fondness for silver and an unswerving conviction that silver was precious, useful, and suited to their condition in life.[64] Silver may have lost liquidity when it ceased to be a major coin in Mediterranean trade, but it did not lose its value in the eyes of merchants who could still wear it. Apparently, Ragusan suppliers understood this and turned it to their advantage.

Seldom do medieval sources prove so compliant in revealing the patterns of trade as in this transition from silver as coin to silver as bullion to support fashion in apparel. There was even a prominent family whose fortune was made by following and promoting the new trade; and, fortunately, it was a family with literary ambitions so the story has been in part, at least, preserved. Bencius del Bono de Flora (identified in Florentine records by the additional surname of Sacchetti), was an ambitious young Florentine who sought his fortune in trade at Ragusa. He recommended

himself to the partners and factors of great Florentine banking houses who
invested in the grain trade, and he transacted much business for them; yet a
considerable portion of his time was spent in accumulating his own trading
empire. At Ragusa he was clever enough to concentrate on the silver trade.
He developed excellent ties with the local merchant aristocracy and took on
Lorino Rici de Flora as an assistant to cope with his increased business. In
appreciation, the Small Council offered Bencius status as *habitator*, which
he accepted, and later citizenship, which he did not. After a lucrative
trading career at Ragusa, he returned to Florence to make a very advantageous marriage, then began his travels again, to Venice this time, which
he was in a position to appreciate as the developing center of the luxury
trade. His son, Franco, composed stories about his father's prolonged visit
to that city.[65] Of one joke played on Giovanni Duccio, an old compatriot of
Bencius in trade, Franco Sacchetti said, "and when they met together they
all laughed in such a way that all Venice was amused at it for the space of a
week."[66] Shrewd, outgoing, and jocular, Bencius had charmed his Ragusan
hosts in much the same way, teaching them much about markets between
witticisms.

    In earlier years, before he had married and moved on, Bencius del
Bono had traded at Ragusa in bulk silver and silver wares: in a real sense,
Balkan silver was his introduction into the market for luxury goods. In 1327,
for example, he accepted the responsibility from a Ragusan silver merchant
for fifty-eight pounds of silver (using a 328-gram, or a Ragusan, pound
weight), and forwarded it on its way to other Florentine agents in Venice to
sell on the open market.[67] In 1330 he sent a smaller amount, sixteen pounds,
eight ounces, but of gold-laden silver from Nova Brdo to market in Venice.[68] His associate Lorino Rici sent seven pounds, seven ounces of fine
silver in 1333 and four pounds, three ounces and three *exagia* of high grade
ore (thought to contain thirty carats of gold) the following year.[69] Other
Florentines, Johannes Faci, Duccio Pucci, and Fortebraccio Charmontesis,
contracted for loads of silver to be conveyed to Venice.[70] The risk of voyage
by sea (since silver only crossed the now well-policed Adriatic) had lessened, but it still held true that a significant benefit accrued to local merchants who used Florentines with links to established Florentine factors
selling on the Rialto or the Campo S. Paolo. Bulk silver, like silver articles,
would only meet the requirements of the law of the mint if one-fifth of it
was turned over to authorities. But once that was done, the market was free
and open to all sellers, and Florentines were adept at working that market.
    Once the silver crossed the Adriatic, Venetian *aurifici* were likely to

purchase it from shipments of bulk silver in order to work it, since a lively industry in jewels, silver and gold artifacts, and other luxury wares flourished at Venice as well as at Ragusa, and *aurifici* were in constant demand.[71] In fact, Venice remained Europe's best supplied and most important market for silver and other luxury wares throughout these decades, and this remained true well into the fifteenth century. Nevertheless, by 1514 Florentine officials could also claim that they had imported enough newly mined silver from Ragusa to purchase Pisa.[72] The luxury market had expanded to Florence, although many affluent foreign consumers still identified the Venetian market with the luxury trade, so Ragusans continued to supply Venice generously with silver. Venice encouraged this supply with special favors since only an adequate supply of precious wares assured their continued primacy in the increasingly competitive arena of the luxury trade.

Back home in their native community, Ragusan merchants carefully adapted their economy to serve this luxury trade. In the thirteenth-century registers of the notary Thomasini de Savere, only eight *aurifici* were mentioned, and most seem to have been local artisans: Bogdanus, Carennus de Tragurio, Dragoe, Marco the son of Grupse, Milcio, Paul de Trano, Tolisclavus, and Vasilio.[73] An Italian from Trani, a Dalmatian from Trau (Trogir), possibly a Greek, and two Slavs were Ragusa's goldsmiths at the time. The earliest notarial registers from Catar (Kotor), Ragusa's silver-rich trading partner, contained references to twenty-four goldsmiths active between 1326 and 1334.[74] At Ragusa by 1300, thirty-five *aurifici* may be identified as serving the trade in silver wares.[75] More than a hundred immigrant *aurifici* set up businesses through the next century, and some of them settled and raised families in the town.[76] They signed their productions, *pro signo,* and apparently developed reputations for skills in certain kinds of work, such as in *aurati* (raised work in either silver or gold) and gold trim, or in variations that are described in commissions for linked silver belts. Their work was offered to silver merchants through a commission:

> Die Viii Januarii, 1335. Angelus, aurifex, fuit confessus et contentus se habuisse et recepise ab Andrea de Mence unam libram puri argenti, de que promisit sibi facere xii cuslerios, habeat ad festem St. Blasii proxime . . .[77]

The quality of the silver with which the goldsmith was to work and the articles to be produced were frequently identified by their weight in silver or gold.

By 1327, the Small Council established a uniform policy for regulating the work of *aurifici.*[78] When working white or pure silver (*argenti blanchi*), goldsmiths might sell their products for sixteen *grossi* an ounce; on a lesser quality silver, the lowest price they might charge was four *grossi* an ounce.[79] The Small Council designated the various qualities of ore from the poorest (present in a lead-laden ore), to the finest (white or pure silver), and even above that another high-quality ore (*glama* or gold-rich ore), which came from the mine at Nova Brdo.[80]

And at home, great silver merchants wracked their brains to invent new articles that could be crafted in silver. One order in 1313 included a footed cup of silver; four bags of silver; thirteen *coclariae* (shell-shaped silver articles, very possibly spoons); a silver casket with two bindings and a footed, jeweled setting of silver; a silver crown set with pearls; and a "jewel" (brooch) of pearls. All this was valued at three hundred *hyperperi*, and it was a handsome order.[81] In March 1319, a Ragusan ordered seven bags of silver, two silver knives, six rings, and two unspecified silver items weighing in all thirty Ragusan pounds. Accompanying this order was another for two chalices, bags of silver, and a silver belt weighing together nine pounds.[82] From 1321 came an order for a belt worked in gold, three silver cups (together weighing about thirty pounds) inset with ninety-six *exagia* or above in pearls and jewels, plus two silver crowns, all estimated to be worth 530 *hyperperi*.[83] In 1327, a pair of silver bracelets, a silver belt, two silver cups, a pair of plaits or necklaces of silver, a necklace of pearls (of silver?), two silver knives, two pairs of gold bracelets, three gold rings, and four buttons with silver work on them provided a tempting cache.[84] A commission from 1330 listed weights more carefully: a bag of engraved silver, with a silver ship weighing twenty-five ounces, a "jewel" of pearls set in gold weighing two ounces and four *exagia*, all for 165 *hyperperi*.[85] A cup, two other bags of silver, and a silver saltcellar (weighing in all three and one-half pounds of silver), with two gold bracelets weighing nine and one-half *saggia* (an alternate spelling of *exagia*) of gold appeared in that same order.[86] In 1333, one order called for fifteen silver bracelets worked with gold, four *frontali*, or head ornaments, and two silver crowns worked in gold. Since the value was placed at only forty *hyperperi* these should be considered a bargain, or rather goods worked in poorer quality silver and destined for the lower or poorer end of the luxury market. Some orders were less varied, such as one for fourteen pounds of belts and a pound of pearls with gold work, but cost much more (290 *hyperperi* in this case).[87]

Religious articles in silver might be expected to dominate the production of silver wares at Ragusa but they were seldom commissioned. Two silver chalices accompanied a long list of articles in 1319, but they were almost lost in the profusion of silver daggers, rings, bracelets, and belts, and it is not even certain that, as chalices, they would be used for sacramental purposes only. Another chalice of silver trimmed in gold was commissioned for eleven *hyperperi* in 1320, but it was not a very valuable object.[88] A cross of gold—probably only a small one since it was one of five items for ten and one-half *grossi*—was commissioned in 1323.[89] One chalice, ordered for the Franciscans in 1347, was a single major consignment of bulk silver for sacramental use: it weighed an impressive five and one-half pounds.[90]

If Ragusan *aurifici* produced more secular than sacred objects, it was also true that their secular production could be put to a wide variety of uses. And what a good joke, intentional or not, Ragusans played on Italian traders who visited their town believing that the many jewels displayed there in the local streets conveyed the same messages about relative wealth and status as they did at home. Ragusans were certainly bejeweled—take bangles for an example. Either as bracelets or earrings (they came in pairs), *cercellis* were ubiquitous in *aurifici*'s commissions. Eight pairs in the pre-ferred new fashion, that is, *sclavoneschis,* were ordered at once, while at least one pair accompanied most large commissions.[91] Silver bangles were trimmed in gold,[92] or with pearls,[93] and a few were made all of gold.[94] Some cost as much as three *hyperperi* a pair but most were much cheaper.[95] They were so popular locally that women from the nobility on down to their servants wore them out in the streets daily. For Italians who thought fashion all the more attractive when it was introduced from the east, *cercellis sclavoneschis* were a novelty to purchase locally and take back home (see note 12).

Ragusan women were perfectly free to wear their finery for all to see. Sumptuary legislation had not begun in the thirteenth century, as it had often elsewhere, in response to admitting the "populo" to some level of responsibility in the commune. Few challenged patrician status at Ragusa, so in a sense all could deck themselves to their pocketbooks' limit without confusing the understanding of social rank. When Kalenda Bocignola did not receive her expected "gift" of gold with her dowry in 1342, she peti-tioned the Small Council to assure her right to it, and she won.[96] The *donaro,* an auxiliary gift accompanying the *dos,* became a matter of some importance to women who liked to display it. Worth only forty *exagia* in gold in the thirteenth century, it was valued at seven hundred *hyperperi,* or almost half again the value of the *dos* or cash award of the dowry, by 1423. Unhindered by laws limiting ostentation and display, women paraded their wealth, particularly in new fashions like bangles and other innovations of the goldsmiths. They liked their heirloom jewels, also. Philippus de Diversis declared that they turned the heads of foreign visitors in the streets.[97] "Le pompe" that foreigners glimpsed in Ragusan streets was forbidden to many at home, and all the more attractive for that reason. As a matter of fact, more than eighty sumptuary laws limited ostentation in Italy's cities in the fourteenth and fifteenth centuries.[98]

The absolute preoccupation with jewels in Ragusan women's wills suggests they were well apprised of their value. Women possessed jewels as *donaro* that could be disposed of at will. With foreigners ready to buy whatever struck their fancy, jewels had only slightly less liquidity than *grossi* or ducats. The noble mothers Nicoletta de Bincola and Blice de Crossio very carefully divided their numerous jewels and their better clothes among their daughters.[99] Ruossa de Mence divided her very considerable holdings of gold and silver, plate and jewels in a careful manner among her descendants.[100] One young noblewoman found a benefactor in her uncle's widow, receiving both *cercellis* and a valuable silver belt from her.[101] The noble gentleman Andreas de Paborra needed pages to deed over an itemized list of his silver goods.[102] It is very possible he was disposing of the inventory of his export business. Other townspeople shared with the nobility a preoccupation with jewels.

On a less lofty level Draga, the daughter of a blacksmith, willed her good mantle, her ring, and six *exagia* of gold to others,[103] and Desa, a *famula,* willed three pairs of *cercellis* and a mantle to her sister.[104]

Jewels signified so little about status that elaborate headdresses (*frontali*) of silver and gold, and even crowns, were worn routinely. *Frontali* were a first order of business for Italian magistrates writing sumptuary law, since they spoke of unearned rank and status. But Ragusans wore them without concern for their symbolic meaning. Some Ragusan *frontali* consisted of *tabulae* or small plates of silver.[105] Gold trim on silver head ornaments enhanced the value of others.[106] Crowns were produced and worn even more frequently, and some were genuine bargains. A silver crown worked in gold and weighing eleven ounces was sold for eight *hyperperi* in 1329.[107] In 1339, two silver crowns cost forty *hyperperi*.[108] In 1343, an *aurifex* elaborated on a design by placing four gold rings on a silver crown.[109] A very small crown could be made using only four ounces and four *exagia* of silver.[110] A *corona alba* or "white crown" cost a mere four *hyperperi,* and it contained so little silver it was little more than lead.[111] Imitation of expensive and hieratic apparel in a less precious medium expanded the market in precious wares to women from the lower social ranks, so Ragusa was home to many crowned heads and tiaras or crowns that told nothing of consequence about status but represented a powerful form of advertising to strangers.

And if crowns could be worn without saying anything of significance about orders, couldn't daggers and knives be worn in the street without threatening the generally pacific nature of urban life? Ragusan men wore them and willed them. One dagger described as a "white" dagger worked with silver was certainly less expensive than the fine silver daggers or knives (*cuslerii*) that were produced in town, but it was also perhaps more functional than most.[112] Much of the production of the *aurifici* inhabited that shady category between luxury and practical use that attracted consumers to new fashions in the fourteenth century. Buttons (*maspellis*) inhabited that category. A line of buttons marching in a row down a woman's dress or a man's coat certainly transcended the functional, but buttons could more easily be justified as useful articles than crowns or knives. Still, forty-eight in a row costing seven *hyperperi*, one *grosso*, represented an investment.[113] *Aurifici* received orders for sets of buttons worked in silver and for buttons of pure silver.

Ragusan streets served then as a catalogue for the imaginative uses of precious metals and jewels. Tacitly at least, the town's councils encouraged the show so great merchants profited from at-home advertisements for their lucrative export industry. Benedetto Cotrugli stated in his fifteenth-century *Perfect Merchant* that a person's apparel no longer mirrored his station and office as it once had in ancient Rome. He regretted this, but he did not find much to censure in it.[114] Neither did his fellow townsmen. The government was not about to prohibit display in the city streets by instituting sumptuary legislation when by allowing display townspeople could stimulate the market for new fashions. If Italian city authorities employed legislation to combat the daily consequences of the newly rich overreaching their station through consuming luxury goods, Ragusans had no reason to be similarly concerned. Ostentation could not disturb the absolutes of social distinction in a community where citizens knew precisely who they were and whom they could and could not marry.

If town fathers were tolerant in the matter of purchasing and wearing jewels made from precious metal, they were absolutely lavish in their appropriation of newly mined silver for their own silver currency. In the fourteenth century, when Venice and every other Italian city ceased coining the silver *grosso*, Ragusans determined that they could afford to do so out of the Balkan mine production they imported from the interior. At some date between 1331 and 1337, Ragusa introduced a run of locally made silver coin. In 1331, Venice had resorted to production of a fractional-weight silver *mezzanino*, and it ceased production of the *grossi* entirely in subsequent years.[115] In the following decades an increase in demand for locally minted, full-weight *grossi* forced the Ragusan mint to hire more *aurifici*. A new Ragusan mint was placed in the second story of the newly constructed customs house located right at the juncture of the *platea*, or business concourse, and the harbor. High silver content in the Ragusa-minted coin had a tonic effect on the local economy. It also encouraged expenditure by visiting foreigners whose gold ducats or florins brought a favorable exchange in silver when they traded on the Ragusan market.[116]

SILVER CONTENT OF THE RAGUSAN *GROSSO*.[117]

| 1337 | 1.951 grams |
| 1348 | 1.673 grams |
| 1356 | 1.673 grams |
| 1370 | 1.518 grams |

This new coinage became a symbol of the community's silver-fed affluence. Silver coin promoted economic growth and contributed to the well-being of wage earners, but like other silver issues of the late Middle Ages it sometimes disappeared with alarming speed and frequency in foreign exchange. In the 1350s Ragusan silver merchants supported their coinage on a tenth of their silver imports from the interior. And, apparently, the scale of silver imports was sufficient to maintain the currency from a tenth, despite silver's occasional rapid exit from the commune when silver's ratio to gold improved for periods of time. The lavish nature of the measures for replenishing the silver currency added to the town's reputation abroad, fueling the growing belief that Ragusa was a pocket of prosperity in the uneasy and capricious world of late medieval commerce.

\*   \*   \*

In conclusion, Ragusans used fashion as one wedge into European markets, and, by learning to read consumption preferences, they promoted their own role from that of a peripheral city in the Mediterranean region to a central supplier of some of the few foreign-made products urban Italians still bought. They identified and built this market despite treaty restrictions on their imports into the Venetian market.[118] To all appearances, luxury imports provided an acceptable opening for Ragusans because they added luster to Venice's reputation. Ragusans labored to make themselves all but indispensable to the Venetians; in return they made great profits on Venice's markets. This required acuity in perception of social preferences as well as in economic bargaining. Ragusans had seized on the nature of the highly emblematic role of jewels in Italy's fluid urban society despite the fact that nothing even closely resembling that phenomenon occurred in their own community. At home, social stratification remained precise and undisturbed by patterns of consumption, so in a certain sense all had a license to consume to the limit of their resources if they so chose.

Ragusans grew very rich in the "hard times" of the late medieval centuries. By the fifteenth century, they had begun to use their accumulated wealth to build a fleet of splendid proportions. Their trading empire ranged over the major maritime sea routes. Noble wealth, if judged by the accumulation of private fortunes, was the equal of any urban elite in the Mediterranean world, yet privately held fortunes were not drained off by overburdening taxes, exorbitant forced loans, confiscations, or the often expensive process of replacing an old ruling elite by new rulers.[119] The cost of living, floated by a silver coinage and regulated by civic legislation, was low by comparative standards. The noble citizenry, when they attracted attention, were not admired merely because they had remained faithful to traditional values and classical republicanism, nor were they admired merely because they practiced seemly customs in their homes and neighborhoods. They were noticed because they had prospered and proved to be remarkably successful at making fortunes, while others around them often lay mired in serious, and expensive, difficulties.[120]

*Notes*

1. C. Jireček, "Die Bedeutung von Ragusa in der Handelsgeschichte des Mittelalters," and *Die Handelsstrassen und Bergwerke von Serbien und Bosnien während des Mittelalters* (Prag: Abhandlungen der kgl. bohm. Gesellschaft der Wissenschaften, 6. Folge, 10. Band, 1879) remain classics on the Ragusan economy. Numerous other works have been produced since; note citations elsewhere to Mihail Dinić's studies of inland trade and the works of Vinko Foretić, Dragan Roller, Jorjo

Tadić, Ivan Božić, and Bariša Krekić. On thirteenth-century trade in the Adriatic, Josip Lučić, "Pomorske-trgovačke veze Dubrovnika i Italije u XIII stoljeću," *Pomorskog zbornika* 5 (1967): 447–75, is particularly valuable; idem., "Gli stranieri a Ragusa nel medie evo," *Bollettino dell' Atlante linguistico mediterraneo* 13–15 (1971–73): 345–48 is useful also. A certain amount of reevaluation has occurred on the extent of Ragusan trade in the Mediterranean in earlier centuries. *Pasquale Longo, Notaio in Corone, 1289–1293,* doc. 52, 63, suggests Ragusans had a wider trading network in the thirteenth century than earlier studies suggested.

 2. The two surviving ratifications of the original Venetian-Ragusan treaty of 1205 date from 1232 and 1252 respectively. See S. Ljubić, *Listine,* vol. 1, pp. 21–22, and T. Smičiklas, *Codex Diplomaticus,* vol. 3, p. 45–47. On Italian markets, see the comments of Richard Goldthwaite in Susan Mosher Stuard, "Medieval Workshop: Toward a Theory of Consumption and Exchange," *Journal of Economic History* 44 (1985): 921–23.

 3. Fernand Braudel, *The Mediterranean,* vol. 1, p. 337.

 4. See F. Cechetti, "La vita dei Veneziani nel 1300," *Archivio veneto* 27 (1884): 31, for discussion of the *curia slavorum;* see also C. Jireček, *Staat und Gesellschaft,* vol. 2, p. 50. V.S.A., *Grazie,* Reg. 8, f. 50, 63, 65; *Grazie,* Reg. 11, f. 5, 54, 71. The charge and pardon for Marinus de Goce concerned the illegal importing of salt in 1302; E. Favaro, ed., *Cassiere della bolla ducale, Grazie, Novus Liber, 1299–1305* (Venice: Il Comitato, 1962), p. 78.

 5. S. Ljubić, *Listine,* vol. 3, p. 224.

 6. Ibid., p. 224.

 7. D.S.A., *Diversa Cancellariae,* XXIV, f. 113v.

 8. See Susan Mosher Stuard, "The Adriatic Trade in Silver, c. 1300," *Studi veneziani* 17–18 (1975–76): 95–143, for the story of Ragusan-Venetian trade negotiations in 1319. The Ragusans actually improved their trading position vis-à-vis the Germans trading silver at Venice. That was not true of other imports. Bariša Krekić noted that trade in hides at Venice decreased after 1319 because of duties, and Ragusans directed their exports henceforth toward the Levant. Bariša Krekić, *Dubrovnik et le Levant au moyen âge* (Paris: SEVPEN, 1961), p. 78.

 9. *MR,* vol. 5, p. 261. The definition of Sclavonia, like that of Romania, presents difficulties. See R. Wolff, "Romania, the Latin Empire of Constantinople," *Speculum* 23 (1948): 1–34. C. Jireček defined Sclavonia as the Adriatic coast between the Istrian peninsula and the Bojana River in Albania as well as the interior. This would include Croatia, Dalmatia, Montenegro, Northern Albania, the Herzegovina, Bosnia, and some of Serbia. C. Jireček, "Die Bedeutung von Ragusa," p. 376. Venice used the term Dalmatia as well as Sclavonia, thus dividing the land with the islands and coast belonging to Dalmatia and the inland territories to Sclavonia. In some instances, Sclavonia appears as a synonym for Rascia or the kingdom of Serbia. Cf. Bariša Krekić, *Dubrovnik et le Levant,* pp. 25–31, and Freddy Thiriet, *La Romanie venetiénne* (Paris, 1959), chap. 1. In distinguishing Romania and Sclavonia, King Dušan of Serbia, on being crowned emperor of the Greeks, formally partitioned his realm and crowned his son king of the Serbs, thereby acknowledging a line between the two that ran a course through Macedonia. Silver was also traded to Florence (see note 72, below). Bogumil Hrabak has found evidence of a silver trade

with Catalonia in which Ragusans traded silver for textiles. Bogumil Hrabak, "Dubrovačko srebro u Italiji i Kataloniji u XIV, XV, i XVI veku," *Istorijski glasnik* 1–2 (1980): 57–78. For details on Ragusa's 1205 treaty with Venice, see Chapter 2.

10. Josip Lučić, *Obrti i usluge u Dubrovniku*, pp. 23–100. See table in Chapter 6.

11. David Herlihy, *Pisa in the Early Renaissance* (New Haven, Conn.: Yale University Press, 1958), pp. 134–61, 178–80.

12. F. Cechetti, "La vita dei Veneziani del 1300," p. 126–27, notes great coats and *zentura d'arzento*, or a silver belt, as well.

13. Pompeo Molmenti, *La storia di Venezia nella vita privata* (Bergamo: Istituto Italia, 1922), vol. 1, pp. 363–66, suggests that Slavic fashions were generally in vogue in the late thirteenth and early fourteenth centuries. Both *le schiavine* (fabric) and *le rasse della Rascia* were in style. See also Rosita Levi-Pisetzky, *Storia del costume in Italia* (Milan: Fondazione Giovanni Treccani degli Alfieri, 1964), vol. 2, *Il Trecento*, and Millia Davenport, *The Book of Costume* (New York: Crown Publishers, 1948). Robert S. Lopez, *Studi sull'economia Genovese nel medio evo*, vol. 14 (Turin: S. Lattes, 1936), provides inventories in which male attire appears.

14. Fernand Braudel, *The Wheels of Commerce*, trans. S. Reynolds (New York: Harper and Row, 1982), pp. 178–80, 312.

15. Roberto Cessi, *Problemi monetari veneziani*, doc. 147, p. 132. See also V.S.A., *Avogaria di Comun, Deliberazioni del Maggior Consiglio, Magnus*, f. 41. For a fuller discussion see Susan Stuard, "The Adriatic Trade in Silver, c. 1300," 95–143. See also F. Lane, "Le vecchie monete di conto veneziane ed il ritorno all'oro," *Atti dell'Instituto Veneto di Scienze, Lettere ed Arti, Cl. science morali e lettere* 117 (1958–59): 58–68.

16. Dante, *Divine Comedy, Paradiso*, ed. Charles Singleton (Princeton, N.J.: Princeton University Press, 1975), canto 19, vol. 3, pt. I, pp. 140–41.

17. Roberto Cessi, *Problemi monetari veneziani*, doc. 57, p. 58; V.S.A., *Zecca, Capitulare massarii all'argento*, vol. 6, fol. 17, 17v, 18, 18v.

18. *MR*, vol. 2, p. 309.

19. Michael Metcalf, *Coinage of the Balkans* (Chicago: University of Chicago Press, 1965), pp. 197–218. M. Dinić, "Krstati groševi," p. 102. Dinić estimates the ratio of the Serbian coin to the Venetian reached 1 to 0.9 in 1303. Gregor Čremošnik, *Spisi, 1278–1301*, "de cruce," doc. 68, pp. 44–45; "de lilia," doc. 307, p. 107; "de macia et de bandera," doc. 68, p. 45.

20. Roberto Cessi, *Problemi monetari veneziani*, doc. 62, pp. 60–61.

21. Desanka Kovačević, "Les Mines d'or et d'argent en Servie et Bosnie," *Annales, économies, sociétés, civilisations* 15 (1960): 248–58; Speros Vyronis, "The Question of the Byzantine Mines," *Speculum* 37, no. 1 (1962): 1–17; and John Nef, "Mining and Metallurgy in Medieval Civilization," in *Cambridge Economic History*, ed. M. M. Postan (Cambridge: Cambridge University Press, 1952), vol. 2, p. 456, assume a later date for major bulk shipments of silver than this study. See also Sime Cirković and Desanka Kovačević-Kojic, "L'Économie naturelle et la production marchande aux XIII<sup>e</sup>–XV<sup>e</sup> siècles dans les regions actuelles de la Yougoslavie," *Balcanica* 13–14 (1982–83): 45–56.

22. V.S.A., *Grazie*, Reg. 3, f. 41, 49.

23. V.S.A., *Grazie,* Reg. 5, f. 50 (1334).

24. V.S.A., *Grazie,* Reg. 7, f. 37 (1336).

25. V.S.A., *Grazie,* Reg. 6, f. 40v and 81v (1344).

26. V.S.A., *Grazie,* Reg. 6, f. 81v.

27. V.S.A., *Grazie,* Reg. 6, f. 81v. For information on Venetian bankers' activities at Ragusa, see Susan Stuard, "The Adriatic Trade in Silver," pp. 118, 123–29.

28. D.S.A., *Diversa Cancellariae,* XII, f. 29, for an example of a commission for silver wares for a goldsmith.

29. The term commonly used was *nappum de argentum.* Frequently one accompanied an order and therefore might be unworked silver. In other instances, however, a number of bags of silver were part of a commission or order, and sometimes these were engraved silver. These might be *tabulae* or ornaments for clothes which were made and sold in the same design.

30. See D.S.A., *Diversa Cancellariae,* IX, f. 168, for a commission with Johannes Fici to take silver of Ragusa, then stored at the mint in Ancona, to Venice. See Susan Stuard, "The Adriatic Trade in Silver," pp. 125–27.

31. See R. Levi-Pisetzky, *Storia del costume in Italia,* vol. 2, for discussion of the change to fashion in Venice and Italy in the fourteenth century. P. Molmenti, *La storia di Venezia nella vita privata,* vol. 1, pp. 363–66.

32. *Croniche de Giovanni, Matteo, e Filippo Villani,* ed. A. Racheli (Trieste, 1957), vol. 1; *Tales from Sacchetti,* trans. Mary Steegman (London: J. M. Dent, 1908).

33. Dante, *Divine Comedy, Paradiso,* canto 15, lines 97–102 (vol. 3, pt. 1, p. 169; see also vol. 3; pt. 2, pp. 258–61).

34. See Robert Lopez, *Studi sull'economia Genovese nel medio evo,* for inventory with male attire in the thirteenth century. Louise Buenger Robbert, "Food and Clothing Prices in Pisa and Venice in the Late Twelfth Century," (forthcoming).

35. The work is located at Worcester Art Museum, Worcester, Mass.

36. R. Levi-Pisetzky, *Storia del costume,* vol. 2, fig. 30, p. 73, silver reliquary from the Treasury of St. Mark. See also F. Cechetti, *La vita dei veneziani nell 1300,* p. 126–27.

37. R. Levi-Pisetzky, *Storia del costume,* vol. 2, fig. 31, p. 74. See also p. 14, donor portrait, *La famiglia del conto Stephano Porro, Affresco databile al 1370, Oratorio, Lentate.* In this donor portrait all the male figures wear large silver belts on their hips.

38. D.S.A., *Diversa Cancellariae,* VIII, f. 176 (1327). Silver wares were historically subject to melting and reworking, so few if any survive from Ragusa's medieval production. In the Bishop's Palace Museum in Dubrovnik there is a silver chalice, possibly fifteenth century. In the same museum: "Madonna with Child." The figure of the Madonna is of the Byzantine type of the thirteenth century. The figures of the saints flanking it are the work of a Dubrovnik painter of the sixteenth century. Silver crowns for the Madonna and Child were also added. The artist is not named, but these crowns may also be the work of a local goldsmith.

39. D.S.A., *Diversa Cancellariae,* IX, f. 211.

40. D.S.A., *Diversa Cancellariae,* X, f. 81v.

41. D.S.A., *Diversa Cancellariae,* II, f. 174.

42. D.S.A., *Diversa Cancellariae*, VIII, f. 2 (1326).

43. D.S.A., *Diversa Cancellariae*, XII, f. 238 (1335).

44. D.S.A., *Diversa Cancellariae*, IX, f. 211.

45. D.S.A., *Diversa Cancellariae*, V, f. 5v, 41.

46. D.S.A., *Diversa Cancellariae*, XII, f. 240v.

47. D.S.A., *Diversa Cancellariae*, X, f. 27 (1333).

48. D.S.A., *Diversa Cancellariae*, VI, 4, 48.

49. D.S.A., *Diversa Notariae*, IV, f. 3.

50. D.S.A., *Diversa Cancellariae*, VI, f. 153.

51. D.S.A., *Diversa Cancellariae*, XII, f. 299v; *Diversa Cancellaraie*, XIII, f. 42v; *Diversa Cancellariae*, XIV, f. 122v; *Diversa Cancellariae*, XI, f. 9v.

52. *MR*, vol. 5, p. 229, distinguished the quality of silver in which goldsmiths might work and what they might charge. See C. Fisković, "Dubrovački zlatari od XIII do XVII stoljeća."

53. D.S.A., *Diversa Cancellariae*, XII, f. 5v.

54. D.S.A., *Diversa Notariae*, VI, f. 149v.

55. D.S.A., *Diversa Cancellariae*, IX, f. 22v.

56. D.S.A., *Diversa Cancellariae*, XII, f. 253v.

57. Roberto Cessi, *Problemi monetari veneziani* (see introduction); see also Gino Luzzatto, *Studi di storia economica veneziana* (Padua: CEDAM, 1954), pp. 74ff., on the mint's standards for precious ores imported into Venice by Slavs and Germans.

58. P. Molmenti, *La storia di Venezia nella vita privata*, vol. 1, pp. 360ff. Cf. Richard Trexler, *Public Life in Renaissance Florence* (New York: Academic Press, 1980), and Edward Muir, *Civic Ritual in Renaissance Venice* (Princeton, N.J.: Princeton University Press, 1981).

59. Rodolfo Pallucchini, *La pittura veneziana del trecento* (Venice and Rome: Istituto per la collaborazione culturale, 1964), fig. 455, *Altichiero de Zevio, Membri della famiglia Lupi di Soragna presentari alla Vergine dai respettivi Santi affresio, 1379–1384*, Padua, Oratorio di S. Giorgio.

60. Guido Ruggiero, "Modernization and the Mythic State in Early Renaissance Venice: The Serrata Revisited," *Viator* 10 (1979): 245–56; Richard Trexler, *Public Life in Renaissance Florence*. Florentines employed the phrase "grave men" for *sapientes*.

61. V.S.A., *Senato Deliberazioni*, Reg. 1333–1334, f. 69; C. Foucard, ed., *Statuto delle nozze a Venezia dell'anno 1299* (pamphlet) (Venice, 1858). For some comments on Venetian sumptuary law in the fourteenth century, see N. Margaret Newett, "The Sumptuary Law of Venice," in *Historical Essays*, ed. T. Tout and J. Tait (London: Longmans, Green, 1902), pp. 235–78. More recently, compare Diane Owen Hughes, "Sumptuary Law and Social Relations in Renaissance Italy," in *Disputes and Settlements: Law and Human Relations in the West*, ed. John Bossy (Cambridge: Cambridge University Press, 1983), pp. 66–99.

62. Desanka Kovačević, "Les Mines d'or et d'argent en Servie et Bosnie," p. 257, gives the following dates for the first references to fourteenth-century mines. Both Brescova (Brskovo) and Rudnica (Rudnik) were producing earlier in the thirteenth century.

| Trepca | 1303 |
| Janejeva | 1303 |
| Rogozno | 1303 |
| Trešnjica | 1312 |
| Lipnik | 1319, 1346, single reference |
| Nova Brdo | 1326 |
| Plana | 1346 |
| Korporici | 1346 |
| Zeleznik | 1350 |
| Kratovo | 1350 |

63. C. Jireček, "Die Bedeutung von Ragusa," pp. 378, 396, 420; Bariša Krekić "Four Florentine Commercial Companies in Dubrovnik (Ragusa)," pp. 25–41, although Krekić does not identify the letters of exchange drawn up at Ragusa for transaction at Venice as such.

64. Gino Luzzatto, *Studi di storia economica veneziana;* idem., *I prestiti della Repubblica di Venezia* (Padua, 1929).

65. Ignacij Voje, "Bencius del Bono," pp. 189–99; see also discussion of Lorino Rici's career in Ragusa in Chapter 5. Bencius del Bono was active in Ragusa from 1318 until the 1330s; D.S.A., *Diversa Notariae,* III, f. 92v, 93.

66. Franco Sacchetti, "Tre Cento Novelle XCVIII," trans. Mary Steegman in *Tales from Sacchetti* (London: Dent, 1908), p. 79.

67. D.S.A., *Diversa Cancellariae,* VIII, f. 144b.

68. D.S.A., *Diversa Cancellariae,* IX, f. 200.

69. D.S.A., *Diversa Cancellariae,* X, f. 83, 228v.

70. D.S.A., *Diversa Cancellariae,* IX, f. 107v, 168; XII, f. 96. Measure for precious metals at Ragusa: 12 ounces = 1 pound; 1 ounce = 6 *exagia* or *saggia* (4.555 g.); 1 *exagia* = 24 carats (0.9 g.); 1 carat = 4 grains (0.0475 g.).

71. S. Stuard, "The Adriatic Trade in Silver," pp. 131ff.

72. V. Makušev, *Monumenta historica slavorum meridionalium vicinorumque populorum e tabulariis et bibliothecis italicis de prompta* (Warsaw, 1874), vol. 1: *Ancona, Bononia, Florentia,* part II, doc. 7, p. 435.

73. Gregor Čremošnik, *Spisi Thomasina de Savere,* doc. 771, 772, 736, 745, 780, 781, 818, 936, 503, 599, 722, 944, 945, 538, 583, 203, 571, 572, 670, 800, 938, 1051, 1075, 1071, 1093, 1123.

74. Anton Mayer, *Kotorski spomenici Prva knjiga notara od god. 1326–1335* (Zagreb: JAZU, 1951), vol. 1, index rerum, p. 635 (henceforth *Monumenta Catarensia*).

75. Josip Lučić, *Obrti i usluge u Dubrovniku,* pp. 62–71.

76. Cvito Fisković, "Dubrovački zlatari od XIII do XVII stoljeća," pp. 241–46.

77. D.S.A., *Diversa Cancellariae,* XII, f. 29, paraphrased, "Angelus, goldsmith swears he has received one pound of pure silver from Andreas de Mence, and he promises to make 12 knives from it by the feast of St. Blasius (Vlah)."

78. *MR,* vol. 5, p. 229.

79. *MR,* vol. 2, p. 46, for definitions of fineness of silver dictated by the council. *MR,* vol. 2, p. 152 for later legislation in 1356 stipulating quality of worked

silver and gold. D.S.A., *Diversa Cancellariae,* V, f. 59v. Goldsmiths were further forbidden to migrate to the interior.

80. C. Jireček, *Die Handelsstrassen und Bergwerke,* p. 43. D.S.A., *Diversa Cancellariae,* X, f. 228v, gives an estimate of gold content in a shipment of silver ore. Thirty carats were estimated to be present in four pounds, three ounces and three *exagia* of silver. There was some uncertainty about the exact amount until the silver had undergone further refining. The various silver ores were called *argento plico, argento biancho, argento fino,* and *argento de glama* by Ragusans in their everyday business; the last mentioned the gold-laden ore from Nova Brdo.

81. D.S.A., *Diversa Cancellariae,* V, f. 42.

82. D.S.A., *Diversa Notariae,* III, f. 121v. In these instances the bags of silver were likely filled with engraved silver or *tabulae.*

83. D.S.A., *Diversa Cancellariae,* VI, f. 90.

84. D.S.A., *Diversa Cancellariae,* VIII, f. 176.

85. D.S.A., *Diversa Cancellariae,* IX, f. 211.

86. D.S.A., *Diversa Cancellariae,* X, f. 81v.

87. D.S.A., *Diversa Cancellariae,* XII, f. 120.

88. D.S.A., *Diversa Notariae,* III, f. 121v. See also Jorjo Tadić, *Građa o slikarskoj skoli u Dubrovniku XII–XVI veku* (Belgrade: SAN, 1952), vol. 1 for other religious art commissioned in the fourteenth and fifteenth centuries.

89. D.S.A., *Diversa Cancellariae,* VI, f. 70v.

90. D.S.A., *Diversa Cancellariae,* VII, f. 38.

91. D.S.A., *Diversa Cancellariae,* XV, f. 134v.

92. D.S.A., *Diversa Notariae,* III, f. 182.

93. D.S.A., *Diversa Notariae,* II, f. 192.

94. D.S.A., *Diversa Notariae,* III, f. 110v.

95. D.S.A., *Diversa Cancellariae,* VI, f. 46.

96. D.S.A., *Diversa Notariae,* III, f. 114v; see Dušanka Dinić-Knežević, *Položaj žena u Dubrovniku,* p. 202.

97. Philippus de Diversis, *Situs aedificiorum,* p. 56.

98. Diane Owen Hughes, "Sumptuary Law and Social Relations in Renaissance Italy," pp. 66–99.

99. D.S.A., *Testamenta,* V, f. 33–33v, 39–40.

100. D.S.A., *Testamenta,* V, f. 57v–58.

101. D.S.A., *Testamenta,* III, f. 25v.

102. D.S.A., *Testamenta,* 5v–6.

103. D.S.A., *Testamenta,* I, f. 6; see also f. 14.

104. D.S.A., *Diversa Notariae,* III, f. 174.

105. D.S.A., *Diversa Notariae,* III, f. 192.

106. D.S.A., *Diversa Cancellariae,* IX, f. 104.

107. D.S.A., *Diversa Notariae,* VI, f. 38v.

108. D.S.A., *Diversa Cancellariae,* XIV, f. 31.

109. D.S.A., *Diversa Cancellariae,* XVI, f. 92v.

110. D.S.A., *Diversa Cancellariae,* XVI, f. 16v.

111. D.S.A., *Diversa Cancellariae,* XIII, f. 45v; see also *Diversa Cancellariae,* XVIII, f. 38v.

112. D.S.A., *Diversa Cancellariae*, XIV, f. 129.

113. D.S.A., *Diversa Notariae*, IV, f. 76; see also *Diversa Cancellariae*, VIII, f. 176.

114. Benedetto Cotrugli, *Della mercatura*, f. 89 (Tucci ed., p. 233).

115. "Monetam similen seu in illo conio seu ligae, quae est illa, quae fit in Ragusio per commune." Milan Rešetar, *Dubrovačka numizmatika*, vol. 1, p. 133. See also Vuk Vinaver, "Der Venezianische Goldzechin in der Republik Ragusa," p. 116–21. *MR*, vol. 2, pp. 10, 86, 156. On the weight of coin minted at Ragusa see Jorjo Tadić, "Les Archives économiques de Raguse," *Annales, E.S.C.* 16 (1961): 1170.

116. Ragusa responded by pegging the exchange rate of the ducat at twenty-four *grossi*, *MR*, vol. 2, pp. 332, 342.

117. Jorjo Tadić, "Les Archives économiques de Raguse," p. 1170.

118. *MR*, vol. 5, p. 261.

119. Investments in the fleet, which grew significantly in the fourteenth and fifteenth centuries, provide a good example of new investment patterns. Stepan Vekarić, "Dubrovačka trgovačka flota, 1599 godine," *Dubrovnik anali* 13 (1974): 427–32; idem., "Vrste i tipovi dubrovačkih brodova XIV stoljeća," *Dubrovnik anali* 10–11 (1966): 19–42. See also Josip Luetić, *O pomorstvu dubrovačke republike u XVIII stoljeću* (Dubrovnik, 1959). Cf. Frederic Lane, "The Funded Debt of Venice," in *Venice and History* (Baltimore: Johns Hopkins University Press, 1966), pp. 87–98, translated by author from Gino Luzzatto, *Il debito pubblico della Repubblica di Venezia* (Milan, 1963), pp. 275–92; Anthony Mohlo, *The Funded Debt of Early Renaissance Florence* (Cambridge, Mass.: Harvard University Press, 1971).

120. Frederic Lane, "The Economic Meaning of War and Protection," in *Venice and History*, pp. 383–98.

# 8. Fame

Sea power, embodied in a merchant fleet, established Ragusa's fame as a city-state of consequence in the Mediterranean. After centuries of persistent attempts to move beyond a peripheral position confined by the Balkans and the Adriatic, Ragusans began to participate on a major scale in the carrying trade. In the decades after 1358, Ragusans achieved some success, but their long-sought prominence as a Mediterranean power came only in the fifteenth century.

In the early years of the fourteenth century, two galleys had carried merchandise from the port; at least fifteen *taridae* were used in transport and five *barcae* or *barcussii*. For swifter voyages, smaller rowed *condurae*, which held only twenty *miliaria* (thousandweight, based on the light Ragusan pound of 328 grams), had served both for short trips along the coast and for voyages along the *intra culfum* route to Venice.[1] This small fleet of a peripheral maritime state could not foreshadow the success that lay ahead.

By the second half of the century Ragusans from a variety of occupations, from aristocrats to skilled laborers, began to invest heavily in shipping and the larger, slow, round-bottomed sailing vessels that had come to dominate the sea routes of the Mediterranean. Now the merchant aristocracy reaped the reward of enriching the *cives de populo,* because this prosperous rank reciprocated their noble patrons by investing in the merchant fleet. At least twelve *cochae,* or cogs, were included in the Ragusan fleet by 1370. Between 1370 and 1391, eight *naves* were added while the galleys and *condurae* (both rowed vessels that had been popular earlier in the century) were evidently retired or, in the case of the two treaty galleys, replaced.[2] Only affluent and adaptable powers rebuilt their fleets swiftly enough to meet changing market conditions in this age. But swift turnover in the type of sailing vessels best suited to the changing demands of sea trade actually brought advantages to the infant merchant marine of Ragusa. Competing larger navies, forced to retire numerous old vessels and at the same time to overhaul their fleets, found it necessary to redesign their shipyard operations radically to suit new conditions. Ragusans had very few old ships to scuttle and only a small amount of capital tied up in them. Since these were the very decades in which substantial fortunes accrued to the noble citizenry and many industrious non-noble inhabitants of the community, Ragusans suddenly found themselves with the capital to build a fleet from scratch. In shipyards near town, particularly at the deep water port at Gruž and on the islands, Ragusans constructed their new fleet, or adapted and refurbished vessels purchased abroad. Lumber, an increasingly scarce Mediterranean commodity, was still available from the Balkan highlands and arrived in town by caravan. The good will of neighbors directly across the sea, the controllers of the Adriatic's last major stand of tall timber for shipbuilding, placed the great forests of timber on Monte Gargano at the disposal of local shipyards.[3] By the fifteenth century, a spanking new merchant navy carried Ragusan products abroad, and the town's sailors and ship captains developed a reputation as reliable carriers in trade.

As the fifteenth century progressed, Ragusans rebuilt their navy anew once more, with the lighter vessels that now dominated Mediterranean trade in ascendence. The fifteenth century saw remarkable growth in the number of ships in the Ragusan fleet. The new, swift small vessels built by the republic competed favorably with great foreign navies involved in the luxury trade, while the pattern of investment in this second reconstruction of the fleet was similar to the first. Ragusans from many walks of life contracted together for partial shares in a vessel, typically investing in quarters, but a vessel might also be owned in shares as small as eighths, and even those shares might be purchased jointly. Ship captains from the Ragusan-held islands and Korcula, salaried employees of the commune, such as physicians; *civis de populo* merchants; and foreign investors, such as the new generation of Florentines staffing banking services in the Adriatic poured fortunes into building or reprovisioning ships.[4] A small ship, of the sort that was now cost efficient in competitive sea trade, required eight to nine months to construct, while a great ship like those in service in earlier decades had required as much as two to three years. The construction of the fifteenth-century fleet of light vessels favored the small investor because it demanded smaller capital sums to buy into shipping interests and a shorter length of time to realize a return on the investment. Ragusan fortunes, based on low living costs and lucrative exports that were not eaten away by voracious war-engendered taxes, paid off in the creation of this fleet. In a sense, those who had tied their business interests to the Ragusan *prijateljstvo* now returned to that merchant aristocracy investment capital for a powerful Mediterranean fleet.

In the half-century between 1520 and 1570, the navy was reconstructed one more time, this time favoring the now-popular large vessels. Mercantile navies again adapted or ceased to compete. The Ragusan fleet soon numbered 180 vessels that carried approximately 38,000 *carra* (one *carra* equals one and a half deadweight tons). The carrying trade grew precipitously in the middle years of the sixteenth century. Josip Luetić estimates the value of shipping at 200,000 ducats in 1540 and 700,000 ducats in 1570. By 1585, the limits of expansion of the fleet had been reached. Within the Ragusan navy forty vessels had a carrying capacity of two hundred to four hundred *carra,* and over thirty vessels possessed capacities over four hundred *carra.* The fleet sailed the Atlantic now, and Argosy (or Ragosy) became a common sight in the harbors of Europe. Ragusans made their presence known by appearing with their fleets in the harbors of maritime powers, where they contracted for loads—"snatching" loads, in the words of Fernand Braudel—before the very eyes of local seamen.[5] The carrying power of this fleet rivaled the navies of Genoa and Venice. Ragusa had become one of the major Mediterranean powers despite the small size of the republic.

Ragusans, then, even before the Dutch, reveal how little numerical strength or geographical size signified under the terms of capitalist trade. With noble family fortunes swollen to at least eight times their size over two centuries, fifteenth-century Ragusans possessed private wealth rivaling that of merchant aristocracies in the greatest cities. A small republic at peace, home and abroad, meant limited demands were placed on personal wealth. Remaining a diminutive city-state promoted the increasing scale of the navy by holding down alternate expenditures, yet obtaining necessary personnel for the navy's expansion was never a problem: the Adriatic was full of eager recruits. Argosy stood for a mighty sea power in the sixteenth-century world.

A great facilitator of trade, and no mean source of Ragusa's growing reputation, was the resident Ragusan consul permanently stationed in foreign ports who shouldered a major responsibility for lading Ragusan vessels with goods for transport. He also promoted Ragusan trade within foreign port cities. The senate had begun developing the office in the fourteenth century, and by the fifteenth century Ragusan consuls sat in twenty-three Mediterranean ports. By the sixteenth century, consuls served in forty-four separate western port cities, with six more in the eastern Mediterranean. Ragusans filled the office themselves when they reckoned the port was absolutely critical to their commerce. Certain strategic consulates, like those at Ancona and at Naples, were always filled by Ragusans, by both noble and *civis de populo* citizens (Benedetto Cotrugli served brilliantly at Naples, where he composed his popular *Perfect Merchant*), but in other ports the Ragusan senate selected an influential local merchant for the position.[6] A network of local and highly respected Italian, French, Spanish, and, in the case of North Africa, Dutch consuls became agents of the republic and in many instances loyal friends of the merchant aristocracy. They became the backbone of an intelligence service second to none in the Mediterranean; oftentimes consuls, native and foreign, served as vocal advocates of the Ragusan way of conducting affairs. A large correspondence to and from these consuls attests to their loyalty and the admiration they awarded to the republic.

Through these foreign consuls the senate cultivated the role of a neutral power and nonaggressor in a Mediterranean world chronically at war. The Ragusan navy fearlessly entered most Mediterranean ports and negotiated for cargoes, at times transporting cargoes between declared enemies. Only a recognized nonaggressor could hope to take and hold such a role in trade, and few rivaled Ragusans in adopting this stance. Armed neutrality, a reputation as devout Catholics enjoying the favor and protection of the papacy, as well as the tolerance and good will of the sultan, kept the fleet mobile in Mediterranean waters.

Meanwhile, Ragusa's reputation fed on prosperity and sea voyaging. It spread by word of mouth in harbors and ports where foreigners serving as Ragusan consuls became mouthpieces for a city-state whose ways of conducting trade and community life were substantively different from the great western powers. Ragusans negotiated successfully with the infidel Turks. They courted and received protection from Catholic powers, even while those powers were at war with each other. Their reputation abroad reflected a growing conviction that the republic of Ragusa did not fit a common mold, although as a Christian city-state involved in commerce it appeared, superficially at least, to be highly conventional. So Ragusan mores and values—as represented by sea captains, sailors, and merchants, as described by foreign travelers and ambassadors, or even as reported as hearsay by foreign consuls serving the republic—became tantalizing, and often perpetuated the city's myth among new observers.

Travelers' accounts of voyages or land journeys to Ragusa as well as ambassadorial journals, particularly the detailed and informative reports of Venetian diplomats traveling to Turkey and the Levant, reinforced Ragusa's reputation as *città felice* of Dalmatia, or, for the classically minded, as Illyria. Caterino Zeno, a sixteenth-century Venetian ambassador to Turkey, commented on the hardships of the land route from Ragusa across the Balkans. He noted that a journey accompanied by pack animals loaded with baggage required twenty-five days, but Vlach runners and pack animals could reach Constantinople in only fifteen days, and Ragusa supplied both.[7] Ragusa was the last Christian outpost on his journey to the east, and an exotic place for that reason alone.

Nicolas de Nicolay, in *Navigations, pérégrinations et voyages faicts en la Turquie* (1576), claimed that Ragusa was prosperous and fair; and he particularly admired its Renaissance summer palaces in the harbor at Gruž, where groves of lemon and orange trees introduced the northern visitor to the moderate and nonseasonal climate of the Levant.[8] Ragusa, then, was an outpost: the language spoken in its streets was already foreign to the western European ear unfamiliar with Slavic; it was the last Catholic outpost an eastward bound traveler visited and the first place he met the seasonless, exotic climate of the south.

Benedetto Ramberti, a sixteenth-century Venetian ambassador who also traveled from his native Venice to Turkey by the land route, found Ragusa exotic for other reasons. It was most noble and ancient, he asserted, as the descendant of Illyrian Epidaurus should be. Now while that old city across the bay was sparsely inhabited, Ragusa itself was very well populated and beautifully situated. Only a cramped harbor marred the excellence of its appointments. Ramberti recognized the signs of a highly successful enterprise in streets filled with commerce and workshops with industry. But in visual appearance Ragusans differed from Italians—not that they were poorly arrayed, for their costumes signified vast wealth. Still, they did not follow Italian fashions, and, in fact, the natives had adopted a common costume, the sort that had not been seen in Italy proper for two hundred years. He was quick to note that noblewomen in particular were curiously dressed. He found the local costume and the cone-shaped headgear quite ugly—a comment to be expected perhaps from a man whose native Venice still remained the hub of latest fashion in Europe. Ragusan women whose bangles, *frontali,* and crowns had introduced fashions from the east into Italy in the fourteenth century had apparently withdrawn from following the continuing round of European fashion cycles. At Venice fifteenth- and sixteenth-century costumes had moved on to entirely new consumer preferences, which Ramberti saw as proper and normal behavior.[9]

Ramberti's terse but acute remarks suggest that for all its superficial ordinariness, Ragusa followed its own distinct course and stood outside the common experience of western European development. And, if Ramberti had remained in town to observe the noble circle and other town dwellers more closely, he would have found even more evidence that townspeople differed in dress, traditions, practices, manners, and values from western Europeans whose behaviors had grown to more closely resemble each other.[10] Travelers and other observers lacked only a schema in which to place the puzzling phenomenon of a town at once so familiar and yet so distinct from the rest of Catholic Europe.

Renaissance humanist discourse was capable of remedying that lack of a category within which to comprehend the republic of Ragusa; Niccolò Machiavelli's thoughts on the nature of republics in his *Discourses on the Ten Books of Titus Livius* provided a *topos* within which the long history of the republic of Ragusa could be considered.[11] Machiavelli recognized that republican governments afforded states two opposing postures: an expansive one like ancient Rome's, which he found the more honorable and worthy of exposition, and a defensive one that he tentatively likened to contemporary Venice, but more confidently to ancient Sparta under the Lycurgan constitution. Machiavelli held out little hope for a middle course between the two types, but while choosing the expansive republic as superior, he still praised the defensive: "If she remains quiet within her limits, and experience shows that she entertains no ambitious projects, the fear of her power will never prompt any one to attack her; and this would even be more certainly the case if her constitution and laws prohibited all aggrandizement. And I certainly think that if she could be kept in this equilibrium, it would be the best political existence."[12] His stated preference for the expansive republic was not, then, a repudiation of the defensive sort, but reflected instead his profound skepticism about the constancy in human endeavors a defensive republic required. "But as all human things are kept in a perpetual movement, and can never remain stable, states naturally either rise or decline, and necessity compels them to many acts to which reason will not influence them."[13] Clearly that "best political existence" was seldom to be hoped for, but not all observers shared this pessimism.

When Machiavelli's audience reflected on distinctions among republics by reference to Mediterranean city-states, some among them expressed strong misgivings about the cost of greatness that expansive city-states had often paid. In Renaissance Europe, when tensions between absolutism and traditional liberties were either worked out or fought over within the ruling classes themselves, Machiavellian notions about expansion were recognized as sure sources for strife and belligerence. Mediterranean cities were Europe's models for development north of the Alps in numerous instances:

what if a pacific sort of city-state could be found whose actual history confounded Machiavelli's skepticism? Its renown would be assured and its myth broadcast. A successful defensive republic, if such ever existed, held attractions.

So by the sixteenth century, the republic of Ragusa began to occupy a place in the thoughts of a European public interested in statecraft and political theory. The town's historical experience, interpreted through chronicles and commentaries, particularly the widely read fifteenth-century *Della mercatura et del mercante perfetto* of Benedetto Cotrugli, posed a documented historical instance where Machiavelli might be proved wrong about the viability of a defensive or nonaggrandizing republic. It came to be generally known that Ragusa's longevity and prosperity had not been achieved at the cost of its ancient republican constitution. Some believed the town embodied virtue in the persons of its citizens—virtue well rewarded by fortune, it should be added. Sedition was known to have been avoided but, to all appearances, not at the expense of ancient constitutional safeguards for civil rights. Church and state lived in apparent harmony, and to cap it all, commendable familial values had been upheld. This was the Ragusan myth that entered the popular imagination of Europe dressed up in the guise of a nonaggrandizing republic. In a certain sense Ragusa served first for developing economies in the role the Dutch played in subsequent centuries and the Japanese more recently: that of a small power that presented a model for development that deviated in its economic and social configurations from more expansion-minded states and realms. Also, Renaissance Ragusans inspired Europeans in a persistent and clearly nostalgic belief that pure aristocracy, that is, a variant of classical republicanism, could flourish in the contemporary world. As this myth grew, Ragusa's practices and institutions took on an aura of probity that attracted comment.

Benedetto Cotrugli is owed a largely unacknowledged debt for providing information on Ragusa to western Europeans in his *Della mercatura et del mercante perfetto,* completed in 1458. This learned treatise, known widely and somewhat inaccurately as a mere late addition to the stock of medieval merchant manuals, actually bridges the gap between that genre and Renaissance treatises on politics, conduct, and governance of the family. Cotrugli stated that his original vocation as a scholar was only reluctantly given up to allow him to pursue a business career. His *Perfect Merchant* and, apparently, his lost treatise on family as well were studded with classical references.[14] Cotrugli had read widely in philosophy, law, theology, and literature; his audience never doubted it. In the *Perfect Merchant* Cotrugli chose a vehicle both practical and scholarly for an exposition of the honorable life open to a noble merchant, drawing specific reference to the values that should be instilled first in youth and then cultivated over a lifetime.[15]

The *Perfect Merchant* was composed in Italian in Naples, where the author served as Ragusan consul, and the treatise found an audience almost immediately. It has had a more enduring impact on western opinion than Ragusan works composed by the author's fellow Ragusan authors in Latin or Slavic because it followed a familiar format in a familiar western language. In fact both Venetians and Neapolitans claim Cotrugli as an exponent of their own outlooks on life. And with the alterations accompanying the sixteenth-century Venetian printed edition, and surviving copy, of the treatise attributable to either Neapolitan or Venetian hands, or both, they may both make claim in part to Cotrugli as exponent of their values.[16] These claims are, however, generally restricted to the arguments that appear in the first book of the treatise, where a straightforward explanation of double-entry bookkeeping and a bold defense of the propriety of taking interest reveal a merchant both practical and advanced in his outlook. Cotrugli's prolix style and considerably more discursive chapters on morals in book 2, and on conduct and family life in books 3 and 4, have not prompted comparable rival claims. But precisely here, in the later arguments, Cotrugli placed the weight of his own understanding of how a merchant succeeds on the project of a perfect life, and here as well he inserted his most choice aphorisms. Perhaps he breathed the "modern" spirit in these later, neglected chapters as well as or better than in his first book on business methods, but if so he did it in a fashion less accessible to today's readers.

In his last chapters, Cotrugli attempted to explain the social world of his native city in the somewhat archaic rhetorical style of his day. Drawing on his own wide business contacts and his reputation as consul, he presented a contemporary, self-conscious, and analytical account of the values that his family had adopted when they accepted citizenship in Ragusa in the late fourteenth century. The order of his chapters signaled his intentions. Cotrugli began with practical business methods that provided a practical link and point of reference for his chosen audience of educated Mediterranean merchants and scholars. He moved his reader from there to a discussion of the morality which should inform business practices. Next he presented the behavior of the merchant who seeks perfection, and in his last book he set forth the foundation of the perfectly ordered merchant life in a discussion of the household and the family. Finally, penetrating to the core of the matter—wise stewardship of private matters and meticulous attention to all familial and domestic questions—Cotrugli revealed to his reader just how, and why, a perfect merchant achieves success. Deference endows life with a rational order, while family inculcates measure in all things.[17] With internalized deference to ensure the preservation of order, prosperity and success follow. The entire exposition is congruent with what the "documents of practice" reveal about the nature of Ragusans' own social achievement; Cotrugli was always alert to the importance of those internal features of his community's history that differed subtly but critically from the internal histories of other city-states.

Cotrugli was profoundly aware of the place of values and conduct. This emphasis, so apparently foreign to the spirit of business manuals, may in fact account for why no modern, annotated edition of his work was undertaken until Ugo Tucci recently set himself to that difficult task. In matter of fact, Cotrugli's discussion of conduct and morals complements the briskly secular approach assumed in his first book.[18] Cotrugli merely breathes a different spirit of secularity when he argues that the first line of attack in creating the perfect life lies in the proper conduct of private life, because he unabashedly harnesses a secular morality to the great matter of self-consciously constructing the course of one's worldly life. To recall, Cotrugli had advised suitability above all else in choosing a bride in order to make marriage the foundation of the planned or "constructed" life.

Cotrugli then carried the argument to the hotly contested issue of partible inheritance. In his third book, in a chapter on the dignity and office of the merchant, Cotrugli made four related assertions that were tailored to appeal to the needs of wealthy Europeans torn by the need to disinherit some of their offspring in order to keep the family fortune intact. The first was that the merchant's vocation advanced the health of the republic; second, it provided for the increase of wealth so that all offspring, sons and daughters, might be provided the wherewithal to further improve their condition rather than face decline over the course of a subsequent generation. Cotrugli presented this as practicable, as in truth it was in Ragusa, rather than as a utopian dream.

Third, the merchant of whom he spoke—that is, the noble and affluent merchant—lived as a man to be trusted, the most likely of all men to be considered a man of good faith toward his children and toward the world at large. The chapter then noted that it was this merchant's "esteem" that, in the private world of his home, he associated with an honorable family in virtuous activity, while in public he mixed with persons of all ranks since others always needed him.[19]

This admirable formula drew foreign attention. Both the Italian humanist scholar Luigi Beccadelli and the French political theorist Jean Bodin were responsible for promoting the myth regarding Ragusan achievements. Beccadelli, archbishop of Ragusa from 1555 to 1563, likened the city-state to an ancient polis and through his poetry practically described his embarkation for Ragusa as a magical return to ancient Illyria where he tasted the joys and pleasures of the virtuous antique world.[20] In the guise of his Renaissance poetic accounts, the notion was alluring but a bit whimsical. It piqued the interest of an educated European public and drew on the increasingly exotic images Ragusa called up in European minds. Beccadelli told of weeks on the storm-tossed winter sea, in sight of the town but unable to land. Ragusa as safe haven finally attained, an enchanted setting along ancient lines preserved as a benefaction for modern eyes and ears, cast the town in the guise of an imagined setting as exotic as the locales of tales gathered from voyages on the great oceans. Beccadelli took satisfaction in this arcadia close by the European heartland, where good manners and geniality created a leisured society conducive to learned discourse and true friendship. For this poet, Ragusa was at once familiar and exotic, a Christian city straddling the gulf between fantasy and fact.

Jean Bodin's classic study of sovereignty was another matter altogether, because it relied on authenticated historical examples of the town's recent history for the stated purpose of confounding the authority of Aristotle on politics. Ragusa, counted as the least or smallest of those who could claim the name of commonwealth, delimited and defined the concept for that reason. Bodin resorted to an analogy: "And as a little family shut up in a small cottage is no lesse to be accounted a familie, than that which dwelleth in the greatest and richest house in the citie"[21] so Ragusa, despite its size, stands as a sovereign state. Perhaps it was this that snared Bodin's interest. If the great states maintained armies, Ragusa did not.[22] If the mighty were brought low by sedition and feared the corruption of officers of state, small Ragusa faced no such difficulty.[23] Even more than the mighty Venetians, he asserted, the Ragusans were an embodiment of republican virtue and the purest of aristocracies to have flourished since ancient times.[24] His admiration for its society of firmly ranked orders ran the risk here of endorsing the very Aristotelian model with which he contended. But Jean Bodin respected historical evidence carefully enough to consider this small city-state even if it challenged his premises, and he sought an explanation for what he found in recent recorded history, in particular in Ragusa's own chronicle accounts.

True to his century, he turned to the private behavior of the Ragusans for reasons to explain the survival of republicanism against modern odds. Even more than the Venetians they were "careful of their nobilitie.... For a Venetian gentleman may marrie a base woman, or a common citizens daughter; whereas the Ragusan gentleman may not marrie a common citizen, neither a stranger how noble soever, if she be not a gentlewoman of Zarasi, or Catharo, or bee farther worth at least a thousand ducats."[25] He proceeded to show how it was that men drawn from only twenty-four houses were members of the Great Council and eligible for offices of state. He returned to Ragusa often in his commentary by way of example, and said in book 6, "And to conclude there is no forme of Aristocratie more perfect and goodly, nor more assured, than where as they make choice of men of virtue and reputation."[26] Bodin, more than any other, assured Ragusa the reputation of a Renaissance utopia, a completed society, hierarchical in character, a marriage of prosperity and stability.[27]

Through proper conduct of family and private life, a naturally virtuous nobility had developed over the ages. In Bodin's words, from "popular estates" they "have little by little as it were without feeling (dissent), changed into Aristocritie."[28] He was impressed by the pacific nature of the change and the deferential stance assumed by the popular classes in preferring rule by the "Aristocritie" to popular government. Even if Bodin was too trusting of his chronicle sources, the notion that lower classes deferred to their betters was sufficiently attractive so that Ragusa as the embodiment of a properly deferential society entered the popular imagination.

Ragusa's fame was poised to travel far. William Shakespeare appropriated the corruption of the name for its fleet, Argosy (from Ragosy) and employed it as a generic term for all navies in *The Merchant of Venice* and *The Taming of the Shrew*, and more imaginatively, in *Henry VI, Part III*.[29] In *Measure for Measure* a plot turn in the last act depended on the substitution of the severed head of a "Rhagozin" pirate for Claudio's. Shakespeare might have had better luck with this ploy if Hungary, the titular lord of Ragusa, had remained the setting of the tale rather than Vienna, to which Shakespeare had moved *Measure for Measure*.[30] But these were only passing references to Ragusans, as it happened the playwright found a more resonant role for the city-state as a setting for drama.

In *Twelfth Night*, Shakespeare's references to the court, to carnival, to

London's taverns and its people, were immediately obvious to a contemporary audience, yet he further enriched plot and character by employing remote Illyria as the setting for the play. It appears to have been anything but a casual choice. Shakespeare mentioned Illyria directly ten times; he made other references to its coast, its sailors and pirates, its tall people, its "robust" wines, and its fabled city. This required more than casual knowledge of contemporary sixteenth-century Illyria—that is, Dalmatia—and it was apparently contemporary Illyria that he had in mind since ancient Illyria supported neither the viticulture and wine production to which he alluded nor the romanticized Christian pirates who preyed on Turkish vessels of which he was so fond. Nearer to home, Shakespeare could find such a wealth of reference to carnivals, misrule, drunkenness, pirates, and the world turned upside down that there was no need to travel to Illyria for that context.[31] Still misrule and disorder, in the sixteenth century at least, were one side of a coin, and Illyria could supply Shakespeare with the obverse: an idyllic city where, so the story went, order and deference were the pleasure and duty of everyone. Jean Bodin's general understanding of proper comportment in a "pure" aristocracy, once it had entered European consciousness, could have informed Shakespeare's choice. The alternative title of the play, "As You Will," takes on resonance in the context of such a properly ordered society—where hierarchy was willed into being by the conscious choice of comportment. The recognition and willingness to live one's life according to one's station takes on resonance by reference to "Illyria's city," if it was Ragusa he had in mind, and some convincing evidence suggests that it was.

The Yugoslav scholar of Renaissance literature, Rudolf Filopović, has argued that Ragusa was the setting for *Twelfth Night,* opposing the opinions of his fellow countrymen who favor Split or Zara (Zadar) as Shakespeare's Illyrian town.[32] English scholars have generally favored either a mythic and more general antique setting as the backdrop for *Twelfth Night,* that is, if they have given the matter consideration at all.[33] Filopović reached his conclusion after comparing travel literature, particularly Hakluyt Society publications of the voyages of John Lock to Jerusalem (1553) and Henry Austel to Constantinople (1585), to Shakespeare's output.[34] While Hakluyt's publications were known to have provided Shakespeare with ideas for settings, there is some question whether he had read an earlier traveler's account written by Sir Richard Guylford and published in 1511. Filopović believes he had, resulting in a claim that *Twelfth Night* includes all the elements of Guylford's description of Ragusa in one place or another. These include relics, monuments of renown and beauty, massive fortifications, vintage wines of great potency, and above all the high spirits, geniality, and mirth that knowledge of one's proper place in a society may bestow.

In III. 3. 18–24 of *Twelfth Night*:

SEBASTIAN:                                        What's to do?
Shall we go see the reliques of this town?
ANTONIO: To-morrow, sir: best first go see your lodging.
SEBASTIAN: I am not weary and 'tis long to night.
I pray you, let us satisfy our eyes
With the memorials and the things of fame
That do renown this city.

Guylford's own description of Ragusa runs: "It is also ryche & fayre in suptuous buyldynge with marveylous strengthe and beautye togyther with many fayre churches and glorious houses of Relygyon . . . there be also many Relyques, as the hed and arme of seynt Blase." The traveler then relates that Ragusa was "the strongest towne of walles, towres, bulwerke, watches, and wardes that euer I sawe in all my lyfe."[35] *Twelfth Night*, Filipović argues, echoes Guylford whenever it partakes something of the tone of a travelogue.

Sounding the note of revels in *Twelfth Night*, I. 3. 42, "I'll drink to her as long as there is a passage in my throat and drink in Illyria," introduces a more central dramatic theme that echoes descriptions found in all three: Lock, Austel, and Guylford. In fact, many sixteenth-century traveler's accounts of Ragusa spoke of order capped by an uncommon good humor, an intoxicating, often intoxicated, measure of jocular well-being open to those who "will" their own happiness through being content with their proper station in life. Were the old nobles of Ragusa fated to be seen as genial aristocrats keeping order as they executed a kind of wine-sodden romp through life?

Needless to say a late sixteenth-century English audience with general knowledge of the republic of Ragusa faced few difficulties in associating its society with Illyria, since Ragusa alone among the Dalmatian cities remained an autonomous state.[36] In *Dubrovnik i Engleska, 1300 to 1650*, Veselin Kostić traced the increased contacts between the English and Ragusans that occurred after 1590.[37] In a much-regretted deviation from policy the republic had been drawn, as Spain's ally, into supplying ships for the Armada in 1588 in consonance with treaty obligations. Perhaps the recent infatuation with Orlando Furioso had unwisely led Ragusans into misdirecting their zeal toward the remote North Atlantic waters; they certainly had little idea what Protestantism was all about. Kostić asserts that the most famous British wreck of the Armada, the galleon in Tobermory Bay, was a Ragusan ship.

Almost immediately regretting this ill-conceived venture, Ragusa's noble merchants reestablished their business network in England through elaborate efforts, and by the end of the sixteenth century, when *Twelfth Night* was written for a court production, the English had tolerantly resumed amicable relations, allowing a Ragusan consul to resettle along with a community of his fellow countrymen bent on trading in London. These men assured themselves of local good will with lavish entertaining, awash in a privately imported stock of "wine of Illyria." Ragusan merchants in London entered the textile trade, and Ragusan ships (the much mentioned Argosy) visited London's docks. Kostić contends from the weight of documentation that resident Ragusan merchants flourished in England, becoming immensely wealthy. Shakespeare could have known about or met these merchants who circulated widely in London society.[38]

On the other side of the trading equation, the new English Levant Company, established in 1582, did not immediately forge trading links at Ragusa because the republic was still Spain's close ally. However, the loss of the Armada, as well as Ragusa's apologetic posture, freed English merchants to redirect their eastern trade through the town. At the end of the century, again, by the date that *Twelfth Night* was written, the Levant Company had already begun to trade at Ragusa, so it appears that *Twelfth Night* was first performed at court at just the time when the republic of Ragusa was coming into favor again.[39] As court entertainment the play's reference to Illyria accurately reflected new initiatives in English foreign policy.

Sixteenth-century Englishmen had other associations with Ragusa as ancient Illyria. In the years after he served as the archbishop of Ragusa, Luigi Beccadelli, that poet of Illyria, composed the *Life* of his long-standing friend, Cardinal Reginald Pole.[40] He had befriended the Englishman in Italy much earlier when both had participated in discourse with other distinguished humanists. After Pole returned to England and Beccadelli left Italy to become archbishop of Ragusa, contacts between the two men were maintained through correspondence. At one point, Luigi Beccadelli wrote to Pole on the behalf of the Ragusan Council in matters relating to trade in cloth.[41] The circle of English scholars who gathered in Pole's household had opportunities to read Beccadelli's prose and poetry and learn of his enthusiasm for Ragusa. In fact it may have been a commonplace among literate Englishmen of that generation that Ragusa was an idyllic republic where deference was cheerfully given and the seemly customs of the ancients were still practiced.

William Shakespeare's choice of Illyria as a setting for *Twelfth Night* was deft and even evocative, if, as he seems to have intended, he wished to fasten attention on the consequence to society of signs of deference: knowing one's station, acting it, propriety, and, particularly, proper marriage. Bodin had made it clear that Ragusans recognized that appropriate marriage partners were the key to a successful society. Shakespeare might easily have drawn material for his dramatic commentary on marriage from the reputation Ragusa had won abroad.[42]

So there was extensive use that could be made of Illyrian Ragusa in dramas like *Twelfth Night*. Although tragedies and tempestuous plays such as *Othello* and *The Merchant of Venice* might be set in Venice, where a violent tenor of life was reputed to have diluted or possibly even destroyed the seemliness and order of a virtuous republic, Illyria or Ragusa was employed for the plot that most turned on knowing one's place in the order of things and performing life's tasks according to that knowledge. As the play begins, order is disrupted by the absence of adequate governance; the duke languishes. Order and rule are both restored in a final, and happy, resolution wherein private order and public rule harmonize once more. Virtue in *Twelfth Night* springs from behaving according to one's rank or condition. This is important in all human discourse, but most important in the most significant of all personal decisions, the choice of a marriage partner. In *Twelfth Night* people of all stations are expected to recognize peers (even in disguise and in extraordinary circumstances) and then to make appropriate choices for life partners. The failure to do so could be a source of humor, as in the countess's ill choice of Viola, Sebastian's twin, or a subject for cruel derision, as in the humiliation of Malvolio. Olivia's household, including Olivia herself, is not exemplary, but by the end of the play it is brought back to propriety. Shakespeare's audience readily accepted his claim that those endowed with nobility by nature, that is, by birth, might be brought to recognize each other. It was significant for Ragusa's reputation abroad that an audience in the west could believe in an Illyria where survived a remnant of persons who still exhibited such seemly behavior.

As Jean Bodin claimed, the cluster of ideas associated with this small

Adriatic city-state included republican virtue and social order with antecedents rooted in the antique world.[43] Preserved in time, so to speak, the town for some observers embodied deference that afforded as close an approximation as late sixteenth-century society offered to the imagined classical world. Virtue among the aristocracy might be believed to be innate and therefore natural, but it was also recognized that it could be taught in a society in which social rank was truly respected.

The cluster of ideas that would come to be associated with Ragusa were finally gathered together. Republicanism took precedence, followed by a virtuous family within which all heirs were provided the means to prosper and to improve their condition, as Cotrugli had explained. A good name and reputation followed. All were premised on maintaining a proper distinction between the private or domestic world and the public sphere, as Bodin noted. The noble merchant linked these worlds together through his own activity. For Ragusa's foreign observers, a reputation for drunken revelry may have served as necessary tempering to draw such paragons back into more truly human dimensions.

From Cotrugli, who was fond of classical citations and proudly compared his beloved republic to ancient republics, the Ragusan myth grew to be associated with the survival of the Roman legal principle of partible inheritance as well as with endogamous marriage. It may have been the avid interest in constitutional debate over the central role of inheritance that accounted, in part, for the lasting interest in Ragusa's republican practices. It had become a commonplace of European thought that partible inheritance, based on Roman law, was suitable for merchants but not for nobles.[44] Cotrugli claimed with considerable authority that Ragusans were both merchants and nobles. The same claim might be made for Venice, but by the late sixteenth century the distributive and equalizing intent of the late Roman law of inheritance had been largely superceded as more and more families allowed only one son, frequently the youngest, to marry in any noble house. For thinkers who saw partible inheritance as the foundation of true republicanism and believed that primogeniture had been imposed on European society by the example of royal houses, Ragusa could stand as living proof of the practicality of an older, yet genuinely noble, system of inheritance.

As P. J. Cooper has suggested, "If there is any trend in the centuries after 1300 in the countries [of western Europe] it would seem to be more towards emphasis on a narrow definition of lineage, in turn fortified by policies of restrictive marriage."[45] By contrast Ragusans continued their old form of marriage within traditionally proscribed limits and divided their estates equitably among their offspring. This was no new trend. The practice relied on a tradition-sanctioned enforcement of social boundaries; buttressed by prosperity, partible inheritance still proved practicable, and further new restrictions on marrying had been avoided. Combining the practice of marriage within social rank with that of partible inheritance was an attractive idea for early European jurists and those constitutional thinkers who feared the concentration of power into the hands of ever smaller elite groups. These ideas continued to be linked in Thomas Starkey's *Dialogue between Reginald Pole and Thomas Lupset,* where reform of marriage practices in England was seen as a first step toward political reform.[46] Starkey advocated partible inheritance and other rights for younger sons as well. In the seventeenth century, James Harrington would continue to see these ideas linked together as the sound foundation of republicanism. It lessened the force of his argument to employ Venice as an example of these virtuous practices, however, since Venice had veered away from them. His "Considerer" pointed out quite clearly that, in following Jean Bodin, he still thought Venice immune from sedition because of its social and familial institutions, which buttressed republican virtue. Ragusa, continuing on its traditional course, better proved Harrington's case.[47] Into the age of the Enlightenment wherever the linking of republican virtue, partible inheritance, "proper" marriage, and deferential behavior continued, Ragusa and its intermarrying families still served as living examples of practical value.[48]

Over time, the cluster of ideas associated with Ragusa's name came to include prosperity understood as solid, reliable fortunes that increased generationally, in an almost miraculous fashion. Again, Benedetto Cotrugli deserves chief credit for promoting the notion through his merchant's manual, but the continued prosperity of Ragusans underwrote his argument. From the thirteenth century until the middle of the seventeenth century, the town had exhibited a remarkably steady growth in wealth, while other Mediterranean powers faced, like as not, cycles of prosperity and decline. As Hans Baron has noted, poverty, an early Renaissance humanist ideal, gave way to acceptance of civic wealth as a possible "organ" of "*virtus.*"[49] Ragusa's small contingent of citizens continued to amass fortunes of enviable proportions. Giovanni Giustiniani, in his *Itinerario* of 1553, stated that many noble households in Ragusa had incomes of 100,000 ducats or more, truly dazzling personal wealth.[50] Merchants visiting the community, its own fleet that sailed the Mediterranean and the Atlantic, and a growing literature broadcast this fact.

The *Perfect Merchant* had described a citizenry morally at ease with their accumulation of material goods. Lack of serious scruples about the destructive properties of vast wealth was an increasingly attractive trait, and it found eager acceptance among prosperous Europeans who had grown tired of morality tales featuring poverty as the soul's best nourishment. In truth, Cotrugli had airily dismissed notions that wealth jeopardized one's chances of salvation; he merely preached moderation in pursuing wealth: any man who used wealth with "measure and reason" could rest assured he warranted heaven's favor. This was a welcome argument by the late fifteenth century that assured Ragusa's fame on its strength alone.[51]

The place that Ragusa came to inhabit in the thoughts of the early modern European audience reveals much about the preferences and values of that age. First, Europeans were not yet as sure about the exact demarcation between private or familial concerns and public welfare as they would be later in the age of the democratic revolution. The English historian G. R. Elton has said somewhat derisively of Thomas Starkey, a thoroughly sixteenth-century thinker, that it was one of his "pet" ideas or "fanciful" notions that reform of marriage was the place to begin the creation of a better commonwealth in England.[52] Yet Starkey's priorities indicate he was a genuine man of his day in that he saw the private or personal as the first line of attack for solving the larger problems of the commonwealth. While this remained a commonplace of social thought, Ragusa figured as a model society for others. Jean Bodin, for one, sincerely believed, as did a number of his contemporaries, that many problems should never rise to the level of public concern but should be managed instead within the economy of the private world of family. Thus marriage as an institution and proper measures for the future welfare of offspring still held pivotal roles in political thought in the sixteenth and seventeenth centuries.

Reference to the experience of Ragusans indicated as well that an early modern audience was no longer as easily convinced by antique authorities as had been the case in earlier Renaissance decades. Jean Bodin's careful illustration of the duration of the Ragusan experiment with republicanism, and his testing of that experience by historical criteria, proved the ascendency of a new historicism in political thought.[53] Nor were Europeans as content with purely hypothetical examples as they had once been. Following Bodin, they were increasingly willing to apply tests of efficacy to authenticated contemporary examples. Since Ragusans passed these new tests to satisfaction, the republic of Ragusa earned a reputation for wisdom and could expect further scrutiny. Historical examples, both proximate and contemporary, served to convince a more cautious, if not yet a thoroughly skeptical, European public.

Above all else, the appeal of Ragusa to the popular imagination of the day reveals just how deeply the social turbulence of the early modern age distressed contemporaries. Ragusa's experience seemed to contain a message that Europeans yearned to believe: that the rewards of a new order need not be purchased at the price of the benefits of inherited familial and social values. There is a kind of longing for the preservation of seemliness and social order in Bodin's reference to the Ragusan gentleman who knows without being told who is the proper partner for marriage. There is longing as well in clinging to the notion that partible inheritance may be a viable system in an often volatile capitalist economy. Certainly many powerful European leaders were loathe to purchase the stability of their political systems at the cost of their younger offspring. In the sixteenth century, people counted the social cost of measures such as primogeniture even while they conceded that such measures kept estates intact and appeared to serve the interests of economic growth and political stability. Ragusa held out to them the possibility that such a price need not be paid. If the price could be avoided through the promotion of aristocratic virtues in an ordered society, aided by a venerable republican constitution, then the Ragusan model should be studied soberly for the lessons it might yield. Such thoughts assured the preservation of a Ragusan myth, but colored as that myth was with nostalgia for a simpler age and traditional values, Europeans were not as discerning as they might have been about how Ragusans managed their success.

The noble citizens of Ragusa, understood in local chroniclers' descriptions, in the typology of Machiavelli's defensive republic, in Cotrugli's *Perfect Merchant,* in Beccadelli's and Shakespeare's classic Illyria, and in Jean Bodin's aristocratic exception among long-lived states, could not in any practical way serve as models for their European neighbors unless those neighbors were willing to undertake a radical overhaul of their marriage practices, family life, and community structure. Ragusan values were not easily assimilated into the main current of European political life because it was precisely here, within the political regime and in privately held values, that Ragusan experience had deviated longest from the norm. Just where the most galvanic changes had occurred in response to a developing commercial economy, that is, within the private sphere of the family, Ragusans were most unchanged in the course of their rise to prosperity. It had been their self-conscious plan to remain an aristocratic republic from as early as the thirteenth century, most likely from a far earlier time; the results of that planning may be seen in their recorded behaviors. All that is missing is their blueprint, and old Ragusans had many reasons to keep that blueprint part of their oral heritage rather than to commit it to paper. Subsequent generations of noblemen and noblewomen had affirmed the plan and devised their own policies in consonance with it. The key to success lay in endogamous marriage among the old dominant families, behavior so far outside the mainstream of social development in most European states that the republic of Ragusa, comprehended in a wry admixture of fantasy and historical fact, came to be in its own way a vision as utopian and unrealizable as the fictional utopias of this new modern age.

*Notes*

1. Stepan Vekarić, "Vrste i tipovi dubrovačkih brodova XIV stoljeća," *Dubrovnik anali* 10–11 (1966–67): 19–23. On carrying capacity and tonnage see Frederic Lane, "Tonnages Medieval and Modern," in *Venice and History,* p. 359. See also Bruno Kisch, *Scales and Weights* (New Haven, Conn.: Yale University Press, 1961), for comparative measures, and Jorjo Tadić, "Le Port de Raguse," pp. 14–15 for estimates of Ragusa's strength in the carrying trade. Ragusa kept two galleys on hand from the earliest documented decades. These carried merchandise and stood ready to fulfill Ragusan treaty obligations to Ragusa's treaty partners were they to be called into action.

2. Stepan Vekarić, "Vrste i tipovi dubrovačkih brodova XIV stoljeća," pp. 23–34. In 1382 the owners of the *Sts. Maria and Nicolas,* a cog, were two noblemen, Marinus Bocignolo and Lamprius Crieva, who owned shares with Matco, Magister Nikolas, *physicus,* and Nikola de Ragusa, none of whom were noble merchants. Tadeus de Flora owned shares with local inhabitants in the *St. Nicola* (pp. 24–25, table 2).

3. On importing of wood from the interior, see Dušanka Dinić-Knežević, "Trgovina drvetom u Dubrovniku u XIV veku," *Godišnjak filoz. fakulteta, Novi Sad* 11 (1968): 9–30. See also Jorjo Tadić, "Le Commerce en Dalmatie et à Raguse et la décadence économique de Venise au XVII^{ème} siècle," *Aspetti e cause decadenza economica veneziano nel secolo XII: Atti del Consegno 27 guigno–2 juglio, 1957* (Venice and Rome, 1961); Frederic Lane, "The Merchant Marine of the Venetian Republic," in *Venice and History,* pp. 143–62. Both histories of Venice and Ragusa note that access to the few existing forests that survived on the western shore of Italy south of Venetian-dominated lands affected the reprovisioning and rebuilding of fleets. Ragusa's amicable relations with the trading cities of Apulia allowed access to stands of timber on the mountainous slopes near the coast.

4. S. Vekarić, "Vrste i tipovi dubrovačkih brodova XIV stoljeća," p. 35–41. Josip Luetić, *Mornarica Dubrovačka republike* (Dubrovnik, 1962), pp. 30–49.

5. Josip Luetić, *Mornarica Dubrovačka republike,* pp. 51–55.

6. Ilija Mitić, *Dubrovački konzuli i konzularna služba o starog Dubrovnika* (Dubrovnik: JAZU, 1973). See also Jorjo Tadić, *Španija i Dubrovnik u XVI veku* (Belgrade: SAN, 1932).

7. Caterino Zeno, *Dei commentarii del viaggio in Persia di M. Caterino Zeno* (Venice, 1558).

8. Nicolas de Nicolay, *Navigations, pérégrinations et voyages faicts en la Turquie* (Antwerp, 1576), p. 157.

9. Benedetto Ramberti, *Libri tre delle cose dei Turchi* (Venice, 1543), pp. 2–11.

10. Ibid., p. 4v. Ramberti seems to be most struck that women dress like each other, in a common fashion, rather than individually or competitively as would be true in cities in Italy.

11. Niccolò Machiavelli, *The Prince and the Discourses,* trans. Luigi Ricci and revised by E. R. P. Vincent (New York: Norton, 1940), p. 129. See also, Felix Gilbert, "The Venetian Constitution in Florentine Political Thought," in *Florentine Studies: Politics and Society in Renaissance Florence,* ed. Nicolai Rubenstein (London: Faber, 1968); idem., *Machiavelli and Guicciardini* (Princeton, N.J.: Princeton University Press, 1965); Gene Brucker, *Florentine Politics and Society* (Princeton, N.J.: Princeton University Press, 1962); Marvin Becker, "The Republican City-State in Florence: An Inquiry into Its Origin and Survival, 1280–1434," *Speculum* 35 (1960): 39–50.

12. Machiavelli, *The Prince and the Discourses,* p. 129.

13. Ibid., p. 129.

14. Benedetto Cotrugli, *Della mercatura.* The treatise was not published for more than one hundred years. See Carl Peter Kheil, *Benedetto Cotrugli Rangeo: Ein Beitrag zur Geschichte der Buchhaltung* (Vienna: Manzsche Buchhaltung, 1906), pp. 23–35, 604ff.

15. See M. Vujić and M. Zebić, *Život i rad Benka Kotruljice i njegov spis o trgovini o savršemen trgovcu* (Titograd, 1963), and Žarko Muljačić, "Benko Kotruljević," *Dubrovnik horizonti* 3 (1970): 32–33.

16. Ugo Tucci makes this claim in "The Psychology of the Venetian Merchant in the Sixteenth Century," *Renaissance Venice,* ed. John Hale (Totowa, N.J.: Rowman and Littlefield, 1973), pp. 346–78. See also his introduction to Benedetto Cotrugli's *Il libro dell'arte di mercantura* (Venice: Arsenale, 1990), pp. 64ff.

17. Class deference is not part of Cotrugli's vocabulary. When matters of class were discussed, Cotrugli used the phrase "mercante e grande et sublime" in contrast to "non da mercanti plebei et vulgari." When deference was at issue Cotrugli tended to use terms like "la dignita del mercante."

18. Robert Lopez and Irving Raymond, *Medieval Trade in the Mediterranean World* (New York: Columbia University Press, 1955), pp. 408–9, 413–14.

19. Benedetto Cotrugli, *Della mercatura,* f. 67–69 (Tucci ed., pp. 206–8).

20. Of Ragusa, Beccadelli wrote

Lasciovi et duolmi et conardente core
Ragusa abbraccio, mi diletta sposa
Specchio d'Illiria et suo pregio maggiore

On Luigi Beccadelli in Ragusa see Josip Torbarina, *Italian Influence on the Poets of the Ragusan Republic* (London: Williams and Norgate, 1931). For Beccadelli's collected works see *Monumenti di varia letteratura, tratti dai manoscritti di Monsignor Lodovico Beccadelli* (Bologna: Instituto delle scienze, 1797; repr. Farnborough, England, 1967). Josip Torbarina has published excerpts from the Beccadelli correspondence in "Fragmenti iz neizdatih pisama nadbiskupa Lodovika Beccadellija," *Dubrovnik revija* 1, nos. 9–10 (1929): 320–40. Illyria was a very popular association for Ragusa among native poets.

21. Jean Bodin, *The Six Bookes of a Commonweale*, facsimile reprint of 1606 English translation, ed. Kenneth D. McRae (Cambridge: Harvard University Press, 1979), p. 10. See also Mirko Deanović, *Anciens contacts entre la France et Raguse* (Zagreb: JAZU, 1950). Bodin was the rare western commentator well read in local chronicle literature.

22. Bodin, *The Six Bookes of a Commonweale*, p. 713.

23. Ibid., pp. 420, 488, 554, and 605.

24. Ibid., p. 235.

25. Ibid., p. 235.

26. Ibid., p. 713.

27. Frank Manuel and Fritzie Manuel, *Utopian Thought in the Western World*, (Cambridge, Mass.: Belknap Press, 1979), p. 153.

28. Ibid., p. 428.

29. See William Shakespeare, *The Merchant of Venice*, I.3.18; III.1.105; V.1.276. *The Taming of the Shrew*, II.1.376; II.1.378; II.1.380. *Henry VI, Part III*, II.6.36. The references to the plays are taken from *The Complete Works and Poems of William Shakespeare*, ed. William Nielson and Charles Hill (Cambridge, Mass.: Harvard University Press, 1942).

30. Shakespeare, *Measure for Measure*, IV.3.75–80; V.1.539.

31. Peter Burke, *Popular Culture in Early Modern Europe* (New York: New York University Press, 1978); Natalie Zemon Davis, "The Reason of Misrule," in *Society and Culture in Early Modern France* (Stanford: Stanford University Press, 1975), pp. 97–123. The ten references to Illyria in *Twelfth Night* are: I.2.2–3; I.3.20, 42, 124, 132; I.5.31; III.4.294; IV.1.37; IV.2.115.

32. Rudolf Filipović, "Shakespeareova Ilirija," *Filologija* (Zagreb) 1 (1957): 123–38.

33. English scholars have given much consideration to Illyria and assumed that Shakespeare's knowledge of Ovid's *Metamorphoses* prompted him to associate *Twelfth Night* with northern or Latin Illyria. This opinion may be found in Edward Sugden's *Topographical Dictionary to the Works of Shakespeare* (Manchester: Longmans, Green, 1925), p. 263, and in John Draper, "Et in Illyria Feste," *Shakespeare Association Bulletin* 16 (1941): 220–28. The New Arden edition of *Twelfth Night*, edited by J. Lothian and J. Craik (London: Methuen, 1975), p. 8, concurs, which suggests opinion has not changed much on the question over the decades.

It is possible, of course, that an English audience of the sixteenth century had a more precise knowledge of Illyria and included in it Greek Illyria or the southern reaches of the Dalmatian coast. W. Borgeaud, *Les Illyriens en Grece et en Italie: Étude linguistique et mythologique* (Genève: S. Roulet, 1943); see also the *Oxford Classical*

*Dictionary,* ed. N. Hammond and H. Scullard (Oxford: Oxford University Press, 1970), p. 541. This more extensive Illyria would include the republic of Ragusa, the only independent city-state on the eastern littoral of the Adriatic in the sixteenth century (which Sugden's Illyria does not include). For English scholars, the assumption that Illyria meant only Latin Illyria to Shakespeare may be the leading reason for suggesting that Split (Spalato) or Zara served as the contemporary setting for *Twelfth Night.* The idea has never been given much weight, however, because most English scholars assume Shakespeare intended an ancient setting for *Twelfth Night.* There is no reason to assume that Shakespeare was unfamiliar with Greek Illyria, however; he did have access to ancient Greek sources translated in Latin.

The Croatian edition and notes for *Twelfth Night* (M. Bogdanović, ed., *Na tri kralja* [Zagreb: JAZU, 1922]), and V. Krisković in "Shakespeare i mi. Česka morska obala u 'zimskoj priči,'" *Hrvatska revija* 14:5 (1941), p. 3, place *Twelfth Night* in Latin Illyria also, following the lead of English editors of the play (Charles Knight and Morton Luce in particular).

In 1988, Joseph Papp's production of *Twelfth Night* in New York's Central Park employed Yugoslavian folkloric motifs, reintroducing contemporary—that is, sixteenth-century—Illyria as setting for the play. The peasant motifs seem somewhat at odds with the aristocratic culture Shakespeare associated with Illyria.

34. See *The Voiage of M(aster) Henry Austel by Venice and thence Ragusa overland and so to Constantinople, Anno 1585,* and *The Voiage of M(aster) John Lock to Jerusalem, Anno 1553,* in Richard Hakluyt, *The Principal Navigations* (London, 1598–1600), vol. 2, pt. 2, pp. 101–12, 194–98.

35. Sir Richard Guylford, *This is the Begynnynge and contynuance of the Pylgrymage of Sir Richarde Guylford, knyght, a controuler unto our late soveraygne lorde kynge Henry the VIII. And howe he went with his servaunte and company towardes Jherusalem* (London: Richard Pynson, 1511; repr. ed. Henry Ellis [Camden Society, 1851]), vol. 51, pp. 11–12. Note also the reference in *Twelfth Night* to St. Blaise (Vlah), Ragusa's patron saint.

36. In addition, the Dalmatian towns north of Ragusa were anything but pacific in the sixteenth century. They were much poorer than the republic and in chronic unrest or open revolt against either Venice or internal aristocratic rule.

37. V. Kostić, *Dubrovnik i Engleska, 1300–1650* (Belgrade: SAN, 1973), doc. 33, pp. 550–56.

38. Ibid., pp. 277–99. Nicola de Goce and the brothers Nicola and Marinus de Mence were most prominent among the long-distance traders in England, and they were joined by another noble, Paul de Gondola. None of these persons appears to have been married, although de Mence left an illegitimate son born in England a legacy in his will. Vast wealth allowed these men to maintain great households, entertain, and forge ties with great merchant families in England. The "Elephant and Castle" in Bankside was a corruption of Infanta de Castile and a gathering place for sailors from Mediterranean countries; Ragusans were habituated to it during their years as Spain's allies. Shakespeare may have learned about the Dalmatian coast and Ragusa from sailors and sea captains who visited London and did their drinking there. Informal sources for information of this nature are, of course, much more difficult to tie down.

39. On the Levant Company see Mortimer Epstein, *The Early History of the Levant Company* (London: G. Routledge and Sons, 1908), p. 19. See also Veselin Kostić, *Dubrovnik i Engleska, 1300–1650,* pp. 334–36, and doc. 28, pp. 534–35. See also Josip Luetić, "English Mariners and Ships in Seventeenth-Century Dubrovnik," *Mariners' Mirror* 64 (1978): 276–84.

40. Luigi Beccadelli, "Vita del Cardinale Reginaldo Polo," in *Monumenti di varia letteratura, tratti dai manoscritti di Monsignor Lodovico Beccadelli* (Bologna, 1797; repr., Farnborough, England, 1967), pt. 1, pp. 271–333.

41. Josip Torbarina, "Fragmenti iz neizdatih pisama nadbiskupa Lodovika Beccadellija," *Dubrovnik revija* 1, nos. 9–10 (1929): 320–40, reprints excerpts from Beccadelli's correspondence with the Pole household in England.

42. Josip Torbarina, "The Setting of Shakespeare's Plays," *Studia Romanica et Anglica Zagrabiensia* 17–18 (1964): 21–59. If the literature on this topic has been largely neglected because it appeared in Croatian, this article, which reviews much of the evidence, should have brought it to the attention of Shakespeare scholars. Torbarina amasses some compelling evidence for Shakespeare's use of contemporary Dalmatia and the city of Ragusa as the setting for *Twelfth Night.*

43. Jean Bodin, *The Six Bookes of a Commonweale,* p. 235.

44. R. Mandrou, *Les Fugger propriétaires fonciers en Souabe, 1560–1618* (Paris: Plon, 1968), p. 75. The idea was articulated by St. Bernard and associated with him in the following centuries.

45. P. J. Cooper, "Inheritance and Settlement by Great Landowners" in *Family and Inheritance,* ed. Jack Goody, Joan Thirsk, and E. P. Thompson (Cambridge: Cambridge University Press, 1976), p. 296.

46. Thomas Starkey, *A Dialogue Between Reginald Pole and Thomas Lupset,* ed. K. M. Burton (London: Chatto and Windus, 1948). The connection between Starkey and Ragusa was entirely personal. As a member of Reginald Pole's household, Starkey was exposed to continental ideas, which Pole brought back with him from his travels in Italy. In Italy, Pole had participated in the literary circles of which Luigi Beccadelli was a member. This was a legendary humanist circle, since it included as well Orsini, Bembo, Michelangelo, and other great artists. Beccadelli maintained a correspondence with Pole once Pole had returned to England, and in later years he wrote the biography of Reginald Pole: "Vita del Cardinale Reginaldo Polo" in *Monumenti de varia letteratura, tratti dai manoscritti di Monsignor Lodovico Beccadelli,* vol. 1, pp. 277–333. J. Torbarina, *Italian Influence on the Poets of the Ragusan Republic* (London: Williams and Norgate, 1931), pp. 47–48. See note 11, above.

47. James Harrington, "The Prerogative of Popular Government," in *The Political Works of James Harrington,* ed. J. G. A. Pocock (Cambridge: Cambridge University Press, 1977), book 1, p. 427. On Harrington and a deferential society, see J. G. A. Pocock, "The Classical Theory of Deference," *American Historical Review* 81 (1976): 516–23.

48. P. J. Cooper, "Inheritance and Settlement by Great Landowners," p. 139; Francesco Favi, *Dubrovnik and the American Revolution,* ed. Wayne Vucinich (Palo Alto, Cal.: Ragusan Press, 1977). Favi served as Ragusan consul in Paris and informed the Ragusan senate about the revolution. See Frederic Lane, "At the

Roots of Republicanism," in *Venice and History* (Baltimore: Johns Hopkins University Press, 1966), pp. 520–39.

49. Hans Baron, "Franciscan Poverty and Civic Wealth as Factors in the Rise of Humanistic Thought," *Speculum* 13, no. 1 (1938): 1–37.

50. Giovanni Battista Giustiniani, *Itinerario*, in *Commissiones et relationes venetae*, ed. Šime Ljubić (Zagreb: JAZU, 1877), p. 249.

51. Benedetto Cotrugli, *Della mercatura*, f. 72–73 (Tucci ed., pp. 221–22). Cf. Hans Baron, "Franciscan Poverty and Civic Wealth," pp. 18–37.

52. G. R. Elton, "Reform by Statute: Thomas Starkey's Dialogue and Thomas Cromwell's Policy," *British Academy Proceedings* 54 (1968): 182.

53. Jean Bodin, *The Six Bookes of a Commonweale*, pp. 10, 235, 433, 605, 713.

# Appendix 1: Timeline

**Circa 667**
Anonymous Chronicler of Ravenna stated "Epidaurum id est Ragusium."

**886–87**
According to tradition Dubrovnik, with Byzantine aid, withstood a siege against Saracens attacking by sea.

**Tenth Century**
According to tradition St. Blasius chosen as patron saint.

**Tenth–Eleventh Centuries**
Town settlement spread across the trough at the foot of the town to Mt. Srdj.

**Circa 999**
Ragusa became an archbishopric.

**1000**
Attack of the Venetian doge, Pietro II Orseolo. The town recognized Venetian rule, according to later tradition.

**1018**
Ragusa returned to Byzantine protection.

**1022**
First written document of Ragusan origin: gift of the Isle of LaCroma (Lokrum) to the Benedictines.

**1023**
First mention of Ragusan *nobiles*.

**1081–85**
Ragusa recognized rule of the Normans and opened trade agreements with cities across the Adriatic.

**1148**
Formal trade agreement with Molfetta, followed by similar agreements with other Adriatic ports.

**1171**

Venetian domination of the town foiled by Ragusan acceptance of Norman protection.

**1181**

First peace agreement with nearby Catar (Kotor).

**1186**

Peace treaty with Serbian Stefan Nemanjić, which included agreements for trade with the Balkan interior.

**1189**

Trade agreement with Ban Kulin of Bosnia.

**1204**

Fourth Crusade attacked Zara; Ragusa capitulated to Venice; treaty followed in 1205.

**1232**

Strengthening of Venetian surveillance over Ragusan trade in the Mediterranean; however, goods brought from Slavonia remained tax-free on the Venetian market.

**1272**

Eight books of *Liber Statutorum* codified.

**1277**

*Liber Statutorum doane* (customs) codified.

**1278**

Fiscal books and files preserved in chancellery.

**1296**

Fire destroyed much of the old *sexteria* of the town.

**1301**

Minutes of councils preserved henceforth.

**1332**

Great Council "closed."

**1333**

Ragusa acquired fortresses at Ston and Pelješac.

**1348**

Black Plague rages.

**1358**

Ragusa freed itself from Venetian domination and placed the town under the protection of the ruler of Hungary.

**1371**

Rectorship defined.

**1377**

*Trentino* for plague protection devised.

**1390**

First Ragusan consulate installed in Siracusa, Sicily.

**1399**

Turkish ruler, Sarhan, guaranteed Ragusans free trade in Turkish lands.

**1419**

Ragusa expanded borders as far as the eastern portion of Canali (Konavli).

**1435**

Town established classical grammar school for boys.

**1436–38**

Dubrovnik constructed an aquaduct from Ombla and a town fountain built by Onofrio de la Cava.

**1440**

Philippus de Diversis wrote *Situs aedificiorum*.

**1442**

Charter from the Sultan allowing trade in return for 1,000 ducats in tribute; tribute rose thereafter. (By 1481 tribute stabilized at 12,500 ducats.)

**1458**

Benedetto Cotrugli wrote *Della mercatura e del mercante perfetto*.

**1516**

Customs House constructed.

**1525**

Shipyard constructed at Gruž.

**1543**

Construction of the Rupe (granary) dug into the limestone of *Castellum*.

**1567**

Death of comedist Marinus Dersa (Marin Držić).

**1568**
Committee of Five established to handle maritime insurance (*ordo super as-sicuratoribus*).

**1588**
Ragusan ships joined Spanish Armada in raid on England.

**1580–1600**
Ragusa possessed 170 to 200 large ships in its navy as well as smaller, coastal vessels. Mediterranean trade peaked.

**1638**
Death of tragedian Ivan Gundulić.

**1662**
First commoner families or noble foreigners allowed to join Great Council.

**1667**
Great earthquake; ten commoner families accepted into nobility.

**1673**
Five more commoner families allowed into nobility.

**1683–99**
So-called Long War with Venice; Ragusa sent emissaries to Habsburg Emperor Leopold.

**1703**
Ragusans reduced tribute to Turkey to payment every third year.

**Circa 1780**
Ragusan ships sailed the Mediterranean and the Black Sea and appeared in Atlantic ports such as New York, Philadelphia, and Baltimore.

**1806**
French general Lauriston occupied Ragusa, and France imposed a war tribute on the republic.

**1808**
By the decision of Marshal Marmont, the Ragusan republic was abolished. Marmont became "duke."

This timeline follows Josip Lučić, in Slobodan P. Novak, *Dubrovnik Revisited* (Zagreb: Sveucilisna naklada Liber, 1987), pp. 177–88.

# Appendix 2: The Later Centuries of the Republic of Ragusa

In the later Middle Ages, Ragusans reaped their rewards. They gained independence as a city-state after 1358, and they grew prosperous beyond belief. If the lessons inculcated by occupation had not been sufficient to set them on a future pacific course, the success of the citizens' elaborate and sometimes secret negotiations to withdraw from Venetian rule in the fourteenth century (when Venice was occupied by its war with Genoa) drilled that lesson into their heads. Traditionally, Rome took more leaders from Ragusa than it supplied, but at that time Elias de Saraca, the rare native son appointed to the local see, held the office of Ragusan archbishop. Brilliantly, and secretly, Saraca served as emissary to the Hungarian court. The terms of nominal rule and token tribute he secured from Hungary, conditions that would allow Ragusa to part from Venice, achieved a long-cherished dream. But the very boldness of Saraca's exploit created grave misgivings among his noble peers. In Saraca's political acumen lay that possibility for preference above others feared by the Great Council. The council formally requested of the pope that a native son never again be elevated to the archbishopric at Ragusa.

The pope honored this request and the senate, Great and Small Councils, freed from the immediate fear of dominance by one of their own number, began experiments with various weak elected executive offices to replace the function of appointed foreign counts. The Great Council settled on a single rector elected by the Great Council who would serve a six-month term and not repeat his term of office; later the council appointed a rector who would serve a one-month term but could only repeat his term two years later.

Power within the government continued to rest with the town's councils. All noble males over the age of eighteen served in the Great Council. Entry at eighteen became the practice in the mid-fourteenth century, the era of plague, but settled at twenty, its former thirteenth-century level, in the middle years of the fifteenth century, when the absolute numbers of the nobility had recovered from the inroads of plague.

The decades after 1358 brought realization of long-term plans for commercial expansion and urban development. A centralized chancellery, a model of efficient organization and bilingual services to merchants, provided both public and private services to the community and to foreigners who came to town to register charters. In these years, Ragusans developed a workable system of quarantine and continued to provide medical care at communal expense to the inhabitants of the town. A waterworks was constructed at great expense to augment the cisterns in use within the town, and great *rupe* or grain storage bins, were carved into the higher-elevation limestone formation of the town to accommodate the increasing scale of foreign grain shipments entering the town. The walls continued to be fortified in a calculated fashion so that observers were made aware that Ragusa was improving its defenses and keeping up with advances in ballistics and weaponry. Officials supervised the Astarea and the islands, thus making it possible for the land under the town's jurisdiction to be turned toward productive uses such as viticulture. The Great Council required members to live within the town, at least in the winter months; nobles continued to count their unrecompensed hours spent in government service as proper and necessary.

Diplomacy with great powers continued to be the great challenge facing the city-state. By the middle years of the fourteenth century, Ragusans recognized the threat posed by Turkish expansion in the Balkans.[1] In the 1390s the senate entered into negotiations with the Ottoman Turks and began the essential but exhaustive process of resecuring the town's commercial network in the newly conquered Balkan lands of the interior. By 1397, Ragusans arranged a treaty with the Turks that secured peace, freedom of the seas, and access to markets of the interior. The Turks demanded a steadily mounting yearly tribute over the following decades; in return Ragusan merchants pursued their trade at the mining sites and trading centers of the Turkish-dominated lands on progressively more favorable terms.

The extraordinary care taken to avoid direct confrontation with the Turks and maintain conditions favorable for trade eventually yielded excellent results for land trade, but problems never fully abated in maritime trade in the eastern Mediterranean Sea. In regard to the Balkans, Ragusans could negotiate virtually alone for their privileges, constrained only by the interests of the Hungarian monarchy, to whom they owed nominal allegiance.

On the sea, Ragusan negotiations with the Turks were complicated by the diplomatic initiatives of other Christian powers. Although Ragusans had earned a reputation as far and above the great powers among their Christian neighbors in their ability to negotiate with the Turks, the restrained behavior they displayed did not serve as a model for others. After the Battle of Mohacs in 1526, Ragusa no longer acknowledged Hungary as overlord by the payment of a tribute. But the increasing demands of the Sublime Porte more than compensated for this cessation. In the sixteenth century, Ragusans found in Spain a powerful and distant Christian power with whom to form an alliance, and this alliance dominated the last centuries of Ragusa's experience as an independent republic and commercial power.[2]

At home, aristocratic Ragusans cultivated the arts and classical learning, and found the leisure to develop circles dedicated to humanist discourse in Italian and Slavic. This Renaissance output has had a lasting influence on the culture and language of Slavic-speaking peoples. Nevertheless historians' commentary on this era of the town's history has grown increasingly irrelevant by focusing narrowly on what Ragusans failed to do in comparison with their Italian neighbors' development: They did not produce a large literature in Italian. They did not imitate the Venetians by introducing the printing press.[3] They did not always follow the fashion in literary or artistic style set across the Adriatic. On a more positive note, a substantial portion of Ragusan literary output was dedicated to the sciences, particularly the practical sciences of mathematics and geography. Ragusans delighted in the drama of their playwrights, and the small theater close by the rector's palace became a favorite haunt of patrician and affluent bourgeois men and women. Summer palaces constructed on the shoreline accurately represented to the outside world the cultivated life of prosperous noble families. A highly evolved indigenous culture followed a course largely its own rather than one that followed the fashion in Italian city-states.

Ragusa became a wealthy city in the fifteenth and sixteenth centuries. Much religious and civic art was of local manufacture, and some of Italy's most eminent artists were commissioned to build or decorate important monuments in the city. While Ragusa owes the great regularity of the *platea* or *stradun,* which forms the main concourse of the city, to rebuilding after the great earthquake of 1667, other unique visual elements that mark the town as distinctive speak to the Great Council's frugal expenditures, but to restrained taste as well. The *sponza* (customs house) and the rector's palace (see Figures 7 and 6); Dominican and Franciscan monasteries at the town's two gates; the harbor facilities; and the town fountains and squares created an esthetic whole.

Frugality within the Great Council helps account for this simplicity in design, but it is also true that Ragusans developed their own esthetic, which brought an austere style to their town. They avoided much of what was Mannerist and Baroque. Ragusans held very sure notions of what suited their small city within its enormous battlements in these prosperous centuries. Even the villas that studded the landscape outside of the town were constructed in a restrained style.

Ragusan merchants and seamen sons of the old noble families, and men from the coast and islands, traveled the Mediterranean and collected together fleets that sailed the Atlantic Ocean. They participated in the battles to which their treaty alliances and duties as a Christian state obligated them, but always with a reluctance conveyed by diplomatic countering and delay. For the most part, the town's stand was nonaggressive. Foreign consulates through the Mediterranean region, merchants stationed in cities as distant as London and Paris, and the fleet on the seas promoted trade and eased diplomatic relations for the republic. Some of the most turbulent decades of Mediterranean history were peaceful and prosperous for the Ragusan citizenry, and many in Europe knew Ragusa's name because of this. The town's reputation grew into a myth, surely not one as riveting and glorious as the myth of Venice, but one impressive nonetheless because of the pacifist achievements of this small republic.

Two events in the seventeenth century did irreparable damage to Ragusa's prosperity and stability. The first was the great earthquake of 1667.[4] Ragusans knew earthquakes well; and one damaging earthquake in the sixteenth century delivered the worst damage to date in a long history of seismic activity. The great earthquake of 1667 was followed immediately by fire that spread over much of the town, leaving the population severely reduced and most of the city in ruins. The physical damage was repaired in time but at great cost. The current uniformity in the reconstruction of the *platea* (*stradun*), the business center of the town, clearly attests to the care and attention devoted by the Great Council to rebuilding. Damage to the citizenry itself was less easily repaired because the number of males eligible to sit on the Great Council was reduced to eighty-four in the aftermath of the earthquake, too few to staff a complex civic bureaucracy, carry out an elaborate foreign policy, and provide an extraordinary array of urban services.

One new citizen had been created from the ranks of the growing merchant bourgeois just prior to the earthquake. Afterward, nine more citizens were given full hereditary rights to nobility, that is, to pass on to their sons their eligibility to sit on the Great Council. The immediate crisis of staffing civic government was met through this expedient move, but a long-term crisis was precipitated by this unprecedented enfranchisement. The old families, often called the Salamanca coterie because they favored educating their sons at that Spanish university, refused to marry with the Sorbonne coterie, the new families who sent their sons to Paris. Creating new citizens was perhaps a political necessity for the Great Council, but it destroyed the perfect congruity between the noble *prijateljstvo,* or marrying circle, and the enfranchised families. Since the two had been one and the same for centuries, their interaction was finely tuned. Disturbing this congruity meant disturbing social equilibrium in the old republic, which produced grave consequences in the political life of the community.

A second blow was sustained when Venice initiated the dredging and enlarging of the harbor at Split (Spalato), its occupied Dalmatian dependency. Ragusan dominance of the land routes across the Balkans was effectively challenged for the first time by an economically viable land route from the east, which terminated in the more northerly reaches of Dalmatia. This occurred in the last years of the seventeenth century, and while Ragusa sprang back to some extent from these two blows, like many other Mediterranean ports its overall relative position in trade declined. Even in the Adriatic, new ports like Trieste and Rijeka drained off local trade. Ragusa could no longer claim to be the major port of call on the eastern shore of the Adriatic Sea. Ragusan traders, diplomats, and councillors might still employ their most clever stratagems in search of trade, but they did so with diminishing success. Venice faced a similar decline, and Turkey did so as well.

Responsibility for a last flourish of commercial activity in Atlantic trade in the eighteenth century fell to the *cives de populo,* in particular the seafaring inhabitants of the coastal villages and islands that lay within the town's authority. In the walled town itself, this last century was perhaps the most placid in the generally pacific course of the community's history. The old noble citizenry's deep affection and pride in their city was expressed as unwillingness to destroy traditional modes of social and political behavior, even if this constituted an ultimately destructive program for the nobility itself. The old nobility refused to marry outside their circle, and fewer and fewer marriages were celebrated. Ragusa's greatness lay in the past that the last few noble citizens revered, but did not disturb.

*Notes*

1. Ivan Božić, *Dubrovnik i Turska u XIV i XVI veku* (Belgrade: SAN, 1952). Most of the important works on the later centuries of the Old Republic are noted in chapters in this study.

2. J. Tadić, *Španija i Dubrovnik u XVI veku* (Belgrade: SAN, 1932). In the eighteenth century, Ragusans broke free from Spain to the extent that they traded in the North Atlantic.

3. Traian Stoianovich, "Ragusa: Society Without a Printing House," in *Structure sociale et développement culturel des villes sud-est* (Bucharest: Association internationale d'études du sud-est-européen, 1975), pp. 43–73. See Chapter 8 for discussion of humanist literature in Ragusa.

4. R. Samardžić, *Borba Dubrovnika za opstanak posle velikog zemljotresa 1667* (Belgrade: Nauc delo, 1960).

# Appendix 3: Text of 1377 Law Establishing a Trentino

Anno MCCCLXXVII, die XXVII Julii. In Consilio Majori Consiliariorium LXVII captum per XXXIV, quod tam Nostrates, quam Advenae, venientes de locis pestiferis non recipiantur in Ragusium, nec ad ejus Districtum, nisi steterint prius ad purgandum se in Mercana, seu in Civitate veteri per unum mensem. Item per consiliarios XLIV ejusdem Consilii captum fuit, quod nulla persona de Ragusio, vel ejus districtu audeat vel presumat ire ad illos, qui venient de locis pestiferis, et stabunt in Mercana, vel Civitate veteri sub poena standi ibidem per unum Mensem; et qui portabunt illis de victualis seu de aliis necesariis, non possint ire ad illos sine licentia officialium ad hoc ordinandorum, cum ordine ab ipsis officialibus eis danda dicta sub poena standi ibidem per unum Mensem. Item per Consiliarios XXIX ejusdem Consilii captum fuit et firmatum, quod quinqunque non observaverit praedicta, seu aliquod praedictorum, solvere debeat de poena hyperperos L, et nihilominus praedicta teneatur observare.[1]

27 July 1377. In the Great Council of sixty-seven councillors it was balloted by thirty-four that our own citizens as well as strangers, when they come from plague-carrying areas, should not be admitted into Ragusa, nor into its territory, unless they have first remained in Mercana or in Civita Vecchia to be cleansed for one month. Moreover, it was balloted by forty-four councillors of the same Council that no person from Ragusa or its territory should venture or presume to go to those who come from plague-carrying areas, and are staying in Mercana or Civita Vecchia, under penalty of [themselves] remaining in the same place for one month; and those who bring [the quarantined people] food or other necessities may not go to them without the permission of the officials who have been appointed to this task, with an order given to them by the same officials under the said penalty of remaining in the same place for one month. Moreover, it was decided and confirmed by twenty-nine councillors of this same council, that whoever does not observe the aforesaid [regulations] or any part of the

aforesaid should pay as a fine fifty *hyperperi* and should be nonetheless bound to observe the aforesaid.[2]

*Notes*

1. D.S.A., *Liber Viridis,* cap. 49, f. 78, 27 June 1377; quoted in Karl Lechner, *Das Grosse Sterben in Deutschland . . . in 1348–1351* (Innsbruck: Wagner, 1884), pp. 67–68.

2. I am indebted to Deborah Roberts for this translation.

# Bibliography

ARCHIVAL SOURCES
DUBROVNIK STATE ARCHIVES (D.S.A.)

fr. A.D. 985, *Pismo Kneza Crnomira Knezu i Općini Dubrovačkoj*
*Acta Sanctae Mariae Maioris*
*Testamenta Notariae*
(1) 1282–83; (2) 1295–1324; (3) 1324–48; (4) 1347–65; (5) 1345–65; (6) 1365–79; (7) 1381–91; (8) 1391–1402; (9) 1402–14; (10) 1416–18; (11) 1419–30; (12) 1430–37
*Distributiones Testamentorum*
(1) 1349–54; (2) 1364–68; (3) 1371–72; (4) 1374–84; (5) 1385; (6) 1395–1405
*Diversa Notariae*
(1) 1310–13; (2) 1314–17; (3) 1318–20; (4) 1324–25; (5) 1324–30; (6) 1339–41; (7) 1352–58; (8) 1362–70; (9) 1370–79; (10) 1387–91; (11) 1402–8
*Diversa Cancellariae*
(3)1295; (4) 1305; (5) 1312–14; (6) 1320–22; (7) 1323; (8) 1325–27; (9) 1328–30; (10) 1333–34; (11) 1334–36; (12) 1334–37 and 1350–51; (13) 1341–51; (14) 1328–29 and 1343–45; (15) 1347–48; (16) 1348–50; (17) 1351–52; (18) 1354–56; (19) 1362–71; (20) 1365–66; (21) 1367–68; (22) 1369–70
*Libri Dotium Notariae*
(1) a. 1348, b. 1349, c. 1348, d. 1349, e. *Testamenta* 1348; (2) 1380–91; (3) a. *Dotes* 1396–98, b. *Venditiones* 1385–1412; (4) 1412–20; (5) 1420–39; (6) 1439–50; (7) 1460–72; (8) 1472–85; (9) 1485–96
*Pacta Matrimonialia*
(1) 1447–53; (2) 1453–64
*Apti de Misericordia* 1 and 2
*Lamenta de Intus et de Foris* 1, 1372–74
*Lamenta de Intus*, 1404–7
*Liber Rosso*
*Liber Viridis*
*Libri Reformationes*
(1) XXVII, 1338–90; (2) XXIX, 1390–92; (3) XXXI, 1397–99; (4) XXXIV, 1412–14


FRANCISCAN LIBRARY, DUBROVNIK, YUGOSLAVIA

*Zibaldone, Memorie storiche su Ragusa vacolte G. Mattei, Testamenta, 1348.*
Venetian State Archives (V.S.A.)

*Avogaria di Comun, Deliberazioni del Maggior Consiglio, Magnus Cinque Savii,* Reg. 9
*Grazie,* Reg. 2–11
*Senato Deliberazioni,* Reg. 1333–1334
*Zecca, Capitulare massarii all'argento,* vol. 6

The following abbreviations are used in the entries below: IJK (Zbornik za Istoriju, Jezik i Književnost); JAZU (Jugoslavenska Akademija Zanosti i Umjetnosti); *MR* (*Monumenta Ragusina*); SAN (Srpska Akademija Nauka). All titles are given in Roman alphabet.

PUBLISHED SOURCES

Beccadelli, Luigi. *Monumenti di varia letteratura, tratti dai manoscritti di Monsignor Lodovico Beccadelli.* Bologna: Instituto delle scienze, 1797; repr. Farnborough, England, 1967.
Bodin, Jean. *Method for the Easy Comprehension of History.* Trans. Beatrice Reynolds. New York: Columbia University Press, 1945.
———. *Six Bookes of a Commonweale.* Facsimile reprint of the English translation of 1606 by Kenneth D. McRae. Cambridge, Mass.: Harvard University Press, 1979.
Bogišić, V., and C. Jireček, eds. *Liber statutorum civitatis Ragusii compositus anno 1272 cum legibus aetate posteriore insertis atque cum summariis, adnotationibus et scholiis a veteribus iuris consultis ragusinis additis.* Monumenta historico-juridica Slavorum meridionalium, vol. 10. Zagreb: JAZU, 1904.
Božić, Ivan. "Filip de Diversis *Opis Dubrovniku.*" *Časopis Dubrovnik* (1983).
Burr, Malcolm. "The Code of Stefan Dušan." *Slavonic and East European Review* 28 (1949–50): 198–217, 516–39.
Cessi, Roberto, ed. *La regolazione delle entrate e delle spese (sec. XII–XIV).* Documenti finanziari della Repubblica di Venezia, ser. I, vol. I. Padua: Libreira Editrice A. Draghi, 1925.
———. *Problemi monetari veneziani.* R. Academia dei Lincei, ser. 4, vol. 1. Padua: PAN, 1937.
Charrier, Ernest. *Négociations de la France dans le Levant.* Collection des documents inédits sur l'histoire de France, ser. 1, vol. 3. Paris: Imprimerie nationale, 1840–60.
Constantine Porphyrogenitus. *De Administrando Imperio.* Ed. Gy. Moravcsik, trans. R. J. H. Jenkins. Budapest: Pétar Tudományegyetani Görög Filológïaï Intezet, 1949.
Cotrugli, Benedetto. *Della mercatura e del mercante perfetto.* Venice: Elefanta, 1583. New edition: *Il Libro dell'arte di mercatura.* Ed. Ugo Tucci. Venice: Arsenale, 1990.
Čremošnik, Gregor. *Kancelarijski i notarski spisi 1278–1301.* Belgrade: Zbornik za Istoriju, Jezik i Književnost (IJK). III, sec. III, bk. I.

————. *Spisi dubrovačke kancelarije*. Bk. 1: *Zapisi notara Thomazina de Savere 1278–1282*. Monumenta historica Ragusina. Zagreb: JAZU, 1951.

Dandolo, Andrea. *Chronicum Venetum*. Ed. Ester Pastorello. 2nd ed., *Rerum Italicarum Scriptores* 12. Bologna: Zanichelli, 1938–40.

Dante Alighieri. *The Divine Comedy*, Trans. and ed. Charles Singleton. 3 vols. Princeton, N.J.: Princeton University Press, 1975.

de Diversis de Quartigianis de Lucca, Philippus. *Situs aedificiorum, politiae et laudabilium consuetudinum inclytae civitatis Ragusii*. Ed. Brunelli. Estratto dai programmi del Ginnasio superiore di Zara degli anni 1880–1882. Zara, 1882.

Dinić, Mihail. *Odluke veća dubrovačke republike*, I. Belgrade: Zbornik za IJK, 1951. Sec. III, bk. 1.

————. *Iz dubrovačkog arhiva*. I, Belgrade: SAN, 1967.

Evans, Sir Arthur. *Illyrian Letters, Correspondence Addressed to the Manchester Guardian During 1877*. London: Longmans, Green, 1878.

————. *Through Bosnia and the Herzegovina on Foot*. London: Longmans, Green, 1876; reprint, Oxford, 1973.

Favoro, Elena, ed. *Cassiere della bolla ducale, Grazie, Novus Liber, 1299–1305*. Venice: Il Comitato, 1962.

Fermendžin, P. E. *Acta Bosnae Potissimum Ecclesiastica*. Monumenta spectantia historiam Slavorum meridionalium. Zagreb: Jugoslavenka Akademija Zananosti i Umjetnosti (JAZU), 1892.

Foucard, C., ed. *Statuto delle nozze a Venezia dell'anno 1299*. Nozze (pamphlet). Venice, 1858.

Freidberg, Emil, ed. *Corpus Juris Canonici*, vol. I. Gratianus, *Decretum*. Graz: Bernard Tauchnitz, 1911.

Gondola, Nicola de. *Discorsi sopra la metheora d'Aristotle*. Venice, 1584.

Giustiniani, Giovanni Battista. *Itinerario*, in *Commissiones et relationes venetae*, ed. Šime Ljubić. Zagreb: JAZU, 1877.

Guylford, Sir Richard. *This is the Begynnynge and contynuance of the Pylgrymage of Sir Richard Guylford, knyght, a controuler unto our late soveraygne lorde kynge Henry the VIII. And howe he went with his servaunte and company towardes Jherusalem*. London: Richard Pyson, 1511; repr. edited by Henry Ellis. Vol. 51. London: Camden Society, 1951.

Harrington, James. *The Complete Works of James Harrington*. Ed. J. G. A. Pocock. Cambridge: Cambridge University Press, 1977.

Kukuljević-Sakcinski, I. *Regesta documentorum Regni Croatiae, Slavoniae et Dalmatiae, Saeculi III, Starine* 21, 22, 23, 24, 27, 28. Zagreb: JAZU, 1889–96.

Ljubić, Šime. *Listine ob odnošajih između južnoga slavenstva i mletačke republike*, vols. 1–10. Monumenta spectantia historiam Slavorum meridionalium, vols. 1–5, 9, 12, 17. Zagreb, 1868–93.

Lučić, Josip, ed. *Spisi dubrovačke kancelarije*. Bk. III, Monumenta Historica Ragusina. Zagreb: JAZU, 1988.

Lukarević (di Luccari), Giacomo. *Copioso ristretto degli annali di Rausa*. Vienna, 1605.

Luzzatto, Gino. *I prestiti della repubblica di Venezia (sec XIII–XV)*. Documenti finanziani della repubblica di Venezia, ser. II, vol. I, pt. I. Padua: A. Draghi, 1929.

Machiavelli, Niccolò. *The Prince and the Discourses*. Trans. Luigi Ricci and revised E. R. P. Vincent. New York: Norton, 1940.

Makušev, Vincentio. *Monumenta historica Slavorum meridionalium vicinorumque populorum e tabulariis et bibliothecis italicis deprompta*. Vol. 1, Warsaw, 1874; vol. 2, Belgrade: Typographia Regni Serbiae, 1882.

Mayer, Anton. *Kotorski spomenici Prva knjiga notara od god. 1326–1335*. Monumenta Catarensia, vol. 1. Zagreb: JAZU, 1951.

Nicolay, Nicolas de. *Navigations, pérégrinations et voyages faicts en la Turquie*. Antwerp: Guillaume Silvius, 1576.

Nodilo, N., ed. *Annales Ragusini anonymi item Nicolai de Ragnina*. Monumenta spectantia historiam Slavorum meridionalium, vol. 14, scriptores I. Zagreb, 1883.

———. *Chronica Ragusina Junii Restii (ab origine urbis usque ad annum 1451), item Joannis Gundulae (1451–1484)*. Monumenta spectantia historiam Slavorum meridionalium, vol. 25, scriptores II. Zagreb, 1893.

Orbini, Mauro. *Il Regno degli Slavi*. Pesaro: Apresso Girolamo Concordia, 1604.

*Pasquale Longo, Notaio in Corone, 1289–1293*. Ed. A. Lombardo, Venice: Monumenti storici pubblicati dalla deputazione di storia per le Venezie, n.s. vol. 6, 1951.

Pliny, *Natura Historiae*. Ed. and trans. H. Rackham. Liber II. Cambridge, Mass.: Harvard University Press, 1938.

Racheli, A., ed. *Chroniche de Giovanni, Matteo, e Filippo Villani*. Trieste: Sezione letterario-artistica del Lloyd Austriaco, 1957.

Rački, Fr. *Monumenta Ragusina, (MR)* 5 vols., Monumenta spectantia historiam Slavorum meridionalium, vols. 10, 13, 27, 28, 29. Zagreb, 1879–97.

Radonić, J. *Acta et Diplomata Ragusina* I. Belgrade: Zbornik za IJK, 1934. Sec. III, bk. 2.

———. *Leges et Ordines Ragusii, Fontes Rerum Slavorum Meridionalium*, ser. 5. Monumenta historico-juridica. Belgrade, 1936.

Ramberti, Benedetto. *Libri tre delle cose dei Turchi*. Venice: Aldo, 1543.

*Ravenatis Anonymi Cosmographia*. Ed. M. Pinder and G. Parthey. Berlin: F. Nicolai, 1860.

Rocca, Morrozzo della, and A. Lombardo. *Documenti del commercio veneziano nel secoli XI–XIII*. 2 vols. Rome and Turin: Sede delli Istituto e Libraria italiana, 1940.

Shakespeare, William. *The Complete Works of William Shakespeare*. Ed. William Nielson and Charles Hill. Cambridge, Mass.: Harvard University Press, 1942.

———. *Twelfth Night* (New Arden edition). Ed. J. Lothian and J. Craik. London: Methuen, 1975.

Smičiklas, T. *Codex diplomaticus Croatiae, Dalmatiae et Slavoniae*, vols. 2–15. Zagreb: JAZU, 1904–34.

Solovjev, A., and M. Peterković. *Dubrovački zakoni i uredbe*. Monumenta historico-juridica, vol. 1. Belgrade, 1936.

Stefanuti, Ugo. *Documentazioni cronologiche per la storia della medicina, chirurgia e farmacia in Venezia dal 1258 al 1332*. Venice: F. Organia, 1961.

Starkey, Thomas. *A Dialogue Between Reginald Pole and Thomas Lupset*. Ed. K. M. Burton. London: Chatto and Windus, 1948.

Stojanović, L. *Acta srpske povelje i pisma*. Belgrade: Zbornik za IJK, 1929.
Tadić, Jorjo. *Pisma i uputsva dubrovačke republike*, vol. 1. Belgrade: Zbornik za IJK, 1935. Sec. III, bk. 4.
──────. *Građa o slikarskoj skoli u Dubrovniku XII–XVI*. 2 vols. Istorijski Institut, bks. 3 and 4. Belgrade: SAN, 1952.
*Tales from Sacchetti*. Trans. Mary Steegman. London: J. M. Dent, 1908.
*The Voiage of M(aster) Henry Austel by Venice and thence Ragusa overland and so to Constantinople, Anno 1585*. In Richard Hakluyt, *The Principal Navigations*, vol. 2, pt. 2, pp. 194–98. London: 1598–1600.
*The Voiage of M(aster) John Lock to Jerusalem, Anno 1553*. In Richard Hakluyt, *The Principal Navigations*, vol. 2, pt. 2, pp. 101–12. London 1598–1600.
Vojnović, Kosta. *Statuta confraternitatum et corporationum Ragusinarum (ab aevo XIII–XVIII), I. Bratovštine dubrovačke. II. Dubrovačke obrtne korporacije*. Monumenta historio-juridica Slavorum meridionalium, vol. 7. Zagreb, 1899–1900.
Zeno, Caterino. *Del commentarii del viaggio in Persia di M. Caterine Zeno*. Venice: Per Francesco Marcolini, 1558.

## SECONDARY WORKS

Abulafia, David. "Dalmatian Ragusa and the Norman Kingdom of Sicily." *Slavonic and East European Review* 54 (1976): 419–28.
Aymard, Maurice. *Venise, Raguse et le commerce du blé pendant la seconde moitié du XVIe siècle*. Paris: SEVPEN, 1961.
Ashburner, Walter. *The Rhodian Sea Law*. London: Clarendon, 1909.
Baron, Hans. "Franciscan Poverty and Civic Wealth as Factors in the Rise of Humanistic Thought." *Speculum* 13; no. 1 (1938): 1–37.
Becker, Marvin. "The Republican City-State in Florence: An Inquiry into Its Origin and Survival, 1280–1434." *Speculum* 35 (1960): 39–50.
Bell, Susan Groag. "Medieval Women Book Owners: Arbiters of Lay Piety and Ambassadors of Culture." *SIGNS: Journal of Women in Culture and Society* 7 (1982): 742–68.
Bellomo, Manlio. *Le condizione giuridica della donna in Italia: vicende antiche e moderne*. Turin: Guiffre, 1970.
Beritić, Lukša. *Utvrđenja grada Dubrovnika*. Zagreb: JAZU, 1955.
──────. "Dubrovački vodovod." *Dubrovnik anali* 8–9 (1960–61): 99–117.
Besta, Enrico. *La famiglia nella storia del diritto italiano*. Padua: A. Milani, 1933.
Bistort, G. *Il magistrato alle pompe nella repubblica di Venezia*. Ser. 3, bk. 5. Venice: Regio deputazione veneta di storia patria, 1912.
Bjelovučić, Harriet. *The Ragusan Republic, Victim of Napolean and Its own Conservatism*. Leiden: Brill, 1970.
Bloch, Marc. *La Société féodale*. 2 vols. Paris: A. Michel, 1941. Translated as *Feudal Society* by L. A. Manyon. Chicago: University of Chicago Press, 1964.
Bogdanović, M., ed., *Na tri kralja*. Zagreb: JAZU 1922.
Borgeaud, Willy. *Les Illyriens en Grece et en Italie: Étude linguistique et mythologique*. Genève: S. Roulet, 1943.

Božić, Ivan. "Ekonomski i društveni razvitak Dubrovnika u XIV i XV veku." *Istorijski glasnik* 1 (1949): 21–61.

——. *Dubrovnik i Turska u XIV i XV veku*. Belgrade: SAN, 1952.

——. "Dve Beleške o Filipu de Diversisu." *Zbornik filoz. fakulteta, Belgrade* 11 (1970): 313–29.

Braudel, Fernand. *Civilisation matérielle et capitalisme*. Translated as *Capitalism and Material Life: 1400–1800* by Miriam Kochan. New York: Harper, 1974.

——. *Les Jeux de l'échange*. Volume 2 of *Civilisation et capitalisme*. Paris, 1979. Translated as *The Wheels of Commerce* by Siân Reynolds, New York: Harper and Row, 1982.

——. *La Mediterranée et le monde mediterranéen a l'époque de Philippe II*. Paris: A. Colin, 1949. Translated from 2nd rev. ed. 1966, *The Mediterranean and the Mediterranean World in the age of Philip II* by Siân Reynolds. 2 vols. New York: Harper and Row, 1973.

——. "Personal Testimony." *Journal of Modern History* 44 (1972): 448–67.

Brown, Peter. *The World of Late Antiquity*. Cambridge, Mass.: Harvard University Press, 1978.

Brucker, Gene. *Florentine Politics and Society*. Princeton, N.J.: Princeton University Press, 1962.

——. *Renaissance Florence*. New York: Wiley, 1969.

Buckler, Georgiane. "Women in Byzantine Law." *Byzantion* 11 (1936): 391–416.

Budiša, Dražen. "Humanism in Croatia." In *Humanism Beyond Italy*, vol. 2 of *Renaissance Humanism*, ed. Albert Rabil, Jr. Philadelphia: University of Pennsylvania Press, 1988.

Bullough, Vern. "Population and the Study and Practice of Medieval Medicine." *Bulletin of the History of Medicine* 36 (1962): 65.

Burke, Kenneth. *The Philosophy of Literary Form*. Baton Rouge: Louisiana State University Press, 1941.

Burke, Peter. *Popular Culture in Early Modern Europe*. New York: New York University Press, 1978.

Campbell, Anna. *The Black Death and Men of Learning*. New York: Columbia University Press, 1931.

Carter, Frank W. *Dubrovnik: The Classic City-State*. London: Seminar Press, 1972.

Cechetti, Francho. "Medicina in Venezia nell 1300." *Archivio veneto* 25 (1883): 1–378.

——. "La vita dei Veneziani nel 1300." *Archivio veneto* 27 (1884): 5–54.

Cessi, Roberto. *Storia della repubblica di Venezia*. Milan: G. Principato, 1944.

Chojnacki, Stanley. "In Search of the Venetian Patriciate: Families and Factions in the Fourteenth Century." In *Renaissance Venice*, ed. John Hale. Totowa, N.J.: Rowman and Littlefield, 1973.

——. "Dowries and Kinsmen in Early Renaissance Venice." In *Women in Medieval Society*. Ed. Susan Mosher Stuard. Philadelphia: University of Pennsylvania Press, 1976.

——. "The Power of Love: Wives and Husbands in Late Medieval Venice." In *Women and Power in the Middle Ages*. Ed. Mary Erler and Maryanne Kowaleski. Athens, Ga.: University of Georgia Press, 1988.

Cipolla, Carlo. *Public Health and the Profession of Medicine in the Renaissance.* Cambridge: Cambridge University Press, 1976.

————. *Storia moneta,* vol. 1. Florence, 1976.

Circović, Sime, and Desanka Kovačević-Kojic. "L'Economie naturelle et la production marchande aux XIII<sup>e</sup>–XV<sup>e</sup> siècles dans les regions actuelles de la Yougaslavie." *Balcancia* 13–14 (1982–83): 45–56.

Clavero, Bartolomé. *Mayorazgo propriedad feudal en Castilla.* Madrid: Siglo Veintiuno Editores, 1974.

Cooper, P. J. "Inheritance and Settlement by Great Landowners." In *Family and Inheritance,* ed. Jack Goody, Joan Thirsk, and E. P. Thompson, pp. 192–408. Cambridge: Cambridge University Press, 1976.

Cooper, P. J., ed. "General Introduction." In *The New Cambridge Modern History,* vol. IV, (1609–48/59), 1–27. Cambridge: Cambridge University Press, 1970.

Čremošnik, Gregor. "Nekoliko ljekarskih ugovora iz Dubrovnika." In *Rešetarov zbornik,* 43–45. Dubrovnik: "Jadran," 1931.

————. "Pravni položaj našeg roblja u sredjem vijeku." *Sarajevo zemaljski muzej u Bosni i Hercegovini, glasnik,* n.s. 2 (1947): 69–73.

————. "Izvori za istoriju roblja i servicijalnih odnosa u našim zemljama sr. vijeka." *Istorijski-pravni zbornik* 1 (1949): 146–62.

Davenport, Millia. *The Book of Costume.* New York: Crown Publishers, 1948.

Davis, James Cushman. *The Decline of Venetian Nobility as a Ruling Class.* Baltimore: Johns Hopkins University Press, 1962.

Davis, Natalie Zemon. "Proverbial Wisdom and Popular Errors." In *Society and Culture in Early Modern France,* 227–67. Stanford, Cal.: Stanford University Press, 1975.

————. "The Reason of Misrule." In *Society and Culture* in *Early Modern France,* 97–123. Stanford, Cal.: Stanford University Press, 1975.

Deanović, Mirko. *Anciens contacts entre la France et Raguse.* Zagreb: Institut francais de Zagreb, 1950.

Dedijer, Vladimir. *History of Yugoslavia.* New York: McGraw-Hill, 1974.

Dinić, Mihail. "Krstati groševi." *Zbornik radova vizantološkog instituta* 1 (1950): 86–112.

————. *Za istoriju rudarstva u srednjevekovnoj Srbiji i Bosni.* 2 vols. Belgrade: SAN, 1955.

————. "The Balkans." In *Cambridge Medieval History,* ed. J. M. Hussey, 2nd ed., vol. 4, part 1, pp. 519–66. Cambridge: Cambridge University Press, 1966.

————. "Dubrovačka srednjevekovna karavanska trgovina." *Jugoslavenski istorijski časopis* 3 (1973): 119–46.

Dinić-Knežević, Dušanka. "Trgovina vinom u Dubrovniku." *Godišnjak filoz. fakulteta Novi Sad* 9 (1966): 39–85.

————. "Trgovina žitom u Dubrovniku." *Godišnjak filoz. fakulteta Novi Sad* 10 (1967): 79–131.

————. "Trgovina drvetom u Dubrovniku u XIV veku." *Godišnjak filoz. fakulteta Novi Sad* 11 (1968): 9–30.

―――. "Petar Pantella, trgovac i suknar u Dubrovniku." *Godišnjak filoz. fakulteta Novi Sad* 13, no. 1 (1970): 87–144.

―――. *Položaj žena u Dubrovniku u XIII i XIV veku.* Belgrade: SAN, 1974.

―――. *Tkanine u privredi srednjovekovnog Dubrovnika.* Belgrade: SAN, 1982.

―――. "Gradni briza u srednjovjekovnom Dubrovniku." *Dubrovnik anali* 22–23 (1985): 25–30.

Dockes, Pierre. *Medieval Slavery and Liberation.* Trans. Arthur Goldhammer. Chicago: University of Chicago Press, 1982.

Draper, John. "Et in Illyria Feste." *Shakespeare Association Bulletin* 16 (1941): 220–28.

"Dubrovnik." *Enciklopedija Jugoslavije* 3, (Zagreb, 1958): 126–27.

Duby, Georges. "Lineage, Nobility and Chivalry." In *Family and Society,* trans. Elborg Forster and Patricia Ranum, 16–40. Baltimore: Johns Hopkins University Press, 1972.

―――. *Medieval Marriage. Two Models from Twelfth-Century France.* Trans. Elborg Forster and Patricia Ranum. Baltimore: Johns Hopkins University Press, 1978.

―――. *Le chevalier, la femme, et le pretre.* Paris, 1981. Translated as *The Knight, the Lady, and the Priest* by Barbara Bray. New York: Pantheon, 1983.

Elton, G. R. "Reform by Statute: Thomas Starkey's Dialogue and Thomas Cromwell's Policy." *British Academy Proceedings* 54 (1968): 165–88.

Epstein, Mortimer. *The Early History of the Levant Company.* London: G. Routledge and Sons, 1908.

Ercole, Francesco. "L'istituto dotale nella pratica e nella legislazione statutaria dell'Italia superiore." *Revista italiana per le scienze giuridiche* 65 (1908): 191–302; 66 (1910): 167–257.

Fairchilds, Cissy. *Domestic Enemies: Servants and Their Masters in Old Regime France.* Baltimore: Johns Hopkins University Press, 1983.

Farlati, Daniel. *Illyricum sacrum,* Vol. 6: *Ecclesia Ragusina.* Venice: Sebastianum Coleti, 1800.

Favi, Francesco. *Dubrovnik and the American Revolution,* ed. Wayne Vucinich. Palo Alto, California: Ragusan Press, 1977.

Febvre, Lucien. "Ce que peuvent nous apprendre les monographies familiales." *Mélanges d'histoire sociale* 1 (1942): 31–34.

Ferguson, C. A. "Diglossia." In *Language in Culture and Society,* ed. Dell Hymes, 429–39. New York: Harper and Row, 1964.

Filipović, Rudolf. "Shakespeareova Ilirija." *Filologija* (Zagreb) 1 (1957): 123–38.

Fine, John. *The Bosnian Church: A New Interpretation.* New York and London: East European Quarterly, distrib. by Columbia University Press, 1975.

―――. *The Early Medieval Balkans.* Ann Arbor: University of Michigan Press, 1983.

Fisković, Cvito. "Dubrovački zlatari od XIII do XVII stoljeća." *Starohrvatska prosvjeta* ser. 1, 3 (1949): 143–249.

Foretić, Vinko. "Dubrovačke bratovštine." *Časopis za hrvatsku provijest.* Zagreb: JAZU, 1943.

―――. "Ugovor Dubrovnika sa srpskim velikim Županom Stefanom Nemanjom i stara dubrovačka djedina." *Rad. JAZU* 283 (1951): 51–118.

―――. "Dubrovački Arhiv u srednjem vijeku." *Dubrovnik anali* 6–7 (1957–59): 73–84.

———. *Povijest Dubrovnika,* 2 vols. Zagreb: JAZU, 1980.

Friedl, Ernestine. *Women and Men.* New York: Holt, 1975.

Gečić, Marina. "Dubrovačka trgovina solju u XIV veku." *Zbornik filoz. fakulteta Belgrade* 3 (1955): 92–152.

Gelcich, Giuseppi. "Dubrovački arhiv." *Glasnik zemaljskog muzeja u Bosni i Hercegovini,* Sarajevo, 22 (1910): 537–88.

———. *Instituzioni maritime e sanitarie della repubblica di Ragusa.* Trieste: L. Hermanstorfer, 1882.

Gilbert, Felix. *Machiavelli and Guicciardini.* Princeton, N.J.: Princeton University Press, 1965.

———. "The Venetian Constitution in Florentine Political Thought." In *Florentine Studies: Politics and Society in Renaissance Florence,* ed. Nicolai Rubenstein. London: Faber, 1968.

Goldthwaite, Richard. "Il prezzo del grano a Firenze dal XIV al XV secolo." *Quaderni storici* 28 (1975): 3–36.

———. *Building Trades in Fifteenth Century Florence.* Baltimore: Johns Hopkins University Press, 1982.

Grmek, M. D. "Bilješke o najstarijim dubrovačkim ljekarnicima." *Farmaceutski glasnik* 9 (1953): 367–70.

———. "Quarantine." *CIBA Review* (1957): 30–31.

Guillou, André. "Il matrimonio nell'Italia bizantina nei secoli X et XI." In *Matrimonio nella societa alto-medieval,* vol. 2, 569–86. Spoleto, 1970.

Hammel, Eugene. *Alternative Structures and Ritual Relations in the Balkans.* Englewood Cliffs, N.J.: Prentice Hall, 1968.

Hammel, Eugene, and Joel M. Halpern. "Observations on the Intellectual History of Ethnology and Other Social Sciences in Yugoslavia." *Comparative Studies in Society and History* 7 (1969): 17–26.

Hammel, Eugene, and Karl Wachter. *Statistical Studies of Historical Social Structures.* New York: Academic Press, 1979.

Han, Verena. *Tri veka dubrovačkog staklarstva, XIV–XVI.* Belgrade: SAN, 1981.

Harden, D. B. *Sir Arthur Evans, A Memoir, 1851–1941.* Oxford: Ashmolean Museum, 1983.

Haumant, E. "La Slavisation de la Dalmatie," *Revue historique* 124 (1917): 287–304.

———. *Esclaves et domestiques au moyen âge dans le monde mediterranéen.* Paris: Fayard, 1981.

Heers, Jacques. *L'Occident aux XIV$^e$–XV$^e$ siècles: Aspects économiques et sociaux.* Paris: Presses Universitaires de France, 1966.

———. *Le Clan familial au moyen âge.* Paris, 1974.

Herlihy, David. *Pisa in the Early Renaissance.* New Haven: Yale University Press, 1958.

———. *Open Muliebria.* Philadelphia: Temple University Press, 1989.

Herlihy, David, and Christiane Klapisch-Zuber. *Les Toscans et leurs familles.* Paris: SEVPEN, 1978.

Herrin, Judith. *The Formation of Christendom.* Princeton: Princeton University Press, 1985.

Hexter, J. J. "The Rhetoric of History." In *Reappraisals in History,* 62–66. Bloomington: Indiana University Press, 1971.

Heyd, Wilhelm. *Histoire du commerce du Levant au moyen âge.* 6th ed., 2 vols. Amsterdam: O. Harrassawit, 1855.

Hirst, L. *The Conquest of Plague.* Oxford: Clarendon, 1953.

Hoffman, Johannes. "Venedig und die Narenter." *Studi veneziani* 11 (1969): 3–41.

Horwitz, Sylvia. *The Find of a Lifetime.* London: Weidenfeld and Nicolson, 1983.

Hrabak, Bogumil. "Kuga u balkanskim zemljama pod Turcima od 1450 do 1600 godine." *Istorijski glasnik* 1–2 (1957): 19–37.

———. "Dubrovačko srebo u Italiji i Kataloniji XIV, XV, i XVI veku." *Istorijski glasnik* 1–2 (1980): 57–78.

Hughes, Diane Owen. "Domestic Ideals and Social Behavior: Evidence from Medieval Genoa." In *The Family in History,* ed. Charles Rosenberg, 114–44. Philadelphia: University of Pennsylvania Press, 1975.

———. "From Brideprice to Dowry in Mediterranean Europe." *Journal of Family History* 3 (1978): 278–85.

———. "Sumptuary Law and Social Relations in Renaissance Italy." In *Disputes and Settlements: Law and Human Relations in the West,* ed. John Bossy, 66–99. Cambridge: Cambridge University Press, 1983.

Jireček, Constantine. *Die Handelsstrassen und Bergwerke von Serbien und Bosnien während des Mittelalters.* Praz: Abhandlugen der kgl. bohm. Gesellschaft der Wissenschaften, 6. Folge, 10. Band, 1879.

———. "Die Bedeutung von Ragusa in der Handelsgeschichte des Mittelalters." *Almanach der Kaiserlichen Akademie der Wissenschaften in Wien,* 49, Jg. S., pp. 365–452. Vienna, 1899.

———. *Die Romanen in den Städten Dalmatiens während des Mittelalters.* 3 vols., Denkenschriften der Kaiserlichen Akademie der Wissenschaften in Wien, phil.-hist. Klasse, Bd. 48–49. Vienna, 1901–3.

———. "Die Mittelalterliche Kanzlei der Ragusaner." *Archiv für Slav. Philologie* 16 (1904): 161–214.

———. *Staat und Gesellschaft im Mittelalterlichen Serbien. Studien zur Kulturgeschichte des 13.-15. Jahrhunderts.* 4 vols. Denkschriften der Kaiserlichen Akademie der Wissenschaften in Wien, phil.-hist. Klasse, Bd. 56, 58, 64, 65. Vienna, 1913–20.

Katele, Irene B. "Piracy and the Venetian State." *Speculum* 63, no. 4 (1988): 865–89.

Kedar, Benjamin. "Genoese Notaries of 1382." In *The Medieval City,* ed. Harry Miskimin, David Herlihy, and A. L. Udovitch, 73–94. New Haven: Yale University Press, 1975.

Keenan, Eileen. "Norm Makers, Norm Breakers." In *Explorations in the Ethnography of Speaking.* Ed. Richard Bauman and Joel Sherzer, 125–43. New York: Cambridge University Press, 1974.

Kelly, Joan. *Women, History, and Theory.* Chicago: University of Chicago Press, 1985.

Kelso, Ruth. *Doctrine for a Lady of the Renaissance.* Urbana: University of Illinois Press, 1956.

Kent, Francis W. *Household and Lineage in Renaissance Florence.* Princeton, N.J.: Princeton University Press, 1977.

Kheil, Carl Peter. *Benedetto Cotrugli Raugeo: Ein Beitrag zur Geschichte der Buchhaltung.* Vienna: Manzsche Buchhandlung, 1906.

Kirshner, Julius. "Wives' Claims Against Insolvent Husbands." In *Women of the Medieval World*, ed. Julius Kirshner and Suzanne Wemple, 256–303. London: Basil Blackwell, 1985.

Kirshner, Julius, and Anthony Mohlo. "The Dowry Fund and Marriage Market in Early Quattrocento Florence." *Journal of Modern History* 50 (1978): 403–38.

Kisch, Bruno. *Scales and Weights*. New Haven, Conn.: Yale University Press, 1961.

Klapisch-Zuber, Christiane. *Women, Family, and Ritual in Renaissance Italy*. Trans. Lydia G. Cochrane. Chicago: University of Chicago Press, 1985.

Kostić, Veselin. *Dubrovnik i Engleska 1300–1650*. Belgrade: SAN, 1973.

Kovačević, Desanka. "Les Mines d'or et d'argent en Servie et Bosnie." *Annales. E.S.C.* 15 (1960): 248–58.

———. *Trgovina u srednjovjekovnoj Bosni*. Sarajevo: Naučno društvo NR Bosne i Hercegovine, 1961.

———. "Zore Bokšić, dubrovački trgovac i protovestijar bosanskih Kraljeva." *Godišnjak društvo istoričara Bosne i Hercegovine* 13 (1962): 289–310.

Krekić, Bariša. *Dubrovnik et le Levant au moyen âge*. Paris: SEVPEN, 1961.

———. "Pestes balkaniques des XV^e et XVI^e siècle." *Annales, E.S.C.* 18 (1963): 594–95.

———. *Dubrovnik in the Fourteenth and Fifteenth Centuries*. Norman: University of Oklahoma Press, 1972.

———. "Four Florentine Commercial Companies in Dubrovnik." In *The Medieval City*. Ed. Harry Miskimin, David Herlihy, and Benjamin Kedar, pp. 25–41. New Haven, Conn.: Yale University Press, 1977.

———. "Foreigners in Dubrovnik." *Viator* 8 (1978): 67–75.

———. *Dubrovnik, Italy, and the Balkans in the Late Middle Ages*. Collected articles: articles cited in notes may be found here. London: Variorum, 1980.

———. "Ser Basilius de Basilio." *Zbornik radova vizantološkog instituta SAN* 23 (1984): 172–82.

———. "*Abominandum Crimen:* Punishment of Homosexuals in Renaissance Dubrovnik." *Viator* 18 (1987): 227–345.

Krekić, Bariša, ed. *The Urban Society of Eastern Europe in Premodern Times*. Berkeley: University of California, 1987.

Krisković, V. "Shakespeare i mi. Česka morska obala u 'zimskoj priči.'" *Hrvatska revija* 14, no. 5 (1941): 3–25.

Kuehn, Thomas. "*Cum consensu mundualdi:* Legal Guardianship of Women in Quattrocento Florence." *Viator* 13 (1982): 309–33.

Lane, Frederic Chapin. *Andrea Barbarigo, Merchant of Venice 1418–1449*. Baltimore: Johns Hopkins University Press, 1944.

———. "Le vecchie monete di conto veneziane ed il ritorno all'oro." *Atti dell'Instituto Veneto di Scienze, Lettere ed Arti, Cl. science morali e lettere* 117 (1958–59): 58–68.

———. *Venice and History*. Collected articles; articles cited in notes may be found here. Baltimore: Johns Hopkins University Press, 1966.

———. *Venice, a Maritime Republic*. Baltimore: Johns Hopkins University Press, 1973.

Lane, Frederic Chapin, and Reinhold Mueller. *Money and Banking in Medieval and Renaissance Venice,* vol. 1. Baltimore: Johns Hopkins University Press, 1985.

Lansing, Carol L. *The Florentine Magnates: Lineage and Faction in a Medieval Commune.* Princeton, N.J.: Princeton University Press, 1991.

Laslett, Peter, Karla Oosterveen, and Richard M. Smith, eds. *Bastardy and Its Comparative History.* Cambridge, Mass.: Harvard University Press, 1980.

Lechner, Karl. *Das Grosse Sterben in Deutschland . . . in 1348–1351.* Innsbruck: Wagner, 1884.

Levi-Pisetzky, Rosita. *Storia del costume in Italia.* 3 vols. Milan: Foundazione Giovanni Treccani degli Alfieri, 1964.

Litchfield, R. Burr. "Demographic Characteristics of Florentine Patrician Families." *Journal of Economic History* 19 (1969): 191–206.

Lopez, Robert S. *Studi sull'economia Genovese nel medio evo, vol. 14.* Turin: S. Lattes, 1936.

Lopez, Robert S., and Irving Raymond. *Medieval Trade in the Mediterranean World.* New York: Columbia University Press, 1955.

Lowe, A. E. *The Beneventan Script.* Oxford: Oxford University Press, 1914.

Lučić, Josip. "Dubrovnik astareja." In *Beritičević zbornik,* ed. Slavomir Benić. Dubrovnik: Društvo prijatelja dubrovačke starine, 1960.

———. "O dubrovačkom patricijatu u XIV stoljeću." *Istorijski zbornik* 37 (1964): 393–411.

———. "Pomorske-trgovačke veze Dubrovnika i Italije u XIII stoljeću." *Pomorskog-Zbornika* 5 (1967): 447–75.

———. *Prošlost dubrovačke astareje.* Dubrovnik: Matica hvratska, 1970.

———. "Gli stranieri a Ragusa nel medio evo." *Bollettino dell'Atlante linguistico mediterraneo* 13–15 (1971–73): 345–48.

———. *Dubrovnik's Relations with England: A Symposium.* Department of English, Faculty of Philosophy, University of Zagreb, 1972.

———. *L'Histoire de Dubrovnik.* Zagreb: JAZU, 1974.

———. *Obrti i usluge u Dubrovniku od početka do XIV stoljeća.* Zagreb: JAZU, 1979.

Luetić, Josip. *O pomorstvu dubrovačke republike u XVIII stoljeću.* Dubrovnik: Pomorski muzej, 1959.

———. *Mornarica dubrovačke republike.* Dubrovnik: Dubrovački odbor za Proslavu dvadeset godišnjice mornarice, 1962.

———. "English Mariners and Ships in Seventeenth-Century Dubrovnik." *Mariners' Mirror* 64 (1978): 276–84.

Luzzatto, Gino. *Studi di storia economica veneziana.* Padua: CEDAM, 1954.

MacLean, Ian. *The Renaissance Notion of Woman.* Cambridge: Cambridge University Press, 1981.

Mahnken, Irmgard. *Dubrovački patricijat u XIV veku.* Belgrade: SAN, 1960.

Mandić, D. "Gregorio VII e l'occupazione Veneta della Dalmazia nell'anno 1076." *Venezia e il Levante fino al secolo XV.* In *Storia diritto economica,* vol. 1. Ed. A. Pertusi, 453–71. Florence and Venice: Olschki, 1972.

Mandrou, R. *Les Fugger propriétaires fonciers en Souabe, 1560–1618.* Paris: Plon, 1968.

Manfroni, Camillo. *Storia della marina italiana dalle invasioni barbariche al trattato di Ninfeo.* Livorno: R. Accademia navale, 1899.

Manuel, Frank E., and Fritzie P. Manuel. *Utopian Thought in the Western World.* Cambridge, Mass.: Belknap Press, 1979.

Marinović, Ante. "Prilog poznavanju dubrovačkih bratovština." *Dubrovnik anali* 1 (1952): 233–45.

———. "Local Autonomies in the Ancient Republic of Ragusa." In *Actes du II<sup>e</sup> congrès international des études du sud-est Européen,* II (Athens, 1972), pp. 499–511.

———. "I pubblici registri fondiari nella repubblica di Dubrovnik nel medioevo." *Studi veneziani* 15 (1973): 135–76.

Marković, Zdenka. *Pjesnikinje starog Dubrovnika.* Zagreb: JAZU, 1970.

Marović, I. "Arheološka istraživanja u okolici Dubrovnika." *Dubrovnik anali* 4 (1962): 9–30.

Maza, Sara C. *Servants and Masters in Eighteenth Century France.* Princeton: Princeton University Press, 1983.

Medini, Milorad. *Dubrovnik Gučetića.* Belgrade: SAN, 1953.

Metcalf, Michael. *Coinage of the Balkans, 620–1355.* Chicago: University of Chicago Press, 1965.

Mihailović, J. *Seizmički karakter i trusne katastrofe našeg južnog primorja.* Belgrade: SAN, 1947.

Mitić, Ilija. *Dubrovački konzuli i konzularna služba starog Dubrovnika.* Dubrovnik: JAZU, 1973.

———. *Dubrovačka država u medunarodnoj zajednici (od 1358 do 1815)* Zagreb: JAZU, 1988.

Mohlo, Anthony. *The Funded Debt of Early Renaissance Florence.* Cambridge, Mass.: Harvard University Press, 1971.

Molmenti, Pompeo. *La storia di Venezia nella vita privata.* 6th ed., 3 vols. Bergamo: Istituto Italia, 1922.

Mueller, Reinhold C. "The Procurators of San Marco." *Studi veneziani* 13 (1971): 105–220.

———. "Aspetti sociali ed economici della peste al venezia nel Medioevo." In *Venezia e la Peste,* ed. Assessorato alle culture et belle arte, 2. Venice: Marsilio, 1979.

———. "The Role of Bank Money in Venice, 1300–1500." *Studi veneziani,* n.s. 3 (1979): 47–96.

Muir, Edward. *Civic Ritual in Renaissance Venice.* Princeton, N.J.: Princeton University Press, 1981.

Muljačić, Žarko. "Benko Kotruljević." *Dubrovnik horizonti* 3 (1970): 32–33.

Nedeljković, Branco. "Nekoliko karakteristike i opaske o dubrovačkom pravu i drzavi XIV i XV stoljeća (1348–1460)." *Istorijski časopis* 18 (1971): 95–106.

Nef, John. "Mining and Metallurgy in Medieval Civilization." In *Cambridge Economic History,* vol. 2, ed. M. M. Postan, 430–92. Cambridge: Cambridge University Press, 1952.

Newett, N. Margaret. "The Sumptuary Law of Venice." In *Historical Essays* by Members of Owen's College, Manchester, ed. T. Tout and J. Tait, 235–78. London: Longmans, Green, 1902.

Novak, Gregor. "Dubrovački potres 1667, i Mletci." *Dubrovnik anali* 12 (1970): 9–25.

## 254    Bibliography

Novak, Slobodan P. *Dubrovnik Revisited.* Zagreb: Sveučilišna naklada Liber, 1987.
Novak, Viktor. "The Slavonic-Latin Symbiosis in Dalmatia During the Middle Ages." *The Slavonic and East European Review* 32 (1954): 1–29.
Novaković, Stojan. "Villes et cités du moyen âge dans l'Europe occidentale et dans la peninsula Balcanique." *Archiv für Slaviche Philologie* 25 (1903): 321–40.
Origo, Iris. "The Domestic Enemy: Eastern Slaves in Tuscany in the Fourteenth and Fifteenth Centuries." *Speculum* 30 (1955): 321–99.
*Oxford Classical Dictionary.* Ed. N. Hammond and H. Scullard. Oxford: Oxford University Press, 1970.
Pallucchini, Rodolfo. *La pittura veneziana del trecento.* Venice and Rome: Istituto per la collaborazione culturale, 1964.
Papadopoli, Nicolo. *Le monete di Venezia.* Venice: Libreria Emiliana 1893.
Petrović, Đurđica. *Dubrovačko oružje u XIV veku.* Belgrade: Vojni Muzej, 1976.
Petrovich, Miodrag. "A Mediterranean City-State: A Study of Dubrovnik Elites, 1592–1667." Ph.D. diss., University of Chicago, 1973.
Pisani, Paul. *Num Ragusini ab omni jure Veneto a saec. X usque ad saec. XIV.* Paris: A. Picard, 1893.
Pocock, J. G. A. *The Ancient Constitution and the Feudal Law.* Cambridge: Cambridge University Press, 1957.
———. *The Machiavellian Moment.* Princeton, N.J.: Princeton University Press, 1975.
———. "The Classical Theory of Deference," *American Historical Review* 81 (1976): 516–23.
Popović-Radenković, Mariana. "Le relazioni commerciali fra Dubrovnik (Raguse) e la Puglia nel periodo angioino (1266–1442)." *Archivio storico per le province napoletane,* n.s. 37–38 (1957–58).
Prelog, Milan, and Jorjo Tadić. *Historija naroda Jugoslavije,* vol. 1, 654–60. Zagreb: Školska knjiga, 1953.
Pullan, Brian. *Rich and Poor in Renaissance Venice.* Cambridge: Cambridge University Press, 1971.
Queller, Donald, and Susan Stratton. "A Century of Controversy on the Fourth Crusade." *Studies in Medieval and Renaissance History* 6 (1969): 233–78.
Queller, Donald, and Thomas F. Madden, "Father of the Bride: Fathers, Daughters, and Dowries in Late Medieval and Early Renaissance Venice." Unpublished ms.
Rashdall, Hastings. *The Universities of Europe in the Middle Ages.* Rev. by F. M. Powicke and A. B. Emden, eds. Oxford: Clarendon Press, 1936.
Rešetar, Milan. *Dubrovačka numizmatika.* 2 vols. Belgrade: SAN, 1924.
Rheubottom, David. "'Sisters First': Betrothal Order and Age at Marriage in Fifteenth Century Ragusa." *Journal of Family History* 13, no. 4 (1988): 359–406.
———. "Hierarchy of Office in Fifteenth-Century Ragusa." *Bulletin of the John Rylands University Library* 72, no. 3 (1990): 155–67.
Riemer, Eleanor Sabina. "Women in the Medieval City: Sources and Uses of Wealth by Sienese Women in the Thirteenth Century." Ph.D. diss. New York University, 1975.
Roglić, J. F. "The Geographical Setting of Medieval Dubrovnik." In *Geographical*

*Essays on Eastern Europe,* ed. N. Pounds, 141–59. Bloomington: Indiana University Press, 1961.

Roller, Dragan. *Dubrovački zanati u XV i XVI stoljeću,* vol. 2. Zagreb: Jugoslavenska Akademija građa za gospodarsku povijest Hvratske, 1951.

Roncière, Charles M. de la. *Prix et salaires à Florence au XIV$^e$ siècle, 1280–1380.* Rome: Ecole francais de Rome, 1982.

Rosembert, André. *La Veuve en droit canonique jusqu'à XVI$^e$ siècle.* Paris: Jouve, 1923.

Ruggiero, Guido. "The Co-operation of Physicians and the State." *Journal of the History of Medicine and Allied Sciences* 33 (1978): 156–66.

———. "Modernization and the Mythic State in Early Renaissance Venice: The Serrata Revisited." *Viator* 10 (1979): 245–56.

———. *The Boundary of Eros.* New York and Oxford: Oxford University Press, 1985.

Samardžić, Radovan. "Podmladak dubrovačkih trgovaca i zanatlija u XVI veku." *Zbornik studentiskih stručnih radova* (1948): 64–78.

———. *Borba Dubrovnika za opstanak posle velikog zemljotresa 1667.* Belgrade: Nauč. delo, 1960.

Saria, B. "O težini najstarijih dubrovačkih dinara." In *Rešetarov zbornik iz dubrovačke prošlosti,* ed. M. Vidoević and J. Tadić, 40–41. Dubrovnik: Matica hrvatska, 1931.

Skok, P. "L'Importance de Dubrovnik dans l'histoire des slaves." *Le Monde slave* 8 (1931): 161–71.

———. "Les Origines de Raguse." *Slavia časopis* 10 (Prague, 1931): 487.

Soloviev, A. "Le Patriciat de Raguse au XV$^e$ siècle." In *Rešetarov zbornik iz dubrovačke prošlosti,* ed. M. Vidoević and J. Tadić, 60–68. Dubrovnik: Matica hrvatska, 1931.

*Spomenica 650–godišnjice ljekarne »Male Braće« u Dubrovniku.* Ed. M. D. Grmek. Zagreb: JAZU, 1968.

Stoianovich, Traian. *A Study in Balkan Civilization.* New York: Knopf, 1967.

———. "Ragusa: Society Without a Printing House." In *Structure sociale et développement culturel des villes sud-est,* 43–73. Bucharest: Association Internationale d'etudes du sud-est européen, 1975.

Stuard, Susan Mosher. "A Communal Program of Medical Care: Medieval Ragusa/Dubrovnik." *Journal of the History of Medicine and Allied Sciences* 28 (1973): 126–42.

———. "The Adriatic Trade in Silver, c. 1300." *Studi veneziani* 17–18 (1975–1976): 95–143.

———. "Women in Charter and Statute Law: Medieval Ragusa/Dubrovnik." In *Women in Medieval Society,* ed. Susan Mosher Stuard, 199–208. Philadelphia: University of Pennsylvania Press, 1976.

———. "Dowry Increase and Increments in Wealth in Medieval Ragusa (Dubrovnik)." *Journal of Economic History* 41 (1981): 795–811.

———. "Urban Domestic Slavery in Medieval Ragusa." *Journal of Medieval History* 9 (1983): 155–71.

———. "Medieval Workshop: Toward a Theory of Consumption and Exchange." *Journal of Economic History* 44 (1985): 921–24.

Sugden, Edward. *A Topographical Dictionary to the Works of Shakespeare*. Manchester: Longmans, Green. 1925.

Šundrica, Zdravko. *Dubrovački jevreji i njihova emancipacija*. Belgrade: SAN, 1971.

———. "Skandal u velikom vijeću," in "Šetnja koz arhiv (2)." *Dubrovnik* 3 (1973): 114–15.

Tadić, Jorjo. *Španija i Dubrovnik u XVI veku*. Belgrade: Srspska kraljevska akademija, 1932.

———. *Dubrovnik portreti*. Belgrade: Srpska knjiženvna zadruga, 1948.

———. *Dix années d'historiographie Yougoslave*. Belgrade: SAN, 1955.

———. "Le Port de Raguse au moyen âge." Le Navire et l'économie maritime du moyen âge au XVIIIᵉ siècle. In *Travaux du second colloque international d'histoire maritime*. Paris: SEVPEN, 1959.

———. "Le Commerce en Dalmatie et à Raguse et la décadence économique de Venise au XVIIᵉᵐᵉ siècle." In *Aspetti e cause decadenza nel economica veneziano nel secolo XII: Atti del Consegno 27 guigno–2 juglio, 1957*, 1–21. Venice-Rome, 1961.

———. "Les Archives économiques de Raguse." *Annales, E.S.C.* 16 (1961): 1168–75.

Tadić, Jorjo, and R. Jeremić. *Prilozi za istoriju zdravstvene kulture starog Dubrovnika*. 2 vols. Belgrade: Biblioteka centralnog higijenskog zavoda, 1938–1940.

Teichman, Jenny. *Illegitimacy, An Examination of Bastardy*. Ithaca, N.Y.: Cornell University Press, 1982.

Teja, A. "La schiavitu domestica ed il traffico degli schiavi." *Revista Dalmatica* 22 (1941): 33–44.

Tenenti, Alberto. "Gli schiavi di Venezia alla fine de cinquecento." *Revista storica italiana* 67 (1955): 52–69.

———. *Piracy and the Decline of Venice*. Trans. Janet Pullan and Brian Pullan. Berkeley: University of California Press, 1967.

Thiriet, Freedy. *La Romanie venetiénne*. Paris: Editions E. de Boccard, 1959.

Tomaschek, W. *Zur Kunde der Händemus-Halbinsel*, II, *Die Handelswege im 12 Jahrhunderte, nach den Erkundigungen des Arabers Idrisi*. Sitzungsberichte der phil.-hist. Klasse der kaiserlichen Akademie. Vienna, 1881 and 1886. Band. 99, pp. 437–507; and Band. 113, pp. 285–373.

Torbarina, Josip. "Fragmenti iz neizdatih pisama nadbiskupa Lodovika Beccadellija." *Dubrovnik revija* 1, nos. 9–10 (1929): 320–40.

———. *Italian Influence on the Poets of the Ragusan Republic*. London: Williams and Norgate, 1931.

———. "The Setting of Shakespeare's Plays," *Studia Romanica et Anglica Zagrabiensia* 17–18 (1964): 21–59.

Treggiari, Suzanne. "*Digna Conducio:* Betrothals in the Roman Upper Class." *Echo du monde classique*, n.s. 3 (1984): 419–51.

Trexler, Richard. *Public Life in Renaissance Florence*. New York: Academic Press, 1980.

Truhelka, C. "Još o testamentu gosta Radina i o patarenima." *Glasnik zemaljskog muzeja, Sarajevo* 25 (1913): 380–81.

Tucci, Ugo. "The Psychology of the Merchant in the Sixteenth Century." In *Renaissance Venice*, ed. John Hale, 346–78. Totowa, N.J.: Rowman and Littlefield, 1973.

Vekarić, Stepan. "Vrste i tipovi dubrovaçkih brodova XIV stoljeća." *Dubrovnik anali* 10–11 (1966–67): 19–42.

———. "Dubrovačka trgovačka flota, 1599 godine." *Dubrovnik anali* 13 (1974): 427–32.

Verlinden, Charles. "Gli schiavi di venezia alla fine de cinquecento." *Rivista storica italiana* 67 (1955): 52–69.

———. "La Crête, débouché et Plague tournante de la traité des esclaves aux XIVᵉ et XVᵉ siècles." *Studi in onore di Amintore Fanfani,* 594–699. Milan: Guiffre, 1962.

———. "Orthodoxie et esclavage au bas moyen âge." *Melanges Eugene Tiserant, studi e testi* 235 (1964): 427–56.

———. *Les Origines de la civilisation atlantique de la renaissance a l'Âge des Lumières.* Paris: A. Michel, 1966.

———. "Le Recruitment des esclaves à Venise aux XIV et XV siècles." *Institut historique Belge de Rome* 39 (1968): 83–202.

———. *L'Esclavage dans l'Europe mediévale.* Vol. 1, Bruges: de Tempel, 1955; vol. 2, Ghent: Rijksonijersiteit te Gent, 1977.

Villari, Luigi. *The Republic of Ragusa.* London: J. M. Dent, 1904.

Villata di Renzo, Gigliola. *La tutela: Indagini sulla scuola dei glossatori.* Milan: Guiffre, 1975.

Vinaver, Vuk. "Trgovina Bosanskim robljem tokom XIV veka u Dubrovniku." *Dubrovnik anali* 2 (1953): 125–47.

———. "Prilozi istoriji plemenitih metala, cena i nadnica srednjevekovni Dubrovnik." *Istorijski glasnik* 1–2 (1960): 51–94.

———. "Der Venezianische Goldzechin in der Republik Ragusa." *Bollettino dell'Istituto di storia della società e dello stato veneziano* 4 (1962): 116–21.

Voje, Ignacij. "Bencius del Buono." *Istorijski časopis* 18 (1971): 189–91.

Vujić, Mihailo, and Milorad Zebić. *Život i rad Benka Kotruljice i njegov spis o trgovini i o savršemen trgovcu.* Titograd, 1963.

Vyronis, Speros. "The Question of the Byzantine Mines," *Speculum* 37, no. 1 (1962): 1–17.

Wolff, Robert. "Romania, the Latin Empire of Constantinople." *Speculum* 23 (1948): 1–34.

Zdravković, Ivan. *Dubrovački dvorci.* Belgrade: SAN, 1951.

Zordan, Giorgio. "I rari aspetti della communione familiare di beni nella Venezia dei secoli XI–XII." *Studi veneziani* 8 (1966): 129–94.

# Index

Abulafia, David, 52 n.27, 53 n.35, 245
Acciaiuoli (banking company of Florence), 183
*Acta Sanctae Mariae Majoris* (Dubrovnik), 29, 54, n.47, 241
Adriatic Sea, 1–2, 3, 165; coast, 21, 27–28, 35, 71, 148, 237
adultery, canon law of, 139–40
adulthood, legal age: for men, 37, 39, 81, 233; for women, 64, 74
Affresio (St.), church in Padua, 185
Alexandria, 53 n.41
Altichiero de Zevio, 185
ambassadorial accounts, 206–7
ambassadors, Ragusan, 39, 174–77
*ancilla, ancilla babica. See* Slaves
Ancona, 27, 205
Andreas (St.) de Castello convent, 88
*anona. See* Grain; *Massarii bladorum*
Anonymous Chronicler of Ravenna, 2, 13 n.7, 156, 229, 244
Antonini (Confraternity of St. Anthony), 153–54
Antonius, Master (surgeon), 45
Antivari. *See* Bar
aphorisms (proverbs), 40, 59–60
Apulia, 26–27, 43, 128, 157
Archbishop of Ragusa, 2, 4, 29–32, 34, 40, 45, 229, 233
architecture, urban, 115–18, 235–36
Argosy, 205, 213, 216
aristocracy, viii, 4, 6–7, 10, 34, 41, 49, 209, 212–13; criterion for, 60–69, 141; women of, 9, 42, 63, 100–113; in Venice, 186. See *also Nobili viri;* Nobility
Aristotle, 100, 107, 111 n.1, 212, 213
Armada, Spanish, 215–16. *See also* Spain
Arsafius (founder), 16–17
artisans, in Ragusa, 163–65, 186–90; immigration, 145–48; wages of, 162

Ashburner, Walter, 33, 54 nn.51–52, 58 n.97, 113 n.34, 245
Astarea, 3, 34, 35–36, 85, 87, 154
Athens, 2
*aurifici. See* Goldsmiths
Austel, Henry, 214–15, 225 n.34, 245
Austria, 6–7
Aymard, Maurice, 1, 12, 13 n.2, 245

Babalio: Marussa de, 64; Rigussa de Andreas de, 145
bachelors: artisan, 126–27, 147–49; noble, 77
*baiula* (governess). *See* Servants
Balkans, 2, 26; trade with, 26. *See also* West Balkans
Ban of Bosnia, 120
banks, banking companies, 183, 188
baptism, of slaves, 120
Bar (Antivari), 29, 65
barbers, 157–58
barber surgeons. *See* Surgeons
*barcae, barcussii. See* Ships
Bari, 27, 29
Baron, Hans, 219, 227 n.49, 245
Bartholomeus (St.) convent, 88
Basilio: Basilius de, 39; Francho, 86–87
Beccadelli, Luigi, 6, 212, 216, 221, 223 nn.4, 20, 226 nn. 41, 46, 245
Becker, Marvin, 223 n.11, 245
Bell, Susan Groag, 114 n.36, 245
Bellomo, Manlio, 112 n.3, 245
belts (*cinctura*), of precious metal, 177, 186
Benedictine monks (Order of St. Benedict), 24, 30, 229
Benessa: Peter de, 80; Symon de, 93 n.37
Beritić, Lukša, 56 n.75, 245
Besta, Enrico, 92 n.36, 245
bilingualism, 4, 15–20, 39
Bincola, Marinus de, 122; Slava, wife of Marinus, 122

Bisceglie, 27
Bistort, G., 113 n.25, 245
Bjelovučić, Harriet, 245
Black Plague (1347–1350), bubonic plague,
46–49, 62, 118, 158, 230; and subsequent
outbreaks, 67, 239–40; wills during, 79–83
Blaise (St.) (Blasius or Vlah), 29–30, 34, 38,
229
Blasius (St.). *See* Blaise
Bloch, Marc, 245
Bobali lineage (Ragusa), 9
Bocignolo: Kalenda de, 191; Marino, 222 n.2;
Rada de, 63–64
Bocza (Bokžić): Maria, 102; Zore, 102, 154
Bodacia, Vitalis de, 65
Bodin, Jean, 49, 58 n.99, 63, 68, 92 n.29, 114
n.38, 212–14, 217, 220, 221, 224 nn.21–28,
226 n.43, 227 n.53, 245
Bogdanović, M., 245
Bogdanus, goldsmith, 189
Bogišić, Valtazar, 6, 33, 54 n.46
Bologna, 44, 101, 107
Bona: Andreas de, 80; Magdalena de,
daughter of Michael, 81
Bonaventura, Master (surgeon) 45
Bonda, Pasqua de, *filia* Pauluscus, 151
Boni, *famula* de Michel de Bincola, 145
Bora, 21
Borgeaud, Willy, 245
Bosnia, 7, 19, 22, 26, 34; trade with, 87; slaves
from, 120; marriage with, 144
*botarius,* 164
Božić, Ivan, 99 n.97, 196 n.1, 238 n.1, 246
Braudel, Fernand, 1, 7, 13 nn.3–4, 51 n.17, 172,
196 n.3, 205, 246
Brescova (Brskovo), 199 n.62, 200 n.62
Brown, Peter, 50 nn.6–7, 51 n.19, 246
Brskovo. *See* Brescova
Brucker, Gene, 93 n.36, 223 n.11, 246
bubonic plague. *See* Black Plague
Buckler, Georgiane, 93 n.36, 246
Budiša, Dražen, 14 n.14, 246
Budra, *famula,* 145
Bullough, Vern, 57 n.83, 246
Buono de Flora (Bono, also Sacchetti), Ben-
cius del, 126, 148–49, 187–88
bureaucracy, 10; Byzantine, 15–18; Ragusan,
35–42, 43–49
Burke, Kenneth, 246
Burke, Peter, 89 n.2, 224 n.31, 246
Burr, Malcolm, 136 n.21

butchering: prohibited to nobles, 154; regulated, 158–59. *See also* Meat
buttons (*maspellis*), 182, 192–93
Byzantines, 2, 15–16, 24, 26, 43, 229
Byzantium. *See* Constantinople

Caboga: Anusla de, 103, 151; Jura de, 117, 151;
Floria de, 151; Luce de, 151; Mirussa de, 151
Cacciaguida, ancestor of Dante Alighieri,
179
*calafatus,* 164
*calderarius,* 164
*calegarius,* 164
*camerarius,* 26
Campbell, Anna, 57 n.83, 246
Canali (Konavle), 21, 34, 231
capitalism, economic development, 163–65,
174–77, 205, 221
Carennus de Tragurio, goldsmith, 189
Carter, Frank W., 13 n.6, 246
*casa. See* Household
Cassino (Mt.), 24–25
Castellum (*sexterium*), 24, 115, 231
Catar (Kotor), 2, 15–16, 20, 47; marriage
with, 77–79, 189, 213, 230
Catena, Nicoleta de, 99 n.44
Catholic Church. *See* Church
Cavtat, 2, 207, 239
*caza mortae,* 47–49. *See also* Quarantine
Cechetti, Francho, 196 n.4, 197 n.12, 246
Celipa, Rada de, 94 n.44
*cercellis sclavonescha* (slavic earrings), 106, 182,
191
Cessi, Roberto, 170 n.61, 197 nn. 15, 17, 20,
242, 246
chancellery, 4, 38, 230, 234; wills in, 97 n.65.
*See also* Notariat, Notaries
charity, 40, 86, 88; of Miho Pracat, 48–49
Charrier, Ernest, 52 n.21, 242
charters. *See* Notariat; Notaries; Chancellery
chattel slavery. *See* Slavery
cheese, price regulation of, 158–59
Chelmo. *See* Herzegovina
children, aristocratic, 70, 81, 112 n.4; *civis de
populo,* 140–52; illegitimate, 149–51; as servants, 122, 129
Chojnacki, Stanley, 91 n.23, 92 n.36, 95
n.47, 104, 112 nn.16–17, 155, 168 n.42, 246–
47
chroniclers (Ragusa), 2, 50 n.13, 52 n.27, 30;
of Ravenna, 13 n.7, 50 n.3, 50 n.13

church, 2, 29–32, 206–7, 209. *See also* Religion
cinctura. *See* Belts
Cipolla, Carlo, 57 n.83, 58 n.98, 170 n.63, 247
Cirković, Sime, 197 n.21, 247
citizenship: rights of, 32–37; *civis de populo*, 147–49, 237
*città felice*, 3, 124, 206
city-states: Italian, 6, 12, 48, 132; medieval, viii, 3, 10; Mediterranean, 69, 79, 171, 194, 205, 205–6, 208; classic, 1
*cives de populo*, 4, 33, 41; dowries of, 103; families of, 117, 140–53; rights of, 147–53; investing, 203
Civita Vecchia. *See* Cavtat
Clavero, Bartolomé, 166 n.3
Clementis, Tamara de, daughter of Sersius, 77
Climpna, *famula* Maroe Sorgo, 145
*clubucarius*, 164
*cocha. See* Ships
Code of Dusan, 120. *See* Nemanjić
codification of law (Ragusa), 32–33
cogs. *See* Ships
coinage: at Ragusa, 160–62, 175–76; at Venice, 160–62, 175–76, 193–94
*collegantia*, 83
Comneni (Byzantine emperors), 25
*condura. See* ships
confraternities, 49, 153–54; of St. Ivan, 154; of St. Lazarus, 153–54
Constantine Porphyrogenitus, 15–18, 24, 50 n.1, 242
Constantinople, 1, 15–18, 22, 29, 53 n.41, 187, 207, 214
constitution (Ragusan), 32–42, 61, 209
consulate, Ragusan, 205–6, 231
contagion theory, 46–49
Convent of St. Thomas, 32
convents, 32, 74, 88
Cooper, P. J., 166 n.3, 218, 226 n.48, 247
*corona. See* Crowns
Correr, Ludovico (of Venice), 84–85
corsairs. *See* Piracy
cost of living, at Ragusa, 156–60
Cotrugli, Benedetto, 6, 40, 59, 67, 68, 89 nn.1–2, 91 n.22, 95 n.50, 140, 147, 165 n.1, 167 n.33, 193, 202 n.114, 206, 209–12, 223 nn. 14, 19, 224 n.20, 231, 242
Count of Ragusa, 2, 38, 41, 176
Craik, J., 224 n.33

Čremošnik, Gregor, 55 n.64, 57 nn.77, 87, 136 nn. 17, 20, 137 nn. 25, 29, 138 nn. 41, 44, 53, 139 n.59, 166 n.10, 200 n.73, 242
Crieva, Lamprius de, 222 n.1
Crnomir (Knez) of Bosnia, 119, 241
Crossio: Agnes de, 82; Michel de, 80
crowns, 182, 190, 192–93
*curia slavorum*, in Venice, 172–73
customs (taxes), 34, 230; officials, 36
customs house. *See* Sponza Palace; Mint

Dabrica, *ancilla*, 125–27
Dalmatia, 1, 20, 39, 206, 214, 237
*dalmatica*, 173
Dandolo, Andrea, 52 n.22, 243
Dante Alighieri, 175, 179, 197 n.16, 243
Dav, Bishop of, 21
Davenport, Millia, 197 n.13, 247
Davis, James Cushman, 99 n.98, 247
Davis, Natalie Zemon, 89 n.2, 224 n.31, 247
Deanović, Mirko, 114 n.38, 247
Dedijer, Vladimir, 55 n.59, 247
defenses, urban, 4, 37 (Map 2), 164, 236
deference, vii–viii, 12, 89, 165, 211–22
Demetrius's (St.) Day, 34
Dersa: Givche de, 141; Marino, 148–49, 231
Dichna, *famula* de Domina Pana, Abbatissa St. Clara, 145
*di-glossia*, 18, 50 n.9
Dinić, Mihail, 55 n.59, 242, 136 n.20, 166 n.5, 169 n.61, 195 n.1, 197 n.19, 247
Dinić-Knežević, Dušanka, vii, 57 n.77, 90 n.15, 98 n.85, 99 nn. 91, 93, 95, 112 n.10, 113 n.35, 114 n.45, 139 n.67, 167 n.35, 169 n.56, 170 n.67, 222 n.3, 247–48
Dioclea, 25
diplomacy, Ragusan, 25. *See also* Senate; Great Council
disease. *See* Black Plague
Diversis de Quaratigianis de Lucca, Phylippus, 56 n.74, 87–88, 90 n.11, 92 n.28, 99 n.97, 113 n.28, 137 n.24, 201 n.97, 231, 243
Dobra, *famula* de Mathie Georgio, 145
Dockes, Pierre, 138, n.52, 248
doctors. *See* Physicians
documents of practice, 8, 211. *See also* Notariat, records of
Dominican monks (Order of St. Dominic), 32, 45, 88, 235
*donaro*, 76, 103, 150. *See also* Dowry
Donatore Inginocchiato, 179

*dos. See* Dowry
dowry, dowry contracts, 11, 64–79; women's right to, 100–3; non-noble, 149–53
Dragoe, goldsmith, 189
Draper, John, 248
Draysa, servant, 109
Držić, Marin (Dersa), 4, 231
*Dubravchane,* 39
Duby, Georges, 91 n.21, 141, 165 n.2, 248
ducats. *See* Coinage
Duracchium (Durazzo, also Durres), 22
Durazzo. *See* Duracchium
Durres. *See* Duracchium
Dušan (king, later emperor of Rascia), 120, 183
Dutch, 205, 206

earthquakes, 20, 62, 232, 235, 236
ecclesiastical offices. *See* Church
economy. *See* Capitalism
education, 3, 39
Egypt, 28
Elton, G. R., 220, 227 n.52, 248
endogamy, endogamous marriage, 66–67, 141, 212–14, 222
Epidaurus (Epidaurum, Pitaura). *See* Cavtat
Epstein, Mortimer, 226 n.39, 248
Ercole, Francesco, 92 n.36, 248
ethnicity, viii, 19
Evans, Sir Arthur, 7, 13 n.13, 243

*faber, ferrarius* (ironsmith), 164
Faci, Johannes of Florence, 188
faction, 3, 41
Fairchilds, Cissy, 139 n.66, 248
Falcidian quarter, 61, 100. *See* Dowry
family, family networks, 10, 61–69, 115–18
famine, 42
*famulae, famuli. See* Servants
Fano, 27
Farlati, Daniel, 51 n.18, 54 n.49, 248
fashion, Italian, 105–7, 177–87
Favi, Francesco, 226 n.48
Favoro, Elena, 243
Febvre, Lucien, 9, 14 n.17, 248
Ferguson, C. A., 50 n.9, 248
Fermendžin, P. E., 54 n.49, 243
*filiola. See* Godchildren
*filiolus. See* Godchildren
Filipović, Rudolf, 214, 224 n.32, 248
Fine, John, 14 n.16, 54 n.49, 136 n.19, 248

fire (of 1296), 42, 116, 230
firewood, regulation of, 159
Fisković, Cvito, 113 n.28, 118, 199 n.52, 200 n.76, 248
Florence, 101–2; dowry in, 104, 149; trade with, 189
Florentines, at Ragusa, 120, 148–49, 177, 183, 187–88
florins. *See* Coinage
*follari. See* Coinage
*fondacho,* 47, 173, 174
foodstuffs, imported into town, 158–59
Foretić, Vinko, 13 n.6, 56 n.67, 195 n.1, 248
Fortebraccio Charmontesis of Florence, 188
Fortress of St. Lawrence (Lovran), 36
Foucard, C., 243
Fourth Crusade, 27–28, 53 n.43, 230
Franciscans (Order of St. Francis), 32, 45, 88, 191, 235
*fraterna,* 11, 38, 117
freed slaves. *See* Manumission
Freidberg, Emil, 243
Friedl, Ernestine, 111, 114 n.46, 249
*frontali* (forehead ornaments), 182–87, 198–93
fugitives, 125–26. *See also* Slaves
fur, fur garments. *See* Textiles

Galleys. *See* Ships
Gargano (Mt.), 204
Gecić, Marina, 249
Gelcich, Giuseppi, 57 n.76, 249
gender, 100–111
genealogy, 9–10, 50 n.13
Genoa, 3, 63, 101, 172, 205, 233
geography, of Ragusa, 20–22
Georgio: lineage, 66; Matcus de, 109, 146; Radula de Mathias, 145; Slaussa, *filia* de Johannes, 151
Gervasius, Count of Ragusa, 26
Getaldi, Marino de, 146
Gilbert, Felix, 223 n.11, 249
Giustiniani, Giovanni, 219, 227 n.50, 243
glaziers, 57 n.77, 170 n.69
Goce: Clara, 151; Francha, wife of Marino, 82; Marino, 196 n.4; Nicoletta, 85–87; Nicoletta, *filia* Martolus, 151; Pervo, 117; Vita, 117; of the Platea, 115; *de populo,* 142–43
godchildren (*filiolus, filiola*), 90 n.15
godparents, 90 n.15, 153

gold: as wedding gifts, 70, 76, 105–6; in trade, 183–84; manufacture of, 189–94; mining of, 188

"Golden Century" of Ragusan history, 2, 7

goldsmiths (*aurifici*) 104, 118, 140, 164, 178–95

Goldthwaite, Richard, 139 n.64, 169 n.52, 249

Gondola: lineage, 115; Ivan (Gundulić) 4, 232; Maria, 100, 107, 111 n.1; Nicola, 243; Paul, 225 n.38; Pervula, 65; Radoslava de Pervulo, 145

grain. See *Massarii bladorum*

Gratian, 101–3, 112 n.7, 113

Gravosa (Gruž) 20, 51 n.20, 207, 231

*Grazie* (Venice), 177–78

Great Council (Ragusa), 3, 32–49, 63, 73, 79, 119, 142, 151; closing of, 154–55, 232; law in, 239–40

*grebener,* 164

Greek (language), Grecophone, 4, 15–18

Gregory (founder), 16–17

Grmek, M. D., 57 n.76, 249

*grosso. See* Coinage

Gruž. *See* Gravosa

Guillelmo, Jacobo, of Venice, 122

Guillou, Andre, 249

Gundulić. *See* Gondola

Guylford, Sir Richard, 214–15, 225 n.35, 243

*gynaeceum* (women's workshop), 110–11, 114 n.45, 134, 139 nn.67–68, 163

*habitatores,* 117–19, 125–26, 147–48, 188

Halpern, Joel M., 13 n.10, 249

Hammel, Eugene, 13 n.10, 249

Han, Verena, 57 n.77, 170 n.69, 249

harbor, 21–22, 47

Harden, D. B., 13 n.13

Harrington, John, 219, 226 n.47, 243

Hakluyt, Richard, 214, 245

Hakluyt Society, 214

Haumant, E., 50 n.11, 249

health care policy, 42–50

Heers, Jacques, 139 n.64, 249

Hercegovina. *See* Herzegovina

heretics, slaves as, 120

Herlihy, David, 58 n.93, 114 n.45, 139 n.68, 197 n.13, 249

Herrin, Judith, 50 n.8, 249

Herzegovina, 7, 22, 34

Hexter, J. J., 50 n.5, 249

Heyd, Wilhelm, 250

Hirst, L., 52 n.22, 250

historiography, 6–7, 33

Hlum (Chelmo). *See* Herzegovina

Hoffman, Johannes, 52 n.22, 250

Horwitz, Sylvia, 14 n.13, 250

households, Ragusan, 7, 115–35, 159–60, 209–12

housing, urban, 115–18, 159–60

Hrbak, Bogumil, 57 n.76, 250

Hughes, Diane Owen, 97 n.62, 104, 113 nn. 22, 24, 201 n.98, 250

humanism: Italian, 4, 111; Ragusan, 100, 211–12, 235. *See also* Renaissance

Hungary, 2, 34, 35, 40, 231, 234–35

hygiene, 43–49

*hyperperus,* as money of account. *See* Coinage

Idrisi, 224, 52 n.31

illegitimacy, 143–50

Illyria, viii, 211–17

immigration, 141, 147–53

incest law, 140–46, 90 n.15

inheritance law, 79–83

*inter-culfum* route (Adriatic), 1, 13 n.5, 23, 203

irredentism, 6

Istrian peninsula, 2, 22–23

Italy, 4, 6, 10, 25

Ivan (St.) confraternity, 154

Jacob (St.) de Visinica monastery, 88

Jacob of Padua, physician, 46

Jeremić, R., 56 n.76, 112 n.11, 166 n.11

jewels: as wedding gifts, 70, 71, 106; in trade, 182–87; manufacture, 164, 189–93

Jireček, Constantin, 13 n.6, 33, 51 n.14, 53 n.42, 54 n.46, 55 n.58, 56 n.68, 61, 90 n.6, 167 n.29, 195 n.1, 196 n.9, 200 n.63, 201 n.80, 250

Jonchetta, 146

Juecho, the pelter, 145

karst, Bosnian, 22, 43

Katele, Irene B., 52 n.23, 250

Kedar, Benjamin, 166 n.3, 250

Keenan, Eileen, 89 n.2, 250

Kelly, Joan, 113 n.32, 250

Kelso, Ruth, 113 n.32, 250

Kent, Francis W., 93 n.36, 165 n.2, 250

Kheil, Carl Peter, 52 n.31, 250

kinship. *See* Family; Marriage

Kirshner, Jules, 93 n.36, 112 n.13, 250–51

Kisch, Bruno, 54 n.45, 222 n.1, 251
Klapisch-Zuber, Christiane, 58 n.93, 92 n.23, 93 n.36, 249, 251
Konavle (*See* Canali), 21, 104
Korcula, 22–23, 204
Kostić, Veselin, 215, 226 n.39, 251
Kotor. *See* Catar
Kovačević, Desanka, 99 n.96, 168 n.37, 197 n.21, 199 n.62, 247, 251
Krekić, Bariša, 13 nn. 1, 6, 52 n.26, 55 nn. 5, 7, 65, 89 n.4, 96 n.53, 99 n.97, 114 n.40, 167 n.29, 169 n.52, 196 nn. 1, 8, 9, 251
Krisković, V., 251
Kuehn, Thomas, 101–2, 112 n.8, 251
Kukuljević-Sakcinski, Ivan, 51 n.18, 243
Kulin, Ban of Bosnia, 26, 230

La Croma (Lokrum), 22; monastery of, 30, 88, 229
*ladica* (ship), 182. *See also* Jewels
Lagosta. *See* Lastovo
Lane, Frederic Chapin, 52 n.25, 53 n.42, 54 n.45, 58 n.100, 170 n.64, 202 n.120, 222 n.1, 251–52
Lansing, Carol L., 92 n.36, 252
Lapad, 20
Laslett, Peter, 166 n.6, 252
Lastovo (Lagosta), 22
Latin (language), Latinphone, 3–4, 15–18, 39
Laurencius Raguseus (sailor), 53 n.41
Lauriston, general of Napoleon's troops, 232
law codes, South Slav, 6. *See also* Code of Dusan
lazaretto, 46–49
Lazarini (Confraternity of St. Lazarus), 153–54
Lechner, Karl, 58 n.94, 240 n.1, 252
Lepanto, 39
letter of exchange (Florentine), 187
Levant, trade with 157, 216
Levant Company, 216
Levi-Pisetzky, Rosita, 198 nn. 31, 36, 37, 252
*Liber Reformationes* (Ragusa/Dubrovnik), 40, 43, 53 n.45, 61, 118, 163, 241
*Liber Rosso* (Ragusa/Dubrovnik), 61, 241
*Liber Statutorum* (Ragusa/Dubrovnik), 9, 71, 122, 230
*Liber Viridis* (Ragusa/Dubrovnik), 12, 13, 58 nn. 94, 98, 241
*Libertas*, 2
lineage, 10, 61–69, 89

Litchfield, R. Burr, 91 n.22, 92 n.25, 108, 114 nn.34–35, 252
literacy: of women, 3; in Italian, 15–18, in Latin, 15–18; in Slavic, 15–18. *See also* Bilingualism
Ljubić, Šime, 51 n.18, 53 n.43, 54 n.53, 243
Lock, John, 214–15, 243
Lokrum. *See* La Croma
Lombardo, A., 53 n.41, 244
London, 214–15
Lopez, Robert S., 197 n.13, 198 n.34, 223 n.18, 252
Lothian, J., 224 n.33
Lovran. *See* Fortress of St. Lawrence
Lowe, A. E., 52 n.31, 54 n.51, 252
Luchari: Anica de, 64; Giacomo de (chronicler) 50 n.13, 52 n.30, 243; Michael de, 64–65; Nicola de Marco de, 64; Stephen de, 116
Lučić, Josip, vii, 13 n.12, 51 n.20, 53 n.40, 54 n.49, 90 n.13, 118, 164, 170 n.68, 196 n.1, 200 n.75, 243, 252
Luetić, Josip, 202 n.119, 205, 223 n.5, 226 n.39, 252
Lukarević (di Luccari), Giacomo. *See* Luchari
lumber, 204
Lupi de Soragno, 185
Lupset, Thomas, 219, 226 n.46
luxury wares, 172–75. *See also* Sumptuary law
Luzzatto, Gino, 139 n.64, 169 n.52, 170 n.62, 199 n.57, 200 n.64, 202 n.119, 243, 252

Machiavelli, Niccolò, 208–9, 223 nn.11–13, 244
MacLean, Ian, 113 n.32, 252
Madden, Thomas F., 113 n.20
Mahnken, Irmgard, 51, n.16, 61, 90 nn.8–9, 91 nn.16–17, 20, 92 n.26, 94 n.44, 98 n.85, 99 n.92, 166 nn. 4, 9, 167 nn. 26, 36, 170 n.75, 252
Makušev, Vincentio, 200 n.72, 244
Mandić, D., 52 n.22, 252
Mandrou R., 226 n.44, 252
Manfroni, Camillo, 252
*manipulus murator. See* Masons
Mantua, 44
Manuel, Frank E., 137 n.33, 224 n.27, 253
Manuel, Fritzie P., 137 n.33, 224 n.27, 253
manumission, of slaves, 130
*marangonus* (carpenter, woodworker), 164

Marco, son of Grupse, goldsmith, 189
*margarisium,* 34
Maria, *ancilla,* 126
Maria (St.) de Castello convent, 88
Marinović, Ante, 56 n.67, 168 n.38, 253
maritime insurance, 232
Mark (St.) of Venice, 29
Marković, Zdenka, 111 n.1, 253
Marmont, general of Napoleon's troops, 232.
   *See also* Napoleon
Marović, I., 50 n.10, 253
marriage, 9, 209–11; gifts, 68–69; property
   rights in, 103–4; separation in, 99 n.95;
   noble, 61–69; limits on, 143–53; in politi-
   cal thought, 213–20. *See also* Endogamy
Martinussio, Anna de, 82
masons, stone, 116, 140, 164. *See also* Artisans
*maspellis. See* Buttons
*massarii bladorum* (grain office), 71, 119, 157
Mattei, G., 46. *See Zibaldone*
Mayer, Anton, 200 n.74, 244
Maza, Sara, 139 n.66, 253
meat, price regulation of, 158–59
medicine, 43–49
Medini, Milorad, 55 n.56, 56 n.70, 253
Meleta, monastery of, 22, 47, 88
Mence: lineage, 177; Andrea Nicola de, 81;
   Blaise de, 38; Buni de, 115 n.5; Domagna
   de, 38, 112 n.5; Lawrence de, 38; Marinus
   de, 117, 225 n.38; Martinussius de, 38, 83,
   115; Mathias, 37–38; Michel de, 38, 173;
   Nicola de, 225 n.38; Peter de, 80, 144;
   Ruossa de, 192
Mercana (Mrkan), 239–40
Metcalf, Michael, 169 n.61, 197 n.19, 253
*mezzanino. See* Coinage
Michael's (St.) Day, 34
middle class. See *Cives de populo*
Mihailović, J., 51 n.18, 253
Milan, 48
Milcio, goldsmith, 189
Miloslava, *famula,* 145
mining, 177. *See also* Balkans, West Balkans
mint, 160–61, 175–76
Mistral, 22
Mitić, Ilija, 13 n.12, 55 n.61, 253
Mohlo, Anthony, 93 n.36, 202 n.119, 251
Molfetta, 27, 229
Molmenti, Pompeo, 197 n.13, 198 n.31, 253
Monopoli, 27
Montenegro, 22

Moors, 23–24
Morosini, Michael (Count of Ragusa), 38
Mrkan. *See* Mercana
Mueller, Reinhold, 95 n.47, 96 n.53, 113 n.18,
   253
Muir, Edward, 13 n.11, 199 n.58, 253
Muljačić, Zarko, 253
*mundium (mundualdus),* in Florence, 102
*murarius. See* Masons
*murator. See* Masons
Muslims, 23–24. *See also* Moors; Turks

Naples, 141, 205
Napoleon, 2, 232
Narenta (Neretva), 23, 119
navy, 172, 203–5, 232. *See also* Ships
Nedeljković, Branco, 13 n.12, 168 n.40, 253
*nef* (ship). See *Ladica;* Jewels
Nef, John, 197 n.21, 253
neighborhoods, 115–18
Nemanjić dynasty, 120, 175; Dušan, 183;
   Miroslav, Stephen, Strasimir (rulers of
   Rascia), 25–26
Neretva. *See* Narenta
Newett, N. Margaret, 113 n.25, 199 n.61, 253
Nicholas (St., of Bari), 29; de Castello, con-
   vent of, 88
Nicolay, Nicolas de, 207, 223 n.88, 244
Nicoleto de Laurencio (possibly de
   Mence?), 178
*Nikola (St.),* ship, 222 n.2
Nikola de Ragusa, 222 n.2
Nikolas, Magister, *physicus,* 222 n.2
nobility. *See* Aristocracy
*nobili viri,* 42, 59, 61, 229. *See also* Aristocracy
Nodilo, N., 50 n.13, 168 n.45, 244
Normans, 2, 23–26, 28, 229
North Africa, 28.
notariat, Slavic, 4, 56 n.67; Latin, 8; records
   of, 8, 10, 120–22. *See also* Chancellery;
   Notaries
notaries, 56 n.67
Nova Brdo, 190, 200 n.62, 201 n.80
Novak, Gregor, 253
Novak, Slobodan, 232, 254
Novak, Viktor, 50 n.11, 254
Novaković, Stojan, 254
*nutrix* (nurse). *See* Servants

old age, of domestic servants, 131
Old Ragusan, dialect, 34, 39

Ombla (River), 20, 43
Onofrio de la Cava, 56 n.75, 231
Oosterveen, Karla, 166 n.6
Orbini, Mauro, 50 n.13, 254
origin myths, Ragusa, 15–20
Origo, Iris, 137 n.30, 254
orphans, 71, 75, 81, 146–47
Orthodox (Serbian) church, 32

Paborra, Andreas de, 192; Anna de, 65; Maria
    de, 82; Peter de, 65
Padua, 44
palaces: renaissance, 207, 235; urban, 84, 115–
    17
Pallucchini, Rodolfo, 119 n.59, 254
Palmota, Rade de, 145; Vloachus de, 145
Pancratius (St.), church of, 16, 29
Pantella, Peter, 110, 163
Paolo Veneziano, 179
papacy, 30, 206. See also Church; Religion;
    Rome
Papadopoli, Nicolo, 254
Papp, Joseph, 225 n.33
parlementum, 60
Parthey, G., 13 n.7, 50 n.3, 244
partible inheritance, 79–81, 218–20
patriciate. See Aristocracy
Paul de Trano, goldsmith, 189
Pavlimir, grandson of King Radoslav, 18, 20
peasants, in Ragusan countryside, 134
Pelješac (Punta Stagni), 22
pelliparius or pilicarius (tanner, furrier), 164
Perussa, famula de Janius Sorgo, 145
Peter Minor (St.) convent, 88
Peter Reynaldo of Venice, 177
Peter's (St.) (sexterium), 24
Petrana: Johannes de, 80; Maria, daughter of
    Mathias, 81
Petrović, Đurđica, 55 nn.59–60, 254
Petrovich, Miodrag, 55 n.57, 56 n.72, 90 n.14,
    99 n.99, 155, 168 n.40, 254
pharmacy (at Ragusa), 44
physicians, 43–49, 157
Pietro II Orseolo (Doge), 23, 229
Pile (land gate at Ragusa), 32
Pinder, M., 13 n.7, 50 n.3, 244
piracy, 23–24, 213
Pisa, 27, 101, 189
Pisani, Paul, 52 n.24, 254
platea (stradun), 32, 115, 194, 235
Pliny (the Younger), vii–viii, 51 n.19, 244

Poce, Goce de, 81
Pocock, J. G. A., 54 n.51, 226 n.47, 254
Pole, Reginald, 216–17, 226 n.46
Popović-Radenković, Mariana, 169 n.49, 52,
    254
Popovo, 21
population, 3; of noble families, 61–69, 74.
    See also Prosopography
power: of patriciate, 9; of noble women, 9
Pracat, Miho, 40
Prelog, Milan, 13 n.6, 254
prijateljstvo, 11, 61–69, 156, 204, 237. See also
    Aristocracy; Endogamy
private sphere, 9, 60, 88–89
prosopography, 8, 140, 165
prostitution, 112 n.11
Protomagister arsenatus, 158
proverbs. See Aphorisms
public welfare, 42–50
Puccii, Duccio, 183, 188
Pullan, Brian, 14 n.15, 254
Pustijerna, 24

quarantine (quarantino), 47–49, 231, 239–40
Queller, Donald, vii, 53 n.43, 113 n.20, 254
Quintavallo, Catarino of Venice, 177
Quirino, Giovanni, Count of Ragusa, 41

Rabil, Albert, 14 n.14
Racheli, A., 244
Racki, Fr., 53 n.45, 244
Radonić, J., 52 n.29, 53 nn.37–40, 244
Radoslav (King), 18
Ramberti, Benedetto, 207–8, 244
Ranena (Ranina): Marino de, 146; Nicolo
    de (chronicler) 50 n.13, 54 n.48)
Rascia (Old Serbia), 25, 175
Rasdall, Hastings, 57 n.83, 254
Ravenna, 2, 13 n.7, 156, 254
Raymond, Irving, 223 n.18, 252
reclusa, 88
Rector's Palace, 35 (Figure 6)
rectorship, 34, 233
relics. See Reliquaries
religion, 29–32. See also Church
reliquaries, 15–16, 29–32
Renaissance: at Ragusa, 216, 221, 235–36; in
    Italy, 107–8, 212. See also Humanism
republicanism, vii, 2, 12, 218
republica perfetta, 3
Rešetar, Milan, 169 n.61, 202 n.115, 254

Resti: Junius de (chronicler), 50 n.13, 52
nn. 27, 30; Matico de Pasce, 81
Rheubottom, David, vii, 55 nn. 55, 57, 92 n.32,
109, 113 n.27, 114 n.39, 254
Rhodian sea law, 33
Rialto (Venice), 173
Richard I (King of England), the "lion-
hearted," 30
Rici, Lorino, de Flora, 148–49, 188, 200 n.65
*ricordanze,* 9, 171
*ricordi,* 9, 171
Riemer, Eleanor Sabina, 112 n.6, 254
Robert Guiscard, ruler of Sicily, 23
Rocca, Morrozzo della, 54 n.41, 244
Roglić, J., 50 n.2, 254
Roller, Dragan, 168 n.38, 195n, 255
Roman law: in Ragusa, 61, 100, 123; revival
of in Italy, 101
Romania, 169 n.9
*Romanoi,* 17. *See also* Byzantines; Con-
stantinople
Rome, 2, 29–32. *See also* Church; Religion
Roncière, Charles M. de la, 139 n.64, 255
Rosembert, Andre, 255
Rudnica (Rudnik), 175, 199–200 n.62
Rudnik. *See* Rudnica
Ruggiero, Guido, 57 n.83, 109, 114 n.42, 168
n.43, 199 n.60, 255
*rupe* (granary), 231, 234. See also *Massarii
bladorum*

Sacchetti, Franco, 126, 178, 187, 200 n.66
sailors, 46
salaries, at Ragusa. *See* Wages
Salerno, 43, 44
*salinarius* (inspector of salt works), 37, 110
Salona, 15–16
Samardžić, Radovan, 90 n.12, 139 n.56, 238
n.4, 255
Sanuti, Nicolosa, 107–8
Saraca: Elias de (archbishop of Ragusa), 34,
40, 233; Peter de, 117
Sarhan (ruler of Turkey), 231
Saria, B., 169 n.61, 255
*sartor. See* Tailors
Savere, Thomasina de (notary), 38, 70, 189
Savini (St.) de Dasa monastery, 88, 144
*sclavi,* 42, 135
Sclavonia (Slavonia), 196 n.9, 230
Sebaste, 29
sedition, 3, 10, 41

seismic activity. *See* Earthquakes
Senate: Ragusan, 39, 205–6; Venetian, 28
Serbia, 25, 60, 175
Serbo-Croatian, 6. *See also* Slavic; Yugoslavia
Sergius (Mt.), also Srdj, 20–21, 229
*serrata* (closing): of Ragusa, 154–55, 230; of
Venice, 154–55
servants, contract servants, 129–35
*servus. See* Slaves
Shakespeare, William, 213–17, 224 nn.29–30,
33, 225 n.38, 226 nn.41–42, 244
shepherds. *See* Transhumance
ships, shipping, 160–61, 202 n.119, 203–5
Sicily, 17, 26, 43, 157, 231
Siena, 101
silver: as wedding gifts, 70, 76, 105–6; trade
in, 183–84; manufacture of, 189–94; min-
ing of, 188; quality of, 190–91
silversmiths. *See* Goldsmiths
Silvestro (St.), *contrata* in Venice, 172
sirocco, 21
Skok, P., 50 n.2, 51 n.14, 255
slaves, 119–35
Slavic, 6, 15, 19, 39. *See also* Literacy; Bi-
lingualism
Small Council (Ragusa), 2, 27–38, 41
Smičiklas, T., 196 n.2, 244
Smith, Richard M., 166 n.6
*soldino. See* Coinage
Soloviev, A., 61, 90 n.7, 10, 244, 255
Sorento: Iello de, 117; Tisa de, 82
Sorgo: lineage, 66–67, 153; Ancula de, 151;
Jacho de, 85–87; Juncho de Marino, 81;
Lucia *filia* Michael, 145, 151; Maracussa,
151; Pervo de, 117; Vita de, 66; Rada de, 82
South Slavs, 7
Spain, 3, 215–16, 223 n.6, 232
Spalato (Split), 77, 214, 237
Spielman, Danila, vii
Split. *See* Spalato
Sponza Palace, 162 (Figure 7), 231, 235. *See
also* Mint
Stagno, 22, 35, 87, 109
Stahl, Allen, vii
Starkey, Thomas, 219, 226 n.46
statute law. See *Liber Statutorum*
Stefanuti, Ugo, 244
Stephen the Protospatharius (founder), 16–
17
step-parentage, 90 n.15. *See* Marriage
Stoianovich, Traian, vii, 238 n.3, 255

Stojanović, L., 245
Ston. *See* Stagno
Stornado, Marco, of Venice, 177
*stradun*. See *Platea*
Stratton, Susan, 53 n.43
Sugden, Edward, 256
sumptuary display, 104
sumptuary law: at Ragusa, 106; at Venice, 104; in Italy, 105–7
Šundrica, Zdravko, vii, 56 n.72, 256
surgeons, 44–49, 157
Symeon (St.) convent, 88
syndics, 43–49

Tadeus de Flora, 222 n.2
Tadić, Jorjo, 13 nn. 6, 9, 56 n.76, 57 n.80, 96 n.54, 112 n.11, 135 n.1, 136 n.23, 166 n.11, 196 n.1, 201 n.88, 202 n.117, 222 n.13, 238 n.2, 245, 256
tailors, 140, 164, 174–75
*tarida*. See Ships
Tasiligardus, *camerarius* of king of Sicily, 26
taverns, near harbor, 102
taxes, 34. *See also* Customs
Teichman, Jenny, 166 n.6, 256
Teja, A., 256
Tenenti, Alberto, 8, 14 n.15, 138 n.56, 256
Termoli, 27
testaments. *See* Wills
textiles, manufacture, 172–75
Theophrastus, 59
*thesaurus de St. Maria*, 81, 98 n.74
Thiriet, Freddy, 196 n.9, 256
Thoma: lineage, 77–78, 88, 115, Bielce de, 78; Dea de, 78; Drago de, 77–78; Jelena de, 78; Medossius de, 78; Nicoletta de, 78; Nicoleta de, 78; Paulus de, 78 Phylippa de, 78, 83–85, 102; Thoma de, 2, 78, 108; Thomas de, 78
Thomas (St.) convent, 88
Tobermory Bay, 216. *See also* Armada; Spain
Tolislauus, goldsmith, 189
Tomaschek, W., 256
Torbarina, Josip, 224 n.20, 226 nn.41–42, 256
trade: in gold, 148, 176–95; in grain, 148–49, 157; in great coats, 172–75; in lumber, 204; in slaves, 120–22, 129; overseas, 48; in silver, 148, 176–95; inland trade, 48, 119–20; with the Levant, 157; in the Adriatic, 3, 25–27; Mediterranean, 11, 48, 129, 230, 234; treaties of, 25–27; diversification in, 163–65

transhumance, 22
Trau (Trogir), 77
travelers' accounts, 206–7
Travunia (Trebinje), 21, 34
treaties: trading, 25, 27–28 (*see also* Trade); Ragusan-Venetian Treaty of 1205, 27–28, 33, 35, 172–75
Trebinje. *See* Travunia
Treggiari, Suzanne, 256
*trentino*. See Quarantine
Trexler, Richard, 199 n.60, 256
tribute, 34
Tripon, count of Catar, 25, 66
Trogir. *See* Trau
Truhelka, C., 136 n.20, 256
Tucci, Ugo, 223 n.16, 256
Tudisio, Thomasina de, 82; Zive de, 94 n.44
Tuerdive, *famula* de Crize de Beho, 145
Tunis, 28
Turks, 2, 32, 35, 143, 206, 231–32, 234
*tutela*, 100–102, 108, 112 n.3
tutors, 70–71, 81, 112 n.4
Tvrtvo I (Ban of Bosnia), 34
*Twelfth Night*, 213–17

Ulizza, *famula* de Rade Volcassio, 145
universities (schools of medicine), 44, 46; Salamanca and Sorbonne, attended by Ragusans, 237
utopia, utopian vision, vii, 212–22

Valentine, archdeacon (founder), 16–17
Valentine, father of Stephen the Proto-spatharius (founder), 16–17
Vasilio, goldsmith, 189
Vekarić, Stepan, 97 n.63, 222 nn. 1, 2, 4, 257
Venice, 1–3, 8; as overlord, 22–24, 27–28, 32–42, 71, 230, 231–32; republic in, 219; dowry in, 71, 73, 83, 104; slaves in, 120; *serrata*, 154–55; market of, 172–80, 184; shipping to, 205. *See also* Trade; Treaties
Verlinden, Charles, 121, 136 n.22, 137 nn. 26, 28, 138 n.52, 257
vernacular. *See* Literacy; Bilingualism
Via Egnatia, 22
Victorinus (founder), 16–17
Villani de Flora, Giovanni, 161, 178, 198 n.32
Villari, Luigi, 13 n.6, 257
Villata di Renzo, Gigliola, 257
Vinaver, Vuk, 136 n.17, 138 n.52; 139 n.65, 169 n.61, 170 n.62, 202 n.115, 257

Vitalius (founder), 16–17
viticulture, 34, 85–87
Vlachs, 22
Vlah (St.). *See* Blaise (St.)
Voje, Ignacij, 138 n.43, 167 n.28, 200 n.65, 257
Vojnović, Kosta, 245
Volcassio: lineage, 67; Junius de, 67, 88, 94 n.44; Marino de, 177; Pasqua de, 38, 108
Volcigno, Parile de, *filia* Rosini, 151
Volcio, Phylippa de, daughter of Andrea, 77, 108
*vrazda,* 60, 89 n.4
Vujić, Mihailo, 223 n.15, 257
Vyronis, Speros, 197 n.21, 257

wages, 156–63; of barbers, 157–58; *protomagister arsenatus,* 158; communal employees, 157–58; physicians, 43–49, 157–58; surgeons, 44–49, 157; textile workers, 158
walls, of Ragusa, 4, 37 (Map 2), 164, 236
water supply and works, 20–21, 43, 119, 234
West Balkans, 1, 21–22, 27, 34, 130, 234. *See also* Slavic; Bosnia; Balkans
widowers, 66–67

widows, 66–67, 71, 104
William II (king of Sicily), 26
wills, 79–83
wine: drinking, 215; price regulation, 85–87. *See also* Viticulture
Wolff, Robert, 196 n.9, 257
women: legal rights, 100–103; literacy, 108, 114 nn.33–34; in humanist circles, 100; incapacity before the law, 100–102, 108; writing wills, 81–83; in Ragusa, 100–113

Yugoslavia, viii, 6–7

Zadar. *See* Zara
Zara (Zadar), 43, 213, 214, 230, 267–28
Zdravković, Ivan, 257
Zebić, Milorad, 223 n.15, 257
Zeno, Caterino, 206–7, 223 n.7, 245
*zibaldone,* Mattei's, 46, 58 nn. 90, 93
*zonas. See* Belts
Zordan, Giorgio, 89 n.3, 257
Zreva, Slava de, 64
*zupparius,* 174. *See also* Tailor

University of Pennsylvania Press
MIDDLE AGES SERIES
Edward Peters, General Editor

F. R. P. Akehurst, trans. *The* Coutumes de Beauvaisis *of Philippe de Beaumanoir.* 1992
Peter L. Allen. *The Art of Love: Amatory Fiction from Ovid to the* Romance of the
Rose. 1992
David Anderson. *Before the Knight's Tale: Imitation of Classical Epic in Boccaccio's*
Teseida. 1988
Benjamin Arnold. *Count and Bishop in Medieval Germany: A Study of Regional Power,*
*1100–1350.* 1991
Mark C. Bartusis. *The Late Byzantine Army: Arms and Society, 1204–1453.* 1992
J. M. W. Bean. *From Lord to Patron: Lordship in Late Medieval England.* 1990
Uta-Renate Blumenthal. *The Investiture Controversy: Church and Monarchy from the*
*Ninth to the Twelfth Century.* 1988
Daniel Bornstein, trans. *Dino Compagni's* Chronicle *of Florence.* 1986
Betsy Bowden. *Chaucer Aloud: The Varieties of Textual Interpretation.* 1987
James William Brodman. *Ransoming Captives in Crusader Spain: The Order of Merced*
*on the Christian-Islamic Frontier.* 1986
Kevin Brownlee and Sylvia Huot. *Rethinking the* Romance of the Rose: *Text,*
*Image, Reception.* 1992
Otto Brunner (Howard Kaminsky and James Van Horn Melton, eds. and trans.).
*Land and Lordship: Structures of Governance in Medieval Austria.* 1992
Robert I. Burns, S.J., ed. *Emperor of Culture: Alfonso X the Learned of Castile and His*
*Thirteenth-Century Renaissance.* 1990
David Burr. *Olivi and Franciscan Poverty: The Origins of the* Usus Pauper *Controversy.*
1989
Thomas Cable. *The English Alliterative Tradition.* 1991
Anthony K. Cassell and Victoria Kirkham, eds. and trans. *Diana's Hunt/Caccia di*
*Diana: Boccaccio's First Fiction.* 1991
Brigitte Cazelles. *The Lady as Saint: A Collection of French Hagiographic Romances of*
*the Thirteenth Century.* 1991
Anne L. Clark. *Elisabeth of Schönau: A Twelfth-Century Visionary.* 1992
Willene B. Clark and Meradith T. McMunn, eds. *Beasts and Birds of the Middle Ages:*
*The Bestiary and Its Legacy.* 1989
Richard C. Dales. *The Scientific Achievement of the Middle Ages.* 1973
Charles T. Davis. *Dante's Italy and Other Essays.* 1984
Katherine Fischer Drew, trans. *The Burgundian Code.* 1972
Katherine Fischer Drew, trans. *The Laws of the Salian Franks.* 1991
Katherine Fischer Drew, trans. *The Lombard Laws.* 1973

Nancy Edwards. *The Archaeology of Early Medieval Ireland*. 1990

Margaret J. Ehrhart. *The Judgment of the Trojan Prince Paris in Medieval Literature*. 1987

Richard K. Emmerson and Ronald B. Herzman. *The Apocalyptic Imagination in Medieval Literature*. 1992

Felipe Fernández-Armesto. *Before Columbus: Exploration and Colonization from the Mediterranean to the Atlantic, 1229–1492*. 1987

Robert D. Fulk. *A History of Old English Meter*. 1992

Patrick J. Geary. *Aristocracy in Provence: The Rhône Basin at the Dawn of the Carolingian Age*. 1985

Peter Heath. *Allegory and Philosophy in Avicenna (Ibn Sînâ)*. 1992

J. N. Hillgarth, ed. *Christianity and Paganism, 350–750: The Conversion of Western Europe*. 1986

Richard C. Hoffmann. *Land, Liberties, and Lordship in a Late Medieval Countryside: Agrarian Structures and Change in the Duchy of Wrocław*. 1990

Robert Hollander. *Boccaccio's Last Fiction: Il Corbaccio*. 1988

Edward B. Irving, Jr. *Rereading* Beowulf. 1989

C. Stephen Jaeger. *The Origins of Courtliness: Civilizing Trends and the Formation of Courtly Ideals, 939–1210*. 1985

William Chester Jordan. *The French Monarchy and the Jews: From Philip Augustus to the Last Capetians*. 1989

William Chester Jordan. *From Servitude to Freedom: Manumission in the Sénonais in the Thirteenth Century*. 1986

Ellen E. Kittell. *From Ad Hoc to Routine: A Case Study in Medieval Bureaucracy*. 1991

Alan C. Kors and Edward Peters, eds. *Witchcraft in Europe, 1100–1700: A Documentary History*. 1972

Barbara M. Kreutz. *Before the Normans: Southern Italy in the Ninth and Tenth Centuries*. 1992

E. Ann Matter. *The Voice of My Beloved: The Song of Songs in Western Medieval Christianity*. 1990

María Rosa Menocal. *The Arabic Role in Medieval Literary History*. 1987

A. J. Minnis. *Medieval Theory of Authorship*. 1988

Lawrence Nees. *A Tainted Mantle: Hercules and the Classical Tradition at the Carolingian Court*. 1991

Lynn H. Nelson, trans. *The Chronicle of San Juan de la Peña: A Fourteenth-Century Official History of the Crown of Aragon*. 1991

Charlotte A. Newman. *The Anglo-Norman Nobility in the Reign of Henry I: The Second Generation*. 1988

Joseph F. O'Callaghan. *The Cortes of Castile-León, 1188–1350*. 1989

William D. Paden, ed. *The Voice of the Trobairitz: Perspectives on the Women Troubadours*. 1989

Edward Peters. *The Magician, the Witch, and the Law*. 1982

Edward Peters, ed. *Christian Society and the Crusades, 1198–1229:* Sources in Translation, including The Capture of Damietta by Oliver of Paderborn. 1971

Edward Peters, ed. *The First Crusade:* The Chronicle of Fulcher of Chartres *and Other Source Materials*. 1971

Edward Peters, ed. *Heresy and Authority in Medieval Europe.* 1980

James M. Powell. *Albertanus of Brescia: The Pursuit of Happiness in the Early Thirteenth Century.* 1992

James M. Powell. *Anatomy of a Crusade, 1213–1221.* 1986

Michael Resler, trans. *Erec by Hartmann von Aue.* 1987

Pierre Riché (Jo Ann McNamara, trans.). *Daily Life in the World of Charlemagne.* 1978

Jonathan Riley-Smith. *The First Crusade and the Idea of Crusading.* 1986

Joel T. Rosenthal. *Patriarchy and Families of Privilege in Fifteenth-Century England.* 1991

Steven D. Sargent, ed. and trans. *On the Threshold of Exact Science: Selected Writings of Anneliese Maier on Late Medieval Natural Philosophy.* 1982

Sarah Stanbury. *Seeing the Gawain-Poet: Description and the Act of Perception.* 1992

Thomas C. Stillinger. *The Song of Troilus: Lyric Authority in the Medieval Book.* 1992

Susan Mosher Stuard. *A State of Deference: Ragusa/Dubrovnik in the Medieval Centuries.* 1992

Susan Mosher Stuard, ed. *Women in Medieval History and Historiography.* 1987

Susan Mosher Stuard, ed. *Women in Medieval Society.* 1976

Jonathan Sumption. *The Hundred Years War: Trial by Battle.* 1992

Ronald E. Surtz. *The Guitar of God: Gender, Power, and Authority in the Visionary World of Mother Juana de la Cruz (1481–1534).* 1990

Patricia Terry, trans. *Poems of the Elder Edda.* 1990

Frank Tobin. *Meister Eckhart: Thought and Language.* 1986

Ralph V. Turner. *Men Raised from the Dust: Administrative Service and Upward Mobility in Angevin England.* 1988

Harry Turtledove, trans. *The Chronicle of Theophanes: An English Translation of Anni Mundi 6095–6305 (A.D. 602–813).* 1982

Mary F. Wack. *Lovesickness in the Middle Ages: The Viaticum and Its Commentaries.* 1990

Benedicta Ward. *Miracles and the Medieval Mind: Theory, Record, and Event, 1000–1215.* 1982

Suzanne Fonay Wemple. *Women in Frankish Society: Marriage and the Cloister, 500–900.* 1981

This book has been set in Linotron Galliard. Galliard was designed for Mergenthaler in 1978 by Matthew Carter. Galliard retains many of the features of a sixteenth-century typeface cut by Robert Granjon but has some modifications that give it a more contemporary look.

Printed on acid-free paper.